INTERNATIONAL ORGAN
AND PEACE ENFORCE

What distinguishes a peace enforcement operation from an invasion? This question has been asked with particular vehemence since the US intervention in Iraq, but it faces all military operations seeking to impose peace in countries torn by civil war. This book highlights the critical role of international organisations as gatekeepers to international legitimacy for modern peace enforcement operations. The author analyses five operations launched through four organisations: the ECOWAS intervention in Liberia, the SADC operations in the Democratic Republic of Congo and Lesotho, the NATO Kosovo campaign and the UN intervention in East Timor. In all these campaigns, lead states sought the mandate of an international organisation primarily to establish the international legitimacy of their interventions. The evidence suggests that international relations are structured by commonly accepted rules, that both democratic and authoritarian states care about the international legitimacy of their actions, and that international organisations have a key function in world politics.

KATHARINA P. COLEMAN is an Assistant Professor in the Department of Political Science at the University of British Columbia.

INTERNATIONAL ORGANISATIONS AND PEACE ENFORCEMENT

The Politics of International Legitimacy

KATHARINA P. COLEMAN

CAMBRIDGE
UNIVERSITY PRESS

CAMBRIDGE UNIVERSITY PRESS
Cambridge, New York, Melbourne, Madrid, Cape Town, Singapore, São Paulo

Cambridge University Press
The Edinburgh Building, Cambridge CB2 8RU, UK

Published in the United States of America by Cambridge University Press, New York

www.cambridge.org
Information on this title: www.cambridge.org/9780521690348

First published 2007

Printed in the United Kingdom at the University Press, Cambridge

A catalogue record for this book is available from the British Library

ISBN 978-0-521-87019-1 hardback
ISBN 978-0-521-69034-8 paperback

CONTENTS

MAPS

FIGURES

viii

TABLES

ACKNOWLEDGEMENTS

I encountered many kinds of generosity while I was researching and writing this book, and I am very grateful for them all. The empirical chapters could not have been written without the help of the individuals who consented to be interviewed for this project. They are not all quoted directly in this book, but they all helped inform its argument. I would like to thank them for their time and their insights. I would also like to thank the Smith Richardson Foundation, the Christian A. Johnson Endeavor Foundation, the Princeton University Center of International Studies, the Princeton University Research Program in International Security, and the Princeton University Council of Regional Studies for enabling me to travel to Australia, Belgium, Botswana, Ethiopia, Nigeria, and Zimbabwe to conduct these interviews. The success (and fun) of these trips owed a great deal to a few individuals who made me welcome and helped me find my bearings. Heartfelt thanks to Desmond Ball and Robert Ayson in Canberra, Sascha Fong in Brussels, Rumbidzai Mashozhera, Terry Farnham, and Yusuf Hassen in Addis Ababa, Halima Ahmed and Mercedes Mensah in Abuja, and Ngoni Mararike in Harare.

I was also fortunate enough to receive exceptional academic advice and support in writing this book. Jeffrey Herbst and Michael Doyle offered invaluable guidance in the initial stages of planning and executing the research. Together with Aaron Friedberg, they also read multiple drafts of the emerging study and invariably provided insightful and constructive comments. Peter Dauvergne, Brian Job, Richard Price, and Allen Sens all read drafts of chapters and I am deeply grateful for their time, support, and perceptive observations. Angela O'Mahony helped me think through parts of the argument aloud and was fabulous about the maps. My colleagues make UBC a wonderful place to work. Ana-Maria Blanaru proofread a complete draft with unfailing attention to detail. At Cambridge University Press, John Haslam, Carrie Cheek, and Jo Breeze expertly guided this project towards publication, and two anonymous reviewers contributed greatly to the quality of this book. Any remaining flaws, of course, are mine alone.

At a personal level, I would like to thank my wonderful parents, Karin and Heinz Pichler, who waited a long time for this book. Thanks also to Sascha Fong, my sister and reality-check, who actually does what I just study. I am also grateful to Soledad Salas, Debbie Thompson, Rosalie Janowicz and Kathleen Cauley, who made it possible for me to write a book *and* be the happy mother of happy children. Finally, my greatest thanks go to my husband David, who has been there every step of the way – even when I was a continent away. This book is for him, and for Sophia and Alisa.

ABBREVIATIONS

ADF	Australian Defence Force
ANAD	Accord de Non-aggression et d'Assistance en matière de Defense (Mutual Non-Aggression and Defence Pact)
ANC	African National Congress
APEC	Asia-Pacific Economic Cooperation
ARRC	Allied Command Europe Rapid Reaction Corps
ASEAN	Association of South East Asian Nations
AU	African Union
BCP	Basotholand Congress Party
BNP	Basotho National Party
CIS	Commonwealth of Independent States
CTF	Combined Task Force (Operation Boleas)
DPKO	Department of Peacekeeping Operations (UN)
DRC	Democratic Republic of Congo
EAPC	Euro-Atlantic Partnership Council (NATO)
ECOMOG	ECOWAS Ceasefire Monitoring Group
ECOWAS	Economic Community of West African States
FRETLIN	Revolutionary Front for an Independent East Timor
FRY	Federal Republic of Yugoslavia
INTERFET	International Force East Timor
KLA	Kosovo Liberation Army
MNF	Multinational force
MSC	Mediation and Security Council (ECOWAS)
NAC	North Atlantic Council (NATO)
NATO	North Atlantic Treaty Organisation
NPFL	National Patriotic Front of Liberia
OAS	Organisation of American States
OAU	Organisation of African Unity
OSCE	Organisation for Security and Cooperation in Europe
RLDF	Royal Lesotho Defence Force

ROEs	Rules of Engagement
SADC	Southern African Development Community
SANDF	South African National Defence Force
SMC	Standing Mediation Committee (ECOWAS)
TNI	Tentara Nasional Indonesia (Indonesian military)
UN	United Nations
UNSAS	United Nations Standby Arrangement System

Introduction

In the 2004 US presidential debates, Democratic nominee John Kerry strongly criticised the manner in which the Bush administration had launched the war in Iraq in 2003. His foremost criticism was that the campaign was not sufficiently multilateral, leaving the USA to bear '90 percent of the casualties in Iraq and 90 percent of the costs'.[1] He suggested that closer attention to alliance-building and more engagement with the United Nations would remedy the situation. This line of attack was well calculated to appeal to US public opinion. George W. Bush responded that he had in fact engaged the UN and that Kerry was undervaluing the coalition that had been built for the Iraq campaign. However, he was clearly on the defensive and struggled to fend off Kerry's repeated charge that 'we can do better' at coalition-building.

Kerry's second line of criticism was decidedly less successful. He charged that the Iraq campaign failed 'the global test where your countrymen, your people understand fully why you're doing what you're doing and you can prove to the world that you're doing it for legitimate reasons'.[2] Kerry suggested that the Bush administration's refusal 'to deal at length with the United Nations' was part of the reason for this failure. This line of attack backfired. Bush immediately challenged the notion of a 'global test' as undermining the USA's right to protect itself and referred to it in subsequent debates to portray Kerry as insufficiently committed to US security. Bush administration officials echoed this argument on various news networks. Sensitive to the political weight of this accusation, Kerry declined to defend his concept, reiterating instead that he would 'never give any country a veto over [the USA's] security'.[3]

---

[1] First Bush-Kerry Debate, 30 September 2004, transcript by the Commission on Presidential Debates, online at www.debates.org/pages/trans2004a.html
[2] Ibid.
[3] Third Bush-Kerry Debate, 13 October 2004, transcript by the Commission on Presidential Debates, online at www.debates.org/pages/trans2004d.html

The irony of this episode is that Kerry's second criticism showed a far greater understanding of the role of international organisations in military interventions than his first one. The notion that the UN could guarantee fair burden-sharing in an enforcement operation was a red herring. As this book will show, obtaining the auspices of an international organisation for a military intervention does not obviate the need to form a coalition of the willing or save the lead state from shouldering a disproportionate share of the resulting costs. On the other hand, a UN mandate would have greatly improved the Iraq campaign's international legitimacy – which is why the Bush administration did in fact seek such a mandate. In doing so, it mirrored the efforts of lead states in all contemporary peace enforcement operations. What distinguished the Bush administration was its willingness to proceed with its intervention despite its failure to secure an international mandate. In the presidential debates, George W. Bush's rhetoric masked this failure by suggesting that the USA had no need to concern itself with international legitimacy and John Kerry failed to forcefully contradict this stance. Both men were framing their remarks to appeal to the US electorate. The US experience in Iraq, including both US attempts to secure a UN mandate and the international hostility that resulted from intervening without one, has confirmed a different reality: international organisations remain crucial gatekeepers to international legitimacy for interstate military deployments.

This book highlights the central role of international organisations in the politics of international legitimacy surrounding peace enforcement operations. In the contemporary international system, there is a strong norm against interstate aggression but military intervention to bolster international peace and security is increasingly considered acceptable or even laudable. In practice, however, it can be difficult to distinguish between peace enforcement and an act of aggression. Both types of intervention involve substantial and often unsolicited movements of combat-ready troops across international borders, and, regardless of their actual objectives, all intervening states have a strong incentive to portray their activity as benign peace enforcement. The danger, therefore, is that increasing international acceptance of peace enforcement opens the door to partisan invasions for ostensibly altruistic ends. This dilemma has received more widespread attention since the 2003 US invasion of Iraq, but it predates that crisis. In fact, it has been raised by every peace enforcement operation, from the Nigerian-led intervention in Liberia in 1990 to the 1998 US-led Kosovo campaign and the intervention in East Timor spearheaded by Australia in 1999. The issue has surfaced most recently in the 2006 negotiations about an international intervention in Lebanon, and will continue to arise whenever a third-party military intervention in a sovereign state is being considered.

How does the contemporary international system cope with this danger? International relations practitioners frequently invoke international organisations as bulwarks against abuse of the concept of peace enforcement. Despite their inherent problems and limitations, these multilateral organisations have a more credible claim to speak for the international community than any other international entity. Moreover, since their collective decision-making procedures require at least some transcendence of individual states' particularistic interests international organisations are seen as able to make less biased distinctions between genuine peace enforcement and aggression. Thus the 2001 International Commission on Intervention and State Sovereignty reported an 'overwhelming consensus ... around the world' that the United Nations Security Council was the most appropriate body to authorise military interventions.[4] It also identified substantial international support for regional or sub-regional international organisations assuming this role, but it did not mention unilateral authorisation by individual states as a viable option. A mandate from an international organisation is crucial to establishing the international legitimacy of a military intervention.

It is this legitimising function that makes international organisations so central to contemporary peace enforcement operations. Although some pooling of resources does take place through international organisations (e.g. the emerging NATO Response Force), no international organisation can mount a peace enforcement operation on its own. States have stubbornly resisted relinquishing their monopoly on the means of warfare by placing significant forces at the disposal of international organisations. They therefore remain the only actors capable of launching and executing peace enforcement operations. However, states almost invariably choose to launch their interventions through international organisations. This book argues that this regularity can only be understood in light of the role that international organisations play in differentiating between legitimate and illegitimate military interventions in the contemporary international system. The importance of this argument is theoretical as well as empirical. In contemporary international relations

---

[4] International Commission on Intervention and State Sovereignty, *The Responsibility to Protect* (Ottawa: International Development Research Centre, 2001), chapter 6.

theory, international organisations are often viewed as creations of international law, instruments of hegemonic power, or facilitators of inter-state cooperation and burden-sharing. Their central role in the politics of international legitimacy has been neither adequately recognised nor fully explored.[5] This book helps fill that gap.

Within this larger empirical and theoretical project, this introduction serves three main purposes. First, it establishes the central empirical observation that modern peace enforcement operations virtually always occur under the auspices of an international organisation. Second, it describes the methodology used within this book to analyse the role of international organisations in launching peace enforcement operations. Finally, it provides an overview of the remainder of this book.

The empirical pattern: international organisations and peace enforcement

This project is inspired by a simple but as yet inadequately explained empirical pattern. Virtually all contemporary peace enforcement operations take place within the framework of an international organisation. This section will define the core concepts of this assertion and demonstrate its empirical validity. The remainder of this book is dedicated to explaining this regularity.

Peace enforcement operations

Peace enforcement operations are forcible military interventions by one or more states into a third country with the express objective of maintaining or restoring international, regional, or local peace and security by ending a violent conflict within that country. They can be distinguished from invasions in that they do not overtly seek to alter the political or geographical status quo to the invader's benefit. As ideal types, they are also distinct from peacekeeping operations, which despite increasingly robust rules of engagement fundamentally aim at implementing a peace or truce that has already been agreed upon at least in principle by the parties to a particular conflict.

---

[5] A classic formulation of the connection between international organisations and legitimacy can, however, be found in Inis L. Claude, 'Collective Legitimization as a Political Function of the United Nations', *International Organization*, 20:3 (Summer 1966).

The formal legal basis for peace enforcement operations is Chapter VII of the United Nations Charter, which authorises UN Security Council 'action with respect to threats to the peace, breaches of the peace, and acts of aggression'. Specifically, Article 42 allows the Security Council to 'take such action by air, sea, or land forces as may be necessary to maintain or restore international peace and security'. Initially intended to promote collective action against interstate aggression, this provision remained largely dormant during the Cold War, partly because superpower rivalry paralysed the Security Council[6] and partly because the UN's disastrous first experience with intrastate peace enforcement in the Congo (1960–4) discouraged any further experimentation. The UN restricted itself mainly to peacekeeping missions, where lightly armed military observers were deployed to monitor the implementation of interstate ceasefire agreements. These operations were conducted under Chapter VI of the UN Charter, which deals with 'Pacific Settlement of Disputes'. Since they represented a striking innovation from the mediation and fact-finding strategies that chapter was originally intended to cover, UN Secretary-General Dag Hammarsjold famously referred to them as belonging to 'Chapter Six and a Half'. Nevertheless, these operations fell far short of enforcement action since they could not apply military force: UN personnel were allowed to use force only in self-defence.

By the early 1990s, the international strategic environment had changed dramatically. The Cold War had ended, but the much-expected 'peace dividend' did not materialise. Instead, the disintegration of the USSR and Yugoslavia and the collapse of Cold War client regimes in the developing world highlighted a new kind of global instability. The international response to the 'new world disorder' of state failure and civil war was not only a proliferation of peacekeeping operations[7] but also a dramatic evolution in the concept of peacekeeping. Most of the new operations in the early 1990s sought to address civil wars and in so doing took on increasingly ambitious tasks, which included organising

---

[6] The one notable exception was the US-led UN intervention in Korea (1950–3). Using the language of Chapter VII without explicitly invoking it, Security Council Resolution 38 of 27 June 1950 recommended that UN members assist the Republic of Korea 'as may be necessary to repel the armed attack and restore international peace and security in the area'. This resolution was passed only because the USSR was boycotting the UN over its failure to recognise Mao Tse-tung's new government in China. Since the intervention was framed as a response to international aggression rather than to internal turmoil, however, this enforcement action was not strictly a peace enforcement operation.

[7] Having launched only 18 peacekeeping operations in its previous 46 years of existence, the UN created 15 new missions between 1990 and 1993, and 36 new missions between 1990 and 2000.

elections, demobilising combatants, resettling refugees, and in some cases even assuming temporary administrative authority in the host country. Despite the unprecedented breadth of their mandate, however, these so-called 'second-generation' peacekeeping operations remained peacekeeping rather than peace enforcement missions: they did not envision using military force to pursue their mandates and impose a settlement on warring factions.

However, peacekeeping reverses in Angola, Somalia, Croatia, and Bosnia and Herzegovina, as well as the apparent effectiveness of military might during the 1991 Gulf War, led many policy-makers to re-evaluate the role of military force in addressing contemporary civil conflicts. These circumstances allowed UN Secretary-General Boutros Boutros-Ghali to coin and develop the concept of peace enforcement in 1992–3.[8] He originally proposed the creation of 'peace-enforcement units' capable of protecting ceasefires against recalcitrant factions. This idea rapidly evolved into a more general concept of peace enforcement operations as authorised under Chapter VII and independent of the consent of the parties to a particular conflict. The failure of UN peacekeeping forces to prevent massacres and genocide in Somalia (1993), Bosnia (1993), and Rwanda (1994) was widely interpreted as demonstrating both the limitations of peacekeeping methods and the need for enforcement operations that can impose a peace on an on-going conflict, if necessary against some combatants' wishes. Unlike peacekeeping missions, therefore, peace enforcement operations are launched in the expectation that the use of military force will be required. Their personnel are deployed fully armed and are permitted to use force to accomplish their mission. Peace enforcement operations can thus be understood as that small but increasingly significant sub-set of modern peace operations that embrace the use of military force.

International organisations

For the purposes of this study, international organisations are formal associations that comprise three or more states. They are created by an international charter, sustained by regular meetings of member states, and supported by a permanent secretariat. These organisations are thus the most concrete and visible sub-set of the universe of international

---

[8] Jane Boulden, *Peace Enforcement: the United Nations Experience in Congo, Somalia, and Bosnia* (Westport: Praeger, 2001), pp. 14–16.

institutions, which also includes international norms, international laws, and international regimes surrounding particular issue areas. Much of the attention within contemporary International Relations theory has focused on these less tangible international institutions, yielding valuable insights into the evolution and effectiveness of international norms, laws, and regimes. This project, however, focuses on international organisations, which unlike norms and regimes have a physical presence in the world. They generally have physical headquarters as well as staff who are not only employed by but can also speak for their organisation. In 2004, the Union of International Associations recognised some 238 international organisations of this kind.[9] They vary widely in purpose, membership structure and requirements, and in the amount of resources and staff at their disposal. Nevertheless all international organisations are fundamentally formal arenas of regular state interaction created by interstate agreements and sustained by at least a minimal organisational infrastructure.

Peace enforcement operations and international organisations

A brief overview of interventions that either meet or approximate the definition of peace enforcement operations elaborated above confirms that virtually all contemporary peace enforcement operations are launched under the auspices of an international organisation.

Table 1.1 comprises the eighteen interventions since 1945 that are most commonly accepted as peace enforcement operations. They all correspond closely to the definition of peace enforcement offered above: these are interstate military interventions explicitly justified by intervening states as aimed at ending a violent conflict within the host country in order to maintain or restore international, regional, or local peace and security. The table lists each intervention's location (target country) and date, indicates the nature of the intervening force (force status[10]), and where appropriate identifies its primary contributing state (lead state) and mandating international organisation.

---

[9] Union of International Associations, *Yearbook of International Organizations (2003/ 2004)* (Brussels: Union of International Organizations, 2003).

[10] An intervening military force can be: (a) national, i.e. under a single national command; (b) international, i.e. under an international organisation's overall command; (c) a multinational force (MNF) operating for an international organisation but remaining under national commands or under the overall command of the lead state.

Table 1.1: *Peace enforcement operations*

Target country	Lead state	Date	Force status	Mandating international organisation
Congo	n/a	1961–1964	UN	UN
Liberia	Nigeria	1990–1997	ECOWAS	ECOWAS
Somalia	USA	1992–1993	MNF	UN
Bosnia Herzegovina	(NATO/USA)	1993–1995	NATO MNF	UN
Somalia	USA	1993–1995	UN	UN
Tajikistan	Russia	1993–2000	CIS	CIS
Rwanda	France	1994	MNF	UN
Haiti	USA	1994	MNF	UN
Albania	Italy	1997	MNF	UN
Central African Republic	(France)	1997–1998	MNF	IMC
Sierra Leone	Nigeria	1997–1999	ECOWAS	ECOWAS
Guinea-Bissau	(Senegal/Guinea)	1998–1999	ECOWAS	ECOWAS
Lesotho	South Africa	1998–1999	SADC	SADC
Democ. Rep. Congo	Zimbabwe	1998–2002	SADC	SADC
Kosovo	USA	1999	NATO	NATO
East Timor	Australia	1999–2000	MNF	UN
Sierra Leone	n/a	2000–2005	UN	UN
Democ. Rep. Congo	France	2003	EU/MNF	UN

Crucially, all but one of these operations were launched from within the framework of an established international organisation. The sole exception, the 1997–8 intervention in the Central African Republic (CAR), proves rather than disproves the general rule. This intervention was launched by Burkina Faso, Chad, Gabon, Mali, Senegal, and Togo, and financed by France. These states did not share membership in a regional organisation that could have mandated intervention.[11] Instead

[11] The Central African Republic belongs to the Economic Community of Central African States, as do Chad and Gabon. Burkina Faso, Mali, Senegal, and Togo, however, belong to the Economic Community of West African States. France belongs to neither organisation.

of intervening without international auspices, however, they established the International Mediation Committee, which then dispatched an inter-African force to the CAR.[12] Thus in the absence of an established international organisation, states preferred to create an ad hoc international body rather than intervene without any institutional international auspices.

Table 1.1 also reveals three other interesting trends: First, while the UN is the most active international organisation in peace enforcement, it is not the only one. Only ten of the eighteen operations in table 1.1 were launched under a UN mandate, with the remainder occurring through smaller international organisations. Second, although international organisations are ubiquitous as mandating bodies for peace enforcement operations, their presence within these operations is more limited. In eight of the eighteen cases, the mandating international organisation did not assume command of the intervention force it authorised. Instead, it authorised the creation of a multinational force (MNF) that it did not directly control. This trend is particularly noticeable for the UN, which selected the MNF formula in seven of its ten peace enforcement operations. Third, most peace enforcement operations occur under the direction of a lead state. In thirteen of the eighteen operations in table 1.1, a single country officially accepted responsibility for coordinating, launching, and leading the military intervention force. In three further cases (indicated by state names in parentheses), individual states assumed prominent operational roles without declaring themselves lead states. Thus in the vast majority of cases, international organisations effectively ceded immediate operational control over the interventions they mandated to a single nation-state.

The overarching lesson from table 1.1, then, is that all generally recognised contemporary peace enforcement operations occurred under the mandate of a formal international organisation. The mandating organisation was almost always an established formal international organisation, although not necessarily the United Nations. However, the role of these mandating organisations did not always extend to implementing the peace enforcement operation.

Table 1.2 identifies sixteen additional military operations since 1945 that have some peace enforcement attributes even though they do not strictly correspond to the definition elaborated above. These operations

---

[12] Eric G. Berman and Katie E. Sams, *Peacekeeping in Africa: Capabilities and Culpabilities* (Geneva: UN, 2000), pp. 222–5.

Table 1.2: *Interventions with peace enforcement attributes*

Target country	Lead state	Date	Force status	Mandating international organisation
North Korea/ Rep. Korea	USA	1950–1953	MNF	UN
Dominican Rep.	USA	1965	USA/MNF	post hoc OAS
Lebanon	Syria	1976–1977	Syria/MNF	post hoc Arab League
Chad	Nigeria	1982	MNF	OAU
CSSR	USSR	1968	MNF	WTO
East Pakistan	India	1971	Indian	none, UN approval sought
Cambodia	Vietnam	1978	Vietnamese	none
Tanzania	Uganda	1979	Ugandan	none
Grenada	USA	1983	MNF	OECS
Iraq/Kuwait	USA	1991	MNF	UN
Moldova	Russia	1992	Russia/MNF	post hoc CIS
Somalia	USA	1993–1994	US Task Force	none, but in support of UN
Sierra Leone	UK	2000–2001	UK	none, but in support of UN
Afghanistan	USA	2001	MNF	none, but UNSC support
Iraq	USA	2003–?	MNF	none
Lebanon	France	2006–?	UN	UN

must be considered to ensure that the observed ubiquity of international organisations in peace enforcement operations is not simply due to an excessively restrictive definition of this term. Like table 1.1, table 1.2 provides information about the interventions' locations and dates, the nature of the intervening forces, and the identity of any lead state and/or mandating international organisation.

This additional evidence does not substantially detract from the core proposition that virtually all peace enforcement operations are launched from within the framework of an international organisation. Two facts stand out. First, the interventions in table 1.2 that most resemble peace enforcement operations follow the pattern of seeking the auspices of an international organisation most closely. The Korean War and the 1991 Gulf War were enforcement operations that differed from the definition of peace enforcement only in the sense that they were perceived to address international aggression rather than internal conflicts.[13] The 1982 OAU intervention in Chad billed itself as part of an on-going peacekeeping mission, but occurred in the midst of a raging civil war and was thus effectively an attempt at peace enforcement. All three interventions were carried out by multinational forces under mandates from international organisations and thus exactly follow the pattern of peace enforcement operations in table 1.1. The 2006 UN intervention in Lebanon also strongly resembles a peace enforcement operation, although it addresses a cross-border conflict whose main protagonists are a state (Israel) and a non-state militia (Hizbollah) and, as is discussed in the epilogue, the enforcement mandate is subject to some doubt. Like the peace enforcement operations in table 1.1, it is mandated by an international organisation, which in this case also has command of the intervention force. The British and US task forces in Sierra Leone and Somalia were also closely related to peace enforcement operations, but occurred in the context of wider international peacekeeping efforts rather than as fully independent operations. This context also provided a close association with the United Nations. Although they lacked independent mandates, therefore, these deployments do not present a significant challenge to the proposition that peace enforcement occurs in association with formal international organisations.

Second, interventions that did not closely resemble peace enforcement operations but nevertheless claimed that status also sought the auspices of international organisations. The interventions in Grenada and Czechoslovakia hardly qualified as peace enforcement operations given the absence of civil war in these countries, but nevertheless claimed to promote stability in response to dramatic internal developments. Both reproduced the pattern of table 1.1 by featuring multinational forces deployed under the mandate of an international organisation, albeit one with limited credibility.[14] Consistent with this logic, a shift towards a peace enforcement rationale to justify an on-going

---

[13] Neither North Korea's claim to simply be reunifying Korea nor Iraq's contention that it was reclaiming a former province received much international credence. Thus these are not generally regarded as civil wars.

[14] Neither the Organisation of Eastern Caribbean States nor the Warsaw Treaty Organisation enjoyed much credibility as an autonomous international organisation.

deployment also seems to entail the quest for international organisation auspices: when the US deployment in the Dominican Republic expanded its official aim from evacuating US nationals to stabilising the political situation, it presented itself as preparatory to a deployment by the Organisation of American States (OAS). Similarly, when Syria began to present its intervention in Lebanon as an attempt to impose a ceasefire rather than merely a response to an invitation from the Lebanese government, it sought Arab League auspices. Finally, when Russia acknowledged that its intervention in Moldova constituted enforcement action rather than interpositional peacekeeping, it sought the auspices of the Commonwealth of Independent States (CIS).

Thus eleven of the sixteen operations in table 1.2 were in fact closely associated with an international organisation or became so when they claimed peace enforcement status. Of the remaining five, four had some affinities with peace enforcement operations but were not publicly justified or defended as such. For Vietnam, Tanzania, and India, this choice was historically conditioned. Although each of their interventions could in retrospect be justified as humanitarian interventions akin to peace enforcement operations, this justification was not available during the Cold War.[15] This context explains the emphasis on self-defence as a public rationale for each of these interventions. By contrast, the 2001 US invasion of Afghanistan might have been presented as an international enforcement action against terrorism, which UN Security Council resolutions 1368 and 1373 had identified as a threat to international peace and security. However, the US chose instead to defend its deployment as an act of unilateral self-defence in the wake of the 11 September 2001 attacks on New York and Washington. Crucially, in all four cases the lead states did not conceive of their interventions primarily as peace enforcement operations. Their failure to secure a mandate from an international organisation thus does not constitute a significant exception to the observation that states launch peace enforcement operations through international organisations.[16]

---

[15] Nicholas J. Wheeler, *Saving Strangers: Humanitarian Intervention in International Society* (Oxford: Oxford University Press, 2000), chapters 2–4.

[16] India also experimented with a humanitarian justification for its intervention, claiming to address a humanitarian situation that 'shocked the conscience of mankind'. Interestingly, in this context it sought (unsuccessfully) to claim international auspices for its deployment by recalling UN 'conventions on genocides, human rights, self-determination' as well as 'the justice part' of the UN Charter. Ibid., p. 63.

The only true outlier in table 1.2, therefore, is the 2003 US-led invasion of Iraq. This was the only contemporary military intervention that claimed the promotion of international peace and security as its primary motivation but failed to secure a mandate from any international organisation. It is worth noting that the case does not fully fit the definition of peace enforcement: although the intervention claimed to enhance international stability by disarming a potential aggressor, it responded neither to an international nor an internal conflict, and thus billed itself as a preventive action. Moreover, the lead state did attempt to portray its action as enforcing previous UN Security Council resolutions and has returned to the UN for post hoc legitimation of its intervention. Nevertheless, this case represents a significant exception that will be more closely examined in the conclusion of this study.

Overall, however, the evidence for the proposition that virtually all contemporary peace enforcement operations are launched through international organisations is remarkably robust. Tables 1.1 and 1.2 show that all eighteen commonly acknowledged peace enforcement operations follow this pattern, while of the sixteen operations most closely related to peace enforcement, only one claimed peace enforcement status without securing an international organisation's mandate. These tables do not, of course, include all military interventions since 1945. Mark Zacher has identified some thirty-seven territorial conflicts for the period of 1950–2000,[17] in addition to which there have been numerous incursions aimed at installing favourable governments in other states, like the 1956 Soviet deployment in Hungary and apartheid South Africa's destabilisation campaigns. All these deployments occurred without the mandate of an international organisation. However, the definition of peace enforcement simply cannot be stretched to include invasions that openly seek to further national interests rather than at least claiming to promote international peace and security.[18] Therefore these interventions do not represent significant exceptions to the proposition that virtually all contemporary peace enforcement operations are launched through international organisations.

---

[17] Mark W. Zacher, 'The Territorial Integrity Norm: International Boundaries and the Use of Force', *International Organization*, 55:2 (Spring 2001), p. 218.

[18] Note that table 1.2 also excludes peacekeeping operations, because they, too, cannot be subsumed under the definition of peace enforcement. Since peacekeeping tends to occur under UN auspices, however, the inclusion of these operations would merely underscore the ubiquity of international organisations in peace operations.

Methodology

The most promising method for discovering why states so consistently choose to launch peace enforcement operations through international organisations is a series of case studies. Only detailed investigation of individual cases can uncover the motivation of the states involved. However, because the answer might be assumed to depend on either the nature of the intervening state or the kind of international organisation involved, it is important to investigate a set of cases that varies both the states and the institutions under examination. Therefore, this book examines five peace enforcement operations launched by a wide variety of states from within a variety of international organisations. Specifically, it focuses on:

- the 1990 Nigerian-led intervention in Liberia, conducted under the auspices of the Economic Community of West African States (ECOWAS);
- the 1998 Zimbabwean-led operation in the Democratic Republic of Congo (DRC), launched under the auspices of the Southern African Development Community (SADC);
- the 1998 South African-led SADC operation in Lesotho;
- the 1999 US-led NATO operation in Kosovo;
- the 1999 Australian-led UN operation in East Timor.

Map 1.1 illustrates the memberships of NATO, ECOWAS, and SADC. Most independent states on the map are also UN members.

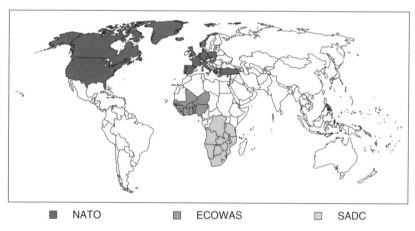

■ NATO   ■ ECOWAS   ▢ SADC

Map 1.1. NATO, ECOWAS, and SADC members

These case studies were selected for two reasons. First, the lead states differed both in their relative international power and in the nature of their regimes. They include the US global superpower, a mid-sized Western power (Australia), two African regional powers of limited international influence (Nigeria and South Africa), and a state that is relatively weak at the international level (Zimbabwe). Two lead states were established democracies (USA, Australia), one was newly democratic (South Africa), one authoritarian (Zimbabwe), and one a military dictatorship (Nigeria in 1990). This variety in the nature of lead states makes it possible to detect similarities and differences in the motivations of different kinds of state for launching peace enforcement operations through international organisations.

Second, the cases selected allow insight into the role of a variety of international organisations in peace enforcement. Each of the operations studied was seminal for the international organisation in which it was launched. Kosovo and Liberia were the first peace enforcement operations for NATO and ECOWAS, respectively. For SADC, the DRC and Lesotho operations were parallel first interventions. East Timor was the UN's most recent and arguably most successful peace enforcement operation. The institutions involved, moreover, represent the range of international organisations active in peace enforcement operations, including a global organisation (UN), an organisation based on military alliances (NATO), and regional organisations (ECOWAS and SADC). In addition to membership differences, these international organisations differ widely in foundational purpose and resource bases, as will be explored in the subsequent chapters.

The analysis within each case study focuses on the lead state as the key actor in deciding how to launch the peace enforcement operation in question. The core question is why lead states decided to operate within the framework of a particular international organisation. What did they hope to achieve by launching their peace enforcement operations within these frameworks – and to what extent were their hopes justified?

It is worth noting the limits of this enquiry. This book is not primarily concerned with isolating the reasons for which peace enforcement operations are launched. These reasons are diverse and likely to vary from state to state and intervention to intervention. Since peace enforcement operations are risky and expensive, states will launch them only if they expect substantial benefits from doing so. However, what benefits they perceive depends in part on their policy objectives, which can include such diverse aims as maintaining international stability, projecting military power, obtaining economic assets, and halting humanitarian disasters. The relative ordering of these objectives is idiosyncratic to each state. Instead of seeking to integrate these varying factors into a general theory about states' motivations for peace enforcement, therefore, this book restricts itself to a different question. Having decided to launch a peace enforcement operation, why do states almost always choose to do so within the framework of an international organisation?

To answer this question, the five case studies in this project draw on four main sources of information. The first are primary documents specifying the function and capacities of the international organisations in question. This includes these organisations' charters, declarations of principle or intent, and budget statements. Particular attention is paid to what institutional structures have been established to cope with peace enforcement operations and how these structures have evolved. The second source of information consists of contemporary media accounts of the launching of the peace enforcement operations in question. These provide not only operational details and timelines of the operation's development, but also editorial comments and politicians' statements about the purpose of the operation. References to the international organisations mandating these interventions are particularly valuable for judging the effect of operating within these frameworks. The third important source of commentary on both the peace enforcement operations in question and the international organisations through which they were launched are academic books and journal articles on these interventions. An effort has been made to include the works of writers from the regions in which the interventions take place.

The fourth source of information for these case studies are a series of interviews conducted by the author in Africa, Australia, Europe, and America.[19] A total of 149 interviews were conducted with 136 interviewees, who included: international civil servants within the international organisations studied; bureaucrats in national governments; diplomats at national missions to the international organisation or at the embassies of member states; military officers of countries that participated in the peace enforcement operations studied; and informed observers of the international organisations under consideration. The diplomats interviewed represented 36 states, of which 18 were African, 9 European,

[19] Research grants from the Smith Richardson Foundation, the Christian A. Johnson Endeavor Foundation, the Princeton University Center of International Studies, the Princeton University Research Program in International Security, and the Princeton University Council of Regional Studies are most gratefully acknowledged.

2 American, and 7 Austral-Asian. Appendix 1 gives an overview of where and when these interviews took place. Interviews were not intended for quantitative analysis and therefore did not follow a standard questionnaire. Instead, interviewees were asked about their areas of special expertise or experience relevant to the peace enforcement operations under investigation. Their insights are drawn upon qualitatively in the case studies of this book.

Chapter overview

In addition to this introduction, this book has seven chapters. Chapter 2 develops the theoretical argument that the central role of international organisations in contemporary peace enforcement operations derives from their function as gatekeepers to international legitimacy where the international use of military force is concerned. The chapter defines the concept of international legitimacy and elucidates the theoretical understanding of world politics upon which it rests. It then describes the special status of international organisations in the politics of international legitimacy. Finally, it suggests that alternative theoretical perspectives focusing on international law, burden-sharing, and power politics do not provide an adequate representation of the role of international organisations in contemporary peace enforcement.

The five subsequent chapters provide empirical support for this theoretical position. They present five chronologically ordered case studies, beginning with the 1990 ECOWAS intervention in Liberia and then focusing on the 1998 SADC operations in the Democratic Republic of Congo and Lesotho, NATO's 1999 Kosovo campaign, and the 1999 UN intervention in East Timor. Each chapter describes the relevant international organisation and provides a historical background of the peace enforcement operation in question before analysing why the lead state chose to operate through this international organisation. Although there are substantial differences between the case studies, all five chapters find considerable support for a legitimacy-centred explanation of the role of international organisations in peace enforcement operations.

Finally, the conclusion summarises the evidence from the case studies and then steps back from this study's exclusive focus on peace enforcement operations to discuss the extent to which a legitimacy-based theory of international organisations might apply to other international military activities. It also argues that the most recent and

high-profile use of military force in world politics, the 2003 US intervention in Iraq, dramatically illustrates both the limits and the importance of legitimacy concerns in shaping states' behaviour in the contemporary international system. The chapter ends by underlining the theoretical implications of this study.

2

States, international organisations, and legitimacy: a theoretical framework

Peace enforcement operations are understudied as a theoretical phenomenon. They have received intense scrutiny from analysts seeking to draw policy guidelines for future operations, but not from international relations theorists enquiring into the nature of the contemporary international system. Nevertheless, these novel and high-profile operations offer a fertile ground for developing international relations theory. Since peace enforcement operations are risky, costly, and controversial, states can be expected to choose their intervention strategies with great care. The fact that virtually all contemporary peace enforcement operations are launched through an international organisation suggests that states see these organisations as playing a critical role in these operations. Yet no international organisation has the resources to launch a peace enforcement operation on its own, or even to significantly decrease its costs and risks to the states that undertake it. Why, then, are international organisations so central to contemporary peace enforcement operations?

This book recognises that states are concerned about how the international community will perceive their interventions. It contends that states launch peace enforcement operations through international organisations because they recognise that these organisations act as gatekeepers to legitimacy in the contemporary international system. This chapter lays the theoretical groundwork for this argument. It begins by elucidating the concept of international legitimacy and explaining its significance to contemporary states. It then offers a theoretical argument for why international organisations affect the legitimacy of peace enforcement operations. Finally, the chapter contrasts this understanding of international organisations with three other conceptions found in international relations theory and among diplomats and pundits: international organisations as embodiments of international law, as facilitators of burden-sharing, and as instruments of power politics.

Understanding international legitimacy

Legitimacy is a social status that can adhere to an actor or an action: it involves being recognised as good, proper, or commendable by a group of others. The basis of this judgement bears scrutiny, since in common parlance there seems to be a qualitative difference between being disliked or unpopular and being perceived as illegitimate. The charge of illegitimacy asserts that a person or action is not (or not only) personally but *socially* offensive, in other words that it offends against a particular set of communal rules. Thus although it may in fact be tainted by the proclivities or aversions of members of the judging group, formally a legitimacy judgement is not based on individual tastes and preferences but on commonly accepted public rules.

This broad definition of legitimacy is, of course, applicable to a multitude of social settings. When thinking about legitimacy in the international context, however, four core issues arise. First, who or what is the subject of international legitimacy judgements? Second, who constitutes the relevant judging group or audience for claims of international legitimacy and illegitimacy? Third, what public rules serve as standards for international legitimacy judgements and how are they related to international law? And finally, why should states, the most powerful actors in the international system and the only ones capable of launching peace enforcement operations, care about international legitimacy? All four questions will be addressed in turn, drawing on arguments from both constructivism and the pluralist strand of the English School. The conception of international legitimacy defended here sees actions as well as actors as subject to legitimacy judgements and identifies the international society of states as a key legitimacy audience. It distinguishes the standards of international legitimacy judgements from international law despite the frequent overlap between legality and legitimacy. Finally, it proposes a relatively thin notion of international society in which a logic of social action rather than either a deep normative consensus or purely instrumental reasoning induces states to value international rules and hence international legitimacy.

Referent object: the international legitimacy of actions as well as actors

The notion of legitimacy is enjoying a surge of interest among international relations theorists after a long period of relative neglect. However, most contemporary writing about international legitimacy remains focused on the legitimacy of entities and actors, providing a rare example of International Relations theorists following Political Theory too closely rather than too loosely. The result has been that a key dimension of international legitimacy – the legitimacy of actions and behaviour rather than of actors and institutions – continues to be unduly neglected.

Political theorists have long struggled with the question of legitimate authority, i.e. of which rulers, regimes, or laws should be obeyed.[1] The question is of crucial importance when thinking of hierarchical political systems, and it is far from being exhausted, as contemporary debates about legitimate governance and the use of ideology, symbols, and language to legitimise or mask authority relations demonstrate. The enquiry into the forms and foundation of legitimacy has also spread beyond political theory, but the focus on legitimacy as concerning the right to rule has largely been maintained:

> Philosophy and political science, law, sociology, and political anthropology have all made of [legitimacy] a privileged object of research ... the various points of view being advanced offer marked differences ... [and] one finds, even within a given discipline, some major divergences. Despite these, there exists a common ground for understanding: the idea of legitimacy concerns first and foremost the right to govern. *Legitimacy is the recognition of the right to govern.*[2]

Although there are good reasons to develop our understanding of legitimacy thus defined, it should be recognised that this conception of legitimacy captures only a sub-section of the phenomena to which the term might otherwise be applied. It excludes not only all actors not asserting a right to govern but also all activities by any actors. Legitimacy, in this definition, is an attribute that only governing entities can have. This obscures the possibility that actions, too, can be (and often are) subject to social judgements of legitimacy and illegitimacy.

With a few notable exceptions,[3] International Relations theorists have tended to adopt the narrow definition of legitimacy as exclusively concerning the right to govern. Ian Hurd defines legitimacy as 'the

---

[1] The question already preoccupies Plato in *The Republic* and Aristotle in *Politics*.

[2] Jean-Marc Coicaud, *Legitimacy and Politics: A Contribution to the Study of Political Right and Political Responsibility* (Cambridge: Cambridge University Press, 2002), p. 10. Emphasis added.

[3] Richard Price, *The Chemical Weapons Taboo* (Ithaca: Cornell University Press, 1997); Nicholas J. Wheeler, *Saving Strangers: Humanitarian Intervention in International Society*

normative belief by an actor that a rule or institution ought to be obeyed'.[4] Mlada Bukovansky describes it as 'the terms by which people recognize, defend, and accept political authority'.[5] Jens Steffek notes that in the debate about international legitimacy, 'the only common denominator ... is that [all approaches] explore the normative conditions of exercising power "above the nation-state".'[6] However, this conception of legitimacy fits uneasily with the traditional view of the international system as anarchical: where no central political authority exists, both authority and obedience are rare. This fundamental contradiction goes a long way towards explaining the relative lack of attention to legitimacy that characterised international relations theory until very recently. Most commonly, the concept was relegated to the state and sub-state level, where it continues to fuel the debate about which entities should be recognised as legitimate participants in international relations.[7] Nevertheless, some theorists persisted in arguing that despite the prevailing anarchy, legitimate authority does exist in international relations. In his seminal treatment of *The Power of Legitimacy among Nations*, for example, Thomas Franck proposed that compliance with international rules largely reflects the degree to which these rules are viewed as legitimate.[8]

Arguments seeking to refocus attention on this kind of international legitimacy have become increasingly common since the end of the Cold War, fuelled in part by the growing role of the United Nations in world affairs in the 1990s. Reflecting this impetus, theorists have tended to

(Oxford: Oxford University Press, 2002); Martha Finnemore, *The Purpose of Intervention: Changing Beliefs About the Use of Force* (Ithaca: Cornell University Press, 2003).

[4] Ian Hurd, 'Legitimacy and Authority in International Politics', *International Organization*, 53:2 (Spring 1999), p. 381.

[5] Mlada Bukovansky, *Legitimacy and Power Politics: The American and French Revolutions in International Political Culture* (Princeton: Princeton University Press, 2002), p. 2.

[6] Jens Steffek, 'The Legitimation of International Governance: A Discourse Approach', *European Journal of International Relations*, 9:2 (2003), p. 252.

[7] Important contributions include Martin Wight, 'International Legitimacy', in Hedley Bull (ed.), *Systems of States: Martin Wight* (Leicester: Leicester University Press, 1977) and Robert H. Jackson, *Quasi-States: Sovereignty, International Relations, and the Third World* (Cambridge: Cambridge University Press, 1990). For a more recent overview, see Allen Buchanan, 'Recognitional Legitimacy and the State System', *Philosophy and Public Affairs*, 28:1 (1999).

[8] Thomas M. Franck, *The Power of Legitimacy among Nations* (Oxford: Oxford University Press, 1990). Zia Mian applies a similar logic to arms control regimes. 'The American Problem: The United States and Non-Compliance in the World of Arms Control and Non-Proliferation', in Edward C. Luck and Michael W. Doyle (eds.), *International Law and Organization: Closing the Compliance Gap* (Lanham: Rowman and Littlefield, 2004).

focus especially on the legitimacy of formal international organisations, most notably (but not exclusively) the United Nations.[9] Some of these treatments challenge the core assumption of anarchy in international relations. Keohane, for example, suggests that the legitimacy of the UN Security Council has become more controversial precisely because it has assumed more intrusive governance functions in the post-Cold War world.[10] Hurd tackles the question even more explicitly: 'The presence of an international organization that states accept as legitimate means that we should not continue to talk of the international system as anarchy. Legitimate institutions suggest the existence of centers of *authority*.'[11]

While the resurgence of debate around the possibility of legitimate authority in the international system is valuable, however, it is also limited in that it retains the traditional focus on the legitimacy of entities and actors. This book argues that the concept of legitimacy can and should also be applied to actions. International diplomacy has a distinctive vocabulary of right and wrong behaviour, of obligations and taboos. Regardless of their actual behaviour, most governments employ this vocabulary to justify their own actions and judge the behaviour of others. States' actions can be – and frequently are – publicly judged as legitimate or illegitimate by other states.

Moreover, the legitimacy of an action is not merely derivative of the legitimacy of the actor: as international reactions to US military activity in Iraq highlighted, a state that is widely recognised as a legitimate actor on the international stage can nevertheless be perceived as acting illegitimately. This independence of the legitimacy of actor and action is not absolute, since over time illegitimate behaviour may cast doubt on a

---

[9] For an early exposition on the UN Security Council, see David D. Caron, 'The Legitimacy of the Collective Authority of the Security Council', *American Journal of International Law*, 87:4 (October 1993). For more recent treatments, see Ian Hurd, 'Legitimacy, Power, and the Symbolic Life of the UN Security Council', *Global Governance*, 8 (2002); Eric Voeten, 'The Political Origins of the UN Security Council's Ability to Legitimize the Use of Force', *International Organization* 59:3, 2005; Robert Keohane, 'The Contingent Legitimacy of UN-Based Multilateralism', paper presented at a conference on 'Legitimacy and Power in the Post-9/11 World', University of Southern California, 27 April 2005. On international organisations more generally, see Hurd, 'Legitimacy and Authority in International Politics' and Jean-Marc Coicaud and Veijo Heiskanen, *The Legitimacy of International Organizations* (Tokyo: United National University Press, 2001).

[10] Keohane, 'The Contingent Legitimacy of UN-Based Multilateralism'.

[11] Hurd, 'Legitimacy, Power, and the Symbolic Life of the UN Security Council', p. 48. Emphasis in text.

state's legitimacy as an international actor. Nevertheless, the legitimacy of a state's or institution's action is at least in the short and medium term independent (as well as analytically distinct) from that state's or institution's legitimacy as an international actor. The most critical consequence of this independence is that even that vast majority of states whose legitimacy as international actors is not challenged cannot assume that the legitimacy of their actions will be similarly uncontroversial. This book will argue that this simple fact informs states' decisions to launch peace enforcement operations under the auspices of international organisations and thus gives international organisations a critical role to play in the contemporary international system.

Audience: whose legitimacy judgement?

Since legitimacy is a social and public status, the concept is inextricably linked to a notion of audience. There must be some social group that judges the legitimacy of an actor or action based on the common standards acknowledged by this group. Yet most discussions of legitimacy in international relations theory are notably silent on the question of audience. They tend to ask whether a particular entity is legitimate or how it can improve its legitimacy, but they do not specify *in whose eyes* this legitimacy is or should be established.

Governments launching peace enforcement operations face at least four potentially crucial legitimacy audiences. The first is domestic public opinion within the intervening state. Peace enforcement operations involve a significant expenditure of national resources abroad. Troops must be deployed, supported, and equipped, military hardware is used and often expended or damaged, and considerable financial costs are incurred. This means that domestic popular support of, or at least acquiescence in, a peace enforcement operation is likely to be important to intervening governments. This can be expected to be especially the case in democracies, but even autocratic regimes must ensure the acquiescence of crucial elements of their support base, since an unpopular peace enforcement operation can result in the violent overthrow of a regime. The 1994 coup in the Gambia, for example, was precipitated by the Gambia's participation in the ECOWAS intervention into Liberia. Public opinion on an intervention can be swayed by many material and strategic factors, but to the extent that legitimacy perceptions also enter the equation, intervening governments have an interest in ensuring that key sections of society see the intervention as corresponding to the standards for deployment of military force accepted among them.

The second potentially important legitimacy audience for states launching a peace enforcement operation is the public within the country of deployment. Although by definition peace enforcement operations do not assume the consent of all parts of the host society (otherwise enforcement would not be necessary), they do require at least acquiescence, if not support, from substantial sections of that society. Peace enforcement contingents generally lack the force ratios as well as the mandate to impose their own rule on the country they are deployed in and are therefore dependent on the collaboration of local powers. Moreover, the population of a host country can typically provide important support to peace enforcement troops, including not only supplies and services but also information on the composition, location, and aims of combatant forces. Since their willingness to provide this support is likely to be linked to their perceptions of the extent to which outside intervention is just and warranted, public opinion in the host country represents a potentially important legitimacy audience for states launching peace enforcement operations.

The immediate neighbours of the intervening state constitute the third potential legitimacy audience. By virtue of their geographical location, these states often have significant importance for and leverage over the intervening state. Few states can afford to ignore regional politics, and many are (or wish to become) members of regional political or trade arrangements. Should the intervening state's neighbours perceive a peace enforcement operation as illegitimate, this might alter regional alliance or trade patterns to its detriment. Reactions are likely to be particularly strong when the intervention takes place within the region, since then neighbouring states can be expected to have ties to and interests in the 'host' country as well as the intervening state. Finally, regional states have a particular incentive to react strongly against a perceived aggression, since their geographical proximity to the offending state renders them more vulnerable to any expansionist tendencies. Thus both normative and security concerns can be expected to lead regional states to balance against a neighbour viewed as launching an illegitimate military intervention.

The final potential legitimacy audience is often referred to as the international community. It has the capacity to issue resounding condemnation, apply global economic sanctions, and even launch a counter-offensive against a state that is perceived to have intervened illegitimately in another state. In its most frequent application, this somewhat nebulous term includes not only all states in the international system, but also transnational and domestic civil societies and the world media. However, the case studies in this book suggest that most states have a more state-centric view of this audience. For them, the international community is in the first instance a community of other states, represented by governments. It is fellow *states* that are recognised as peers and hold the greatest power to apply pressure against a state either bilaterally or through international institutions. Public opinion campaigns and consumer boycotts are often critical in focusing states' attention on a particular issue, but are rarely able to significantly constrain a foreign state unless they are supported, coordinated, and reinforced by state actions.[12] Ultimately, therefore, an intervening state is likely to perceive the international community *of states* as its most immediately crucial legitimacy audience at the global level – though there is no doubt that especially in democracies, the legitimacy judgement of the government will be significantly impacted by the media and domestic civil society.

These groups represent four potential legitimacy audiences for a state launching a peace enforcement operation. They are analytically distinct although their judgements may to some extent be interdependent and the third audience represents a sub-set of the fourth. There are marked differences among them, including the fact that only the latter two can be said to constitute truly international legitimacy audiences: *international* legitimacy concerns must thus be concerns about the legitimacy judgements of one or both of these audiences. Finally, it is worth noting that these are *potential* legitimacy audiences. A particular intervening state may have its own reasons for privileging one audience over another or ignoring one altogether. The following empirical chapters will suggest that states launching peace enforcement operations generally have strong international legitimacy concerns and that the auspices of an international organisation are particularly effective in addressing this type of concern. The current discussion merely seeks to highlight that legitimacy by definition presupposes an audience, so that we cannot fully discuss the one without analysing the nature of the other.

---

[12] Note, for example, the continuing importance of states in the 'boomerang pattern' of pressure identified as a key tool for transnational activists in Margaret E. Keck and Kathryn Sikkink, *Activists Beyond Borders: Advocacy Networks in International Politics* (Ithaca: Cornell University Press, 1998).

Rules and laws: standards for international legitimacy judgements

Legitimacy is a public judgement according to public rules. It does not simply reflect the particular tastes or preferences of an individual, but must be justified with respect to commonly understood and shared standards of behaviour (for actions) or recognition (for actors). Thus for international legitimacy judgements by states to be possible, the international system must be conceived of as a society structured by a set of commonly understood rules. Such a conception has been proposed by both the English School of international relations theory and by constructivism, and it is also espoused in this book.

States are not inanimate objects that act and react to each other mechanically. Instead, governments acting on behalf of states are conscious actors who realise that they are interacting with other, equally conscious, agents. They also realise that this interaction is structured (and rendered possible) by a set of 'rules of the game'. To borrow Finnemore's definition of a norm, there are 'shared expectations about behaviour' in this international 'community of actors'.[13] States acknowledge these rules in their public discourses though not necessarily in their actions. They may engage in aggression, commit war crimes, or violate diplomatic immunity, but they do not publicly admit to doing so. They seek to hide these activities or, if discovered, argue that they comply with internationally accepted standards of conduct. Their public judgements of other states' actions are couched in similar terms. Such justification and judgement – and hypocrisy – only make sense in a context of common rules to apply, appeal, and pay lip service to. Thus, as Hedley Bull put it, the modern state system is a society whose members 'conceive themselves to be bound by a common set of rules in their relations with one another'.[14]

It is tempting to conflate the rules that necessarily underlie international legitimacy judgements with international laws. Both are public standards of behaviour and there is considerable overlap between them. In general, activity that is in strict accordance with international law is unlikely to be perceived as illegitimate, while actors engaging in illegal

---

[13] Martha Finnemore, *National Interests in International Society* (Ithaca: Cornell University Press, 1996), p. 22.

[14] Hedley Bull, *The Anarchical Society: A Study of Order in World Politics* (New York: Columbia University Press, 1995), p. 13.

activity have particular reason to fear that their behaviour will be viewed as illegitimate. This overlap is no coincidence: as Thomas Franck has pointed out, laws that do not reflect the commonly accepted principles of a society are likely to be discredited over time.[15] The fact that there is a tendency among both practitioners and scholars of international relations to use the word 'legitimate' and 'legal' as synonyms is therefore hardly surprising.

Nevertheless, the rules that provide standards for legitimacy judgements in the society of states can and should be distinguished from international laws. Empirically, the legitimacy and legality of actions do not always coincide. Not all actions that violate international law provoke the same amount of international opprobrium, while some legal actions face international censure. It was not illegal for the USA to withdraw from the Anti-Ballistic Missile Treaty but in doing so it provoked an international outcry. NATO's 1999 Kosovo campaign was illegal because it lacked a UN Security Council mandate, but it aroused less protest than Iraq's equally unauthorised and illegal invasion of Kuwait in 1990. The Independent International Commission on Kosovo has in fact explicitly claimed that NATO's campaign in Kosovo was 'illegal but legitimate'.[16] This suggests the need to differentiate between international law and international legitimacy.

This distinction is most easily made with regard to international treaty law. Some rules, like precepts governing the recognition of sovereign states, are not explicitly codified in any international document. Others are codified, but remain analytically prior to their contractual embodiments. As Bull noted, formal international law may 'state the basic rules of coexistence among states and other actors in international society', but it 'can contribute to international order ... only if [it already has] some basis in the actual dealings of states with one another'.[17] This does not make treaties irrelevant, since they may enhance compliance by clarifying obligations, increasing the precision of international rules, or allowing for delegation to settle disputes about

---

[15] Thomas M. Franck, 'Interpretation and Change in the Law of Humanitarian Intervention', in J.L. Holzgrefe and Robert O. Keohane (eds.), *Humanitarian Intervention: Ethical, Legal, and Political Dilemmas* (Cambridge: Cambridge University Press, 2003).

[16] The Independent International Commission on Kosovo, *The Kosovo Report: Conflict, International Response, Lessons Learned* (Oxford: Oxford University Press, 2000).

[17] Bull, *The Anarchical Society*, pp. 135–7.

interpretation.[18] It is nevertheless useful to distinguish between international rules and the international treaties that may codify them.

The distinction between international rules and customary international law is harder to establish. Customary international law emanates from state practice grounded in *opinio juris*, in other words from regular patterns of behaviour that states believe to be enjoined by law. This seems to point towards exactly the kind of commonly accepted but not necessarily codified 'rules of the game' discussed above. The value of distinguishing legality from legitimacy becomes clear, however, when we consider the longstanding controversy among international lawyers regarding the process by which customary law evolves. As Michael Byers notes, the 'chronological paradox' here is that a change in state practice can only be initiated by behaviour that deviates from previous practice – but this requires a state to either knowingly violate existing customary law or be mistaken in its belief of what the law is (its *opinio juris*).[19] For most international lawyers, however, neither violation nor mistake seem satisfactory vehicles for the evolution of international law. The one privileges powerful states able and willing to breach existing law and the other essentially bases the evolution of law on ignorance. Nevertheless, it is clearly essential that customary law be able to evolve in order to stay relevant in a changing international system.

Resolving this apparent conundrum depends on – and therefore highlights – the distinction between international legality and legitimacy. Consider the innovative understanding of the evolution of customary law developed by Byers. Rejecting the notion that customary law evolves by mistake, Byers suggests several ways of attenuating the problem of evolution by violation. First, he argues that state practice is constituted by both actions and statements,[20] which makes it possible to change customary law without a direct act of violation. A statement that distances itself from established state practice does not violate the law, and an accumulation of such statements can alter the content of the law and thus smooth the legal way for the first action to break with previous

[18] Kenneth Abbott, Robert O. Keohane, Andrew Moravcsik, Anne-Marie Slaughter, and Duncan Snidal, 'The Concept of Legalization', *International Organization*, 54:3 (2000). See the remainder of this special issue of *International Organization* for discussions of the possible impact of legalization.
[19] Michael Byers, *Custom, Power and the Power of Rules: International Relations and Customary International Law* (Cambridge: Cambridge University Press, 1999), pp. 130–3.
[20] Ibid., pp. 156–7.

patterns of behaviour. Since states do not necessarily respect this avenue of legal evolution, however, the question remains: when can an action that violates precedent without preparatory collective statements of legal change effect a change in customary law?

In response, Byers suggests two parameters. The first is that fundamental legal rules ('principles') regarding jurisdiction, personality, reciprocity, and legitimate expectations constrain the ways in which international law can be altered even by powerful states willing to break with existing practice to set new precedents for international law.[21] The second is the collective nature of the determination of international law. An act that violates existing practice will only establish a new precedent if most states signal their support of or at least acquiescence in the new international law being proposed – and even a powerful state cannot fully control the reactions of other states.[22] Two things are striking about these parameters. First, as Byers notes, they do not eliminate the advantage powerful states have in shaping customary law, which derives from these states' ability to bear the costs of an action that violates existing practice. Second, as Byers admits, neither parameter resolves the chronological paradox.[23] Even if it is widely supported by other states and seeks change compatible with Byers' four principles, action that is contrary to established practice represents an instance of law being developed by violation. The difference between a successful and an unsuccessful attempt to change customary international law by precedent is therefore not found in the legality of the action but in its acceptance among other states – in other words its *legitimacy*.

Byers does not fully address what determines this legitimacy. He argues that states will decide how to react to proposed changes based on their perceived material and ideational interests. He might be expected to argue for some kind of collective standard influencing state judgements since, drawing on Alexander Wendt, he explicitly proposes conceiving of 'the customary process ... as involving a "collective knowledge" or set of shared understandings'.[24] Yet Byers restricts this collective knowledge to a common understanding of how the *process* of evolution works, rather than imposing any restrictions on the possible *content* of rules.[25] He thus presents the decision about international acceptability as merely an aggregation of individual preferences: 'rules are developed only when they are in the interests of most

---

[21] Ibid., chapters 4–7.   [22] Ibid., p. 157.   [23] Ibid., p. 158.
[24] Ibid., p. 148.   [25] Ibid., p. 150.

if not all States, as those States perceive and manifest those interests to be'.[26] This atomisation of states is incongruous in a context in which they are asked not only to judge a particular action but also to contribute to the development of a common system of laws. Yet, as will be further argued below, there is also little reason to believe that the disparate and often profoundly divided states of the current international system base their legitimacy judgements on 'a common sense of moral justice', as Thomas Franck has suggested.[27]

An intermediate position begins by recognising that the practice which constitutes customary law is also an expression of generally accepted 'rules of the game' in the international system. It also acknowledges, however, that customary law and rules of the game develop differently. Customary law evolves by cumulative accepted precedents: although ultimately determined by states, it has an objectified presence in past practice and current jurisprudence. By contrast, international rules of the game depend entirely on the shared understandings of states about the principles governing their interaction. The shared, intersubjective quality of these rules makes them resistant to change, but even abrupt change is nevertheless possible at any instant, assuming sufficient consensus among states. The international community may at any one time overthrow its precedents and endorse (or reject) a particular activity as corresponding to (or violating) the new rules it now acknowledges.

When a state's action violates existing practice, therefore, it violates international customary law. Legitimacy, however, is a judgement of acceptability independent of legal strictures.[28] The illegal action thus may or may not be judged by other states to also violate the prevailing rules of the game. If states are persuaded that the action merely applies the existing rule to new circumstances, they will be inclined to accept it as legitimate. If states believe that the action violates existing rules, they will be equally inclined to view it as illegitimate – unless they are persuaded that a change in the rules is necessary. Thus legitimacy judgements of states have an element of collectivity: they reflect understandings of what the current rules of the collective game are. They may also, of course, reflect the various individual interests of particular states, and are therefore unlikely to be unanimous. In aggregation,

[26] Ibid., p. 155.
[27] Franck, 'Interpretation and Change in the Law of Humanitarian Intervention', p. 216.
[28] Thanks to an anonymous reviewer for suggesting this formulation.

however, international legitimacy judgements can be seen to reflect common understandings of the rules structuring international politics, though not necessarily a common morality.

It is this difference in the developmental processes of customary law and international rules of the game that opens the possibility of an action being either legitimate but illegal or legal but illegitimate. Over time, as precedents become established, legality and legitimacy can once again be expected to coincide. It is nevertheless important to distinguish the two concepts – not least in order to form a more complete picture of how customary law evolves. The chronological paradox cannot be completely overcome: in the absence of preparatory statements altering practice, an action that establishes a new precedent will constitute a violation of international law. Distinguishing legality from legitimacy, however, allows us to think more systematically about why some such actions are clearly perceived as violations and others accepted as precedents for evolving customary law.

Motivations: why states care about international legitimacy

Having defined and described the concept of international legitimacy, the question that remains is whether and why legitimacy matters in international politics. This question can be broken into two components. First, in general terms, why might states value the international rules that form the basis of legitimacy judgements? Second, more specifically, why might states care whether their own actions are perceived as internationally legitimate? A relatively thin conception of international society provides a starting point for answering both questions while avoiding both the problematic assumption of a deep normative consensus among states and the pitfalls of a purely functionalist understanding of international rules.

The English School is united in affirming the existence of an international society structured by rules but divided in its explanation for why states value these rules. Drawing on Martin Wight and John Vincent,[29] solidarists see international society as capable of moving towards a greater normative consensus that can provide a framework for

---

[29] Barry Buzan, 'From International System to International Society: Structural Realism and Regime Theory Meet the English School', *International Organization*, 47:3 (Summer 1993), p. 334. R. John Vincent, *Human Rights and International Relations* (Cambridge: Cambridge University Press, 1986).

international politics. Wheeler, for example, suggests that the recent acceptance of the legitimacy of UN-mandated humanitarian interventions by the society of states reflects a deepening (but not yet sufficient) collective commitment to human rights.[30] A major advantage of this approach is that it offers a ready explanation for why states care about the rules of the international system. If these rules reflect a substantive normative consensus among states, states can be assumed to value these rules because they endorse and share the moral position that underlies them.

Pluralists, however, argue cogently that such a deep normative consensus is extremely unlikely among the diverse and often deeply divided states of contemporary international society. In this respect, it is important to distinguish the content of a rule from the motivations of states acknowledging it. Although virtually all international rules have a moral dimension, states do not necessarily accept these rules *because of* their moral content. In fact, even solidarists acknowledge that states (or more properly their governments) tend to be decidedly uneven converts to substantive normative principles. One of the strengths of Wheeler's argument, for example, is that it explicitly does not contend that states invoke the norm of humanitarian intervention in good faith but holds that states are constrained by the norm *regardless* of their motivations.[31] This position is echoed in much contemporary constructivist writing, which examines the web of norms that structure international politics without necessarily attributing its effectiveness to a widespread normative consensus among states. Thus Finnemore and Sikkink suggest that only a select group of state and non-state norm entrepreneurs need to exhibit ideational commitment for a new norm to develop. If they secure a critical mass of state support (around one-third of the states in the system) a norm cascade ensues during which ideational commitment plays less of a role than 'peer pressure': states accept the norm not because they are convinced of its intrinsic moral value, but because they wish to appear legitimate to other states, demonstrate belonging to the international system through conformity, and secure the esteem of other states.[32]

---

[30] Wheeler, *Saving Strangers*. Wheeler suggests that this commitment should be further extended to accepting the legitimacy of unilateral humanitarian interventions that meet certain threshold criteria.

[31] Wheeler, *Saving Strangers*, p. 9.

[32] Martha Finnemore and Kathryn Sikkink, 'International Norm Dynamics and Political Change', *International Organization*, 52:4 (1998), pp. 895–904.

To the extent that states constitute the critical audience, therefore, international legitimacy judgements seem unlikely to reflect widely shared moral standards, though solidarists might argue that international society would be much improved if they did.[33] But if there is no consensus on the moral value of the content of international rules, why should states place any value on them? Here pluralists tend to draw on Hedley Bull, who postulated that states must accede to some set of common rules to establish a modicum of international order that allows them to interact in a predictable manner.[34] For pluralists, even states that are fundamentally divided on substantive moral issues can value international rules because they share a common interest in the order of international society that these rules help uphold. The advantage of this view is that it allows for the possibility of international legitimacy judgements even if the international society of states is not united by shared normative principles.[35] Some states may have a normative commitment to the content of existing rules, but it is not necessary for this commitment to be universal for legitimacy judgements to be possible. For many states, the international rules that set standards for legitimacy judgements may simply be commonly acknowledged 'rules of the game'.

In thus rejecting solidarism, it is nevertheless important not to go to the opposite extreme of a purely functionalist explanation of the value of international rules to individual states. Such an argument might run as follows: since most states value stability in the international system and predictability and non-violence in their relations with other states (at least most of the time), they are likely to value (if not always observe) the rules that provide this predictability and order. There are two main problems with this argument.

First, international order can theoretically be preserved by several different sets of rules. Even if all states value order, therefore, they need not value the same set of rules. Indeed, in the absence of a normative consensus the particular set of rules adopted is likely to be rooted in the

---

[33] Wheeler explicitly shifts to a different legitimacy audience to discuss what conceptions of legitimate humanitarian intervention should be: 'it is not sufficient to restrict our understanding of legitimacy to that of the practice of actors themselves . . . The problem with this conception of legitimacy is that it tells us nothing about the normative content of these norms and rules, or why they should be adhered to.' *Saving Strangers*, p. 10.

[34] Bull, *The Anarchical Society*.

[35] For equally thin views of the international society of states as a 'practical association' and 'rule community', respectively, see Terry Nardin, *Law, Morality, and the Relations of States* (Princeton: Princeton University Press, 1983) and Franck, *The Power of Legitimacy among Nations*.

prevailing balance of international power. Bull concedes this, but argues that the benefits of order ensure that even states disadvantaged by prevailing rules value them:

> the particular kinds of limitations that are imposed on resort to violence, the kinds of agreements whose binding character is upheld, or the kinds of rights of property that are enforced, will bear the stamp of those dominant elements. But that there should be limits of some kind on the resort to violence, an expectation in general that agreements will be carried out, and rules of property of some kind, is not in the special interest of some members of society, but a general interest of all of them.[36]

However, as Krasner has noted, if rules have distributional effects their content will be contentious even if all states are made better off by their presence.[37] In the absence of a moral consensus underpinning the prevailing set of international rules, therefore, these rules are likely to be contested, unless international order is held to be so precarious that states value the prevailing set of rules simply because it is the only set in fact providing order at that time. This logic of *après moi, le deluge* stands in contrast to the degree of contestation that in fact surrounds many prevailing international rules. Absent this logic, however, states cannot be held to value prevailing rules simply for their functional contribution to international order.

The second problem with a purely functionalist explanation is that it neglects the essentially social dimension of states' commitment to order in the international system. This dimension is most prominently suggested by the fact that rule contestation is itself generally rule-bound. States appear to recognise an obligation to the international system even as they challenge its specific rules. Andrew Hurrell has argued cogently that purely rationalist approaches cannot satisfactorily explain this phenomenon and insists that states' commitment to ordering rules beyond 'minimum rules of coexistence' must be embedded in a sense of both legal and moral community among states.[38]

While Hurrell thus rejects pluralist versions of the English School as well as rationalist regime theory, however, it is possible to conceive of a

---

[36] Bull, *The Anarchical Society*, p. 53.
[37] S. D. Krasner, 'Global Communications and National Power: Life on the Pareto Frontier', *World Politics*, 43:3 (April 1991).
[38] Andrew Hurrell, 'International Society and the Study of Regimes: A Reflective Approach', in Volker Rittberger (ed.), *Regime Theory and International Relations* (Oxford: Oxford University Press, 1997), pp. 58–65.

commitment to international society even in the absence of a substantive normative consensus among states. Buzan, recognising that 'in a postcolonial world, a global international society can only be multicultural', argues that a sense of shared identity can emerge out of the shared mutual recognition of sovereignty among states.[39] Similarly, Thomas Franck argues that:

> The rules of the international system obligate ... primarily because they are like the house rules of a club. Membership in the club confers a desirable status, with socially recognized privileges and duties and *it is the desire to be a member of the club, to benefit from the status of membership, that is the ultimate motivator of conformist behaviour: that and the clarity with which the rules communicate, the integrity of the process by which these rules were made and are applied, their venerable pedigree and conceptual coherence.*[40]

Franck thus sees international society as a 'rule community' in which states recognise a set of secondary rules (i.e. rules about rule-making), as a 'reciprocal of that [international] community's validation of their nations' statehood'.[41] Summing up this position, Reus-Smit notes, 'An international society can be said to exist when states mutually recognise each other's rights to sovereign authority, when sovereignty comes to be based less on states' material capacities to defend their independence than on institutionalised rules.'[42]

What distinguishes this model is that in it states share not only an understanding of how rules evolve but also a feeling of obligation to following this process because of their membership in international society. They understand themselves as members of a club of sovereign states, and therefore as obliged to respect order in that club, if only to the extent that they recognise certain procedures for changing its rules. Thus even if states disagree on the normative value of the content of prevailing rules, they value the society that these rules are both outgrowths of and

---

[39] Buzan, 'From International System to International Society', pp. 343–51. Constructivists have also noted that the mutual recognition of sovereignty forms the basis of a rudimentary society of states. See Alexander Wendt, 'Anarchy is What States Make of It', *International Organization*, 46:2 (Spring 1992); Christian Reus-Smit, *The Moral Purpose of the State* (Princeton: Princeton University Press, 1999); and Bukovansky, *Legitimacy and Power Politics*, p. 22.

[40] Franck, *The Power of Legitimacy among Nations*, p. 38. Italics in text.

[41] Ibid., p. 196.

[42] Christian Reus-Smit, 'The Politics of International Law', in Christian Reus-Smit (ed.), *The Politics of International Law* (Cambridge: Cambridge University Press, 2004), p. 33.

help to order. States may support changing these rules, but seeing them violated indicates a rejection of the rules' social context as well as of the rules themselves. This means that states have reason to care about international rules – and therefore legitimacy – even if they have no normative commitment to the substance of these rules and do not see them as uniquely able to provide order in the international system.[43]

Understanding the international system as a 'thin' society (i.e. a society not based on substantive normative consensus beyond the value of the society itself) also helps explain why individual states might worry about international legitimacy perceptions of their own actions. Such a motivation is missing in a purely functionalist account of the value of rules to individual states thanks to the familiar free-rider problem: the fact that international rules enhance order in the international system gives states a reason to want other states to obey these rules but does not necessarily mean that they want to follow these rules themselves. In fact, each state's ideal situation may be one in which it is able to free-ride on the order created by others obeying the prevailing rules while breaking these rules itself whenever this suits its strategic, economic, or political interests. States that conceive of themselves as members of an international society, however, face a more complicated calculation.

Following March and Olson's seminal article,[44] it has become common for theorists of international relations to distinguish two types of motivational logic behind state behaviour. The first is the 'logic of expected consequences' in which actors decide on a particular action based on their expectations of the costs and benefits it will entail. The second is the 'logic of appropriateness', where 'action involves evoking an identity or role and matching the obligations of that identity or role to a specific situation'.[45] The tendency to view these alternatives as presenting a strict dichotomy between consequential and identity-based motivations is unfortunate, however, because it obscures a third motivational logic. Based on a notion of states as conscious members of an international society, this logic could be called the logic of social action.

---

[43] The social context of states also helps situate Finnemore and Sikkink's assertion that in a norm cascade peer pressure rather than ideational commitment may be a driving factor for states ('International Norm Dynamics and Political Change', pp. 902–4). States come to accept a new norm as a new 'club rule' rather than because they are necessarily convinced of the inherent value of the rule.

[44] James G. March and Johan P. Olsen, 'The Institutional Dynamics of International Political Orders', *International Organization*, 52:4 (Autumn 1998).

[45] Ibid., p. 951.

According to this logic, states care about the legitimacy of their actions because they recognise themselves to be inevitably social actors. They are members of a society of states that recognises a set of rules of international behaviour and has a general preference for these rules to be observed. Their behaviour is shaped by these rules not because good international citizenship has become an intrinsic part of their identity (a logic of appropriateness) but because they enjoy being seen as good 'club members' by other states. The operative logic is other-regarding rather than self-regarding: states need not inherently want to act as good citizens, they simply want to *be seen* as such. States know that other states will judge their actions according to the prevailing rules, and they care about these judgements because they recognise themselves to be in an on-going social relation with these other states. Empirically, states dislike opprobrium from their peers. They are embarrassed by hostile resolutions in the UN General Assembly, dislike being voted out of prestigious positions within international organisations, and resent adverse or hostile international assessments of their country. By contrast, they enjoy being regarded as valuable members of the international community and eminent global citizens. Ian Hurd has argued convincingly that the politics surrounding the membership of the UN Security Council, for example, can only be fully understood if the social prestige of being associated with the Council is appreciated.[46]

These preferences affect states' behaviour, especially when they engage in high-profile international activities. The more likely an activity is to command international attention, the greater are both the risk of incurring international opprobrium and the chance of garnering international prestige. Because peace enforcement operations are dramatic, expensive, controversial, and relatively rare events, they inevitably attract the attention of other governments and of the world media. They are thus precisely the kinds of state activities in which legitimacy concerns are most likely to arise.

Three caveats should be raised about this position. First, the legitimacy concerns described here differ from the reputational concerns that game theorists analyse. In game theory, reputations are considered important because they offer a way for players to reap the benefits of cooperation with other players in iterated games. Building a reputation for honouring agreements helps players persuade their interlocutors to engage in cooperative activities with them. Reputations also allow

---

[46] Hurd, 'Legitimacy, Power, and the Symbolic Life of the UN Security Council', pp. 41–4.

players to make more credible commitments to cooperative strategies, since staking their reputations increases states' costs of defection, which now include the loss of future benefits from cooperation. These reputational arguments are squarely anchored in the framework of the logic of expected consequences: players care about their reputations only because they allow them to reap benefits in the future. However, reputational arguments lose analytical clarity as they are extended to involve more diffuse reciprocity in large social groups and over longer time periods.[47] The logic of social action does not rely on predictions of future material disadvantages as a result of rule violation. Instead, it suggests that states also value international legitimacy for the immediate and non-material benefits it entails. They value their standing in international society as an end in itself, not simply as a means to other ends, and they chafe at international opprobrium itself, not only at its possible material consequences.

Second, states do not care *only* about international legitimacy. 'Naming and shaming' has been a notoriously weak mechanism for ensuring compliance with international treaties precisely because although states care about the legitimacy of their actions, they also have a myriad of other political, economic, and strategic interests. The same is clear in peace enforcement operations. Even though they occur for ostensibly altruistic reasons, states are unlikely to shoulder the risks and costs involved unless they perceive their national interests to be significantly affected. Therefore launching these operations must, from the point of view of the international community, be an exercise in harnessing partiality: states that already have an interest in intervening in a crisis must be persuaded to do so in a manner that maximises the benefits to the target country and to the international community as a whole. The interests involved vary from state to state and from intervention to intervention and are not necessarily sinister, potentially including bolstering the credibility of an alliance, containing neighbourhood insecurity, or responding to a domestic imperative for action in the face of graphic media reporting as well as economic enrichment and/or power-projection. The fact remains, however, that pure altruism is exceedingly unlikely to be the sole motivation of any lead state launching a peace enforcement operation. Therefore all lead states are open to accusations of sinister or self-serving motives – but then this is precisely why they will *also* be concerned about legitimacy.

---

[47] Hurrell, 'International Society and the Study of Regimes', p. 59.

The final caveat is that states need not only care about legitimacy for purely ideational reasons. In fact, there are three main ways of conceptualising the connection between legitimacy and the mobilisation of resources for a peace enforcement operation. First, international legitimacy may itself have material benefits. The empirical chapters of this book show, for example, that legitimacy makes it easier for a state to convince other states to participate in a peace enforcement operation it is launching, thus diminishing its own share of the material burden imposed by the operation. However, this study will also argue that the material contributions of many participants in peace enforcement operations are in fact symbolic. Thus in many cases participants are courted to bolster the international legitimacy of the intervention instead of legitimacy being sought to attract them.

Second, international legitimacy can help mobilise resources by positively affecting other relevant legitimacy audiences, such as the domestic publics in the lead state or in the host country of the intervention. This book argues, however, that these instrumental benefits of international legitimacy are relatively marginal. Public opinion in the host state is more likely to be swayed by the conduct and effectiveness of peace enforcers than by international assessments of the legitimacy of their deployment. Public opinion in intervening states will also be shown to be less influenced by international legitimacy judgements than might be expected: autocracies generally disregard domestic opinion and established democracies rarely contemplate a peace enforcement operation unless its domestic legitimacy is already established. Appreciable interdependence between international and domestic legitimacy is thus usually limited to new democracies (where public legitimacy is more tenuous) and interventions that last long enough to erode initial public support (which is not the scenario usually anticipated by states launching a peace enforcement operation).

Finally, constructivism points to a more fundamental way in which international legitimacy makes resources available for peace enforcement operations. At the core of this perspective is the notion that international politics is structured by normative and ideational as well as material factors.[48] Particular types of activity only become possible as shared understandings of this activity emerge in international society. Thus Martha Finnemore has argued forcefully that humanitarian interventions have only become possible because of an increasing

---

[48] Reus-Smit, 'The Politics of International Law', p. 21.

international acceptance of humanitarian justifications for military intervention since World War Two.[49] In this sense, it is only international legitimacy that makes a particular kind of activity possible. If the concept of legitimate peace enforcement did not already exist in the international system, a state could still intervene in another conflict. However, it would be hard pressed to explain or justify this action either to its domestic public or to other states in the international system, which in turn would make it supremely difficult to mobilise international or domestic resources for this intervention. This study accepts the constructivist notion that peace enforcement operations can only occur if there is already 'normative space' for them in the international system. Still in keeping with constructivism, however, it also argues that states do not *only* care about occupying this space because it leads to greater resource mobilisation. They *also* seek the legitimacy made possible by the existence of this space as an inherent good because they fundamentally care about their standing in the international society structured by these shared understandings.

International organisations and the international legitimacy of peace enforcement operations

Having established the relevance of international legitimacy theoretically, we can now examine the dynamics of international legitimacy judgements in the particular case of peace enforcement operations. This section will describe the rules that currently apply to these interventions, elucidate how these rules create a role for international organisations as gatekeepers to international legitimacy, and delineate the scope for strategic state behaviour within this framework. Together, these elements provide an explanation for why states launch peace enforcement operations through international organisations.

Contemporary international rules regarding peace enforcement

Three main rules are relevant for international legitimacy judgements of peace enforcement operations: respect for state sovereignty, the

---

[49] Martha Finnemore, 'Military Intervention and the Organization of International Politics', in Joseph Lepgold and Thomas G. Weiss (eds.), *Collective Conflict Management and Changing World Politics* (Albany: State University of New York Press, 1998), pp. 185–9.

prohibition on aggressive war, and the endorsement of military action to promote international peace and security.[50] These rules derive from different historical periods and stand in considerable tension with each other, but together they limit the kinds of military activity that can be judged legitimate in the current international system.

Military intervention in other polities is as old as international relations itself. Thucydides' *History of the Peloponnesian War* chronicles scores of such interventions, including into civil wars.[51] Nevertheless, the first rule relevant to the peace enforcement operations today has its roots in the emergence of the Westphalian sovereignty regime from the seventeenth century onwards. Although the 1648 Peace of Westphalia invented neither the principle of *cuius regio, eius religio* nor the modern state system, it did reflect the emergence of territorially defined states as the major actors of world politics – and the beginnings of their attempt to regulate their interactions with each other. The parties at Westphalia sought to forestall another war of religion by curtailing the tendency of states (and other actors) to interfere in each other's religious life. From this impulse, there gradually grew a more general system enjoining non-intervention in domestic governance, which is what we understand as the rule of state sovereignty today. The principle has often been honoured only in the breach, but as argued above international rules do not require genuine normative commitment by states to structure international society. Even as 'organized hypocrisy',[52] the rule of state sovereignty and its logical corollary, the principle of non-intervention into the internal affairs of other states, remain relevant in framing legitimacy judgements in the current international system. Though the extent of immunity sovereignty provides for states is currently deeply contested, in part for reasons discussed below, the principle itself is far from having been superseded. Few other principles are as frequently affirmed in

---

[50] Once peace enforcement operations have deployed, the conduct of operations may also affect legitimacy judgements. In this study, however, the focus is primarily on the legitimacy of launching peace enforcement operations.

[51] Thucydides argues that Athens' intervention in the civil war in Corcyra set the trend for further interventions by Athens and Sparta in civil wars throughout the Hellenic world. Thucydides, *History of the Peloponnesian War*, translated by Rex Warner (London: Penguin Classics, 1972), pp. 236–45.

[52] Stephen D. Krasner, *Sovereignty: Organized Hypocrisy* (Princeton: Princeton University Press, 1999).

diplomatic discourse and in the debates and resolutions of the various bodies of the United Nations.

The second international rule relevant to contemporary peace enforcement operations is the prohibition on aggressive war. For centuries, war was widely perceived as a legitimate activity of sovereign states. Statehood was thought to entail a right to wage war in pursuit of one's interests in matters ranging from acquiring colonies to collecting debts owed to a state's nationals.[53] However, the carnage of World War One and the stalemate of trench warfare raised questions both about the glory of modern war and its utility as a means of policy. Modern warfare seemed both dangerously inconclusive (leading to wars of attrition) and devastatingly costly, leaving victors and vanquished almost equally ruined. This set the stage for a revolution in international rules.

At Versailles in 1918 war was still officially deemed legitimate if it aimed at national self-determination. By 1928, however, sixty-five states were ready to sign the Kellogg-Briand Pact, thereby renouncing war as a means of diplomacy and declaring self-defence the only legitimate reason for war. The treaty codified into international law what had already become an international rule: that the aggressive use of military force was not an acceptable activity for sovereign states. Despite repeated violations since the 1920s, both the law and the rule against aggression remain intact. Aggressive warfare was one of the main charges at the Nuremberg trials. The UN Charter commits member states to use force only in self-defence or as part of a Security Council mandated mission.[54] The core purpose of the Security Council, meanwhile, is to preserve international peace and security and counter aggression.[55] Thus despite the débâcle of World War Two and repeated violations during the Cold War, the rule against aggression not only survived the twentieth century but emerged strengthened from it. Since 1945 no major power (and only very few minor ones) has declared war.[56] In the contemporary international system, it is simply not

---

[53] Regarding debt collection, see Finnemore, *The Purpose of Intervention*, chapter 2. For an early objection to aggressive war, however, see John S. Mill, 'A Few Words on Non-intervention', in Gertrude Himmelfarb (ed.), *J. S. Mill Essays on Politics and Culture* (Garden City: Doubleday, 1963).

[54] UN Charter, Articles 2, 42–49, and 51. The only exception, concerning actions against World War Two enemies (Article 107), is now outdated.

[55] Ibid., Article 39.   [56] Finnemore, *The Purpose of Intervention*, p. 134.

acceptable (as well as illegal) to wage a war of aggression. Iraq's international isolation after its 1990 invasion of Kuwait is testimony to this fact, as were the USA's emphatic efforts to reject allegations of aggression during the 2003 invasion of Iraq.

The prohibition on aggressive warfare modifies the earlier rule of state sovereignty, since sovereign states are denied their previously accepted prerogative of declaring war to further their national interests. Both rules militate against peace enforcement operations, however, since these operations involve interference in the internal affairs of a sovereign state and an unsolicited military deployment into its territory. The fact that it is at all possible to justify contemporary peace enforcement operations derives from a third and most recent set of international rules: the rules of justified intervention.

The only established exception to the rule of state sovereignty in the contemporary international system is the acknowledgement that international military intervention may be necessary in the interest of international peace and security.[57] This rule has its roots in the failure of the British and French appeasement policies in the 1930s, which not only did not prevent World War Two but arguably encouraged Nazi aggression and prolonged the war by allowing Germany to increase its military strength and access to raw materials. The lesson states learned was that the stability of the international system (and ultimately their own security) might require a collective military intervention to check some countries' activities. This realisation underlies the collective security system enshrined into law by Article 2.7 of the UN Charter, which explicitly authorises the violation of state sovereignty in order to counter acts of aggression and threats to or breaches of the peace. The

---

[57] Historically, there have been other attempts to establish exceptions to the Westphalian sovereignty system. In the nineteenth century, the conservative powers in the Concert of Europe argued for a right to intervene in liberal revolutions but no broadly accepted rule emerged because Britain opposed the notion. Louise Richardson, 'The Concert of Europe and Security Management in the Nineteenth Century', in Helga Haftendorn, Robert O. Keohane, and Celeste A. Wallander, *Imperfect Unions: Security Institutions over Time and Space* (London: Oxford University Press, 1999), p. 58. However, colonial intervention into less 'civilised' nations was permitted in the nineteenth century. Marc Trachtenberg, 'Intervention in Historical Perspective', in Laura W. Reed and Carl Kayson (eds.), *Emerging Norms of Justified Intervention* (Cambridge, Mass.: American Academy of Arts and Sciences, 1993), pp. 21–7. This rule essentially decreed that the Westphalian sovereignty system did not apply to the non-European world. It was abandoned by the 1960s, and decolonisation brought the developing world into the Westphalian system.

reason is made clear in the Charter's first preamble: 'to save succeeding generations from the scourge of war, which twice in our life-time has brought untold sorrow to mankind'.

This rule of intervention for the sake of international peace and security has undergone a remarkable evolution since the end of the Cold War. The drafters of the UN Charter envisioned strong aggressor states as the major threat to international stability. Intervention in the internal affairs of states was not deemed necessary to promote international peace and security.[58] In the 1990s, however, civil wars in weak and failing states emerged as primary international concerns. This new threat perception combined with the pre-existing rule allowing military intervention to protect international peace and security to open the possibility of legitimate peace enforcement operations within sovereign states.

The key criterion of legitimacy is that the intervention should serve the international system, distinguishing peace enforcement operations from both purely self-serving and purely humanitarian interventions. Advocacy for the latter has made considerable inroads into the contemporary international discourse. Most recently, the Canadian-sponsored International Commission on Intervention and State Sovereignty saw its concept of an international 'Responsibility to Protect' individuals whose government is unable or unwilling to shield them from genocide, war crimes, ethnic cleansing, or crimes against humanity adopted by the 2005 UN World Summit.[59] The Summit document also stressed that intervention should remain subject to Security Council decisions on a 'case-by-case basis', however, reflecting the fact that states are still far from a consensus on a new rule of purely humanitarian intervention. At the interstate level, interventions are likely to continue being defended as necessary for international peace and security as well as warranted on humanitarian grounds. Academics have argued since the early 1990s that in the contemporary threat environment humanitarianism and international peace and security

---

[58] The failure to prevent the Holocaust shamed states into creating the Convention against Genocide, but a rule for intervention to stop genocide (much less other humanitarian catastrophes) was not established after World War Two. For a US-focused overview of this failure, see Samantha Power, *A Problem From Hell: America and the Age of Genocide* (New York: Basic Books, 2002).

[59] International Commission on Intervention and State Sovereignty, *The Responsibility to Protect* (Ottawa: International Development Research Centre, 2001). UN General Assembly Resolution 60/1, 24 October 2005, Articles 138–139.

are closely linked.[60] UN Security Council resolutions also began equating humanitarian disasters with threats to international peace and security in order to authorise military action under Chapter VII of the UN Charter.[61] Until a new rule permitting humanitarian interventions in their own right is fully established, hybrid justifications citing international peace and security will remain central to establishing the international legitimacy of an intervention.

Thus an international rule justifying military interventions for the sake of international peace and security has emerged alongside the older rules of state sovereignty and non-aggression, and since the 1990s this rule has increasingly been understood to include interventions in civil wars. This raises the possibility of internationally legitimate peace enforcement operations. Aggressive war and violations of state sovereignty in pursuit of national interests remain taboo, however, which imposes a strict requirement of public justification on states wishing undertake legitimate international interventions. Unsolicited international military deployments can be justified – but only if other states accept that they serve international interests rather than (or at least as well as) purely national priorities. This caveat creates a key role for international organisations in peace enforcement operations.

International organisations and peace enforcement operations

The existence of international rules makes it possible to talk about legitimacy in international relations, and the rules regarding the use of military force described above set the parameters for legitimacy judgements of peace enforcement operations. Nevertheless, arriving at an international legitimacy judgement about any particular intervention is fraught with two difficulties.

The first problem lies in determining the facts of a situation and measuring them against the standards set by prevailing rules. Two questions are particularly relevant for legitimacy judgements of peace enforcement operations. First, what is the extent of the conflict in the

---

[60] A. Dowty and G. Loescher, 'Refugee Flows as Grounds for International Action', *International Security*, 21:1 (Summer 1996); Kevin Hartigan, 'Matching Humanitarian Norms with Cold, Hard Interests: The Making of Refugee Policies in Mexico and Honduras, 1980–89', *International Organization*, 46:3 (Summer 1992).

[61] International Institute for Strategic Studies, 'The Shifting Sands of Sovereignty', *Strategic Survey 1999/2000* (London: Oxford University Press, 1999). The only partial exception, INTERFET, is examined in chapter 7 of this book.

host country and what are its probable international consequences? Second, does or will a particular military intervention remedy the situation, and thus serve international rather than (or as well as) national interests? Even unbiased observers can differ in their answers to these questions – and few states are unbiased observers. Not only the intervening and target states but also their neighbours, rivals, and allies all have national interests affecting their responses to an intervention, as do states that are not directly affected by a particular deployment but either welcome or fear the precedent it may set.

The second difficulty arises from the fact that international legitimacy judgements require the interpretation of prevailing general rules in light of a specific situation. For example, in 1999 Lesotho's prime minister (and thus head of government) requested a military intervention opposed by the country's king and official head of state. What does respect for state sovereignty prescribe in such circumstances? Even more critical are interpretations of what constitutes a threat to international peace and security and therefore warrants intervention despite the rule of state sovereignty. As noted above, this conception evolved in the 1990s to include internal wars and has tended to embrace humanitarian catastrophes as having security consequences. Moreover, 'international security' has increasingly been interpreted as including regional as well as global dimensions.

This issue is further complicated by the fact that, as argued above, international rules are social conventions that exist purely through the assent or acquiescence of the states of the system. Unlike international law, they are not anchored in treaties, precedent, or established practice. What constitutes the 'prevailing rules' is thus open to amendment at any time if the members of the international system accept this change. An action that breaks previously accepted understandings of international rules can still be legitimate if the international community is persuaded to accept either a new rule or a new interpretation of existing rules. But who speaks for the international community? Individual states have only a partial view of it: they have their own beliefs about prevailing rules, which they confirm over time in interactions with other states, but they have no direct way of assessing what the international community as a whole accepts as legitimacy standards at any one point in time.

In the contemporary international system, international organisations are called upon to address both of these difficulties. The theoretically obvious solution to the problem of bias in assessing the facts of a situation is to delegate this task to a more neutral third party.[62] In the contemporary international system, this is often an intergovernmental organisation. As Keohane and Nye observe, since World War Two specific issue areas of international relations have 'typically [been] managed by an international organisation with a specific headquarters and a secretariat'.[63] These international organisations are presumed to overcome (or at least attenuate) the problem of bias by the institutionalised aggregation of the preferences of individual member states, perhaps combined with the input of a professional international secretariat. Thus Article 39 of the UN Charter charges the Security Council with recognising threats to international peace and security but Article 99 authorises the Secretary-General to bring potentially relevant situations to the Council's attention. Farer aptly summarises the belief underlying this dispensation: 'submitting the self-help impulse to the discipline of multimember organizations ... [is useful because] collective authorization will credential the intervention as authentically humanitarian rather than a seizure of assets or the imposition of a client regime'.[64]

Moreover, their multilateral nature generally allows international organisations to speak for the international community with more credibility than any individual state.[65] When a prevailing rule has either been challenged or opened for reinterpretation, individual states may feel uncertain about the standards by which the international legitimacy

---

[62] Alec Stone Sweet, 'Judicialization and the Construction of Governance', *Comparative Political Studies*, 32:2 (April 1999), p. 149. Nardin, *Law, Morality, and the Relations of States*, p. 90.

[63] Robert O. Keohane and Joseph S. Nye, 'The Club Model of Multilateral Cooperation and Problems of Democratic Legitimacy', paper prepared for the American Political Science Convention, Washington D.C., 31 August–3 September 2000, p. 2. See also Harold Hongju Koh, 'Why do Nations Obey International Law?', *The Yale Law Journal* 106:2599 (1997), p. 2614. Nardin, however, traces the roots of this function for international organisations back to the eighteenth century: *Law, Morality, and the Relations of States*, chapter 5.

[64] Tom Farer, 'A Paradigm of Legitimate Intervention', in Lori F. Damrosch (ed.), *Enforcing Restraint: Collective Intervention in Internal Conflicts* (New York: Council on Foreign Relations Press, 1993), p. 339.

[65] Note that this credibility is tied to a perception that the international organisation is truly multilateral, rather than an instrument of a single state. If this perception (and therefore the legitimacy of the international organisation itself) is challenged, its legitimising capacity will decline over time – a threat that is currently very keenly felt within the United Nations. Still, a multi-member international organisation inherently has more credibility than any single state when it claims to speak for the international community.

of a particular action should be judged. Many – especially those whose national interests are not immediately affected – will look for clues about the international community's reaction before voicing their own legitimacy judgements. International organisations provide both a forum and a focal point for this reaction. Their legitimacy judgements reflect not an individual opinion of prevailing rules but the aggregated perceptions of at least a section of the international community. Their approval of a particular state action is thus the most potent signal of that action's correspondence to commonly acknowledged rules (i.e. international legitimacy) available in the contemporary international system.

In sum, international legitimacy judgements are difficult to formulate because they are intrinsically collective value judgements about often ambiguous or controversial situations that are structured by commonly acknowledged but not immutable international rules. In this context of uncertainty, international organisations are in a privileged position for making authoritative judgements of both value and fact. Inis Claude recognised this as early as 1966, when he suggested that 'collective legitimization' is a core function of the United Nations:

> the function of legitimization in the international realm has tended in recent years to be increasingly conferred upon international political institutions . . . [I]t is the political judgement by their fellow practitioners of international politics that [statesmen] seek, not a legal judgement rendered by an international judicial organ . . . the legitimizing function performed by the United Nations organs is less a matter of purporting either to apply or to revise the law than of affixing the stamp of political approval or disapproval.[66]

The 'stamp of approval' of an international organisation for a peace enforcement operation indicates a collective judgement that the intervention both corresponds to the international community's interests and accords with its acknowledged rules. Individual states have only their particular judgements to set against this collective verdict. Unless motivated by significant national interests, few will be inclined to take up such an unequal contest.

With respect to peace enforcement operations, this legitimising function is not absolutely unique to the United Nations, although legally the UN Security Council is the only body empowered to authorise military

---

[66] Inis L. Claude, 'Collective Legitimization as a Political Function of the United Nations', *International Organization*, 20:3 (Summer 1966), pp. 370–2.

action to redress a threat to international peace and security.[67] As Claude points out, the UN's 'status as an institution approximating [membership] universality gives it obvious advantages for playing the role of custodian of the seals of international approval and disapproval'.[68] The more inclusive an international organisation's membership is, the more credible its claim to represent the international community as a whole becomes. Nevertheless, as Claude recognises, 'the function of collective legitimization is not, in principle, reserved exclusively to the United Nations'.[69] In the specific case of peace enforcement operations, there are two reasons why other international organisations may also play a legitimising role.

First, the UN is not necessarily the best-placed organisation to assess a particular conflict situation and its possible consequences for international peace and security, especially if this is understood to include regional as well as global security. This recognition is reflected in Chapter VIII of the UN Charter, which enjoins member states to seek to peacefully resolve local disputes through 'regional arrangements or agencies' before referring them to the Security Council.[70] It was also central to justifying an increasing emphasis on regional conflict management in the 1990s, which was spearheaded by UN Secretary-General Boutros-Ghali and reflected genuine enthusiasm as well as a more cynical disengagement by major UN members from intervention in 'Third World' conflicts.[71] Regional states are more aware of crises in their midst and more likely to understand the complexities of a local civil war and its impact on the wider region. Regional international organisations, as aggregations of these states, thus have considerable standing in evaluating whether a crisis constitutes a regional security threat. A regional organisation's declaration that a given situation constitutes a regional security threat or that a particular intervention serves a regional interest is hard to dispute from the outside. By contrast, confidence in the UN's ability to assess and willingness to acknowledge

---

[67] UN Charter, Articles 42, 53.1.
[68] Claude, 'Collective Legitimization as a Political Function of the United Nations', p. 371.
[69] Ibid., p. 372.
[70] UN Charter, Article 52.2. However, Article 53.1 explicitly forbids regional organisations engaging in enforcement action without Security Council authorisation.
[71] Boutros Boutros-Ghali, *An Agenda for Peace* (New York: United Nations, 1992), p. 35. For an account of cynical motives for some cases of regionalisation, see Eric Berman, 'The Security Council's Increasing Reliance on Burden-Sharing: Collaboration or Abrogation?' *International Peacekeeping*, 4:1 (Spring 1998).

impending security threats has been shaken by such notable instances as the UN failure to recognise the 1994 genocide in Rwanda.

Second, smaller international organisations become relevant when the UN refuses to react to a particular intervention. The UN has a superior claim to speaking for the international community thanks to its near-universal membership. Within the UN, the fifteen-member Security Council bears primary responsibility for maintaining international peace and security.[72] If the Council declines to announce its interpretation of international rules by neither granting nor withholding its seal of approval from an intervention, however, other international organisations may try to take its place. Much depends on why the Council does not pronounce on a case. In some cases examined in this book, the Security Council failed to respond because a particular conflict was not of sufficient interest to its members. In these cases, no pronouncement about the legitimacy of intervention was implied and regional organisations could step into the resulting void relatively easily. By contrast, if the Security Council does not respond to a crisis because its members are openly deadlocked on the question of intervention, the message is that at least part of the international community considers an intervention illegitimate. To replace the UN as gatekeeper to international legitimacy under these circumstances, a smaller organisation must seek to show that it is a truer reflection of the international community than the Security Council. The Kosovo case study in this book falls in this category. Overall, however, an unofficial effect of the regionalisation of conflict management in the 1990s was to shift some responsibility for approving peace operations towards regional organisations. Since several interventions launched without a UN mandate received at least partial post facto UN endorsement, regional organisations' claims to be effective interpreters of the international community's rules in moments of regional crisis were partially validated.

In sum, on the first dimension of facilitating international legitimacy judgements (assessing the facts of a situation), regional organisations have some advantages over the UN, although as subsequent chapters will show they also face problems of bias. On the second dimension (reflecting the international community's interpretation of prevailing rules) smaller international organisations lack the privileged status conveyed to the UN by its universal membership. However, they enjoy some legitimising potential in cases where the UN chooses to neither grant

---

[72] UN Charter, Article 24.1.

nor formally withhold its seal of approval. Thus although the UN remains the most important gatekeeper to international legitimacy for peace enforcement operations, other international organisations can also play a legitimising function.

The scope for strategic state behaviour

Thirty-five years ago, Inis Claude recognised the potential for strategic state behaviour within a system where international organisations act as guardians of international legitimacy. Referring specifically to the UN, he argued:

> Collective legitimization is an answer not to the question of what the United Nations can *do* but to the question of how it can be used. Statesmen have been more perceptive than scholars in recognizing and appreciating the significance of this potentiality for utilization of the Organization. They have persistently, and increasingly, regarded the United Nations as an agency capable of bestowing politically weighty approval and disapproval upon their projects and policies.[73]

Claude's insight holds true for peace enforcement operations. As argued above, lead states care about international legitimacy but also have a host of other policy goals. They thus have an incentive to act strategically o seek to legitimise the furthest possible pursuit of their national interests. The fact that international legitimacy judgements occur in a structure provided by public rules and international organisations does not rule out such strategic behaviour. On the contrary, this structure provides both the parameters and the forum for such strategic action.

Constructivists have long recognised that the existence of a structure does not preclude innovative action by agents. As Alexander Wendt has argued, agents and structure are mutually constitutive: while states cannot be conceived independently of the social structure in which they are embedded, this structure itself depends entirely on its recognition by states and can be changed by alterations in state practice.[74] This opens the possibility of strategic behaviour by agents to alter or reinterpret structure in line with national interests. With respect to international legitimacy, the scope for strategic state behaviour arises in the first

---

[73] Claude, 'Collective Legitimization as a Political Function of the United Nations', p. 373.
[74] Alexander Wendt, 'The Agent-Structure Problem in International Relations Theory', *International Organization*, 41:3 (1987).

instance from the flexibility of prevailing rules, understood both as their indeterminacy and their capacity for change. As regards indeterminacy, Bukovansky notes that several regime types can claim legitimacy even in an international political culture that recognises a single dominant form of legitimate authority.[75] Similarly, as the debate about humanitarian intervention reveals, several kinds of deployment can claim the legitimacy of bolstering international peace and security. Such ambiguity allows states to advance interpretations of prevailing rules that maximise their own international legitimacy or that of their preferred actions. However, as both Bukovansky and Wheeler cogently argue, rules are not infinitely flexible: some regime types or actions simply cannot be legitimated under existing rules.[76]

There is a second dimension to the flexibility of international rules, however: they are also open to outright change. States can seek to modify international rules to accommodate activities that would not qualify as internationally legitimate under the existing dispensation. Byers, for example, analyses how the USA has sought to change the international rules governing self-defence and the treatment of detainees.[77] However, since international rules are public conventions among all states in the system, they cannot be changed unilaterally. Change requires the assent of other members of the international society, and, as Byers shows, even a hegemon cannot force other states to accept new rules.

Thus the flexibility of international rules provides scope for strategic behaviour by states while the limits of this flexibility impose constraints on states seeking international legitimacy for their interventions. In the case of peace enforcement operations, however, strategic state behaviour has an additional dimension. States recognise that in the contemporary international system international organisations act as gatekeepers of international legitimacy for peace enforcement operations. Because international organisations have a privileged role in pronouncing on the content of prevailing rules and their applicability to particular interventions, the struggle for international legitimacy gains a concrete institutional forum. It becomes first and foremost a struggle to secure the mandate of an international organisation capable of generating that legitimacy.

---

[75] Bukovansky, *Legitimacy and Power Politics*, pp. 8–9.
[76] Ibid., p. 9; Wheeler, *Saving Strangers*, pp. 7–9.
[77] Michael Byers, 'Not Yet Havoc: Geopolitical Change and the International Rules on Military Force', forthcoming.

As discussed above, the benefit of such a mandate from the point of view of a state launching a peace enforcement operation is that it certifies an intervention as fulfilling an international interest and thus corresponding to the prevailing rules acknowledged by the international community. Although international organisations are presumed to transcend the biased perspectives of individual member states through aggregation, however, the pursuit of narrow domestic interests is far from impossible in this framework. As Michael Walzer notes, 'states don't lose their particularist character merely by acting together'.[78] The decision-making process within international organisations is charac-terised by intense political bargaining, and decisions on whether to grant or withhold a mandate for a peace enforcement operation do not escape this profoundly political logic. As Claude recognised, 'in final analysis the problem of legitimacy has a political dimension that goes beyond its legal and moral aspects . . . the process of legitimization is ultimately a political phenomenon, a crystallization of judgment that may be influ-enced but is unlikely to be wholly determined by legal norms and moral principles'.[79]

Crucially, moreover, states launching a peace enforcement operation are typically members of the international organisations whose stamp of approval they seek. They can use this insider position in their quest to marry the fullest possible pursuit of their interests with the requirements of international legitimacy. This may involve not only lobbying other member states for their support of the intervention but also seeking to manipulate the organisation's approval process in order to secure a mandate.

In these endeavours, states launching peace enforcement operations have three major assets. First, the intervention has a much higher priority for them than for most other member states, whose attention may be distracted by a multitude of other items on the organisation's agenda. They are therefore likely to enjoy a considerable advantage in terms of both their knowledge of an on-going crisis and their commit-ment to a particular strategy for resolving it. Second, by approaching the international organisation for a mandate, potential interveners reassure their fellow states of their general commitment to resolving the crisis

---

[78] Michael Walzer, *Just and Unjust Wars: A Moral Argument with Historical Illustrations* (New York: Basic Books, 1992), p. 107.
[79] Claude, 'Collective Legitimization as a Political Function of the United Nations', p. 369.

within the parameters set by prevailing international rules. Subsequent 'minor' attempts to manipulate the organisation's decision-making process are likely to be seen as a natural corollary of the state's operating within this framework, which helps limit the resulting alarm and protests. Finally, states wishing to launch peace enforcement operations are often the only ones willing to address a particular international crisis. If they experience difficulties obtaining their organisation's mandate for intervention on their own terms, they can threaten not to intervene at all, which would increase the pressure on other states to address the potential threat to international peace and security. To avoid this pressure, states may be willing to certify a dubious intervention as legitimate.

Despite these advantages, states wishing to launch a peace enforcement operation cannot wholly mould the international organisations within which they operate to their wishes. International organisations are composed of sovereign states that may be vulnerable to pressure or incentives but retain the capacity to choose whether or not to support a proposed intervention. International organisations also have established rules and regulations, most notably regarding their decision-making procedures. States seeking to legitimise an intervention face a fine balancing act: they may seek to manipulate the decision-making process, but excessively blatant violations raise questions about the validity of the mandate obtained and may damage the international organisation's internal unity and international credibility. Finally, the rules of the international system themselves impose limits on the kinds of activities international organisations can endorse. Manipulating international organisations allows intervening states some latitude to legitimise activities that are controversial under existing rules, but since these rules are not infinitely flexible, the discretion of international organisations is also limited. An organisation that succumbs to political pressure from member states to endorse a blatant violation of prevailing rules loses its own credibility as custodian of those rules. Although these factors constrain the exercise of state power within international organisations, however, manipulation of the mandating process by prospective lead states remains a reality.

There is one further avenue for strategic behaviour for states launching a peace enforcement operation. It arises from the fact that the ability to legitimise an intervention does not belong exclusively to any single international organisation. As argued above, the United Nations' stamp of approval for an intervention carries special weight, but in its absence a mandate from a smaller international organisation can also bolster an intervention's international legitimacy. Lead states benefit from this multiplicity of potential legitimising organisations because it offers them a choice of forums to operate in, even if not all the options are equally desirable.

Ideally, lead states would like to secure a UN mandate, thus both ensuring their intervention's legality and maximising its legitimacy. Note, however, that the legitimacy bestowed by the UN is not simply derivative of its unique legal status. The UN Charter suggests the reverse: the Security Council's legal ability to mandate enforcement action (Article 42) is grounded in the prior stipulation that it acts for all members of the UN on matters of international peace and security (Articles 24–25). The ultimate source of the Council's legal power, therefore, is precisely what makes the UN uniquely able to bestow legitimacy on a peace enforcement operation: its claim to represent the international community as a whole.

This priority of legitimacy over legality is also evident from the interactions of smaller international organisations with the UN during peace enforcement operations. The mandates of these organisations do not offer the same advantages to lead states in peace enforcement operations. They cannot ensure the legality of an intervention because under the UN Charter only the UN Security Council is legally empowered to mandate enforcement action.[80] They also represent the endorsement of only a limited group of states rather than the international community as a whole. Nevertheless, as argued above, they do have some legitimising potential, deriving from both their multilateral nature and their advantages in assessing proximate threats to regional peace and security. Moreover, from the point of view of lead states smaller international organisations have the advantage of being easier to obtain a mandate from. Their restricted membership and the fact that members are often close allies or regional neighbours maximise the influence of aspiring lead states. By contrast, UN mandates require the assent of nine of the fifteen diverse Security Council members and the acquiescence of all five veto-endowed permanent member states. This can be exceedingly difficult to achieve, especially for lead states with limited international leverage that are not themselves Security Council members. Smaller

---

[80] UN Charter, Article 53.1. Under Article 51, states retain the right to individual or collective self-defence without Security Council authorisation. NATO is founded on this article. Peace enforcement operations, however, rarely respond to a direct military attack on another state and thus do not fall under this provision.

organisations thus represent a viable though not ideal legitimising alternative for lead states that are unable to obtain a UN mandate.

The utility of smaller international organisations to lead states does not end there, however. These organisations are also platforms from which efforts to further improve an intervention's international legitimacy can be launched. Where the Security Council has been unresponsive to an intervention, smaller international organisations are useful bases for renewed lobbying for a UN mandate. If a regional organisation certifies the existence of a threat to regional peace and security, it highlights the issue for Security Council attention, since under Article 24 of the UN Charter the Council bears the 'primary responsibility for the maintenance of international peace and security'. The Council is not only challenged to react, however: it is also presented with a solution to the issue that is backed by the most affected section of the international community. While legally the Security Council retains the right to provide an alternative solution, politically this becomes more difficult as the number of states that have already endorsed an intervention through other international bodies grows.

One strategy for lead states with little direct influence in the Security Council, therefore, is to treat international organisations as forming a legitimacy pyramid. They scale the first rung by obtaining a mandate from a regional or even sub-regional organisation, and then use that organisation as a platform from which to lobby for endorsement by larger international organisations, with the UN forming the apex of the pyramid. In the case studies of this book, all three African lead states pursue exactly this strategy. It is worth noting, however, that *post hoc* endorsement by the UN, even if it is obtained, cannot retroactively eliminate the illegality of a deployment launched without Security Council authorisation. Scaling the legitimacy pyramid, therefore, represents a quest of international legitimacy, not legality.

Progress up the legitimacy ladder is not automatic, however. Although there is pressure on the Security Council to approve an intervention already approved by other international organisations, hostility by key Council members (notably veto-wielding states) can block the endorsement process. Even in these cases, however, smaller international organisations can provide useful platforms for increasing an intervention's international legitimacy even beyond the levels directly generated by their mandate. One strategy, which was used in the case of NATO's Kosovo intervention, is to seek to displace the Security Council as the beneficiary of the legitimating capacity generated by the UN's universal membership. The first step is to confirm, both by the declaration of the smaller international organisation and if possible by drawing on UN resolutions, that a threat to international peace and security exists. The second step is to argue that the Security Council is not fulfilling its Charter function of mandating 'prompt and effective action' to address this threat.[81] Finally, it is suggested that the smaller international organisation is serving the wider international community by substituting its mandate for that of the incapacitated Security Council.

Again, this strategy aims at securing international legitimacy, not legality. What is challenged is not the Security Council's legal right to authorise peace enforcement operations but its capacity to recognise efforts to address security threats in the name of the international community – i.e. legitimate interventions. The success of this argument depends both on challenging the Security Council's authority and on proposing a suitable substitute for it. It is in the latter respect that the platform provided by a smaller international organisation is crucial. As debates about the 2003 Iraq intervention made clear, the judgements of individual states are unlikely to make internationally acceptable substitutes for those of the Security Council. Smaller international organisations have a greater chance of success because they are already acknowledged to have some capacity to launch legitimate peace enforcement operations.

In sum, smaller international organisations provide alternative sources of international legitimacy, though they are inferior to the UN in that respect. As rungs in a global legitimacy ladder, they also act as platforms for lobbying for a UN mandate and thus further improving an intervention's international legitimacy. In the context of sufficient disgruntlement with the Security Council's fulfilment of its obligation to ensure prompt and effective action to address international security threats, they may even be able to present themselves as substitutes for the Council in recognising legitimate interventions. In all these cases, smaller international organisations breach the UN's monopoly on legitimising peace enforcement operations. The result is that the avenues for strategic action by lead states seeking to legitimise their intervention are multiplied. Thus although international legitimacy judgements are structured by international rules interpreted through international organisations, there remains ample room for strategic state behaviour within the parameters of this framework.

---

[81] Ibid., Article 24.

Alternative perspectives on international organisations

Although the image of international organisations as gatekeepers to international legitimacy is commonly endorsed by diplomats, this function has received little recognition in international relations theory. In part, this reflects the fact that peace enforcement operations themselves have received relatively little sustained theoretical attention. The literature on all kinds of peace operations has burgeoned since the 1990s, but remains dominated by policy rather than theoretical concerns. Scholarly attention has largely focused on the crucial questions of when an intervention is morally justifiable and under what circumstances it is likely to succeed.[82] The role of international organisations in launching peace enforcement operations has attracted far less attention. International organisations are occasionally cited as guarantors for genuinely humanitarian interventions, but this proposition is rarely fully explored. Moreover, the politics of legitimacy and legality are often conflated, leaving an image of international organisations as guardians of international law rather than gatekeepers to legitimacy.

There has, however, been a protracted debate about the role of international organisations in international relations theory. Legitimacy does not feature prominently in this debate either, however, perhaps in part because its contributors rarely focus on the specific issue of peace enforcement. The continuum of positions ranges from theorists who envision international organisations as significant independent actors in international politics to those who believe that they merely provide a

---

[82] On the moral conditions for intervention, see, among others, Mill, 'A Few Words on Non-intervention'; Walzer, *Just and Unjust Wars*; Walzer, 'The Politics of Rescue'; International Commission on Intervention and State Sovereignty, *The Responsibility to Protect*. Examples of studies seeking, in diverse ways, to draw lessons for future interventions include: Walter Clarke and Jeffrey Herbst (eds.), *Learning from Somalia: the Lessons of Armed Humanitarian Intervention* (Boulder: Westview Press, 1997); John L. Hirsch and Robert B. Oakley, *Somalia and Operation Restore Hope: Reflections on Peacemaking and Peacekeeping* (Washington, D.C.: United States Institute of Peace Press, 1995); Michael W. Doyle, Ian Johnstone, and Robert C. Orr (eds.), *Keeping the Peace: Lessons from Multidimensional UN Operations in Cambodia and El Salvador* (New York: Cambridge University Press, 1997); Patrick M. Regan, *Civil Wars and Foreign Powers: Outside Intervention in Intrastate Conflict* (Ann Arbor: University of Michigan Press, 2000); Michael W. Doyle and Nicholas Sambanis, 'International Peacebuilding: A Theoretical and Quantitative Analysis', paper prepared for delivery at the 2000 Annual Meeting of the American Political Science Association, Washington, D.C., 31 August–3 September 2000; S. J. Stedman, 'Spoiler Problems in Peace Processes', *International Security*, 22:2 (Fall 1997), pp. 5–53.

smokescreen for state-centred power politics. In the peace enforcement case, however, the conception of international organisations as independent actors[83] is implausible. Although some organisations involved in these operations have relatively large bureaucracies and distinctive corporate goals, none disposes of the military forces necessary for peace enforcement. Moreover, the nature of peace enforcement operations severely limits the scope for independent action by international organisations. Neo-functionalism argues cogently that these organisations have most influence in nominally apolitical contexts and on issues that states perceive as technical or non-controversial.[84] By contrast, peace enforcement operations are risky, expensive, and command a great deal of domestic and international attention. When the stakes are this high, governments do not delegate decisions to international organisations. Therefore states, rather than international organisations, are the primary agents launching peace enforcement operations.

Contemporary international relations theory does, however, offer two main explanations for why states consistently choose to launch peace enforcement operations through international organisations. Associated with neo-liberal institutionalism and realism, respectively, these explanations focus on burden-sharing and power politics. Along with the international law explanation just alluded to, these propositions constitute the three main explanations to rival the legitimacy-centred theory proposed in this book. The following sections analyse each proposition in turn.

Requirements of international law

One popular explanation for the ubiquity of international organisations in peace enforcement operations is simply that unilateral interventions violate international law. The UN Charter severely restricts states' use of military force. UN member states pledge to 'refrain in their international relations from the threat or use of force against the territorial integrity or political independence of any state'.[85] There are only three exceptions. The first, which authorised military action against an Axis state in

---

[83] M. N. Barnett and M. Finnemore, 'The Politics, Power, and Pathologies of International Organizations', *International Organization*, 53:4 (Fall 1999).

[84] A. M. Burley and W. Mattli, 'Europe Before the Court: A Political Theory of Legal Integration', *International Organization* 47:1 (Winter 1993).

[85] UN Charter, Article 2.4.

World War Two,[86] is not relevant to contemporary peace enforcement operations. The second is the right to individual or collective self-defence,[87] which justifies military action after an international attack but has only limited relevance for interventions into civil wars. It is the third exception that provides the legal basis for most contemporary peace enforcement operations. The Charter permits the Security Council to 'take such action by air, sea, or land forces as may be necessary to maintain or restore international peace and security'.[88] All UN members undertake, in principle, to provide the 'armed forces, assistance, and facilities' necessary for such enforcement activities.[89] The Security Council has the prerogative of determining whether the required action 'shall be taken by all Members of the United Nations or by some of them'.[90] It can also authorise 'regional arrangements or agencies' to carry out military operations on its behalf.[91]

Thus the UN Charter, a foundational document of contemporary international law, clearly outlines a prominent role for international organisations in peace enforcement operations. Moreover, international law is cited with remarkable regularity by both practitioners and observers of world politics commenting on particular enforcement operations. Intervening states almost invariably present a legal case for their deployments, while objections are also frequently couched in legal terms. This was most recently demonstrated by vociferous debate about the precise legal implications of UN Security Council Resolution 1441 for the 2003 US-led intervention in Iraq. Especially in the aftermath of the March 2003 Blix report on Iraq's weapons stock, diplomats and media correspondents alike argued at length about whether Iraq was indeed in 'material breach' of its obligation and whether this provided a legal basis for intervention. The underlying assumption in this debate was that international law does indeed help determine state behaviour. One implication might be that states turn to international organisations to launch peace enforcement operations to meet the requirements of international law.

This proposition receives some support in the academic literature. International legal scholars often cite Louis Henkin's observation that 'almost all nations observe almost all principles of international law and almost all their obligations almost all the time' to establish the impact of

---

[86] Ibid., Article 107.   [87] Ibid., Article 51.   [88] Ibid., Article 42.
[89] Ibid., Article 43.1.   [90] Ibid., Article 48.1.   [91] Ibid., Article 53.1.

international law on state behaviour.[92] One prominent explanation for this perceived compliance is that the process of elaborating international laws favours their incorporation into states' policy-making matrix. Thus Abram and Antonia Chayes argue that the iterative process of debating an international agreement increases states' commitment to this agreement once it becomes international law.[93] Similarly, Harold Koh maintains that 'domestic decision making becomes "enmeshed" with international legal norms as institutional arrangements for the making and maintenance of an international commitment become entrenched in domestic legal and political processes'.[94] There is ample scope for these processes to have shaped contemporary states' policies on the use of military force. States debated the clauses of the UN Charter when they joined the organisation, and their diplomats and bureaucrats serving at the UN are exposed to a continuing debate reaffirming these laws. Most states are also members of smaller international organisations, where they are exposed to similar socialisation processes. On this analysis, states' tendency to obey international law by launching peace enforcement operations through international organisations is hardly surprising.

Within international relations theory, some strands of constructivism also envision states as capable of so internalising norms (including those codified in international law) that they become standard modes of conduct. In March and Olsen's terms, states may make behavioural decisions based on a 'logic of appropriateness', i.e. by 'following internalized prescriptions of what is socially defined as true, normal, right, or good, without, or in spite of, calculation of consequences and expected utility'.[95] Thus states might choose to launch peace enforcement operations through international organisations simply because international law indicates that this is the appropriate mode of behaviour. Indeed, if internalisation is complete, this may not even be a conscious choice. As Finnemore and Sikkink put it, 'norms may become so widely accepted

---

[92] Koh, 'Why do Nations Obey International Law?', p. 2599.

[93] Abram Chayes and Antonia Chayes, 'On Compliance', *International Organization*, 47:2 (1993).

[94] Koh, 'Why do Nations Obey International Law?', p. 2654.

[95] James G. March and Johan P. Olsen, 'The Logic of Appropriateness', ARENA working paper 04/09, University of Oslo. Quoted in Ian Hurd, 'Legitimacy and Strategic Behaviour', paper prepared for the conference on 'Legitimacy and Power in the Post 9/11 World' at the University of Southern California, 27–28 April 2005.

that they are internalized by actors and achieve a "taken-for-granted" quality that makes conformance with the norm almost automatic'.[96]

However, the notion that states launch peace enforcement operations through international organisations out of internalised respect for international law suffers both theoretical and empirical flaws. At the theoretical level, Downs, Rocke and Barsoom have cogently criticised the tendency of international legal scholars to infer the strength of international law from perceived state compliance, since non-violation may simply reflect the low demands that international law places on states.[97] With respect to constructivism, Finnemore and Sikkink note that norm internalisation is an extreme case. Many norms do not reach the internalisation stage of their 'life cycle'. Thus although constructivists generally accept that states' identities and interests – and therefore their behaviour – can be shaped by international institutions, most maintain that there remains ample scope for strategic or outright norm-violating behaviour by states. Automatic norm-conformance is especially unlikely concerning an activity as high-profile, exceptional, and controversial as launching a peace enforcement operation.

Empirically, the explanation based on international law suffers from the fact that not all international organisations are legally empowered to authorise a peace enforcement operation. The UN Charter explicitly reserves the right to authorise enforcement action for the Security Council.[98] Yet only ten of the eighteen peace enforcement operations listed in table 1.1 of this book's introduction were launched under UN auspices. The remainder occurred through smaller international organisations that could not substantially affect the legality of the intervention. International law cannot explain why states chose to operate through these organisations. UN auspices, by contrast, do have a legal impact, but this alone does not prove that states turn to the UN primarily out of concern for international law. In fact, assuming consistency in states' motivations for turning to international organisations to launch peace enforcement operations suggests that international law is not the primary motivator for states operating within the UN framework, either. The case studies in this book will confirm that although states typically do construct a legal case for their interventions, their primary motivator

[96] Finnemore and Sikkink, 'International Norm Dynamics and Political Change', p. 904.
[97] George Downs, David M. Rocke and Peter Barsoon, 'Is Good News about Compliance Good News about Cooperation?', *International Organization*, 50:3 (Summer 1996).
[98] UN Charter, Articles 42 and 53.1.

for turning to any international organisation, including the UN, to launch a peace enforcement operation relates to international legitimacy rather than international law. This underlines a central tenet of this chapter, which is that despite a popular tendency to conflate legality and legitimacy in international relations, the distinction between the two concepts is both theoretically and empirically important.

Facilitators of burden-sharing

The second major alternative explanation for the prominent role of international organisations in peace enforcement operations focuses on their capacity to promote burden-sharing. International organisations by definition comprise at least three states, and many have far more members. The United Nations, the world's largest international organisation, currently counts 192 members. If a peace enforcement operation is launched through an international organisation, all its members are at least potential military and financial contributors to the intervention. Some international organisations even have institutionalised burden-sharing mechanisms. The UN, for example, maintains a peacekeeping budget that totalled US$2.8 billion in 2003/2004, to which each member state must contribute based on a predetermined scale of assessment. It thus seems more than reasonable to suggest that states decide to launch peace enforcement operations through international organisations to take advantage of these burden-sharing mechanisms. Indeed, this perception of the role of international organisations is prevalent among politicians. As noted at the beginning of this book, for example, during the 2004 US presidential election campaign John Kerry charged that launching the Iraq intervention without a UN mandate was a mistake because it left the USA shouldering most of the costs of the operation. A similar perception exists among contributors to the policy-oriented literature on peace operations. Patrick Regan, for example, argues that burden-sharing is the crucial motivation for multilateralism in these operations:

> The ability of a decision maker to participate [in a peace operation] will be a function of the ease with which costs are distributed and benefits accrue collectively. One way to overcome this constraint ... is to spread out the costs among a large number of actors. The UN serves this role well, though it is not the only multilateral organization capable of such a tasks. The European Union (EU), the North Atlantic Treaty Organization

(NATO), the Organization of American States (OAS), and the Organization of African Unity (OAU) are examples of other organizations able to orchestrate multilateral interventions.[99]

Within international relations theory, this conception of international organisations finds support from neo-liberal institutionalism. Theorists in this tradition argue that international organisations matter because they help states reap the rewards of mutually beneficial cooperation.[100] They work from the premise that states are rational actors that seek to maximise benefits relative to costs in pursuit of their national interests. Interstate cooperation, defined as a mutual adjustment of policy, is possible only when it benefits all the states involved. However, even the existence of potential joint gains does not guarantee cooperation if unilateral defection is more profitable than joint cooperation or cooperative behaviour leaves states exposed to exploitation.[101] Although mutually beneficial cooperation can arise spontaneously even under these conditions,[102] neo-liberal institutionalists tend to stress the role of international institutions in addressing these difficulties. Institutions can limit free-rider problems by monitoring state behaviour to ensure that defection is detected.[103] They also provide structures to facilitate the collective punishment of defectors.[104] Finally, they can help states make credible commitments to cooperation by increasing the publicity of these commitments.[105]

Neo-liberal institutionalists differ in the kinds of international institutions they study. Many focus on international regimes, seminally defined as 'principles, rules, norms, and decision-making procedures around which actor expectations converge in a given issue-area'.[106]

---

[99] Regan, *Civil Wars and Foreign Powers*, pp. 106–7.

[100] Robert O. Keohane, *After Hegemony: Cooperation and Discord in the World Political Economy* (Princeton: Princeton University Press, 1984).

[101] Lisa Martin, 'Interests, Power, and Multilateralism', *International Organization*, 46:4 (Autumn 1992), pp. 768–75 and 780–3.

[102] Robert Axelrod, *The Evolution of Cooperation* (New York: Basic Books, 1984).

[103] Keohane, *After Hegemony*, chapter 6.

[104] Paul Milgrom, Douglass North, and Barry Weingast, 'The Role of Institutions in the Revival of Trade', *Economics and Politics*, 2 (1990).

[105] Lisa L. Martin, *Coercive Cooperation: Explaining Multilateral Economic Sanctions* (Princeton: Princeton University Press, 1992) and 'Credibility, Costs, and Institutions: Cooperation on Economic Sanctions', *World Politics*, 45:3 (April 1993).

[106] Stephen Krasner, 'Structural Causes and Regime Consequences: Regimes as Intervening Variables', in S. Krasner, *International Regimes* (Ithaca: Cornell University Press, 1983).

Abbott and Snidal suggest that this broad and relatively abstract focus is in part a reaction to the excessively 'legal-descriptive' tradition that preceded today's more theoretical approaches to the study of international relations.[107] They also contend, however, that formal international organisations can be more effective in facilitating interstate cooperation than more abstract international regimes, because they provide a centralised and moderately independent forum for state interaction and collective activities. Similarly, Milgrom, North, and Weingast suggest that once actors' interactions reach a certain level of complexity, a more concrete institutional framework becomes necessary to sustain cooperation.[108] Neo-liberal institutionalists agree, however, that the importance of all these international institutions derives primarily from their capacity to facilitate interstate cooperation. These institutions may originally be created by the dominant powers in a system for their own advantage. However, they persist despite changes in relative power because of their crucial function in promoting mutually beneficial cooperation.[109]

Peace enforcement operations differ from many activities traditionally modelled by neo-liberal institutionalists in two important ways. First, non-cooperation in peace enforcement operations is easily detectable: troop and resource contributions to peace enforcement operations are public and empirically verifiable. Since the problem of hidden defection is thus sidelined, states will turn to international organisations more for their ability to generate cooperation than for their monitoring capacities. Second, the goal of peace enforcement operations is not to attain untapped mutual benefits from cooperation but to protect the public good of international stability. Thus states wishing to launch peace enforcement operations seek cooperation not to increase their benefits but to diminish their costs by sharing the burden of intervention among the largest possible number of states. In the case of peace enforcement operations, the neo-liberal institutionalist perspective thus essentially revolves around a logic of burden-sharing. Nevertheless the basic vision of international organisations as facilitators of mutually beneficial interstate cooperation remains intact.

---

[107] Kenneth W. Abbot and Duncan Snidal, 'Why States Act through Formal International Organizations', *Journal of Conflict Resolution*, 42:1 (February 1998).
[108] Milgrom, North, and Weingast, 'The Role of Institutions in the Revival of Trade'.
[109] Keohane, *After Hegemony*; S. Krasner, 'State Power and the Structure of International Trade', *World Politics*, 28:3 (1976).

This vision of the role of international organisations in peace enforcement operations is theoretically sound and provides a clear sense of the practical importance of these organisations to intervening states. Empirically, however, the case for burden-sharing is easily overstated. Since sovereign states retain the exclusive command of their militaries, an international organisation's mandate cannot guarantee that all member states will contribute troops to a peace enforcement operation. Financial burden-sharing mechanisms are also typically in abeyance for peace enforcement operations: in all five interventions studied in this book, participating states were responsible for funding and equipping their troops. Thus international organisations offer no direct burden-sharing advantage that could not be captured in an ad hoc coalition of the willing, and they often impose costs associated with multilateral decision-making. Their contribution to building an intervention force is at best indirect: some countries may find it easier to participate in an intervention because of the legitimacy bestowed by an international organisation's mandate. The case studies in this book suggest, however, that most of the ensuing troop contributions are token forces designed to further enhance the legitimacy of the intervention rather than to produce a significant military impact. They also demonstrate that intervening states value the legitimacy generated by the mandate of an international organisation as a good in itself rather than as a vehicle for encouraging burden-sharing.

Instruments of state power

The final alternative explanation for the role of international organisations in peace enforcement operations is that powerful states find them useful and inexpensive masks for the exercise of their power. In this view, states operate through international organisations because they give a veneer of multilateralism to essentially self-interested endeavours, which is useful for minimising the international affront caused by this exercise of power. International organisations are so responsive to state power, moreover, that dominant members incur no significant costs in obtaining this figleaf. If such costs should unexpectedly arise, they would either operate through another international organisation or dispense with an international mandate altogether. This view of the (virtually non-existent) role of international organisations underlay John Bolton's now-notorious assertion that 'This kind of mindless creation of the United Nations as something different from what is in the United

States' interest to do isn't going to sell here or anywhere else.'[110] The same perception fuelled the 'No Blood for Oil' protests during the 1991 Gulf War and has become even more widespread since the 2003 US decision to intervene unilaterally in Iraq when it found the UN mandating process excessively cumbersome.[111] In the literature on peace operations, this view is represented among others by Phyllis Bennis, who views the Security Council as a cartel dominated by the USA that easily offers its members the political cover to intervene militarily at will in other parts of the world – or to ignore crises they do not wish to address.[112]

Within international relations theory, this view of international organisations emerges from realism. In this paradigm, 'international relations is ... a state of relentless security competition, with the threat of war always in the background'.[113] Classical realists explain this state of affairs by reference to human nature,[114] while neo-realists attribute it to the anarchic nature of the international system.[115] Both agree that in such a system, states must embrace *Realpolitik*: they must be concerned primarily with promoting their own national interests, defined in terms of either power or security. This stark logic leaves little room for international organisations to influence international politics. States are jealous of their sovereignty and power, and do not allow international organisations to become independent actors in world politics. They also decline to be swayed by international norms or international law, depriving international organisations of any moral or legal status that would allow them to influence international affairs. Finally, realists counter neo-liberal institutionalism by insisting that in an anarchic world where every state is a potential enemy states must care not only about the magnitude but also about distribution of gains from cooperation. 'While each state wants to maximize its absolute gains, it is more important to make sure that it does better, or at least no worse, than the

---

[110] 'John Bolton: In His Own Words', video clip online at www.truthout.org/multimedia.htm.

[111] US frustration with the UN also indicates that the organisation was less pliant than cynics might expect. A fuller examination of the complex evidence about the role of the UN arising out of the 2003 Iraq intervention is provided in the conclusion of this book.

[112] Phyllis Bennis, *Calling the Shots: How Washington Dominates Today's UN* (New York: Olive Branch Press, 2000), chapter 6.

[113] John J. Mearsheimer, 'The False Promise of International Institutions', *International Security*, 19:3 (Winter 1994–5), p. 9.

[114] Hans Joachim Morgenthau, *Politics Among Nations; The Struggle for Power and Peace* (New York: Knopf, 1960).

[115] Kenneth N. Waltz, *Theory of International Politics* (Reading: Addison-Wesley, 1979).

other state in the agreement.'[116] This means that international organisations' capacity to promote cooperation merely by increasing information flows or remedying commitment problems is severely restricted.

In the realist world, therefore, international organisations play at best a superficial role. Lack of cooperation reflects a lack of sufficient common interests – and international organisations cannot change that. Meanwhile, when states' interests do coincide, international organisations are basically superfluous. They offer an arena for states to meet and learn about each other's preferences, but in their absence bilateral diplomacy could serve the same purpose. Why, then, would states operate through international organisations to launch peace enforcement operations? Robert Gilpin has suggested that international organisations institutionalise hegemony: powerful states invent a set of international norms, rules, and institutions that favour their interests and that other states become accustomed to obeying because they are backed by the might of the hegemon.[117] This allows the hegemon to dominate world affairs without having to reassert its power every time other states face policy decisions. Institutions thus simply ensure more efficient hegemonic control. Translated to the case of peace enforcement operations, this logic implies that international organisations should allow powerful states to intervene in other countries with less exertion than if they acted outside these forums. States should face very few costs from operating in the framework of these institutions, because they both erected and continue to dominate them. On the other hand, operating within this framework should bring at least some material benefits.

It is worth distinguishing this perspective from the legitimacy-based one championed in this book because both suggest that states turn to international organisations to make their peace enforcement operations more acceptable to other states. One key difference lies in the theories' predictions about the pliability of international organisations. Realism expects international organisations essentially to rubber-stamp any policies proposed by powerful states. By contrast, this chapter has argued that international organisations' discretion of what types of behaviour to legitimise is limited not only by other sovereign member states but also by the limited flexibility of the rules that provide standards for international legitimacy judgements. The second main

---

[116] Mearsheimer, 'The False Promise of International Institutions', p. 12.
[117] Robert Gilpin, *War and Change in World Politics* (New York: Cambridge University Press, 1981).

difference lies in the fact that in a realist world, powerful states neither expect nor are willing to incur significant costs from operating within an international framework. By contrast, this chapter has argued that states value international legitimacy as a good in itself, which suggests a much greater willingness to incur costs in pursuit of an international mandate for their interventions. Empirically, the case studies in this book suggest that international organisations are less pliable than realism suggests and that operating through these organisations does impose substantial costs on intervening states.

Conclusion

The aim of this chapter was to establish the theoretical framework for investigating the central thesis of this book, namely that states launch peace enforcement operations through international organisations primarily because of their concern with the international legitimacy of their intervention. The chapter began by elaborating a theoretical understanding of the concept of international legitimacy, taking as its starting point the general definition of legitimacy as a social status judged according to commonly accepted rules. It noted that actions as well as actors are subject to legitimacy judgements and that legitimacy is inextricably bound to an audience: legitimacy and illegitimacy are always in the eyes of a particular social group. Four potential legitimacy audiences were identified for peace enforcement operations, of which only two are international: regional states directly affected by the intervention and the wider international community of states. The challenge, then, was to conceptualise the rules according to which these groups form legitimacy judgements. This chapter argued that in the contemporary society of states, these rules should be distinguished from international laws and understood, following Franck, as 'club rules' acknowledged by sovereign states as structuring their common interactions. States value these rules because they value the international society that recognises them as its sovereign members, and individual states care about international legitimacy judgements of their own behaviour because they realise that they are essentially social actors.

The second section of this chapter described the politics of international legitimacy judgements in the more specific case of peace enforcement operations. It identified three rules as crucial to these judgements: respect for state sovereignty, non-aggression, and intervention in the service of international peace and security. It also highlighted the crucial role of international organisations under this dispensation. These organisations are widely accepted as both relatively unbiased judges of facts and the most credible mouthpieces of the international community in the current international system. The United Nations is particularly well-suited to these tasks, but they can also be undertaken by smaller international organisations. International organisations are therefore in a privileged position to offer judgements of what the prevailing rules of the international community are and whether a particular intervention accords with them. This makes them gatekeepers of international legitimacy for contemporary peace enforcement operations.

Within this structure of rules and international organisations, there remains ample opportunity for strategic behaviour by states. Intervening states use their status as members of international organisations to legitimise a maximal pursuit of their national interests, and they may use smaller and more easily influenced international organisations as rungs in a global legitimacy pyramid whose apex is the United Nations. Nevertheless, the limited flexibility of prevailing rules limits the kinds of behaviour even international organisations can legitimise. International organisations are not mere rubber-stamps, and even powerful states modify their behaviour to approximate the prevailing international rules.

This theory will not surprise most international diplomats. Legitimacy is a constant watchword in modern world politics, especially since communications technology has made states aware of each other's actions to an unprecedented degree. Thus one high-ranking military officer was able to summarise this book's argument in the following eloquent – and unprompted – manner:

> It's all about the international legitimacy. It's doing what is deemed to be right – and in the national and international interest – but with legitimacy . . . It's the way the international environment works today, that global matters are managed. It comes down to regional problem, resolved within global rules. And the global rules we ideally work through are [embodied in] the UN. If that is impossible or impractical, you step down to the next level, which is a coalition force with a UN mandate. And if that is impossible, you end up with sort of an MFO [multinational force] type of operation. But certainly the responsible nations in the international community – except in absolute extremis – will always act . . . under an international paradigm.[118]

---

[118] Author's interview with Air Marshal Douglas Riding, Vice Chief of the Australian Defence Force during INTERFET, Canberra, Australia, 1 May 2002.

Nevertheless the notion of international organisations as gatekeepers of international legitimacy requires more sustained attention. Practitioners of world politics are quick to assert the importance of international legitimacy but often struggle to define the term. Contemporary commentators on world affairs often conflate legitimacy with legality, suggesting that states launch peace enforcement operations through international organisations out of respect for international law. In international relations theory, meanwhile, the role of international organisations in the politics of international legitimacy has been neglected. Inis Claude, who identified the UN's collective legitimisation function as early as 1966, found that 'this function has been given relatively little attention … most studies have tended to focus upon the operational functions of the Organization … Our action-oriented generation has concentrated on the question of what the United Nations can and cannot *do* … rather than on its verbal performance.'[119] It is perhaps this focus on operational functions that informs the realist vision of international organisations as ineffective entities that at best serve as figleaves for great power politics. Neo-liberal institutionalists seek to save international organisations by arguing that they can affect international politics by facilitating interstate cooperation, but they, too, neglect the 'verbal performance' of international organisations as far as international legitimacy is concerned.

This book seeks to focus attention squarely on the crucial role international organisations play in the politics of international legitimacy surrounding peace enforcement operations. Its case studies argue that neither international law nor burden-sharing nor power politics can explain why states have so consistently sought the auspices of international organisations for their peace enforcement operations. The explanation for this behaviour lies in states' recognition of the role of international organisations as gatekeepers to international legitimacy for military interventions. An important corollary, which will be explored in the concluding chapter, is that the price of not operating within the framework of an international organisation goes beyond the loss of burden-sharing and the problem of illegality. A state that intervenes in another country without the mandate of an international organisation will face the real and adverse consequences of being seen to be acting illegitimately by the international community of states.

[119] Claude, 'Collective Legitimization as a Political Function of the United Nations', p. 372.

3

Peace enforcement through sub-regional organisations: the Economic Community of West African States and Operation Liberty in Liberia

The activities of African international organisations evolved dramatically in the 1990s. A proliferation of internal wars coupled with the relative disengagement of the developed world from Africa in the wake of the Cold War thrust the continent's sub-regional organisations into an unprecedented role as instruments of conflict management. Among other tasks, several of these organisations have assumed the responsibility of launching peace enforcement operations into their member states.

The Economic Community of West African States (ECOWAS) has become Africa's most prominent interstate organisation in this regard. Its first peace enforcement operation (codenamed Operation Liberty by Nigeria) began on 24 August 1990, when 3,500 West African soldiers deployed in Liberia under Nigerian leadership to halt an armed rebellion against Liberia's President Samuel Doe. Although named the ECOWAS Ceasefire Monitoring Group (ECOMOG), the force predictably encountered a hostile reception by the rebel army, and formally received a peace enforcement mandate on 20 September 1990.

This intervention was a watershed in several respects. It was the first peace enforcement operation launched by an African sub-regional organisation. It was internationally recognised as a test case for regional conflict management. It has served as a model for other African organisations considering regional peace enforcement operations. And it prompted a spurt of institutional development within ECOWAS that transformed the organisation into Africa's most advanced conflict management body.

This chapter analyses why ECOMOG's lead state, Nigeria, chose to launch Operation Liberty under ECOWAS auspices. It begins by providing some historical background on ECOWAS and its engagement in the Liberian civil war. It then demonstrates that the Nigerian decision to intervene through the ECOWAS framework cannot be explained by focusing either on international law or on burden-sharing. Instead, it finds that Nigeria displayed a consistent preoccupation with the intervention's international legitimacy, which it sought to bolster by placing the operation under ECOWAS auspices. Moreover, Nigeria incurred significant costs in this pursuit of international legitimacy, which were not balanced by any material benefits. Nigeria valued international legitimacy as a good in itself and adjusted its behaviour in pursuit of that good.

Historical background

The Economic Community of West African States was founded on 25 May 1975. It comprises fifteen West African states (sixteen in the 1990s) and spans the most densely populated region of Africa along the Gulf of Guinea (Map 3.1).[1] Although ECOWAS was originally conceived as a purely economic organisation, its members rapidly recognised the link between economic development and regional security. In 1978, they annexed a Protocol on Non-Aggression to the ECOWAS Treaty. In 1981, they added a Protocol on Mutual Assistance on Defence, in which they pledged to respond collectively to both external aggression and internal conflicts instigated by other states. However, these early attempts to build a West African security community foundered on mutual suspicions between francophone and anglophone ECOWAS member states. Francophone states were in a numerical majority in West Africa, but they feared anglophone Nigeria's economic and military dominance in the region and its tremendous influence within ECOWAS. They had already created their own exclusive mutual non-aggression and defence pact (ANAD) in 1977, and were reluctant to move to a more inclusive regional security arrangement. In turn, anglophone states resented ANAD as a threat to regional unity inspired by France's machinations in its erstwhile colonies. The 1980s thus saw no further development towards a regional security community.

---

[1] ECOWAS founding members were Benin, Burkina Faso, Ghana, the Gambia, Guinea, Guinea Bissau, Côte d'Ivoire, Liberia, Mali, Mauritania, Niger, Nigeria, Senegal, Sierra Leone, and Togo. Cape Verde acceded to the Treaty in 1977, Mauritania announced its withdrawal on 26 December 1999.

Map 3.1. Economic Community of West African States (ECOWAS)

The Liberian civil war violently revived the issue. It began in December 1989, when a Liberian exile named Charles Taylor crossed into Liberia from Côte d'Ivoire to lead an armed rebellion against the incumbent military regime of Samuel Doe. He mobilised support so successfully that by June 1990 his National Patriotic Front of Liberia (NPFL) controlled 90 per cent of Liberia's territory and was besieging the capital, Monrovia. On 14 July 1990, Doe appealed for help from his fellow ECOWAS heads of state. Reflecting the language of the Protocol on Mutual Assistance on Defence, he argued that Taylor's rebellion would devastate the entire ECOWAS sub-region and requested an ECOWAS peacekeeping force.[2]

The West African region was divided on how to respond. Nigeria's military head of state, Ibrahim Babangida, favoured intervention, not

[2] M. Weller (ed.), *Regional Peace-keeping and International Enforcement: The Liberian Crisis* (Cambridge: Cambridge University Press, 1994), pp. 60–1.

only because he was concerned about the security of Nigerians living in Liberia but also because he was a personal friend of Doe's. By contrast, Côte d'Ivoire and Burkina Faso, West Africa's leading francophone states, supported Taylor's rebellion and opposed any intervention to save Doe. Their heads of state despised Doe, in part because of family ties with Adolphus Tolbert, whom Doe had killed when he seized power in 1980. Responding to Nigerian pressure despite protests from francophone member states, ECOWAS called for an immediate cessation of hostilities and dispatched an ECOWAS Ceasefire Monitoring Group (ECOMOG) to 'help ensure strict compliance with' this ceasefire.[3] The NPFL, however, rejected the ECOWAS Peace Plan. Determined not to be deprived of his imminent military victory, Taylor announced that his forces would resist ECOMOG's deployment. From the beginning, therefore, Operation Liberty was effectively a peace enforcement mission.

The first ECOMOG troops landed on 24 August 1990. By October 1990, ECOMOG had established control over Monrovia, thwarting Taylor's attempt to seize power though failing to save Doe, who was captured at ECOMOG headquarters and subsequently executed by the Independent National Patriotic Front of Liberia, a splinter group from the NPFL and supposed ECOMOG ally. Since the NPFL remained deeply entrenched in the countryside a seven-year war for control of Liberia ensued between the NPFL and ECOMOG. It was punctuated by a dozen failed peace accords, complicated by a proliferation of warring factions, and characterised by the widespread use of child soldiers and intense brutality against civilians. The war formally ended in 1997, when substantially free and fair elections held under ECOMOG auspices brought Charles Taylor to power, in part because he threatened to renew hostilities if he was not elected. Within two years, however, armed rebel groups began to form against Taylor's regime. Civil war broke out again in 1999, and in 2003 Taylor was forced to relinquish power and go into exile in Nigeria. ECOWAS again became involved in peacekeeping during this second civil war, but this time with a UN mandate and under the understanding that the ECOWAS force would be replaced by a UN peacekeeping mission as soon as possible. The official hand-over took place on 1 October 2003.

---

[3] Ibid., pp. 67–76.

ECOMOG and international law

Operation Liberty provides clear evidence against the popular perception that states launch peace enforcement operations through international organisations out of respect for international law. In fact, despite its ECOWAS auspices Operation Liberty violated both international law and internal ECOWAS rules.

Crucially, ECOWAS had no authority to launch a peace enforcement operation under contemporary international law. According to the United Nations Charter, only the UN Security Council can authorise the international use of military force, unless it occurs as an act of individual or collective self-defence.[4] Regional organisations are possible participants in UN peace enforcement actions, but 'no enforcement action shall be taken under regional arrangements . . . without the authorization of the Security Council'.[5] Since the Liberia intervention was the first peace enforcement operation launched by a sub-regional organisation, moreover, it cannot be argued that precedent had in any way changed the interpretation of these Charter clauses.

Nevertheless, Operation Liberty occurred without a UN mandate. Indeed, ECOWAS had made no official effort to secure such a mandate. The Standing Mediation Committee (SMC) that established ECOMOG sought international financial support for the intervention but did not request a UN mandate for it.[6] Nigeria's Minister of External Affairs officially informed the UN Secretary-General of ECOMOG's creation two days after it occurred, but made no mention of a possible UN mandate. He simply concluded:

> in view of our shared responsibility for the maintenance of international peace and security, we have no doubt that you will lend your considerable moral support to the ECOWAS initiative in Liberia. We are also confident that [you will] generously contribute materially towards the attainment of the stated ECOWAS objective in the Republic of Liberia.[7]

---

[4] UN Charter, Chapter VII and Article 51. The only other exception, the authorisation to continue war against the Axis power (Article 107), has lapsed since the end of World War Two.

[5] Ibid., Article 53.

[6] ECOWAS Standing Mediation Committee, 7 August 1990, in Weller, *The Liberian Crisis*, pp. 67–70.

[7] Letter from Nigeria's Minister of External Affairs of the Federal Republic of Nigeria to the United Nations Secretary-General, 9 August 1990 in Weller, *The Liberian Crisis*, pp. 75–6.

The reasons for ECOWAS's failure to secure a UN mandate for Operation Liberty are subject to dispute. ECOWAS Chairman Dauda Jawara initially claimed to have been advised that UN approval was not necessary, and then argued (equally implausibly) that he had believed that a 'good luck' letter from the UN Secretary-General had constituted authorisation.[8] A more compelling argument is that the urgency of the Liberian crisis did not allow time to engage in the lengthy process of seeking a UN mandate. One Acting Executive Secretary of ECOWAS has even claimed that as the Liberian war developed, 'all along ECOWAS was in touch with the UN, warning that the situation was getting worse, but there is no help forthcoming. Therefore ECOWAS countries decide to act together.'[9] However, the official communications of the SMC and the Nigerian Ministry of Foreign Affairs contain no hint that a UN mandate had been requested. Whatever the practical merit of these arguments, moreover, the fact remains that when ECOMOG troops landed in Liberia on 24 August 1990, they were acting without a UN Security Council mandate and therefore illegally. As one West African diplomat put it, 'From a legal point of view it was not correct. The [UN] Charter requires states to seek authorisation before intervening. It's a big decision to decide to shoot people. One cannot simply give oneself the right to make this decision.'[10]

In addition to defying international law as formulated in the UN Charter, Nigeria and its ECOMOG allies violated internal ECOWAS rules when they launched Operation Liberty. Within the ECOWAS framework, the legal basis for the intervention would have been the 1981 Protocol on Mutual Assistance on Defence, which called for collective action in cases of 'internal armed conflict within any Member State engineered and supported actively from outside and likely to endanger the security and peace in the entire community'(Article 4.b). In his request for ECOWAS support on 14 July 1990, Doe implicitly appealed to this clause by claiming, with some credibility, that the war in Liberia threatened 'the socio-political and economic tranquility of ... the sub-region of the

---

[8] Max Sesay, 'Civil War and Collective Intervention in Liberia' *Review of African Political Economy*, 67 (1996), p. 44. Jimmi Adisa, 'The Politics of Regional Military Co-operation: The Case of ECOMOG', in Margaret A. Vogt (ed.), *The Liberian Crisis and ECOMOG: A Bold Attempt at Regional Peace Keeping* (Lagos: Gabumo, 1992), p. 213.

[9] Author's interview with Frank Ofei, Acting Deputy Executive Secretary (Economic Affairs) and Director of Studies, ECOWAS, Abuja, Nigeria, 18 September 2000.

[10] Author's interview with Ambassador Pierre L. Yéré, Head of the Embassy of Côte d'Ivoire in Ethiopia. Addis Ababa, Ethiopia, 9 November 2000. Author's translation from French.

ECOWAS as a whole'.[11] Moreover, since the NPFL was actively supported by Burkina Faso, Ivory Coast, and Libya, the conflict qualified for ECOWAS attention under the Protocol on Mutual Assistance on Defence.

However, Article 6 of the Protocol reaffirmed that only the ECOWAS Authority could decide 'on the expediency of military force'. This body, which unites the heads of state and government of all ECOWAS member states, was created by Article 5.1 of the ECOWAS Treaty as 'the principal governing institution of the Community'. The Treaty also stipulated that the Authority would take its decisions by consensus. Since Côte d'Ivoire and Burkina Faso supported Taylor's rebellion, however, Authority consensus on ECOWAS action to assist Doe was effectively precluded. To circumvent this obstacle, Doe did not address his appeal for help to the Authority. Instead, he petitioned the five-member ECOWAS Standing Mediation Committee (SMC), which had been created on Nigeria's initiative in May 1990 and was dominated by anglophone states, including Nigeria.[12] It was the SMC that created ECOMOG on 7 August. In doing so, it ignored the Authority's executive prerogative and violated the ECOWAS principle of consensus decision-making. Burkina Faso promptly publicly voiced its 'total disagreement' with the decision and challenged the SMC's ability to act for ECOWAS.[13]

Nigeria was complicit in this flouting of ECOWAS's internal rules, and may even have suggested this course of action to Doe. When the SMC was formed, at Nigeria's insistence, the Liberian civil war was already under way and Doe had already contacted Babangida for possible assistance. Earlier that month, as Nigeria's ambassador to Liberia until 1992 recalled:

> Doe did come to Nigeria to ask for assistance. He played down the situation, but he did come – although I would not know what exactly happened at [his] meeting [with Babangida] . . . I don't know if there was a promise to help . . . But Doe was beaming at the press conference on his way out. He was a very happy man. I felt there must have been a promise of assistance.[14]

As the dominant member of the SMC, Nigeria was also involved in a further decision regarding ECOMOG that violated ECOWAS principles.

---

[11] Weller, *The Liberian Crisis*, pp. 60–1.
[12] The SMC comprised the Gambia (chair), Ghana, Mali, Nigeria, and Togo.
[13] Weller, *The Liberian Crisis*, p. 85.
[14] Author's interview with Ambassador A. Ajakaiye, Nigeria's Ambassador to Liberia until 1992, then Director of Training, Nigerian National War College, Abuja, Nigeria, 28 September 2000.

Article 13 of the 1981 Protocol stipulated that any ECOWAS military intervention would be undertaken by the Allied Armed Forces of the Community (AAFC), a stand-by military force drawn from the national armies of all member states. This force was never created, in part because of mutual suspicions between anglophone and francophone West African states, but the principle of collective action it embodied remained in effect. The SMC, however, made no attempt to create an intervention force composed of units from all ECOWAS member states. Only SMC members and Guinea and Sierra Leone were invited to contribute to ECOMOG.[15] Thus although it claimed to be an ECOWAS force, ECOMOG was designed to include only seven of ECOWAS's sixteen member states. Important francophone states like Senegal, Côte d'Ivoire, and Burkina Faso were excluded.

ECOMOG's defenders have tended to justify these breaches of both international law and internal ECOWAS rules by highlighting the urgent need to respond to the Liberian crisis. Whatever the justification, however, Nigeria clearly displayed little regard for either the UN Charter or internal ECOWAS rules in launching ECOMOG. The ECOWAS framework did not and could not guarantee Operation Liberty's legality. The fact that Nigeria nevertheless opted to launch the intervention within this framework suggests that it sought something other than legal status from these auspices.

ECOWAS as a vehicle for burden-sharing

The neo-liberal institutionalist proposition that Nigeria turned to ECOWAS to ensure maximal burden-sharing for Operation Liberty is also empirically unsustainable. Not only did ECOWAS prove a poor vehicle for promoting burden-sharing, there is little evidence that Nigeria expected more positive results when it chose to lead the intervention under ECOWAS auspices.

ECOWAS had virtually no internal resources to contribute to Operation Liberty. It had no standing army and no expertise in peace-keeping or military affairs. It was also virtually bankrupt, having failed to convince its members to provide the funds for even its tiny annual budget. By June 1991, ECOWAS was owed some US$12.3 million in membership arrears, which amounted to almost three times its annual budget.[16] The only way for ECOWAS to generate burden-sharing for

---

[15] ECOWAS Standing Mediation Committee Decision A/DEC.1/8/90 in Weller, *The Liberian Crisis*, pp. 67–9, Article 2.

[16] 'ECOWAS to sanction defaulting member states', *Agence France Presse*, 18 June 1991.

Operation Liberty, therefore, was to encourage member states to participate in ECOMOG or to contribute to it financially. It failed on both counts.
Troop contributions to the intervention were extremely uneven
across ECOWAS member states. Indeed, the most striking feature of
the ECOMOG force was how few ECOWAS members actually participated in it. ECOMOG's original deployment comprised soldiers from
Gambia, Ghana, Guinea, Nigeria, and Sierra Leone and thus represented
only one-third of ECOWAS member states. From then until the very end
of the campaign, ECOMOG remained almost entirely in the hands of a
tiny minority of ECOWAS states, led by Nigeria, which consistently
accounted for 60–80 per cent of ECOMOG troops. Figure 3.1 illustrates
both the low number of participants and Nigerian dominance in
ECOMOG at the beginning, middle, and end of the operation.
There were only two brief exceptions to the overall trend of low
participation and Nigerian dominance of ECOMOG. First, in 1991–2,
having failed to defeat the NPFL militarily, Nigeria agreed to share
ECOMOG's leadership in order to facilitate a peaceful settlement. The
largely francophone Committee of Five (comprising Senegal, Togo,
Guinea-Bissau, and the Gambia and headed by Côte d'Ivoire) was
invited to initiate peace negotiations, and the USA persuaded Senegal
to join ECOMOG to help 'de-Nigerianize' the force.[17] Even during this
interlude, however, ECOMOG represented only six ECOWAS member
states. Moreover, by 1992 Nigeria reversed course. Fearing that franco-
phone/NPFL collaboration was harming Nigeria's regional interests, it
encouraged new Liberian armed factions to emerge as rivals to the
NPFL, hoping to force a military solution to the Liberian civil war
with their help. In response, the NPFL launched Operation Octopus,
a major counter-offensive against ECOMOG, sealing the collapse of
francophone-led peace negotiations and leading to the withdrawal of
Senegalese troops from ECOMOG in January 1993.[18] The second partial
exception arose after the 1997 Peace Plan, which was made possible by a
grudging accommodation between Nigeria and Charles Taylor. Given
the real prospect of peace, ECOMOG participation became less risky
and, for the first time, a majority of ECOWAS states (nine out of sixteen)
joined ECOMOG. Despite this wider participation, however, Nigeria

[17] Robert Mortimer, 'ECOMOG, Liberia, and Regional Security in West Africa', in
    E. Keller and D. Rothchild (eds.), *Africa in the New International Order* (Boulder:
    Lynne Rienner, 1996), pp. 154–5.
[18] Mortimer, 'ECOMOG, Liberia, and Regional Security in West Africa', p. 159.

3.1.A. Troop contributions to ECOMOG, 1991/92

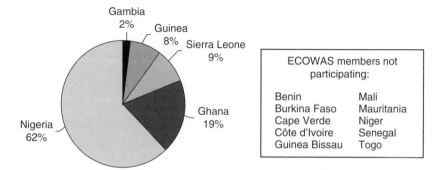

3.1.B. Troop contributions to ECOMOG, 1993/94

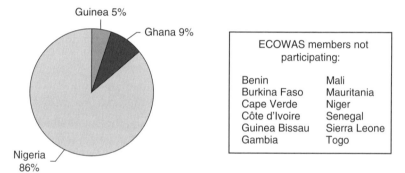

3.1.C. Troop contributions to ECOMOG 1997

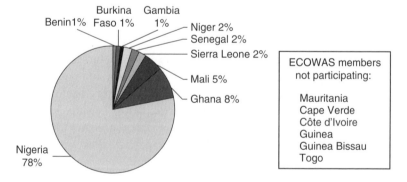

Figure 3.1. Troop contributions to ECOMOG

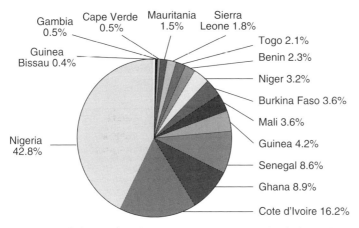

Figure 3.2. National shares of total 1989/90 ECOWAS GDP (excluding Liberia)

still provided 78 per cent of the troops and continued to dominate ECOMOG operations.

Nigeria's dominance in ECOMOG cannot be fully explained by its relative size in the region. Although Nigeria dwarfs its neighbours in population and GDP size, this cannot justify the huge disparities in ECOWAS states' contributions to ECOMOG. Figure 3.2 uses ECOWAS states' contributions to the total West African GDP in 1989/90 to capture the differences in size of ECOWAS members.[19] It excludes Liberia, since the aim is to depict the size differentials among potential contributors to Operation Liberty.

Thus in 1989/90, Nigeria accounted for 42.8 per cent of the combined GDP of these states. This figure increased to 45.7 per cent by 1999.[20] It does not, however, account for the fact that Nigeria shouldered 60–85 per cent of the military burden for ECOMOG. Using GDP proportions as a proxy for relative size, figure 3.3 visualises deviations from a fair burden-sharing arrangement for ECOMOG. It plots the difference between an ECOWAS member's share of ECOMOG troops and its share of regional GDP. Thus a negative score indicates that the country shouldered a smaller proportion of the ECOMOG burden than its relative size would suggest it was responsible for and a positive score has the opposite implication. The figure shows that throughout the intervention, Nigeria shouldered more than its fair share of the ECOMOG military burden.

---

[19] Data from World Bank Country Data database, through http://www.worldbank.org.
[20] Ibid.

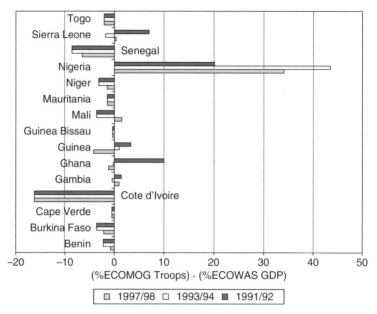

Figure 3.3. Deviations from burden-sharing for ECOMOG

Nigeria's military contribution to ECOMOG also translated directly into a disproportionate share of the financial burden. There was no mechanism to encourage financial burden-sharing for Operation Liberty among ECOWAS members. ECOMOG's regulations explicitly stated that ECOMOG members had to finance their own troop contributions: 'Responsibility for pay of members of the [ECOMOG] Group shall rest with their respective national State.'[21] The only partial exception was the Special Emergency Fund created by the Standing Mediation Committee, which sought financial contributions to ECOMOG from both within and beyond the West African region. Contributions to the fund were strictly voluntary, however, and remained negligible: by January 1991, just over US$3 million had been collected, most of it from ECOMOG states.[22] The burden of financing ECOMOG thus remained squarely on the troop contributors. Since each

[21] Weller, *The Liberian Crisis*, pp. 77–85, Article 39.
[22] Festus B. Aboagye, *ECOMOG: A Sub-Regional Experience in Conflict Resolution, Management and Peacekeeping in Liberia* (Accra: Sedco Publishing, 1999), p. 288. The contributors were the Gambia, Mauritania, Nigeria, and Sierra Leone.

country paid its own troops, moreover, the size of a country's financial obligations was directly linked to the size of its troop contribution.

Even figure 3.3 does not fully convey Nigeria's disproportionate share of the financial burden generated by Operation Liberty, however. In addition to supplying by far the largest proportion of ECOMOG troops, Nigeria provided 80 per cent of ECOMOG's logistics, including most of ECOMOG's airpower and its transport from its staging area in Sierra Leone to Liberia.[23] Moreover, although theoretically ECOMOG states were responsible for bringing their troops to this staging area, in practice the Gambian and the Guinean troops were airlifted there by Nigeria.[24] Nigeria also subsidised other ECOMOG contingents in Liberia, notably by providing the entire force with petrol, oil and lubricants.[25] Thus Nigeria's share of Operation Liberty's financial burden exceeded even its disproportionate share of ECOMOG's military presence. Nigeria is estimated to have spent some US$4 billion on ECOMOG. Ghana, ECOMOG's second largest troop contributor, spent around US$25 million.[26] Even assuming that the other three main ECOMOG contributors matched Ghana's financial contribution, which is unlikely, total non-Nigerian ECOMOG contributions would not exceed US$100 million. This suggests that Nigeria shouldered well over 90 per cent of the financial cost generated by ECOMOG's deployment. As Nigerian Major-General Ndiomu (rtd.) succinctly summed up: 'ECOMOG was ostensibly a regional operation, but the burden was entirely on Nigeria.'[27]

Operating through ECOWAS did not, therefore, generate significant military or financial burden-sharing for Operation Liberty. This came as no surprise to Nigeria. As far as financial burden-sharing was concerned, Nigeria knew that ECOWAS had no formal cost-sharing mechanisms for peace enforcement operations in 1990, and it helped draft ECOMOG regulations requiring states to pay for their own troop contributions.

---

[23] Larinde Laoye, 'Logistics Support in ECOMOG Operations', *Defence Studies*, Special Issue on ECOMOG (1996), p. 53.

[24] Segun Aderiye, 'ECOMOG Landing', in Vogt (ed.), *The Liberian Crisis and ECOMOG*, p. 97.

[25] Mitikishe Maxwell Khobe, 'The Evolution and Conduct of ECOMOG Operations in West Africa', in Mark Malan (ed.), *Boundaries of Peace Operations: The African Dimension*, Institute for Security Studies Monograph No. 44, February 2000, p. 8.

[26] Author's interview with Colonel Festus B. Aboagye, Senior Military Expert for OAU on Ethiopia-Eritrea Mission, Addis Ababa, Ethiopia, 6 November 2000.

[27] Author's interview with Major General (rtd.) Charles B. Ndiomu, Provost, Centre for Peace Research and Conflict Resolution, Nigerian National War College, Abuja, Nigeria, 22 September 2000.

Even more striking is the fact that Nigeria explicitly did not seek to use the ECOWAS framework to generate military burden-sharing. The SMC, led by Nigeria, initially restricted ECOMOG membership to its five member states plus Guinea and Sierra Leone. Nigeria thus deliberately forestalled ECOWAS-wide military burden-sharing for ECOMOG, in exchange, perhaps, for greater control over ECOMOG's deployment and strategy. This policy was only reversed in November 1990, when the SMC had to disavow it as a manifest contradiction to ECOWAS principles.[28] Thus burden-sharing considerations do not appear to have been Nigeria's main motivation for launching ECOMOG within the ECOWAS framework.

Nigerian legitimacy concerns for ECOMOG

If operating through ECOWAS could neither guarantee Operation Liberty's legality nor ensure significant burden-sharing for intervention, why did Nigeria choose to launch the operation in this framework? A British diplomat in Nigeria summed up the answer succinctly: 'It's a legitimacy issue. If you're doing it on behalf of a regional organisation, it's more politically acceptable on the international stage.'[29] This section delineates Nigeria's legitimacy concerns for ECOMOG and identifies the international community as its primary legitimacy audience. The next section will demonstrate how ECOMOG's ECOWAS auspices helped address these concerns.

As chapter 2 argued, peace enforcement is inherently controversial because it contravenes international rules enjoining respect for state sovereignty and prohibiting aggressive warfare. States launching such interventions must prove that their operations serve international peace and security to establish the international legitimacy of their actions. Although ECOMOG was initially called a peacekeeping force, its enforcement character was obvious from the beginning. Charles Taylor made it abundantly clear that he would militarily oppose ECOMOG's deployment. Three days before ECOMOG deployed to Liberia, he warned that the NPFL would consider an intervention 'a flagrant act of aggression'

---

[28] ECOWAS Heads of State and Government, 'Final Communiqué of the First Extra-Ordinary Session of the Authority of Heads of State and Government held in Bamako, Mali, 27–28/Nov/1990', *Official Journal of the Economic Community of West African States*, Vol. 21 (1992).

[29] Author's interview with Colonel Graham G. Davies, Defence Adviser, British High Commission, Abuja, Nigeria, Abuja, 21 September 2000.

and would 'fight to the last man . . . I've given orders to open fire on any strangers setting foot in our territory.'[30] ECOMOG's hostile reception in Liberia was thus no surprise, and the decision to formally revise its mandate from peacekeeping to peace enforcement on 20 September was no more than a belated admission of reality.

Nigeria, ECOMOG's lead state, defended itself against charges of violating state sovereignty by emphasising that it was responding to an appeal for help by Liberia's ruler, Samuel Doe. It also stressed the humanitarian catastrophe taking place in Liberia and NPFL threats against foreign nationals (including Nigerians) living in Liberia. Finally, it underlined the regional security implications of the Liberian civil war, both in terms of the refugee flows it generated and because the NPFL recruited soldiers from neighbouring countries by promising to support their rebellions in the future.

This defence suffered from several weaknesses. First, Doe's right to invite intervention was undermined by the fact that at the time of his appeal he was a deeply unpopular military dictator who had all but lost control of Liberia. Doe's death within the first three weeks of ECOMOG's deployment was a further blow to the argument that ECOMOG served the sovereign Liberian government. Second, the fact that Nigeria was ruled by a military dictator with close personal ties to Samuel Doe made the intervention appear like an act of mutual assistance among dictators. It severely undermined the credibility of Nigeria's claim to be intervening to safeguard human rights and popular sovereignty. As one former Nigerian official put it:

> The basic problem was this: here we were saying we were advancing democracy in Liberia, and then Babangida annuls the elections at home . . . There must be congruence between domestic policy and foreign policy – only then can you project yourself credibly onto the international arena. But here the champion of democracy was undemocratic internally, and that undercut its foreign policy. That was our real Achilles heel.[31]

Finally, Nigeria was vulnerable to accusations of aggression. West Africa's most powerful state had launched a military intervention into a weaker state that was vigorously resisted by the local movement that controlled 90 per cent of the country. To make matters worse,

---

[30] Weller, *The Liberian Crisis*, p. 86.
[31] Author's interview with Dr Jimmi Adisa, Information Analyst, UNDP Project for Capacity Building of the OAU Mechanism for Conflict Prevention, Management, and Resolution, Addis Ababa, Ethiopia, 18 October 2000.

ECOMOG had acted without a UN Security Council mandate. Nigeria's sheer size prompted fears that it was seeking to assert its regional hegemony. In addition, there was persistent suspicion about Nigeria's motives, which Nigerian President Babangida indirectly acknowledged by insisting: 'For the avoidance of doubt, Nigeria has no territorial ambition in Liberia or anywhere in Africa or world-wide ... For the avoidance of doubt, neither Nigeria nor the members of ECOMOG forced their way into the Liberian conflict in a manner remotely resembling military adventurism.'[32] Despite these protestations, Nigeria was accused of benefiting economically from Operation Liberty. The issue was not only that individual ECOMOG soldiers (especially Nigerians) supplemented their irregular pay-cheques by resorting to the black market and to theft.[33] Much more damaging was the organised and systematic exploitation of Liberia's natural wealth by whole divisions of ECOMOG soldiers. For example, ECOMOG troops collaborated with ULIMO-J faction fighters to control western Liberia's diamond market, and they 'backed' a rubber plantation in Buchanan run by the misnamed Liberia Peace Council at a profit of around US$1.5 million.[34] They also stripped Liberia of its fixed assets, including railroad stock and public utilities. 'Liberians watched the "peacekeepers" tear down their country's limited infrastructure and sell it for scrap abroad.'[35] In Monrovia, cynics maintained that ECOMOG was an acronym for 'Every Car Or Moving Object Gone'.

Even this large-scale looting did not cover Nigeria's full expenditures in Liberia, and many Nigerians understandably resent allegations of economic profiteering. However, individual Nigerians did benefit greatly from the intervention – and the Nigerian regime found itself accused of complicity in this profiteering. As one Nigerian diplomat noted:

> There are people who believe that [the Liberia intervention] was an adventure based on people in the military who wanted to make a profit.

[32] Ibrahim Babangida, 'The Imperative Features of Nigerian Foreign Policy', *Contact* (Publication of the Economic Community of West African States) 2:3 (November 1990), pp. 12–14.

[33] Herbert Howe, 'Lessons from Liberia', *International Security*, 21:3 (Winter 1996/97), p. 169.

[34] William Reno, *Warlord Politics and African States* (Boulder: Lynne Rienner, 1998), p. 105.

[35] S. Ellis, 'Profiteering from War', in the South African *Weekly Mail and Guardian*, 25 July 1997.

There is no proof of that, but I have spoken to a minister who says he was aware of arms leaving Nigeria to go to the rebels. So maybe somebody made a profit. But there is no proof.[36]

Under these circumstances, Operation Liberty's legitimacy was subject to considerable doubt. The question that remains is why Nigeria's military leadership was concerned about this controversy. This question can only be answered by distinguishing among the four possible legitimacy audiences for ECOMOG delineated in chapter 2.

As might be expected of a military regime, Nigeria's leadership showed little concern for how Operation Liberty would be perceived by the Nigerian public. Babangida's regime may have hoped to derive domestic advantages from the deployment. Some observers suggest that Babangida saw the operation as an opportunity to send potential coup-makers abroad.[37] One Nigerian military officer also argues that he hoped to divert public attention from Nigeria's domestic problems:

> Things were too hot for [Babangida] in Nigeria, so he looked to a foreign quarrel ... By 1990, civilians were fed up with military government ... [So] Babangida imposed ECOMOG on Nigeria ... [He] wanted to keep giddy minds busy by diverting them to other quarrels, by telling them we must help our neighbours ... Babangida thought that if people are thinking about Liberia, they will stop grumbling at home.[38]

Given the dismal state of Nigeria's economy, however, many Nigerians opposed the intervention, arguing that the resources being poured into Liberia would be better invested within Nigeria itself. The Nigerian government responded to these questions with a mixture of propaganda, obfuscation, and intimidation:

> Nigerians never knew how many casualties there were ... nor how much money was being spent. And under that rule, people were not bold enough to criticise the government. Also, academics came forward to give palatable reasons for the intervention, especially the 'African theory': when the neighbour's house is burning, Africans always help.[39]

---

[36] Author's interview with Ambassador Ekpang, Director Jakubo Gowon Centre, Abuja, Nigeria, 28 September 2000.

[37] Several interviewees referred to this allegation, but preferred their remarks to remain off the record.

[38] Author's interview with Major General (rtd.) Charles B. Ndiomu, 22 September 2000.

[39] Ibid.

This strategy suggests a relatively cavalier attitude towards domestic public opinion on the part of the Nigerian regime, which is not surprising in a dictatorship. Some efforts were made to soothe domestic discontent, but ultimately the government sought less to reassure those concerned about the intervention's legitimacy than to silence them.

The Nigerian government similarly disregarded the Liberian public as a legitimacy audience for Operation Liberty. Its efforts to win Liberian 'hearts and minds' were limited by its virulent distaste for Taylor and his supporters. As Nigeria's ambassador to Liberia at the time recalls, 'the Nigerian perception was that Taylor was a rebel. Once you use the vocabulary of government and rebels you cannot be even-handed. That's not possible.'[40] The ambassador opposed this stance, reasoning that 'the problem would have been solved at less cost if we were not totally partisan'. He was opposed, however, by influential military officials, including General Joshua Dogonyaro, who assumed command of the ECOMOG forces in Liberia from September 1990 to February 1991. These 'hawks' argued that the solution to the Liberian conflict was the military defeat and destruction of Taylor's NPFL. This antagonistic mindset meant that Liberians who questioned Operation Liberty were viewed less as an audience to be convinced of the operation's legitimacy than as enemies to be defeated. 'Good' Liberians were assumed to appreciate ECOMOG's efforts in Liberia without further persuasion.

From the point of view of the Nigerian government, the West African region and continental Africa enjoyed somewhat greater importance as a legitimacy audience. At the regional level, Nigeria saw itself as a natural leader thanks to its population size and natural resources. It was frustrated by the tendency of francophone West African states to look to France rather than to Nigeria for international leadership. In addition, Nigeria's sheer size tended to intimidate its neighbours, further undermining its ability to unite the region behind its leadership. Operation Liberty had the potential to alter these perceptions by demonstrating Nigeria's beneficial commitment to the West African sub-region. As one official put it, 'other countries [have to] understand that Nigeria is not out to oppress and expand, but is prepared to assist them with internal difficulties. To persuade them, Nigeria must put its money where its mouth is, and risk money and even lives for the sub-region.'[41] This effect

---

[40] Author's interview with Ambassador A. Ajakaiye, Abuja, Nigeria, 28 September 2000.
[41] Author's interview with Humphrey Orjiako, Deputy Director, Office of Conflict Resolution, The Nigerian Presidency, Abuja, Nigeria, 22 September 2000.

could only be achieved, however, if Operation Liberty was perceived as legitimate. If it was viewed as illegitimate, regional fears of Nigerian hegemony would increase and francophone states might be driven even further towards France to balance Nigerian dominance.

Nigeria has also consistently seen itself as a natural leader at the continental level. As one government official put it, 'Nigerians believe that Nigeria is very highly gifted in terms of human resources and also of natural resources, which we have in abundance ... [So] the elites ... believe seriously that Nigeria could be the political and economic leader, the real focus of authority on the continent.'[42] Establishing itself as Africa's leader was therefore a fundamental tenet of Nigerian foreign policy:

> Pax Nigeriana is the attempt by Nigeria to establish itself as a regional leader in Africa through political, economic, and military actions taken in Africa or on issues related to Africa. Politically, Nigeria has attempted to act as Africa's spokesman at the United Nations, the OAU, and other international fora; militarily, it has sent peacekeepers to the Congo, Chad, Liberia, Somalia, and Sierra Leone, provided military training to armies from Gambia to Tanzania, and supplied military assistance to liberation movements in southern Africa; economically, it has promoted sub-regional integration through ECOWAS and provided bilateral aid and technical assistance to African countries.[43]

Operation Liberty offered Nigeria a chance to bolster its continental profile. Babangida insisted that the Liberian crisis portended 'danger and international embarrassment ... for all of us in the sub-region in particular, and to Africa and the black race in general'.[44] Nigeria could earn considerable prestige within Africa by providing welcome proof that Africans could solve their own security crises. Again, however, this could only be achieved if ECOMOG was perceived as a legitimate peace enforcement operation rather than an act of aggression.

However, the Nigerian government's concern with West Africa and other African states as a legitimacy audience for Operation Liberty was mitigated by Nigeria's relative power within Africa and in particular in its region. Nigeria felt secure within West Africa. It did not need ECOMOG to demonstrate its power in the region. It felt somewhat

---

[42] Ibid.
[43] Adekeye Adebajo, *Liberia's Civil War: Nigeria, ECOMOG, and Regional Security in West Africa* (Boulder: Lynne Rienner, 2002), pp. 43–4.
[44] Babangida, 'The Imperative Features of Nigerian Foreign Policy', p. 12.

less certain of its leadership at the continental level, but again its relative power guaranteed it status and respect in this community.

By contrast, the Nigerian government felt insecure and insufficiently respected on the wider international stage. Here, Nigeria's relative weakness (compared to the developed world) made it dependent on international recognition and prestige as a resource for power and influence. Nigeria has traditionally been deeply concerned about both factors. By 1990, however, its military regime faced increasing international disapprobation because of its repressive domestic policies. A show of leadership on regional peace and security issues might remedy the situation. As one observer argued:

> Liberia was an opportunity to break back into the international community, to show how good Nigeria and Nigerians are, and that although we still might also be isolated by the Western powers, that we are doing good things in Liberia and Sierra Leone. I think that was part of the calculation – breaking out of the isolation of the international community.[45]

This tactic became increasingly important later in the 1990s, when Sani Abacha's authoritarianism threatened to reduce Nigeria to international pariah status. 'Nigeria's internal policies attracted a lot of enmity from outside Africa, so the Abacha government felt that it could recover some outside glamour by taking on the [Liberia] intervention.'[46] The tactic had some success: as one Western diplomat commented, 'we praised [the Nigerians] for Liberia, even during the worst part of the Abacha regime. We were forced to cooperate with them because they were willing to do this job.'[47]

Nigeria also had more positive international ambitions, which included asserting itself as spokesman for Africa in world affairs. This goal could also be promoted by pointing to Nigeria's leadership on regional peace and security issues. For example, some Nigerian diplomats used Nigeria's leadership in Operation Liberty to argue for a Nigerian permanent seat on the UN Security Council.[48] Their argument is ambitious, but its logic is not unreasonable. Article 23 of the UN Charter already specifies that the primary selection criterion for

---

[45] Author's interview with Dr Kole A. Shettima, Country Coordinator, John D. and Catherine T. MacArthur Foundation, Abuja, 25 September 2000.

[46] Author's interview with Ambassador Ekpang, 28 September 2000.

[47] Author's interview. Remarks not for attribution.

[48] Ehiedu E. Iweriebor and Martin I. Uhomoibhi, *UN Security Council: A Case for Nigeria's Membership* (Lagos: Times Books, 1999).

non-permanent members of the Security Council should be their contribution to international peace and security. The allocation of any
further permanent seat may also follow this logic. Moreover, service to
regional security also has the more immediate benefit of generating
international gratitude. As one African diplomat described it, 'There
are important issues, like the expansion of the UN Security Council. If
Nigeria shows leadership [in Africa], it might win a few votes – maybe as
a quid-pro-quo for massive involvement in areas that Western powers
don't want to be involved in.'[49]

However, Operation Liberty could only improve Nigeria's international status if it was perceived to be legitimate. An act of aggression
cannot be used as an indicator of a state's commitment to regional
security or as an argument for granting this state prominence on the
international stage. It was therefore above all the wider international
community that would have to be convinced of the legitimacy of the
Nigerian-led ECOMOG intervention in Liberia. The broad international
community of states was thus the crucial legitimacy audience for
ECOMOG in the eyes of the Nigerian government.

ECOWAS and ECOMOG's international legitimacy

The ECOWAS framework had no significant effect on Liberian or Nigerian
public perceptions of Operation Liberty's legitimacy. Liberians judged
ECOMOG by its performance on the ground. ECOMOG contingents
provided a modicum of security, especially around Monrovia, and were
less prone to human rights abuses than Liberian factions in the civil war.
However, ECOMOG's economic excesses, including black marketeering,
theft, looting, and the wholesale exploitation of Liberia's natural resources,
diminished its popular support. The ECOWAS framework also had only a
limited, though positive, effect on Nigerian public opinion. Many
Nigerians feel considerable pride in Nigeria's regional leadership, and an
ECOWAS endorsement of Operation Liberty would help confirm this
leadership role. Nevertheless, critics remained unconvinced of the wisdom
of risking Nigerian lives in Liberia and of pouring scarce Nigerian resources
into ECOMOG.

However, the ECOWAS framework did have a significant impact
on international perceptions of Operation Liberty's legitimacy. As a

---

[49] Author's interview, remarks not for attribution.

member of the Nigerian War College noted, this was Nigeria's key motivation for operating in this framework:

> as Liberia widened in scope, ECOWAS was brought in to discuss it. Nigeria still had to bear the bulk of the intervention, but it needed greater legitimacy, and so there was a need to bring in other states ... It was an ECOWAS decision, probably made under Nigerian pressure, for ECOWAS to get involved. There are benefits at the regional and international level: greater potency, more legitimacy.[50]

The Nigerian government knew that the international legitimacy of its actions in Liberia depended crucially on the international community being persuaded that Nigeria was leading a genuinely regional response to a local security issue. Babangida took care to stress this regional dimension: 'Nigeria is a member of a sub-regional group that took a solemn decision to restore peace by separating the warring factions in a sister country, Liberia ... We are participating in ECOMOG at the level of our capacity and expectations of other members within the sub-region.'[51] ECOWAS auspices were crucial for credibly placing ECOMOG in this regional context. As a member of Nigeria's Ministry of Foreign Affairs put it, ECOWAS 'is a regional body. We need the support of everybody in the region so that we don't give the impression as if it's our own personal agenda.'[52] Thus, as another Nigerian observer noted, operating through ECOWAS 'gives legitimacy, the basis for legitimate action. There's an institutional structure given by ECOWAS, rather than going through the bilateral process – that might be seen as aggression ... [They] legitimised it as an ECOWAS or ECOMOG intervention.'[53] In short, as a Sierra Leonean diplomat summed up: going through ECOWAS was 'for not looking like an invasion'.[54]

ECOWAS was more than a name to be affixed to the intervention, however. It was a platform for encouraging West African states to publicly coalesce into a united front behind Operation Liberty. This

---

[50] Author's interview with Dr Ochoche, Director of Research and Publications, Centre for Peace Research and Conflict Resolution, Nigerian National War College, Abuja, Nigeria, 26 September 2000.

[51] Babangida, 'The Imperative Features of Nigerian Foreign Policy', p. 12.

[52] Author's interview with Abubakar Hassan Fulata, Special Adviser to the Nigerian Minister of Foreign Affairs, Abuja, Nigeria, 9 October 2000.

[53] Author's interview with Dr Kole A. Shettima, 25 September 2000.

[54] Author's interview with Colonel K. S. Mundeh, Defence Adviser to the Sierra Leone High Commission, Lagos, Nigeria, 13 October 2000.

was crucial because ECOWAS's ability to generate international legitimacy for the intervention was fundamentally linked to its multilateral
nature. If Nigeria claimed ECOWAS auspices but other member states
disowned the intervention, Operation Liberty's international legitimacy
would not be much advanced. Such dissent was a very real possibility.
Two ECOWAS members, Côte d'Ivoire and Burkina Faso, vehemently
opposed the intervention. Others felt uneasy about the manner in which
Operation Liberty had been launched. Expressing this concern, Guinea
Bissau responded to the SMC's decision to create ECOMOG by calling
for an extra-ordinary session of the ECOWAS Authority to 'define a
platform for joint action in Liberia based strictly on the respect of the
supreme interests of the Liberian people'.[55]

Two characteristics of the ECOWAS framework favoured the emergence
of a publicly united regional front in support of Operation Liberty when
this summit met on 28 November 1990. First, ECOWAS lacked burden-
sharing mechanisms, making it possible for member states to assent to the
intervention without incurring any obligation to contribute to it either
financially or militarily. Second, the ECOWAS Authority takes decisions by
consensus rather than by voting. Nigeria could thus block any Authority
motion to censor ECOMOG. Even more importantly, the consensus rule
muted formal opposition to Operation Liberty by ECOWAS member
states. Although it theoretically afforded each member a veto over the
operation, exercising this veto was extremely costly. Doing so would offend
Nigeria, which, as one Nigerian diplomat put it, 'is a very powerful country
[within West Africa] whose friendship is not entirely without benefits'.[56]
Vetoing an Authority resolution endorsing the SMC's decision would also
reveal embarrassing regional divisions to the outside world and risk tearing
ECOWAS apart by humiliating and disowning the SMC members that had
claimed to act in the region's name. Thus,

> when you have an organisation that has had some history, and you want it
> to continue, issues are discussed on the basis of consensus. And if you find
> yourself not quite agreeing with the mainstream of the consensus, you
> kept quiet, and find an excuse to be absent, make no commitment, and do
> not participate in solving that particular issue. But you do not come and
> say No, I disagree.[57]

---

[55] Weller, *The Liberian Crisis*, p. 100. See also Adisa, 'The Politics of Regional Military
Co-operation', p. 217.
[56] Author's interview with Ambassador A. Ajakaiye, 28 September 2000.
[57] Author's interview with Ambassador A. Ajakaiye, 3 October 2000.

Under the consensus system, however, the only alternative to exercising a veto was acquiescing to ECOMOG. States could not dissociate themselves from the operation or register their dissent without vetoing the operation. These circumstances favoured acquiescence.

Under the combined influence of the consensus rule and the lack of burden-sharing mechanisms, states at the extra-ordinary Authority session decided overwhelmingly to acquiesce to a decision endorsing the SMC's actions. This left Côte d'Ivoire and Burkina Faso isolated in their opposition to Operation Liberty. Once a majority of ECOWAS states were willing to certify that ECOMOG was acting in the interest of regional peace and security, moreover, opposition became difficult to justify. Côte d'Ivoire decided merely to distance itself from ECOMOG's militaristic methods, rather than openly oppose the intervention itself.[58] It was finally brought fully into the ECOWAS fold when Nigeria, appealing to Côte d'Ivoire's vision of itself as a major player in West African politics, invited it to lead the 1991–2 Committee of Five peace negotiations.[59] Côte d'Ivoire's ambassador to Ethiopia summarised his country's stance: 'we were worried about a certain partiality on the Nigerian side ... [Still,] Côte d'Ivoire was involved from the beginning [though] her method was dialogue.'[60] This put Burkina Faso in the untenable position of being the only ECOWAS country openly opposed to Operation Liberty. It backed down. Thus, as a Ghanaian diplomat noted: 'ECOWAS politics are very interesting. All states ... meet and decide by consensus. When they convene a summit, if the majority is in favour of something, the others are bound to toe the line.'[61]

Thus the initially hostile extra-ordinary session of the Authority ultimately endorsed the SMC Peace Plan, appealed to ECOWAS states to contribute troops and funds to the ECOMOG, and offered 'warm congratulations' to the SMC for its 'timely initiatives taken on behalf of the entire community'.[62] This official façade of united support for ECOMOG persisted throughout Operation Liberty. As Ambassador

---

[58] Author's interview with Roger Laloupo, Head of the ECOWAS Department of Legal Affairs, Abuja, Nigeria, 11 October 2000.

[59] Author's interview with Ambassador A. Ajakaiye, 3 October 2000. The USA also urged Côte d'Ivoire to head the peace negotiations. Author's interview with Mr Jankey, Political Officer, Embassy of Ghana to Ethiopia, Addis Ababa, Ethiopia, 25 October 2000.

[60] Author's interview with Ambassador Pierre L. Yéré, 9 November 2000.

[61] Author's interview with Mr Jankey, 25 October 2000.

[62] ECOWAS Heads of State and Government, *Final Communiqué*, Bamako, Mali, 28 November 1990.

Ajakaiye recalls, 'you could observe [some countries'] nonchalance, non-participation, evasiveness, and draw your conclusion. But nobody came to attend and said, no, we don't agree with this.'[63] A member of Nigeria's Ministry of Foreign Affairs noted triumphantly: 'In the end they all supported [ECOMOG]. Even if they opposed it, it was subtle opposition. They didn't come out openly to challenge ECOMOG and Nigeria. There was very little they could do to stop the intervention. But that doesn't stop [dissenters] from supporting the rebels ... You don't expect 100%, total compliance.'[64]

The impact of this ECOWAS mandate on Operation Liberty's regional legitimacy was limited. West African states had followed the developments within ECOWAS closely. They knew that Nigeria had initially launched ECOMOG through the SMC, contrary to ECOWAS rules. They also knew that the apparent unity behind the Authority's endorsement of the intervention owed more to internal ECOWAS politics than to real consensus. As one diplomat pointed out, 'there were no open cracks, but whoever knew the politics of ECOWAS ... would have seen the line'.[65] Nevertheless, the ECOWAS mandate made it easier for West African states to accept ECOMOG. Regional states would have been outraged if Nigeria had intervened in Liberia alone and without an ECOWAS mandate. By operating through ECOWAS, Nigeria at least showed a willingness to submit the intervention to regional scrutiny and acknowledge the concerns it raised among other states in the region. The ECOWAS mandate also made it easier for Ghana, the Gambia, Guinea, and Sierra Leone to accede to Nigeria's request for their participation in ECOMOG. Thanks to this mandate, they could claim to be acting as responsible members of their region. Gambian diplomats, for example, explained that 'Gambia wanted to fulfil its quota in ECOMOG' because 'we felt obliged to, being a sister republic'.[66] Liberian interim president Amos Sawyer confirmed: 'We owe an unending debt to ECOWAS and the cooperative governments that have given a new viability to this subregional organisation.'[67]

[63] Author's interview with Ambassador A. Ajakaiye, 3 October 2000.
[64] Author's interview with Abubakar Hassan Fulata, 9 October 2000.
[65] Author's interview with Ambassador A. Ajakaiye, 3 October 2000.
[66] Author's interviews in Abuja, Nigeria with Mr Amoa-Awua, Acting Head of Mission, Ghana High Commission (2 October 2000); Alasan Barrow, Financial Adviser, The Gambia High Commission (2 October 2000); and Maba J. O. Jobe, High Commissioner, The Gambia High Commission (6 October 2000).
[67] Liberian Interim President Dr Amos Sawyer, 'Address to the Nation on the Outcome of the Lomé Cease-Fire Talks', Radio ELBC, Monrovia, 19 February 1991, transcribed by BBC Summary of World Broadcasts 22 February 1991. Note that Sawyer lists only the ECOMOG countries, plus Togo, the fifth SMC member.

It was at the global level, however, that the ECOWAS framework made its most substantial contribution to Operation Liberty's legitimacy. As noted in chapter 2, there was a trend towards the regionalisation of peacekeeping efforts in the 1990s, and the slogan of 'African solutions to African problems' featured prominently in international discourse. Regionalisation was, however, anchored in Chapter VIII of the UN Charter and thus conceived of within the framework of formal organisations. The ECOWAS framework qualified Operation Liberty for international legitimacy under this dispensation. By going through ECOWAS, 'at the UN level, the operation gained greater respectability, it was easier to invoke the Charter'.[68] In fact, UN Secretary-General Boutros Boutros-Ghali recognised that ECOMOG might 'herald a new division of labor between the United Nations and regional organizations'.[69] Major powers also stressed the regional framework when voicing their appreciation for ECOMOG. The USA declared its 'belief that ECOWAS mediation in the peace process supports our goals of regional solutions to regional problems',[70] In 1992, the UK claimed: 'We have consistently welcomed and supported the initiatives of the countries of the Economic Community of West African States (ECOWAS) to try to resolve, through regional efforts, the crisis in Liberia.'[71]

The fact that the ECOWAS Authority mandate for ECOMOG was arrived at under the consensus rule also affected international judgements of the operation. Despite the divisions within the region, the Authority formally proclaimed that all sixteen ECOWAS heads of state and government approved of the SMC's decision to launch ECOMOG. Their apparently unanimous assent made ECOMOG hard to criticise at the international level. The day before the summit, the USA had cautioned that 'in view of the split within ECOWAS on the issue of military intervention, the United States maintained its neutrality while continuing to support the stated goals of ECOWAS'.[72] A day later, there was formally no split anymore. By 1992, the US ambassador to the UN was

---

[68] Author's interview with Dr Ochoche, 26 September 2000.
[69] Boutros Boutros-Ghali, *Supplement to An Agenda for Peace* (New York: UN, 1995), p. 32.
[70] Subcommittee on African Affairs of the US Senate Foreign Relations Committee, Statement by Herman Cohen, Assistant Secretary of State for African Affairs, 27 November 1990.
[71] Sir David Hannay, UN Security Council Provisional Verbatim Record of the 3138th Meeting, in Weller, *The Liberian Crisis*, p. 267.
[72] Statement by Herman Cohen, Assistant Secretary of State for African Affairs, 27 November 1990.

insisting: 'The dispatch of a six-nation West African peacekeeping force in 1990 demonstrated unprecedented African determination to take the lead in regional conflict resolution ... we have supported this effort from its inception.'[73]

In addition to directly generating legitimacy for Operation Liberty, the ECOWAS framework also provided an effective platform for lobbying larger international organisations. It thus represented the first rung on a global legitimacy pyramid of the kind identified in chapter 2. The second rung, in this case, was the Organisation of African Unity (OAU, now African Union, AU), Africa's only continental organisation. The OAU was (and the AU still is) a cumbersome organisation hampered by the need to forge consensus among fifty-three member states before it could take any action. However, it was the point of contact between Africa and the rest of the world. As one Western diplomat remarked, 'we have to try to work with the OAU because it is the only continental organization and it has a broad mandate ... There is no alternative to the OAU – we need the interlocutor at the continental level.'[74] OAU endorsement of ECOMOG thus represented the approval of the entire African continent.

Nigeria recognised that the OAU had a greater capacity to generate international legitimacy for ECOMOG than ECOWAS. As one diplomat put it, 'We needed ... the OAU political umbrella, as a continental organisation ... For political legitimation, we needed the OAU. When we started, there was cynicism about the OAU – it can't do anything, it has no troops. But we needed the political legitimacy ... The OAU is very weak, but it has the political umbrella.'[75] The ECOWAS framework maximised ECOMOG's chances of receiving the OAU's blessing. As one ECOWAS diplomat commented: 'we are sixteen out of the fifty-three members, we are the largest group in the OAU. A Secretary-General taking sniper shots at ECOWAS will not last.'[76]

The OAU made considerable efforts to legitimise Operation Liberty. The OAU Secretary-General defended the intervention from August 1990 onwards, brushing aside complaints about the intervention's illegality without a UN mandate: 'to argue that there is no legal basis for the

---

[73] E. Perkins, UN Security Council Provisional Verbatim Record of the 3138th Meeting, in Weller, *The Liberian Crisis*, p. 266.
[74] Author's interview, remarks not for attribution.
[75] Author's interview, remarks not for attribution.
[76] Author's interview, remarks not for attribution.

intervention is surprising. Should the countries in West Africa just leave Liberians to fight each other? Will that be more legitimate?'[77] The OAU even assumed responsibility for ECOMOG. The director of the OAU's Political Department has claimed that 'the OAU gave ECOWAS the mandate' for the intervention and that, more generally, 'we have no recollection of any ECOWAS decision made without the [OAU] Secretary-General.'[78] The OAU's key contribution to Operation Liberty lay in these declarations of support. One West African diplomat put it bluntly: 'From the ECOWAS point of view, we needed one thing and one thing only from the OAU – we needed political legitimation.'[79] A Nigerian diplomat put this more politely: 'We were content to deal with Liberia on our own. But the OAU did have observers there for legitimacy . . . Legitimacy is very key in the implementation of a foreign policy.'[80]

The OAU also acted as a conduit for lobbying the highest rung on the global legitimacy pyramid, the United Nations. The OAU had formal observer status at the UN and represented 53 of the UN's then 185 states. It also coordinated closely with the Africa Group in the UN, and together these organisations were understood to 'speak for Africa' in the global forum. Thus 'if the OAU legitimises something, it is hard for the US, the UK, or others to criticise this position. If the OAU accepted it, it was the African position – and that made it hard to criticise from outside.'[81] The OAU was well aware of this conduit role. In 2000, the Director of the OAU's Political Department noted:

> We see a pyramidal relationship between the OAU, the UN, and sub-regional organisations – the UN is at the top, the OAU in the middle and the sub-regional organisations at the bottom . . . The first to engage [a crisis] is the sub-region, but the sub-region needs the OAU's continental endorsement, and the OAU then takes it to the UN . . . The OAU is a

---

[77] Adisa, 'The Politics of Regional Military Co-operation', p. 216.

[78] Author's interview with Sam Ibok, Director of the OAU Political Department, Addis Ababa, Ethiopia, 1 November 2000.

[79] Author's interview, remark not for attribution. In 1993, following the Cotonou Accord's call for a more international (i.e. less Nigerian) ECOMOG, the OAU attempted to recruit other African states to participate in ECOMOG. These efforts produced limited results. Egypt, Tanzania, Uganda, and Zimbabwe announced troop contributions, but Egypt and Zimbabwe later withdrew their offers. Tanzania deployed 800 men in January 1994, but withdrew them when the Cotonou peace efforts collapsed.

[80] Author's interview with Dr Martin Uhomoibhi, Deputy Head of Mission, Nigerian Embassy, Addis Ababa, Ethiopia, 21 October 2000.

[81] Author's interview with Dr Jimmi Adisa, 18 October 2000.

continental organisation, and therefore has more possibilities of getting the international community's attention. Our role is to mobilise the international community.[82]

He also acknowledged that this was a key factor in the OAU's continental importance: sub-regional actors consult with the OAU Secretary-General 'because they want him to explain this to the [UN] Security Council'. The Head of the UN Liaison Office with the OAU in Addis Ababa confirmed that these links are the OAU's greatest strength:

> [sub-regional organisations] need the blessing of the [OAU] Council of Ministers and the Heads of State to be in a better position to deal with the international community ... In New York, you have the office of the OAU observer mission and the Africa Group. All issues are pressed through the Africa Group – it is they who submit decisions to the UN bodies. Sub-regional organisations do no exist at that level. It's only the OAU.[83]

Ultimately OAU lobbying, combined with direct appeals by ECOWAS to the UN and the West's preference for an 'African solution' to the Liberian civil war, helped produce formal UN recognition of ECOMOG in 1993. The UN Security Council had previously been tentative in its reaction to ECOMOG. In January 1991, the Security Council president 'commended the efforts made by the ECOWAS Heads of State and Government to promote peace and normalcy in Liberia',[84] but the Council refrained from formally endorsing ECOMOG. In November 1992 it relented somewhat by exempting 'the peace-keeping forces of ECOWAS' from the embargo it decided to impose on all military equipment exports to Liberia.[85] It recalled Chapter VIII of the UN Charter and welcomed both ECOWAS efforts to bring peace to Liberia and the OAU's endorsement of these efforts. In March 1993, again acknowledging Chapter VIII, ECOWAS, and the OAU, UN Security Council Resolution 813 took the further step of condemning armed attacks against the ECOWAS forces. Finally, on 22 September 1993, the Security Council Resolution 866 officially 'commend[ed]

---

[82] Author's interview with Sam Ibok, 1 November 2000.

[83] Author's interview with Mamadou Kane, Head of the United Nations Liaison Office with the OAU, Economic Community of Africa Headquarters, Addis Ababa, Ethiopia, 19 October 2000.

[84] Weller, *The Liberian Crisis*, p. 128.

[85] UN Security Council Resolution 788, 19 November 1992, in Weller, *The Liberian Crisis*, pp. 273–4.

ECOWAS for its continuing efforts to restore peace, security and stability in Liberia'.[86]

This resolution responded to the Cotonou Peace Agreement signed by the parties of the Liberian civil war on 25 July 1993. The agreement called for an expanded ECOMOG presence supervised by a UN Observer Mission. Resolution 866 accepted this arrangement, 'noting that this would be the first peacekeeping mission undertaken by the United Nations with a peace-keeping mission already set up by another organisation'. The UN Observer Mission in Liberia (UNOMIL) simultaneously represented an endorsement of ECOMOG and an implicit wariness of it. The UN would cooperate with ECOMOG – in fact, the Security Council emphasised that ECOMOG would bear the 'primary responsibility' for helping to implement the Cotonou Agreement. This signalled the UN's official acceptance of the force as a legitimate presence in Liberian conflict management. Nevertheless, UNOMIL's presence also suggested a degree of mistrust of ECOMOG's impartiality. In the event, however, UNOMIL did not prove an effective monitoring force. Mandated to withdraw from all areas of combat, UNOMIL personnel spent most of their deployment confined to Monrovia. They also depended on ECOMOG for their security and transport, and could not move without ECOMOG escort.[87] Bereft of the means to effectively monitor ECOMOG, UNOMIL tried to preserve both forces' reputations by refusing to criticise ECOMOG. Thus 'United Nations peacekeepers [were] surprisingly complimentary concerning ECOMOG ... [arguing that] ECOMOG only lacked the necessary resources' to bring peace to Liberia.[88]

If UNOMIL's supervision role was thus compromised, however, its role of validating ECOMOG's deployment in the eyes of the international community only became all the more prominent. As one UNOMIL member put it, even when ECOMOG 'borrowed' the UN's own equipment, 'we would just keep patting them on the back and say what a great job they're doing'.[89] UNOMIL symbolised, and Security Council Resolution 866 formalised, the UN's seal of approval on

[86] Weller, *The Liberian Crisis*, p. 412.
[87] Clement Adibe, 'The Liberian Conflict and the ECOWAS-UN Partnership', *Third World Quarterly*, 18:3 (1997), p. 478.
[88] Eric Berman, ' "Successful" Elections in Liberia: Hold the Applause', *UN Watch*, online at unwatch.org/pas/97/pas008.htm (current in 2000 but now no longer available at this site), p. 1.
[89] Author's interview, remark not for attribution.

ECOMOG operations in Liberia. This finalised the process of inter-national legitimation. As a West African diplomat put it:

> Liberia may not have been legal. But when we eventually went there, they lauded the initiative. This is retrospective legitimisation. If you do some-thing that is illegal but then you go to court and you're found not guilty, was it really illegal? It was accepted by the OAU, and then the UN cooperated. In strict legal terms, the critics are right – ECOMOG was not legal – a Security Council mandate was needed, and we never got it – but we did get retrospective legitimation.[90]

Thus achieving the ECOWAS mandate helped further the inter-national legitimacy of Operation Liberty both directly and because it opened the way to formal approval of the operation by larger inter-national organisations with greater legitimising potential. By 1993, whatever the private misgivings of individual countries, the interna-tional community as a whole had officially endorsed ECOMOG through the UN Security Council's agreement to cooperate with the force.

The costs and benefits of the ECOWAS framework

So far, this chapter has argued that Nigeria's decision to launch its intervention in Liberia under ECOWAS auspices owed far more to its concerns about Operation Liberty's international legitimacy than to respect for international law or desire for burden-sharing. Yet if Nigeria's recourse to ECOWAS was relatively cost-free, or if the costs incurred were balanced by material benefits, then its decision to operate within this framework would tell us very little about the value it attached to the international legitimacy this generated. To counter this objection, this section demonstrates that Nigeria incurred significant costs in obtaining and operating under an ECOWAS mandate, which were not balanced by material benefits.

The costs of obtaining the ECOWAS mandate

Nigeria was able to manipulate the internal dynamics of ECOWAS in order to secure the organisation's mandate for Operation Liberty. However, obtaining this mandate entailed material and political costs for Nigeria. Although Nigeria dominates the West African region, it

---

[90] Author's interview, remark not for attribution.

could not force its sovereign fellow states in ECOWAS to endorse ECOMOG. Therefore Nigeria relied in part on the distribution of economic benefits to persuade hesitant ECOWAS members. As Nigerian Major-General Ndiomu explained:

> Babangida granted a lot of largesse. We became a very charitable organisation. At times, we even contributed to the equipment of our neighbours – Benin, Togo ... If we had to phase out an aeroplane, we would give it to them. Niger and Chad, too – if they find it difficult to pay their salaries, they come here, and we give them the money. It's the heads of state that collect the money – the nationals don't benefit. I don't like to use the word bribery, but they did benefit from the gifts of Babangida and Abacha ... Babangida provided gifts and security, which favoured most of them.[91]

The most grievous cost to Nigeria of obtaining the ECOWAS mandate, however, was the political damage the process did to the organisation. Nigeria was the driving force behind ECOWAS's creation and remains one of the organisation's most ardent supporters. It hosts the ECOWAS headquarters. It is also responsible for a lion's share of the ECOWAS budget and is one of very few ECOWAS members to pay its dues regularly. This is not an altruistic stance:

> Lagos extended its influence in West Africa through the creation of ECOWAS and became a respected actor on the wider continental scene ... Overcoming the opposition of France and the vast majority of francophone states, Lagos created a vehicle through which it could extend its political, economic, and military influence in the subregion ... [ECOWAS] provided a forum through which Nigeria could mobilize support for its goals of forging closer subregional and economic cooperation.[92]

Thus 'ECOWAS remained Nigeria's greatest foreign policy achievement until 1990'.[93]

Launching Operation Liberty under ECOWAS auspices nearly tore the organisation apart. Relations between anglophone and francophone West African states were traditionally tense, and Côte d'Ivoire and Burkina Faso, key francophone states in the region, opposed the Liberia intervention. They were outraged at the subterfuge of having

---

[91] Author's interview with Major General (rtd.) Charles B. Ndiomu, 22 September 2000.
[92] Adebajo, *Liberia's Civil War*, p. 47.   [93] Ibid.

the SMC create ECOMOG. Even Nigerian head of state Ibrahim Babangida was forced to admit that a permanent rift was imminent, noting in November 1990 that 'the supposed threat of disintegration of ECOWAS over the Liberian crisis' was an 'issue of serious concern'.[94] Ultimately, Nigeria was able to persuade ECOWAS members to maintain a façade of unity. Nevertheless, insisting on ECOWAS auspices for Operation Liberty was fraught with risk and created substantial divisions within the organisation that have proved slow to heal. Both factors represented significant and predictable costs to Nigeria.

The benefits and costs of operating under an ECOWAS mandate

The material benefits generated by the ECOWAS mandate were minimal. At the international level, ECOMOG members, including Nigeria, received only paltry financial support. ECOWAS's Special Emergency Fund for ECOMOG had received only just over US$3 million by January 1991, most of it from ECOMOG members.[95] The UN Trust Fund for Liberia created in 1993 by UN Security Council Resolution 866 received only $15.16 million by April 1994, growing very slowly to $24 million by January 1996.[96] In terms of bilateral assistance, the USA was the largest extra-regional contributor to ECOMOG. By November 1992, it had contributed a total of $8.6 million to ECOWAS directly, plus $18.75 million in bilateral military aid to ECOMOG states.[97] By 1996, its contributions averaged around $10 million a year.[98] These sums are insignificant compared to Nigeria's expenditures.

At the regional level, as noted above, the ECOWAS mandate facilitated the participation of Ghana, Guinea, Sierra Leone, and the Gambia in ECOMOG. With the exception of Ghana, however, these countries provided only token forces.[99] The Gambia only contributed 100–150 troops in 1990–1, then withdrew entirely until 1997. The Sierra Leonean,

[94] Babangida, 'The Imperative Features of Nigerian Foreign Policy', p. 12.
[95] Aboagye, ECOMOG, p. 288. The contributors were the Gambia, Mauritania, Nigeria, and Sierra Leone.
[96] Third and Fifteenth Progress Reports of the Secretary-General on the United Nations Observer Mission to Liberia, 18 April 1994 and 23 January 1996 respectively, UN documents S/1994/463 and S/1996/47.
[97] Statement of E. Perkins, US Ambassador to the UN, in Weller, The Liberian Crisis, p. 266.
[98] Sesay, 'Civil War and Collective Intervention in Liberia', p. 47.
[99] Data from Military Balance (International Institute for Strategic Studies, London), annual reports 1990–2000.

Gambian, and Guinean contingents together never amounted to more than 1,600 troops. In comparison, Nigeria's commitment in Liberia escalated to 10,000 troops between 1993 and 1995. The military contribution these forces could make within ECOMOG was thus strictly limited. They also entailed costs for Nigeria. First, Nigeria offered economic incentives to persuade hesitant states to join ECOMOG. For one observer, this included 'supplying of oil to other countries below the official price, funding political campaigns and elections, paying their civil servants' salaries'.[100] Another suggested, 'the position that Nigeria was coming from was not so different from that of the US in the Gulf War. It was important for the US to have a widespread international presence. People were literally paid to be in the Gulf.'[101] Ensuring the continued participation of these allies demanded further resources:

> whenever there was a hitch, diplomacy was employed to make sure that the rank of the countries whose support we had did not break . . . There would be a mission . . . they'd speak to them – why the decision was taken, explain that it was not a slight, that it was necessary to take it immediately, and so forth. I wouldn't be in a position to know whether there were other forms of appeasement. But I know that the diplomatic and perhaps material weight of Nigeria was put behind the effort to maintain solidarity among the participating countries. During those moments of tension, some delegation would go . . . and probably some envelope or some briefcase might change hands.[102]

Second, Nigeria subsidised its ECOMOG partners by providing their forces with logistics, transport, and oil supplies as well as financial support. A member of Nigeria's Ministry of Foreign Affairs explained:

> When NATO intervened in Kosovo, the principal actor was the US. It had to mobilise other NATO members, and it disbursed material and financial support for the intervention. It was the same with Nigeria . . . In military terms we are better equipped and trained, in terms of resources we are better endowed than most countries of the region. So it was a matter of resources both human and material.[103]

---

[100] Author's interview with Dr Kole A. Shettima, 25 September 2000.
[101] Author's interview with Dr Ochoche, 26 September 2000.
[102] Author's interview with Ambassador A. Ajakaiye, 3 October 2000.
[103] Author's interview with A. H. Fulata, 9 October 2000.

This applied to Ghana as well as to smaller troop contributors. One Nigerian diplomat noted:

> What is probably true is that there were times when Nigeria made grants of money to the government of Ghana, perhaps not saying directly 'this is to pay for your troops' . . . That was the kind of informal way things were done. But as for direct payment, it's not true that Nigeria was paying Ghana's troops . . . But that was the impression a lot of people had – that there were times when Nigeria said yes you are with us, have this – and of course that would encourage Ghana to stay on further.[104]

Thus the presence of other ECOMOG troops in Liberia taxed Nigerian financial and military resources. Of course, some other ECOMOG countries also contributed to the intervention. Ghana, for example, had spent US$10 million on ECOMOG by 1996 and spent a further US$10 million in 1997–8.[105] However, these contributions were relatively small and had to be supplemented by Nigerian funds that could otherwise have been spent on Nigeria's own troops. Moreover, from Nigeria's point of view, the value of other states' contributions was partially offset by Nigeria's lack of control over these resources. ECOMOG's force commander was Nigerian, but his control over ECOMOG troops was tenuous:

> Because of the high level of control from home governments, the contingent commanders enjoy[ed] considerable autonomy from the control of the force commander. There have been instances where contingent units have been pulled out of their area of deployment without the approval or even knowledge of the force commander, thus endangering the deployment of flanking contingents. Some contingents have also at times refused to come to the aid of other contingents without clearance from their home governments.[106]

These costs were not justified by the negligible military contribution of these forces. With the exception of Ghana, most states' participation in ECOMOG was a losing proposition for Nigeria in purely materialistic terms. It resulted in a sub-optimal allocation of Nigerian resources from a military or financial point of view. Nigeria's willingness to assume these costs can only be explained in the context of its concerns about

---

[104] Author's interview with Ambassador A. Ajakaiye, 3 October 2000.
[105] Sesay, 'Civil War and Collective Intervention in Liberia', p. 47. *The Military Balance 1999/2000* (London: International Institute for Strategic Studies), p. 248.
[106] Khobe, 'The Evolution and Conduct of ECOMOG Operations in West Africa', p. 9.

Operation Liberty's international legitimacy. Nigeria realised that a multinational deployment was key to fully legitimising the intervention. Its ECOMOG partners helped validate the ECOWAS mandate and confirmed that ECOMOG was a truly regional effort. From the very beginning of Operation Liberty, Nigerian officials were aware of the crucial importance of multilateralism to ECOMOG's international legitimacy: 'As Nigerian troops were arriving at the staging post in Sierra Leone, frantic efforts were being made to convince other Africans to come along ... the administration saw immediately that it would be hue and cry if they decided to go in alone.'[107] Nigeria was willing to spend scarce resources for this legitimacy effect: 'Nigeria still had to bear the bulk of the intervention, but it needed greater legitimacy, and so there was a need to bring in other states.'[108]

Nigeria also faced another kind of regional cost from operating within the ECOWAS framework. In addition to seeking to entice its regional allies to join and remain in ECOMOG, the ECOWAS framework forced Nigeria to allow its regional rivals into the force. For ECOMOG to credibly claim to be a regional force, it also had in principle to be open to all ECOWAS members. Nigeria recognised this when it agreed in November 1990 to reverse the Standing Mediation Committee's earlier restriction of ECOMOG participation. Nigeria did not encourage other ECOWAS states to join ECOMOG in part because it feared losing control over ECOMOG. However, it was occasionally forced to accept their contributions. In 1991–2, Senegalese troops were sent to augment ECOMOG during the francophone-led Committee of Five peace negotiations. Sierra Leone's Defence Adviser in Nigeria illustrated the loss of cohesion this entailed in ECOMOG:

> The Senegalese battalion that went to Liberia was not taking commands from the Force Commander – they were getting direct instruction from Dakar. When they clashed with the NPFL – they lost 6 men in October 1992 – they pulled out ... They were not really working as part of ECOMOG. The Force Commander did not know that they were deploying – he just saw troops withdrawing from their forward position and getting on a boat.[109]

After the 1997 Peace Plan, ECOMOG expanded again to include contingents from previously hostile ECOWAS states. Again, there were

---

[107] Author's interview with Ambassador A. Ajakaiye, 28 September 2000.
[108] Author's interview with Dr Ochoche, 26 September 2000.
[109] Author's interview with Colonel K. S. Mundeh, 13 October 2000.

problems: 'Burkina Faso ... used its troops as moles to get information from the ECOMOG High Command ... they were passing information of operational importance to Charles Taylor, and Côte d'Ivoire did the same.'[110]

In short, the legitimacy that the ECOWAS mandate conveyed on Operation Liberty did not translate into significant material benefits in terms of international or regional financial or military contributions to the operation. Achieving and operating under this mandate did, however, impose substantial financial, political, and military costs on Nigeria, which suggests that Nigeria valued legitimacy as an independent end in international relations.

Conclusion

Nigeria decided to launch Operation Liberty within the ECOWAS framework in order to bolster the intervention's international legitimacy. The decision was clearly not motivated by respect for international law, since ECOMOG was launched in violation of both international law and internal ECOWAS rules. Nigeria also knew that the ECOWAS framework would not generate significant financial or military burden-sharing for the operation. ECOWAS auspices did, however, strengthen Nigeria's claim to be acting in the interest of regional peace and security, and the organisation provided a platform to lobby the OAU and the UN for their endorsement of the intervention.

The key to this success was ensuring that ECOWAS spoke with one voice on the international stage. ECOWAS' institutional structures helped achieve this. The Standing Mediation Committee allowed the intervening states to present other ECOWAS members with a *fait accompli* and the consensus rule of decision-making forced these other states to choose between acquiescence and the possible destruction of ECOWAS. Acquiescence was facilitated because the lack of burden-sharing mechanisms within ECOWAS severed any link between assent and military or financial contributions to the operation. Nevertheless, Nigeria's decision to obtain and operate under ECOWAS auspices was neither easy not costless. Nigeria incurred financial costs in persuading its fellow states to approve the mandate, military costs in occasionally having to accept untrustworthy regional allies, and political costs in

---

[110] Ibid.

terms of the rift ECOWAS suffered over the issue of intervention in Liberia.

The notion that ECOWAS states (and Nigeria in particular) view the role of their organisation in peace enforcement operations primarily as generating international legitimacy is further confirmed by the institutional developments that Operation Liberty triggered within ECOWAS. Efforts to rebuild the organisation after the rift caused by the intervention led to the revised ECOWAS Treaty of July 1993, which formally supersedes the 1975 Treaty. Article 58 of the Treaty commits member states 'to co-operate with the Community in establishing and strengthening appropriate mechanisms for the timely prevention and resolution of intra-State and inter-State conflicts'. However, it took another Nigerian-led peace enforcement operation – launched into Sierra Leone in May 1997 and granted ECOWAS auspices the subsequent August – to galvanise ECOWAS members to agree on specific institutional structures to this end. The eventual result was the ECOWAS Mechanism for Conflict Prevention, Management, Resolution, Peacekeeping and Security, whose implementation protocol was signed on 10 December 1999.

The Mechanism created a Mediation and Security Council (MSC) composed of nine elected member states, which is to meet regularly at three levels – heads of state, ministers, and ambassadors. The MSC is subordinate to the Authority of Heads of State but is mandated in Article 7 to take 'appropriate decisions' on the Authority's behalf. The Mechanism also established departments of Political Affairs, Humanitarian Affairs, Defence and Security, and an Early Warning System within the ECOWAS Secretariat. It created a Defence and Security Commission to unite regional chiefs of defence staff and a Council of Elders to mediate during crises. Finally, ECOMOG was institutionalised in Articles 21 and 22 as 'a structure composed of several stand-by multi-purpose modules (civilian and military) in their countries of origin and ready for immediate deployment' whose functions include 'peacekeeping and restoration of peace'. The Mechanism has not yet been fully implemented, but the tenor of the reform efforts provides a good indication of the lessons ECOWAS states drew from the Liberia intervention.

Significantly, these institutional reforms did nothing to ensure the legality of future peace enforcement operations launched within the ECOWAS framework. The ECOWAS Mechanism does not require states to secure UN Security Council approval before launching a peace enforcement operation. This was no oversight: both member states and experts raised the issue of a UN mandate during the process of elaborating the protocol.[111] However, ECOWAS member states chose to ignore this legal requirement for peace enforcement operations, mostly because they 'did not want to tie their own hands. They do not trust the Security Council to decide in the interest of the region: it is too removed and too slow.'[112] Whatever the pragmatic merits of this argument, it is not compatible with a vision of states launching peace enforcement operations through ECOWAS out of respect for international law.

ECOWAS reforms have also done little to improve the organisation's capacity to promote interstate burden-sharing for peace enforcement operations, although some efforts were made in this direction. As noted, the Mechanism institutionalised ECOMOG as a stand-by force drawn from all ECOWAS countries. There were joint military training exercises for the stand-by force in 1998 and 2000, and by October 2000 the ECOWAS Secretariat began identifying and registering the stand-by troops offered.[113] Moreover, the Mechanism suggested that the ECOWAS Community Levy (a tax on imports from outside the ECOWAS region proposed in 1993) could help finance future ECOMOG deployments,[114] obviating the need for a separate ECOWAS peacekeeping fund.

However, both innovations met obstacles. Some ECOWAS members, including Nigeria, proved unwilling to fully institute the Community Levy, prompting ECOWAS Executive Secretary Lansana Kouyate to complain in 2000: 'The hopes pinned on the Community Levy as the panacea to the problem of irregular payment of contributions have failed to materialise.'[115] As for the ECOMOG stand-by arrangement, many national minimum pledges are too small (120–150 troops) to

---

[111] Draft Protocol for an ECOWAS Mechanism submitted by Benin in 1998. Author's interview with Dr Gervais Houndekindo, Minister Counsellor at the Embassy of Benin Republic in Nigeria, Abuja, Nigeria, 25 September 2000. Author's interview with Professor Margaret Vogt, Special Assistant (African Affairs) to Assistant UN Secretary-General, UN Department of Political Affairs in 2000, in 1999 expert seconded by the International Peace Academy to help elaborate the ECOWAS Mechanism, New York, USA, 27 June 2000.

[112] Author's interview with Professor Margaret Vogt, 27 June 2000.

[113] Author's interview with Lansana Kouyate, Executive Secretary of ECOWAS, Abuja, Nigeria, 7 October 2000.

[114] ECOWAS Defence, Interior, and Security Ministers, *Projet de Mécanisme*.

[115] Lansana Kouyate, *2000 Interim Report of the Executive Secretary* (Abuja: ECOWAS, 2000), p. 51.

represent significant contributions to a peace enforcement operation – total ECOMOG forces in Liberia, for example, fluctuated between 7,100 and 11,710 troops. Moreover, any force deployment remains heavily dependent on Nigeria, especially for transportation or air support. As one observer put it, 'Without Nigeria, there is no peacekeeping in this region. They always provide the logistics.'[116] Most crucially, ECOWAS states tend to insist that troops earmarked for ECOMOG are not automatically available for future peace enforcement operations. The Mechanism states that 'given the fact that the security of each individual country depends on the capacity to guarantee the security of the whole sub-region, every member state should make troops available to ECOWAS every time the organisation asks for them.'[117] ECOWAS Executive Secretary Kouyaté stressed that this implies automaticity: 'you read the Protocol, which is signed: when the stand-by unit is composed, it is obligatory for each member state to contribute.'[118] However, diplomats from individual ECOWAS states indicated that their states consider that they retain the right to decide on the deployment of these troops on a case-by-case basis.[119] Thus both financial and military burden-sharing remains highly uncertain for peace enforcement operations launched in the ECOWAS framework. ECOWAS itself remains an overwhelmingly economic organisation with few human and financial resources to contribute to peace enforcement operations.

By contrast, ECOWAS reforms have firmly institutionalised the internal features that facilitated the legitimation of Operation Liberty. First, despite the divisiveness of the intervention, ECOWAS states reaffirmed their commitment to speaking with one voice. The 1991 Declaration of Principles announced that ECOWAS members were:

> Determined, therefore, to consult among ourselves ... with a view to adopting common policies and enhancing our international negotiating position ... We reaffirm our determination to speak with one voice under the aegis of ECOWAS on all international issues which touch and concern our development and prosperity. We will therefore resist any attempt by

---

[116] Interview with Sean Pike, South African High Commission, Abuja, Nigeria, 5 October 2000.

[117] ECOWAS Defence, Interior, and Security Ministers, *Projet de Mécanisme*.

[118] Author's interview with Lansana Kouyate, 7 October 2000.

[119] Author's interviews in Abuja, Nigeria with Mr Amoa-Awua, Acting Head of Mission, Ghana High Commission in Nigeria (2 October 2000) and with Maba J. O. Jobe, High Commissioner, The Gambia High Commission (6 October 2000).

forces outside our sub-region to undermine the expression of our collective will.[120]

Article 9 of the 1993 Revised ECOWAS Treaty did open the possibility of deciding issues 'by unanimity, consensus, or by a two-thirds majority', depending on the subject area. However, it stipulated that these matters would be determined by a future protocol and that 'until the entry into force of said protocol, the Authority [of ECOWAS heads of state] shall continue to adopt its decisions by consensus'.[121] At the time of writing, there has been no such protocol in the area of regional peace and security.

Second, the committee structure that allowed Nigeria to present its fellow ECOWAS members with the *fait accompli* of ECOMOG's creation was formalised. The 1999 ECOWAS Mechanism replaced the ad hoc five-member Standing Mediation Committee with a permanent Mediation and Security Council (MSC) composed of nine ECOWAS members elected for renewable two-year terms. The MSC is empowered to 'authorise all forms of intervention and decide particularly on the deployment of political and military missions' in the name of the ECOWAS Authority, although the Authority's endorsement must be sought at its first subsequent ordinary summit.[122] The MSC is as open to Nigerian domination as the SMC was. Its nine members include the past and present ECOWAS chairs, effectively leaving seven open seats. The election system coupled with renewable terms virtually guarantees Nigeria a place on the MSC, and the anglophone vote within West Africa also favours Ghanaian participation. Moreover, in stark contrast to the Authority, the MSC makes decisions based on a two-thirds majority vote of member states present. A quorum of two-thirds of MSC members is necessary for an MSC meeting to be properly constituted.[123] Technically, therefore, the MSC could authorise a military

---

[120] ECOWAS Heads of State and Government, *Declaration of Political Principles of the Economic Community of West African States*, signed at the 14th Session of the Authority of Heads of State and Government in Abuja, Nigeria, 4–6 July 1991.

[121] ECOWAS Heads of State and Government, *Treaty of the Economic Community of West African States*, signed 24 July 1993 in Cotonou, Benin. Accessed online at http://www.ecowas.int/sitecedeao/english/stat-1.htm; document no longer available at this site.

[122] ECOWAS Heads of State and Government, *Protocol Relating to the Mechanism for Conflict Prevention, Management, Resolution, Peacekeeping and Security*, signed on 10 December 1999 in Lomé, Togo, Article 10.2.c. ECOWAS Defence, Interior, and Security Ministers, *Projet de Mécanisme*.

[123] ECOWAS Heads of State and Government, *Rules of Procedure of the Mediation and Security Council*, Abuja, Nigeria, 27 May 2000, Rules 46, 45.

intervention by the vote of only four ECOWAS members. This decision would then be forwarded to the Authority, where the consensus rule favours endorsement of the decision.

Finally, as noted, the ECOWAS Mechanism failed to institutionalise burden-sharing for peace enforcement operations, ensuring that acquiescence to an ECOWAS mandate for intervention remains relatively costless. Meanwhile the tiny minimum commitments that most states have made to ECOMOG, if honoured, help ensure any future operation's international legitimacy rather than its military effectiveness: these token forces have little military value, but they suffice to give any deployment the multilateral character necessary to gain credibility as a regional operation.

In sum, the institutional developments that have taken place within ECOWAS since its Liberian intervention have tended to strengthen the organisation's capacity to legitimise peace enforcement operations. ECOWAS states have not transformed their organisation in any significant way. It remains much better adapted to the task of helping to legitimise a peace enforcement operation than for ensuring burden-sharing or strict compliance with international law. The 1999 Mechanism simply eliminated the ad hoc nature of the arrangements that helped Nigeria legitimise the ECOMOG intervention in Liberia. In fact, it acknowledged that some aspects of ECOMOG 'remained subjects of controversy' and explicitly aimed to 'consolidate' ECOWAS's institutional ability to launch peace operations.[124]

The main thrust of ECOWAS reforms with respect to peace and security, therefore, has been to build an increasingly well-equipped organisation for generating legitimacy for regional peace operations. In part, this suggests that dominant ECOWAS states – including Nigeria – were basically pleased with the manner in which the organisation functioned during Operation Liberty. However, a deeper trend is also at work. Unease over Nigeria's regional dominance and possible military imperialism remains. Nevertheless resistance to Nigerian hegemony has abated in the face of the multiple crises that shook the region in the 1990s, notably in Sierra Leone, Guinea-Bissau, Guinea, and Côte d'Ivoire. West African states note that conflict tends to spread from one state to another and feel increasingly insecure. They also believe that the West, and therefore the UN, cannot be counted on to address these instabilities. Therefore, off the record, the region's reliance on Nigeria to

---

[124] ECOWAS Defence, Interior, and Security Ministers, *Projet de Mécanisme*.

ward off regional instability is a frequent refrain among diplomats from smaller ECOWAS nations. One diplomat confided that 'we want to hide behind Nigeria as a means to an end. Nigeria . . . has to be encouraged to take on ECOWAS responsibilities, because it is the only country capable of doing so. So we use Nigeria for the benefit of the region. We court Nigeria assiduously so that it does not tire of its role.'[125] States feel dependent on Nigeria to contain regional conflagration and therefore accede to Nigeria's leadership. A Nigerian bureaucrat put this succinctly: 'if the conflict expands, you may become a victim yourself. And if somebody is prepared to take up the tab for the intervention, for goodness' sake, why not?'[126] In order to encourage Nigeria to take this responsibility, states have to ensure that it can launch peace enforcement operations that enjoy international legitimacy. That is precisely what ECOWAS's peace and security structures are built for.

[125] Author's interview, remark not for attribution.
[126] Author's interview with Humphrey Orjiako, 22 September 2000.

4

Peace enforcement through sub-regional organisations: the Southern African Development Community and Operation Sovereign Legitimacy in the Democratic Republic of Congo

Founded in 1992, the Southern African Development Community (SADC) is the youngest and perhaps the most paradoxical organisation studied in this book. Throughout the 1990s, it lacked functional institutional structures for dealing with regional peace and security issues. As late as December 2000, the SADC secretariat insisted that it had no mandate to address political peace and security questions.[1] Nevertheless, in 1998 two major military interventions were launched under SADC auspices. In August 1998, Zimbabwe, Angola, and Namibia sent troops into the Democratic Republic of Congo (DRC) to counter an invasion from Rwanda and Uganda that threatened to topple the DRC's President Laurent Desiré Kabila. One month later, South Africa and Botswana intervened in Lesotho to support Prime Minister Pakalitha Mosisili against internal unrest and an army mutiny following a controversial general election. Both interventions, codenamed Operation Sovereign Legitimacy and Operation Boleas, respectively, claimed SADC auspices, and together they helped define SADC's role in regional peace enforcement.

This chapter focuses on SADC's role in Operation Sovereign Legitimacy, leaving the analysis of Operation Boleas for chapter 5. After providing an explanation for SADC's lack of security institutions and some background information on the DRC intervention, it examines why Zimbabwe chose to launch Operation Sovereign Legitimacy through SADC. It argues that neither international law nor burden-sharing concerns can explain this decision. Instead, Zimbabwe's core motivation for operating in this framework, despite the ensuing costs, was its preoccupation with the international legitimacy of its intervention, particularly in the eyes of other African states.

---

[1] Author's interview with Ester V. Kanaimba, Public Relations Officer, SADC Secretariat, Gaborone, Botswana, 7 December 2000.

Institutional background: SADC's lack of functioning security institutions

SADC's creation in 1992 reflected hope for a new era of cooperative regional politics following the decline of the apartheid state in South Africa. Two institutions born out of the struggle against white minority rule in Southern Africa were transformed into a single organisation devoted to cooperation throughout the region. The Front-Line States (FLS) alliance had been formed in 1975 to provide a forum for political cooperation among the region's majority-ruled states and liberation movements. From 1981 onwards, the Southern African Development Co-ordination Conference (SADCC) sought to integrate the economies of these states and thus decrease their economic dependence on South Africa. Both institutions lost their *raison d'être* when the apartheid regime in South Africa began to crumble. Given the twin challenges of integrating the newly democratic South Africa into Southern Africa and preventing the region's political and economic marginalisation in the post-Cold War world, however, the perceived need for a regional institutional framework remained strong.

Thus SADC was created on 17 August 1992 on the foundations of the FLS and SADCC, with South Africa joining in 1994 and membership reaching its current total of fourteen members in 1998 (map 4.1).[2] The organisation is more institutionalised than either of its predecessors, most notably in the sense of having a central decision-making body, the Summit of SADC Heads of State and Government, which meets regularly and is supported by a permanent secretariat based in Gaborone, Botswana. SADC inherited SADCC's primary focus on economic development, but as simultaneous heir to the FLS it was never meant to be a purely economic organisation. The SADC Treaty listed 'promoting and defending peace and security' as one of the organisation's objectives (Article 5.c), and member states agreed to cooperate in the area of 'politics, diplomacy, international relations, peace and security' (Article 21.3.g).

However, a leadership struggle between South Africa and Zimbabwe soon marred attempts to accommodate security concerns into SADC's institutional structure. Zimbabwe claimed a right to lead any new SADC

---

[2] SADC members include Angola, Botswana, the DRC, Lesotho, Malawi, Mauritius, Mozambique, Namibia, Seychelles, South Africa, Swaziland, Tanzania, Zambia, and Zimbabwe.

Map 4.1. Southern African Development Community (SADC) in 1998

body on peace and security based on its earlier central position in the FLS and President Mugabe's status as the region's longest serving states-man. Initially unsure of its ability to press its own leadership claims, South Africa countered by arguing for a rotating chairmanship. This debate was resolved, seemingly in South Africa's favour, when the SADC Organ for Politics, Defence and Security (known as the Organ) was formally launched in June 1996 under a troika leadership consisting of a rotating elected chair and his immediate predecessor and successor. Mugabe was consoled by being elected as the Organ's first chairman, while South Africa staked out its own regional leadership claim by being elected Chair of the SADC Summit in August 1996.

Crucially, however, the Organ's relationship to SADC as a whole had been left underspecified, though it was announced that the Organ would 'function independently of other SADC structures'.[3] In the Summit and the Organ, SADC therefore now had two summit-level bodies with no

---

[3] SADC Heads of State and Government, *Summit Communiqué*, Gaborone, Botswana, 28 June 1996.

clear authority relation between them, opening a new avenue for rivalry between South Africa and Zimbabwe. Zimbabwe insisted that the Organ was autonomous from the Summit and capable of making final decisions on security matters in SADC's name. South Africa countered that the Organ must be subordinate to the SADC Summit, which Article 10.1 of the SADC Treaty had declared 'the supreme policy-making institution of SADC'. The 1997 SADC Summit meeting in Blantyre, Malawi, was scheduled to resolve this controversy by adopting a Protocol on Politics, Defence and Security in which the structure and rules of the Organ would be fully specified. Instead, South African President Mandela and Zimbabwe's President Mugabe clashed openly at the Summit and no agreement was reached on the proposed Protocol. The Organ was thus effectively paralysed, and SADC remained bereft of functioning institutions for dealing with regional peace and security issues.

The DRC crisis and Operation Sovereign Legitimacy: historical background

The DRC, Africa's third largest country, became independent from Belgium as the Republic of Congo in 1960. It almost immediately descended into civil war, which ended when Joseph Mobutu seized power in a coup in 1965. Mobutu changed the Congo's name to Zaire and ruled autocratically for 32 years, amassing enormous wealth while failing to improve Zaire's development levels. Since the longevity of his rule owed much to the massive Cold War patronage he received from the West, Mobutu's hold on power became precarious with the end of the Cold War. The immediate impetus for his downfall, however, arose from his decision to shelter elements of the genocidal Rwandan government and its ethnic Hutu militia in refugee camps in eastern Zaire in the wake of the Rwandan genocide of 1994. In 1996, the new Rwandan government and its ally Uganda invaded Zaire, emptied the refugee camps, and pursued fleeing Hutu groups. They sought to legitimise this pursuit by placing it under the nominal leadership of the Congolese Alliance de Forces Démocratiques pour la Libération du Congo-Zaïre (AFDL), headed by Laurent Désiré Kabila. The campaign had military support from Angola and political support from many Western nations eager to see an end to Mobutu's kleptocratic regime. Its success surprised even its sponsors: the AFDL swept across the country to capture its capital, Kinshasa, in May 1997. Mobutu was deposed, Zaire became the Democratic Republic of Congo, and Kabila assumed the presidency.

However, Kabila was unable to establish a stable power base in the DRC.[4] The AFDL was an alliance of exiles that lacked grassroots structures and had built little popular support in Zaire before seizing power. Kabila's close connections with Rwanda and Uganda were viewed with suspicion, the army was fragmented, and civil society organisations resisted Kabila's attempts to centralise political power. Moreover, Kabila alienated his international allies by cancelling lucrative concession contracts promised to Western firms at the beginning of his campaign and snubbing UN efforts to establish a presence in the DRC. He also disappointed his regional backers by forcing Rwanda and Uganda to reduce their troop presences in the DRC and refusing to move against Rwandan, Ugandan, and Angolan rebel movements operating within the DRC. Instead of cultivating his existing regional allies, Kabila looked for support from Sudan (Uganda's long-time rival) and Libya as well as allying with Zimbabwe and joining SADC in February 1998.

The cost of these policies soon became clear. On 2 August 1998, a mutiny broke out among elements of the DRC military stationed on the border with Rwanda. The soldiers announced a general rebellion to topple Kabila. They were backed by Rwanda, although the Rwandan government initially denied its involvement. On 4 August, the rebellion gained a second front as Congolese rebels and Rwandan and Ugandan soldiers were airlifted to the Kitona army base in the Lower Congo (west of Kinshasa) to instigate an uprising there. Within two weeks, troops from Kitona were poised to take control of Kinshasa. Meanwhile, rebel forces also took over large swathes of eastern DRC. The uprising gained a wider political umbrella on 12 August, when a group of Congolese opposition politicians led by Wamba Dia Wamba created the Rassemblement Congolais pour la Democratie (RCD). The collapse of Kabila's regime seemed imminent.

Kabila appealed for help to the United Nations, the Organisation of African Unity, and fellow SADC leaders. Southern African states reacted most promptly. On 8 August 1998, the presidents of Zimbabwe, Zambia, Tanzania, and Namibia met their counterparts from the DRC, Uganda, and Rwanda in Victoria Falls, Zimbabwe, and dispatched an investigative team to the DRC to ascertain the extent of international involvement in the rebellion. However, Kabila's defeat became imminent while this team was still in Goma. On 18 August, SADC defence ministers met

---

[4] 'How Kabila Lost His Way: The Performance of Laurent Désiré Kabila's Government', International Crisis Group Republic of Congo Report No. 3, 21 May 1999.

in Harare, Zimbabwe, without the benefit of the team's report. At the end of this meeting, Mugabe announced that SADC had decided to 'respond positively' to Kabila's requests for military assistance.[5] Within days, 2,800 Zimbabwean troops were airlifted to Kinshasa while around 2,500 Angolan troops entered the DRC from Angola's Cabinda enclave.[6] This was the beginning Operation Sovereign Legitimacy.

Together with Congolese troops loyal to Kabila and 300 Namibian reinforcements, the Zimbabwean and Angolan forces defeated the western prong of the rebellion, relieved Kinshasa, and preserved Kabila's government. However, the RCD still controlled much of the eastern DRC. What followed was first a stalemate and then a gradual escalation and complication of the conflict. Within the DRC, warring factions and local militia proliferated. Internationally, the DRC became the 'first African world war',[7] involving thousands of troops from Angola, Burundi, Chad, Namibia, Rwanda, Uganda, and Zimbabwe as well as the DRC. The Lusaka Ceasefire Agreement of August 1999 also involved the UN in the conflict, but brought no peace. In fact, violence worsened when Rwanda and Uganda broke their alliance and became battling rivals for influence in eastern DRC. Prospects for peace finally improved for most of the DRC in 2001 and Angola, Namibia, and Zimbabwe largely withdrew their troops during 2002, leaving the responsibility for peacekeeping in the DRC to the UN. The conflict was not fully resolved, however, and Uganda and Rwanda continued to maintain troop presences in eastern DRC. Companies from several states also remained active in the illegal exploitation of the DRC's natural resources.[8] Escalating violence in the Ituri region gave rise to a French-led UN peace enforcement operation in 2003. The death toll continued to rise, reaching 3.5 million war-related deaths by 2003.[9] SADC operations in the DRC had ended, however.

---

[5] 'Zimbabwe defence minister says SADC to send men, arms to DRC', *Deutsche Presse-Agentur*, 19 August 1998.

[6] Eric G. Berman and Katie E. Sams, *Peacekeeping in Africa: Capabilities and Culpabilities* (Geneva: United Nations Publication, 2000), p. 180.

[7] Term coined by Susan Rice, the US Assistant Secretary of State for Africa.

[8] Final report of the UN Panel of Experts on the Illegal Exploitation of Natural Resources and Other Forms of Wealth of the Democratic Republic of the Congo, 8 October 2002, online at www.un.org/Docs/journal/asp/ws.asp?m=S/2002/1146.

[9] 'Peace, they say, but the killing goes on', *The Economist*, 27 March 2003.

Operation Sovereign Legitimacy and international law

Why did Zimbabwe, the lead state in Operation Sovereign Legitimacy, decide to launch the intervention under SADC auspices? Respect for international law can be excluded as a motivating factor both because SADC auspices could not substantially contribute to the intervention's legality and because Zimbabwe violated SADC rules in launching the intervention.

Operation Sovereign Legitimacy was explicitly launched as a regional peace enforcement operation. As Zimbabwe's President Mugabe put it, 'We are going to ... help the government of President Laurent Kabila restore peace and stability ... in the DRC.'[10] As a peace enforcement operation, however, Operation Sovereign Legitimacy, like ECOMOG before it, required a UN Security Council mandate.[11] SADC states refused to acknowledge this when they created the SADC Organ in 1996[12] and given the West's political disengagement from Africa in the 1990s, there were good practical reasons for this stance. However, SADC members had no legal right to overrule the UN Charter. In fact, signatories of the UN Charter explicitly acknowledge its precedence over all other formulations of international law.[13] Therefore SADC auspices could not legalise Operation Sovereign Legitimacy as a peace enforcement operation in the absence of a UN mandate.

The legal case for Operation Sovereign Legitimacy is much stronger when the intervention is viewed as an act of collective self-defence. Article 51 of the UN Charter acknowledges states' 'inherent right of individual or collective self-defence if an armed attack occurs against a member of the United Nations'. Kabila consistently depicted the conflict in the DRC as essentially an invasion by Rwanda and Uganda and based his appeals for international assistance on that assertion. This interpretation was contested. The Congolese rebels explicitly presented their struggle as a domestic political uprising. One spokesman insisted: 'There has been no invasion, what's going on here is that the Congolese themselves are fighting for their freedom.'[14] Moreover, Rwanda and Uganda initially denied any involvement in the crisis. The fact that the

---

[10] SAPA, 'DR Congo: SADC Defence Ministers Agree to Aid to Kabila against Rebels', BBC, 19 August 1998.

[11] UN Charter, Article 53.

[12] SADC, *Summit Communiqué*, Gaborone, Botswana, 28 June 1996.

[13] UN Charter, Article 103.

[14] 'Zimbabwe to send troops to Congo', CNN, 19 August 1998.

8 August 1998 meeting of Southern African states in Victoria Falls dispatched an investigative team to the DRC reflects genuine initial uncertainty about the nature and origins of the violence.

In fact, the conflict in the DRC combined deeply intertwined elements of both internal rebellion and international intervention. Kabila's regime was undeniably unpopular and the rebellion against him had genuine local roots. However, it was also militarily supported by the Rwandan and Ugandan governments, who by January 1999 had deployed at least 4,000 troops each into the DRC.[15] Kabila's insistence on the sanctity of Congolese national sovereignty rang hollow since he himself had seized power with Rwandan and Ugandan military support just fifteen months earlier, but his regime had been internationally recognised as the DRC's legitimate government. It was allowed to occupy Zaire's seat at the UN and SADC admitted the DRC as a member under Kabila's leadership. Moreover, on 18 August 1998, the SADC defence ministers formally endorsed Kabila's assessment of the conflict at their meeting in Harare. Zimbabwe's Defence Minister announced: 'We are convinced that the rebel force is supported from Uganda and Rwanda ... It became very clear that our sister country has been invaded.'[16] The legal case for Operation Sovereign Legitimacy as an act of collective self-defence upon invitation by a government undergoing international armed attack is thus relatively strong. It certainly compares favourably to the alternative legal argument for Operation Sovereign Legitimacy as a peace enforcement operation. If Operation Sovereign Legitimacy was an act of collective self-defence, however, its SADC auspices were irrelevant from a legal point of view. Under current international law, no international institutional framework is necessary for collective self-defence. Individual states can respond to each other's requests for assistance against an international armed attack as freely as international organisations.

Thus the SADC framework offered no legal advantages for Zimbabwe. It was insufficient to legalise a peace enforcement operation and unnecessary for legalising collective defence activities. The notion that Zimbabwe launched Operation Sovereign Legitimacy through SADC out of respect for international law is also inconsistent with Zimbabwe's willingness to break internal SADC rules in launching the operation. Zimbabwe claimed

---

[15] International Institute for Strategic Studies, *Strategic Survey 1998/99* (Oxford: Oxford University Press, 1999), p. 28.
[16] 'DRC: Zimbabwe says SADC to back Kabila', *IRIN*, 19 August 1998.

that SADC authorised intervention at the Harare meeting of 18 August 1998. This meeting took place under the auspices of the Inter-State Defence and Security Committee (ISDSC), a gathering of Southern Africa's defence ministers and the only component of the Organ that had remained active after the Blantyre SADC Summit of 1997. The meeting was called by Zimbabwean President Mugabe in his capacity as the Chairperson of the SADC Organ. It was chaired by Zambia, the current ISDSC chair. After the meeting, Zambia's Defence Minister Chitalu Sampa briefed Mugabe, who then publicly announced SADC's decision to intervene. Mugabe 'made it clear that he believed he was speaking for all members of the fourteen-nation Southern African Development Community'.[17] Sampa confirmed that 'all SADC countries would assist Kabila in his efforts to thwart the rebellion', and Zimbabwe's Defence Minister added that the decision to intervene had been unanimous.[18] The meeting opened the way to Operation Sovereign Legitimacy.

> The same night, the first Zimbabwean contingent left for Kinshasa. By morning of the next day – the 19th – they were digging trenches outside the Kinshasa airport. At the same time, Angolan forces went into Kabinda, and Angolan forces stationed in Brazzaville crossed over into Kinshasa. So within 24 hours, SADC forces (as we believed at the time that they were) were in the DRC.[19]

However, the Harare meeting had no power to confer a SADC mandate for an intervention. It barely qualified as an ISDSC meeting, since only nine of SADC's fourteen member states were in attendance and of these only four were represented by their Defence Ministers.[20] Moreover, the ISDSC can only make recommendations to SADC heads

---

[17] 'Mugabe says Southern African states will back Kabila', *Deutsche Presse-Agentur*, 18 August 1998.
[18] SAPA, 'DR Congo: SADC Defence Ministers Agree to Aid to Kabila against Rebels', BBC, 19 August 1998; 'Zimbabwe defence minister says SADC to send men, arms to DRC', *Deutsche Presse-Agentur*, 19 August 1998.
[19] Author's interview with Lieutenant-Colonel A. W. Tapfumaneyi, Staff Officer Grade One (Policy), Zimbabwe Ministry of Defence, Harare, Zimbabwe, 29 November 2000.
[20] The quorum for all SADC meetings is two-thirds of all SADC member states (SADC Treaty, Article 18). Only Angola, Namibia, Zambia, and Zimbabwe were represented by their Defence Ministers ('DRC: Zimbabwe says SADC to back Kabila', *IRIN*, 19 August 1998). South Africa and Botswana sent their Deputy High Commissioner and High Commissioner to Zimbabwe, respectively. Both announced that they were attending the meeting as observers only. Author's interview with Lieutenant-Colonel A. W. Tapfumaneyi, 29 November 2000.

of state, not reach decisions in their name. Since the SADC Organ was inoperative, only a SADC Summit could have legally launched a SADC operation. Yet there was no SADC Summit on this issue until 13–14 September 1998, almost a month after Operation Sovereign Legitimacy was launched. Legally, therefore, Operation Sovereign Legitimacy was not a SADC operation. Indeed, Botswana, Mozambique, and South Africa vociferously opposed the intervention and publicly disputed Zimbabwe's contention that it had been launched by a unanimous SADC decision. A spokesman for South African President Mandela stressed 'that there was no uniform SADC view on the DRC as neither the grouping's heads of state summit nor organ on security and defence [*sic*] had met to discuss the issue'.[21] Zimbabwe must have known that the Harare meeting did not legally constitute a SADC decision. However, it proved willing to break SADC's internal rules in order to claim the organisation's auspices for Operation Sovereign Legitimacy. This behaviour does not indicate a substantial respect for international law on Zimbabwe's part.

In sum, Zimbabwe's decision to launch Operation Sovereign Legitimacy through SADC cannot be explained by reference to international law. Depending on whether the intervention is viewed as a peace enforcement operation or an act of collective self-defence, SADC auspices were either insufficient or unnecessary for establishing its international legality. Meanwhile Zimbabwe's willingness to violate SADC's internal rules to claim the organisation's auspices for the intervention belies the notion that it was motivated by an internalised respect for international law.

Burden-sharing during Operation Sovereign Legitimacy

The evidence from Operation Sovereign Legitimacy also fails to support the notion that states turn to international organisations to promote burden-sharing for their peace enforcement operations. SADC has some highly developed burden-sharing structures – but none of them promote cooperation for military interventions.

As an economic organisation, SADC promotes burden-sharing to an exceptional degree. Throughout the 1990s, SADC states argued that sovereign equality required a strictly equal distribution of responsibilities and burdens among SADC members. Thus, for example, all SADC

---

[21] SAPA, 'Mandela rules out sending military assistance to DR Congo's Kabila', BBC, 20 August 1998.

states contributed exactly equal amounts to SADC's budget, irrespective of their GDP. This extreme burden-sharing within SADC was supplemented by extraordinary levels of burden-sharing between SADC and the wider international community. In 1996, only 15 per cent of SADC's economic programme was funded by SADC members.[22] In 1998, a US$133 million five-year grant from the European Union to SADC dwarfed the organisation's internal annual budget of around US$16 million.[23] In short, SADC's economic programme 'is predominantly externally funded, and financial contributions from member states and private sector institutions are negligible'.[24]

However, SADC failed to mobilise any international funding for Operation Sovereign Legitimacy. There was considerable donor interest in developing a SADC peacekeeping capacity in the 1990s. Denmark funded a Regional Peacekeeping Training Centre (RPTC) in Harare, Zimbabwe, and the British Military Advisory and Training Team (BMATT) offered peacekeeping training courses. Western donors also sponsored two major SADC peacekeeping exercises, Blue Hungwe (1997) and Blue Crane (1999). Since these initiatives focused exclusively on peacekeeping rather than peace enforcement, however, they made virtually no contribution to Operation Sovereign Legitimacy. Direct financial support for the intervention from outside Southern Africa was also scarce. Chad, China, Libya, Cuba, Iran, Sudan, and North Korea were reported to be assisting Kabila's regime, but only Libya provided direct financial aid to Zimbabwe for Operation Sovereign Legitimacy.[25]

SADC also failed to promote burden-sharing for Operation Sovereign Legitimacy within Southern Africa. With no military capacity, just 30 staff members, and an annual budget of only US$16 million, SADC

---

[22] Mark Malan and Jakkie Cilliers, 'SADC Organ on Politics, Defence and Security: Future Development', *ISS Occasional Paper* No. 19 (March 1997), p. 2.

[23] European Union, 'Regional Cooperation between the European Commission and the Southern African Region', online at www.europa.eu.int/comm/development/publicat/sadc_en.htm, April 2003. Document no longer available at this site. Christof Maletsky, 'Regional defence organ wrested from Mugabe', *The Namibian*, 12 March 2001.

[24] Guy Lamb, 'The Realities of Regional Security in Southern Africa', paper presented at the Globe Southern Africa Conference on 'Partnership for Sustainability II' Environmental Security in Southern Africa, at the Parliament of South Africa, Cape Town, 21–22 September 2000.

[25] International Crisis Group, 'Scramble for the Congo: Anatomy of an Ugly War', *ICG Africa Report No. 26*, 20 December 2000, p. 65. 'Africa' in International Institute for Strategic Studies, *Strategic Survey 1998/99*, pp. 239, 283.

headquarters had few resources to contribute to the operation, while the SADC Organ was paralysed and had neither a budget nor a permanent secretariat. SADC also proved unable to promote military or financial burden-sharing for Operation Sovereign Legitimacy among its member states.

Table 4.1 lists the troop contributions by SADC members to Operation Sovereign Legitimacy from August 1998 to December 1999.[26] Its most outstanding feature may well be the amount of '0' values it contains. Only three SADC members participated in Operation Sovereign Legitimacy, indicating that the SADC framework was not very effective at helping Zimbabwe recruit allies for the intervention.

The impression is confirmed when the motivations of the states that did participate in Operation Sovereign Legitimacy are considered. Zimbabwe's most important ally, Angola, participated primarily because it correctly feared that turmoil in the DRC would allow the Angolan rebel movement UNITA to strengthen its supply lines and military bases on the DRC/Angola border. Namibia, the junior partner in Operation Sovereign Legitimacy, was motivated by its historical alliance with Angola and by fears that a UNITA resurgence would destabilise its border with Angola.[27] Both Angola and Namibia welcomed the SADC framework because it allowed them to present their actions as motivated by regional solidarity rather than national interests. However, their participation in Operation Sovereign Legitimacy was agreed to in bilateral talks with Zimbabwe rather than through SADC institutions and did not spring from any obligations imposed by SADC or through the SADC framework.

Thus from August 1998 to December 1999, Zimbabwe shouldered an ever-increasing share of the military burden while the vast majority of SADC states declined to participate and Angola decreased its deployment to respond to renewed civil war within its own borders. Clearly, the SADC framework elicited no significant military burden-sharing for Operation Sovereign Legitimacy among its members.

---

[26] Sources for troop numbers: International Crisis Group, 'Scramble for the Congo', pp. 4, 12; 'Strategic Geography – Africa', *Strategic Survey 1998/99*, p. 283; Taylor Seybolt, 'The War in the Democratic Republic of Congo', *SIPRI Yearbook 2000* (Oxford: Oxford University Press, 2000), p. 64.

[27] Chris Gordon, 'Africa's Wars All Becoming One', *Jane's Intelligence Review*, 5:10 (October 1998).

Table 4.1: Troop contributions to Operation Sovereign Legitimacy

	Aug 1998	% OSL troops	Oct 1998	% OSL troops	Jan 1999	% OSL troops	Dec 1999	% OSL troops
Angola	7,000	68.6	7,000	57.4	2,500	20.0	2,500	16.1
Botswana	0	0	0	0	0	0	0	0
Lesotho	0	0	0	0	0	0	0	0
Malawi	0	0	0	0	0	0	0	0
Mauritius	0	0	0	0	0	0	0	0
Mozambique	0	0	0	0	0	0	0	0
Namibia	200	2.0	200	1.6	2,000	16.0	2,000	12.9
Seychelles	0	0	0	0	0	0	0	0
South Africa	0	0	0	0	0	0	0	0
Swaziland	0	0	0	0	0	0	0	0
Tanzania	0	0	0	0	0	0	0	0
Zambia	0	0	0	0	0	0	0	0
Zimbabwe	3,000	29.4	5,000	41.0	8,000	64.0	11,000	71.0
TOTAL	10,200		12,200		12,500		15,500	

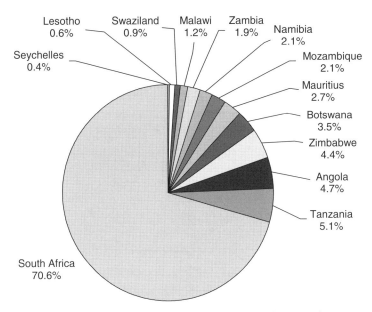

Figure 4.1. National shares of total 1998 SADC GDP (excluding DRC)

The SADC framework also failed to promote financial burden-sharing for Operation Sovereign Legitimacy within Southern Africa. If the equal-shares norm that governed SADC's budget had been applied to Operation Sovereign Legitimacy, Zimbabwe would have been responsible for only $\frac{1}{13}$ of the operation's costs, or just under 7.7 per cent. As figure 4.1 shows, a distribution of the operation's costs based on the relative size of countries' economies would have benefited Zimbabwe even more: in 1998, Zimbabwe accounted for only 4.4 per cent of total regional GDP, while South Africa's share was over 70.6 per cent.[28]

The financial burden generated by Operation Sovereign Legitimacy was not shared among all SADC members, however. Each troop contributor was fully financially responsible for its deployment. SADC states that did not participate in Operation Sovereign Legitimacy also declined to fund the intervention. With the exception of some Libyan funding for Zimbabwe, each troop contributor had to meet this

[28] Data from SADC, *SADC Statistics: Facts and Figures 1999* (Gaborone: SADC, 1999).

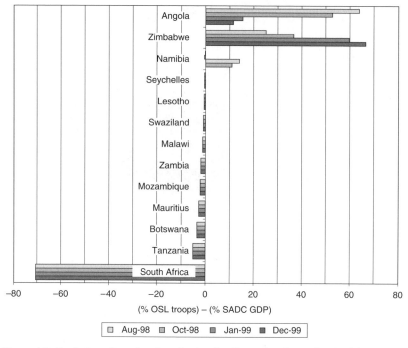

Figure 4.2: Deviations from burden-sharing for Operation Sovereign Legitimacy

responsibility unassisted. Figure 4.2 shows the financial winners and losers from this arrangement. It takes each SADC country's share of total troop contributions to Operation Sovereign Legitimacy as a rough proxy for the percentage of the operation's financial cost that this country incurred. From this figure, it subtracts the percentage of the total 1998 SADC GDP (excluding the DRC) that this country generated. Thus each bar on the graph represents how much more or less a country contributed than it would have been responsible for under a burden-sharing arrangement reflecting the relative size of each country's GDP.

The greatest winner from the lack of financial burden-sharing within SADC for Operation Sovereign Legitimacy was South Africa. Under a financial burden-sharing arrangement sensitive to the relative sizes of SADC countries' economies, it would have been responsible for 70.6 per cent of Operation Sovereign Legitimacy's costs. In the event, South Africa funded 0 per cent of the operation. The biggest loser was

Zimbabwe. Whereas under a scheme of financial burden-sharing relative to GDP size Zimbabwe would only have been required to fund 4.4 per cent of Operation Sovereign Legitimacy's troops, it in fact consistently contributed – and therefore had to fund – between 60 per cent and 70 per cent of the troops for the intervention.

Even figure 4.2 does not fully capture the imbalance in the financial burdens during Operation Sovereign Legitimacy, however. In addition to financing their own troops, Angola and Zimbabwe jointly provided the operation's air power. Zimbabwe also provided equipment for the coalition as well as arms for DRC troops loyal to Kabila.[29] Thus by October 1999, Zimbabwe was estimated to be spending around US$27 million a month on its involvement in the DRC.[30] This translates into a yearly cost of US$324 million, which represents over 5 per cent of Zimbabwe's total GDP for 1998 (US$6.4 billion). For comparison, in 1999 *total* defence expenditure for the USA was 3 per cent of GDP, on average 2.3 per cent of GDP for European NATO members, and on average 2 per cent of GDP for SADC states not undergoing civil war. Even this cost estimate may be low, however: by September 2002, Zimbabwe was reported to have spent a total of Zim$100 billion (US$1.9 billion) in the DRC.[31]

Thus SADC failed spectacularly to encourage financial and military burden-sharing for Operation Sovereign Legitimacy, much to Zimbabwe's disadvantage. Yet Zimbabwe never expected the SADC framework to help distribute the financial burdens of Operation Sovereign Legitimacy among fellow member states. It knew that SADC had no institutional mechanism to facilitate such burden-sharing. Unlike other international organisations, SADC had no roster of stand-by forces potentially available for peace enforcement operations, and there was no budget or financial assessment mechanism for regional military interventions. Zimbabwe also declined to seek the establishment of a voluntary SADC fund to help finance Operation Sovereign Legitimacy. Instead, Zimbabwe sought to recoup its costs from the DRC itself. Kabila had initially promised to reimburse his allies' deployment expenses. Unable to raise the necessary funds, he granted them mining contracts and other joint ventures instead. Several Zimbabwean

---

[29] Wuyi Omitoogun, 'Military Expenditure in Africa', *SIPRI Yearbook 2000* (Oxford: Oxford University Press, 2000), p. 293.
[30] Omitoogun, 'Military Expenditure in Africa', pp. 296–7.
[31] Sydney Masamvo, 'Government Owed $100 Billion', *Financial Gazette (Harare)*, 12 September 2002.

parastatal companies became active in the DRC, including OSLEG, an army firm named after Operation Sovereign Legitimacy. Given their lack of capital, graft, and the difficulty of extracting resources in a conflict environment, these ventures failed to replenish Zimbabwe's state coffers, although some individuals benefited immensely.[32] Zimbabwe made no moves to supplement this income by seeking better financial burden-sharing through SADC, correctly recognising the futility of such a gesture.

Zimbabwe's legitimacy concerns during Operation Sovereign Legitimacy

Zimbabwe chose to launch Operation Sovereign Legitimacy through SADC because it was intensely concerned with how the intervention would be perceived by other African and especially South African states. This section examines the nature of Zimbabwe's legitimacy concerns and identifies its key legitimacy audience.

Zimbabwe's legitimacy concerns

African states are well aware of the inherently controversial character of military interventions in the contemporary international system. As one African scholar put it:

> Intervention of one country in the affairs of another . . . is normally done after careful consideration because it could boomerang, causing embarrassment and complicating the security problem at hand. After all it is contrary to the principle of sovereignty implicit in independent statehood. It is true that this concept of sovereignty has been diluted somewhat in recent times, especially in the case of gross human rights abuses. Nevertheless, wanton intervention in pursuance of rabid national interests is still considered illegitimate.[33]

In these circumstances, the onus is on intervening states to prove that they are not intervening for narrow national interests. In Operation Sovereign Legitimacy's case, accusations of aggression could in part be countered by pointing to the fact that Kabila had requested the intervention. Nevertheless, allegations that Zimbabwe was pursuing national interests in the DRC threatened the operation's international legitimacy.

[32] International Crisis Group, 'Scramble for the Congo', p. 63.
[33] Akiiki B. Mujaju, 'How to Make Sense of the Events Taking Place in the Great Lakes Region', in Mwesiga Baregu (ed.), *Crisis in the Democratic Republic of Congo* (Harare: SAPES Books, 1999), p. 85.

The most widely believed charge was that Zimbabwe intervened in the DRC to exploit the country's tremendous mineral wealth. In this regard, however, it is important to distinguish Zimbabwe's initial motivations from subsequent developments. In August 1998, Mugabe deployed 3,000 troops to save Kinshasa for Kabila, hoping, in return, to gain political influence and preferential commercial access to the DRC's vast resources.[34] An agreement reached with the DRC on 4 September 1998 gave a Zimbabwean company a 37.5 per cent share and management control in the DRC state mining company Gecamines,[35] but granted no exclusive mining rights. Mugabe did not foresee that Zimbabwe would become embroiled in a protracted war for control of the vast Congolese territory. Yet although Kinshasa was secured by September 1998, the rebellion against Kabila continued to gain ground in eastern DRC. Thus 'what was initially seen as a short military adventure [was] increasingly becoming a substantial military exercise'.[36] Zimbabwe was trapped:

> [Mugabe] has already made a substantial investment in the DRC, which compels him to maintain ZNDF forces in the DRC ... [Moreover] Zimbabwe is not strong enough to sign a deal without the permission of its allies. In particular, it would be difficult to withdraw the several thousand Zimbabwean troops from Mbuji Mayi without the permission of the far more numerous Congolese and Interahamwe.[37]

To compensate for the enormous expense of this entanglement, Zimbabwe established increasingly massive and intrusive business interests in the DRC, branching into electricity, aviation, and agriculture as well as diamond and cobalt mining.[38] Yet these ventures only mushroomed around September 1999,[39] and they were the consequence of a

---

[34] Mugabe may also have hoped to secure outstanding loans made to Kabila. Michael Nest, 'Ambitions, Profits and Loss: Zimbabwean Economic Involvement in the Democratic Republic of Congo', *African Affairs*, 100 (2001), p. 471.

[35] International Crisis Group, 'Scramble for the Congo', p. 61.

[36] Economist Intelligence Unit, *Country Report: Zimbabwe*, 4th Quarter (October 1998), p. 6.

[37] International Crisis Group, 'Scramble for the Congo', p. 65.

[38] Ibid., p. 61. UN Panel of Experts, 'Report on the Illegal Exploitation of Natural Resources and Other Forms of Wealth of the Democratic Republic of the Congo', 8 October 2002, pp. 6–13.

[39] Although the first deal for the 'self-financing' of Zimbabwe's intervention force was signed on 4 September 1998, the real boom of official Zimbabwean/Congolese joint ventures only began around September 1999. International Crisis Group, 'Scramble for the Congo', p. 61. Reuters, 'Zimbabwe, Congo set up joint ventures to fund war', *GO Network News*, 23 September 1999; Justin Pearce, 'Mugabe's costly Congo venture', *BBC*

miscalculation. They enriched Mugabe and his entourage, but the war was ruining Zimbabwe. Mindful of the political costs of this predicament, Mugabe urged Kabila to negotiate a political settlement with the rebels as early as November 1998.[40] Thus Zimbabwe did not initially launch Operation Sovereign Legitimacy as a bid for direct appropriation of the DRC's resources. 'Whatever economic interests Zimbabwe subsequently acquired in Congo were not part of its initial calculus.'[41] Nevertheless, Zimbabwe was concerned about the impact of allegations of rapaciousness on the intervention's international legitimacy because they threatened a fundamental political objective behind the intervention. Zimbabwe intended Operation Sovereign Legitimacy to demonstrate its regional leadership and continental importance, and this was only possible if the operation was accepted as legitimate.

This motivation for Zimbabwe's leadership of Operation Sovereign Legitimacy has frequently been linked to Mugabe's personal desire for prestige and international status. One report asserts: 'Zimbabwe sent troops to the Congo because President Robert Mugabe wants to establish himself as a powerful regional military leader.'[42] Another highlights 'Mugabe's personal desire to be recognized as one of sub-Saharan Africa's foremost leaders' as a critical factor in explaining the intervention.[43] In the 1980s, Mugabe was one of Africa's most prominent statesmen thanks to his leadership of Zimbabwe's independence movement and of the region's struggle against apartheid. Thereafter, however, he was progressively upstaged, first by Yoweri Museveni of Uganda and then by Nelson Mandela of South Africa, the anti-apartheid icon who became president of Southern Africa's most powerful state in 1994. As one diplomat noted: 'Mugabe feels threatened by Mandela – he used to be the Old Man of Africa, but now, with Mandela, he has become little more than an upstart.'[44] Intervening in the DRC gave Mugabe an

News Online, 25 July 2000; Lawrence Bartlett, 'War and riches inspire new African economic deal making', *Agence France Presse*, 30 September 1999.

[40] International Crisis Group, 'Africa's Seven Nation War', *ICG Democratic Republic of Congo Report No. 4*, 21 May 1999, p. 31.

[41] Martin R. Rupiya, 'A Political and Military Review of Zimbabwe's Involvement in the Second Congo War', in John F. Clark (ed.), *African Stakes of the Congo War* (New York: Palgrave Macmillan, 2002), pp. 96–7.

[42] 'Congo: Less Fighting, but No Peace', in International Institute for Strategic Studies, *Strategic Survey 2000/2001* (Oxford: Oxford University Press, 2001), p. 230.

[43] Taylor Seybolt, 'Major Armed Conflicts', *SIPRI Yearbook 2000* (Oxford: Oxford University Press, 2000), p. 67.

[44] Author's interview with Mac Okwechima, Senior Counsellor, Nigeria High Commission, Gaborone, Botswana, 11 December 2000.

opportunity to reassert his political importance while countering both Museveni (whose troops were fighting against Kabila) and Mandela (who opposed military action in the DRC). As one critic put it, 'Mugabe ... wanted to show President Yoweri Museveni of Uganda and President Nelson Mandela of South Africa that he still counted.'[45] A more sympathetic observer noted: 'Robert Mugabe of Zimbabwe ... is a man that the world has not given adequate recognition ... Mandela emerged in South Africa and completely overshadowed him. Congo gave him the opportunity to both cut Mandela down to size and thwart Museveni's grand plans [of leadership in Africa].'[46]

Focusing exclusively on Mugabe's psyche to explain Zimbabwe's intervention in the DRC is excessively simplistic, however. The rivalry between Zimbabwe and South Africa was not just the consequence of the personal antipathies of their leaders. It was also a struggle for regional hegemony between Southern Africa's two most prominent states. After the end of apartheid, South Africa asserted itself as a regional power-house because of its economic and military power. Mugabe's regime bristled at this assertiveness. As one Southern African diplomat commented:

> Zimbabwe is fighting to be a regional powerhouse. When Zimbabwe talks, it talks about South Africa as competition. The trade balance between Zimbabwe and South Africa favours South Africa, but Zimbabwe wants to compare to South Africa and compete with it. [After apartheid ended] they went to second largest economic base in the region, and so they are spiteful of South Africa.[47]

Zimbabwe also questioned South Africa's leadership aspirations on equity grounds:

> We are not equal in resources [in the region], so some will contribute more than others – but this should not translate into power equations. Then we would lose the original principle on which SADC was first based: sovereign equality ... Zimbabwe ... dwarfed the rest of SADC during its own time, but it did not impose itself as a hegemon on the region.[48]

---

[45] Robert I. Rotberg, 'Africa's Mess, Mugabe's Mayhem', *Foreign Affairs*, 79:5 (September–October 2000), p. 53.
[46] Mujaju, 'How to Make Sense of the Events Taking Place in the Great Lakes Region', p. 94.
[47] Author's interview, remarks not for attribution.
[48] Author's interview with Lieutenant-Colonel A. W. Tapfumaneyi, 29 November 2000.

Most importantly, however, Zimbabwe challenged South Africa's ideo-logical leadership credentials. As one Zimbabwean official put it: 'there is the view that the South African bureaucracy is still very white. It has been suspected, especially during the Mandela period, that the bureau-cracy is working . . . to protect the old South Africa that dominated the region and did what it wanted with the countries in the sub-region.'[49] In this sense, the rivalry between Zimbabwe and South Africa took place across a deep political fault line within Southern Africa.

Some Southern African countries, including Botswana and Mozambique, embraced the newly democratic South Africa as a positive regional force of the future and supported its efforts to claim a leader-ship role in the region. Others, like Angola and Namibia, were more sceptical about the extent of South Africa's transformation, especially since it declined to sacrifice its national economic interests to promote regional development: 'Post-apartheid South Africa . . . effectively doused the euphoria that accompanied the advent of majority rule there, from a subregional perspective, to pursue an isolationist foreign policy and a protectionist trade policy.'[50] Critics pointed to the con-tinued dominance of whites in South Africa's bureaucracy and army and questioned whether the country had fully overcome its apartheid heri-tage. As a high-level Angolan military official commented, there was 'concern that, so soon after the end of apartheid, vestiges of the old way of doing things might still remain and how the country would develop in the future was still uncertain'.[51] Throughout the 1990s, Zimbabwe saw itself as leading a regional effort to balance against this 'new' but not fully reconstructed South Africa.

This agenda provided the context for Zimbabwe's decision to inter-vene in the DRC. The DRC could rival South Africa in population and resources, though not in levels of development. After Kabila's ascent to power in 1997, therefore, Zimbabwe hoped for an alliance with the DRC that would help balance South Africa's regional dominance.[52] Mugabe

---

[49] Ibid.

[50] A. W. Tapfumaneyi, 'Some Reflections on the Current Conflict in the DRC: Explaining Zimbabwe's Military Intervention', in Baregu (ed.), *Crisis in the Democratic Republic of Congo*, p. 122.

[51] Vice Admiral André Gaspar Mendes de Carvalho, 'The Position of Angola', in Baregu (ed.), *Crisis in the Democratic Republic of Congo*, p. 102.

[52] Colette Braeckman, *L'Enjeu Congolais: L'Afrique Centrale Après Mobutu* (Paris: Fayard, 1999), p. 293.

assiduously courted Kabila, extending bilateral aid and lobbying to bring the DRC into SADC. The outbreak of the second DRC war threatened this scheme. However, it also provided an opportunity for Zimbabwe to demonstrate its regional leadership capacity. If Zimbabwe could spearhead the region's response to its most severe challenge of the post-apartheid era, its continuing regional leadership role would be reaffirmed.

To reap this reward, it was vitally important that Operation Sovereign Legitimacy was accepted as a legitimate endeavour for the benefit of the entire Southern African region. Zimbabwe consistently stressed that Operation Sovereign Legitimacy aimed to bolster regional peace and security. Announcing the operation, Mugabe insisted, 'We have considered it our duty to respond to the call ... for assistance so that peace and stability can be restored in the Congo and in our region.'[53] In January 1999, Zimbabwe's Foreign Minister specified that:

> allowing aggression and rebellion in the DRC would set a bad precedent with very negative consequences for the entire region. First, we can talk about the flood of refugees into neighbouring countries ... Secondly, allowing the disintegration of the DRC into ethnic based [sic] units is the last thing any country in Africa wants. Such a meltdown into ethnicism would inevitably affect every country where there is more than one ethnic group. No African country would be spared, leading to continental chaos.[54]

For Zimbabwe, the stakes were high. If Operation Sovereign Legitimacy was accepted as a legitimate response to a regional crisis, Zimbabwe would reap significant prestige from having led it. If not, Zimbabwe would appear as a bully that invaded neighbouring countries. The credibility of its claims to regional leadership would be seriously, perhaps terminally, undermined. This dilemma was at the heart of Zimbabwe's legitimacy concerns during the launching of Operation Sovereign Legitimacy.

---

[53] Robert Mugabe, 'Announcement of Zimbabwe's Intervention in the DRC', Harare 18 August 1998, accessed online through the Zimbabwe government's website at www.gta.gov.zw on 16 April 2003. Site not currently accessible.

[54] 'Zimbabwean Minister of Foreign Affairs on Zimbabwe's Foreign Policy', 20 January 1999, accessed online through the Zimbabwe government's website at http://www.gta.gov.zw on 16 April 2003. Site not currently accessible.

Zimbabwe's main legitimacy audience

As chapter 2 noted, a state launching a peace enforcement operation has four potential legitimacy audiences: its domestic public opinion, public opinion in the host state of the intervention, regional states, and the broader international community of states. For Zimbabwe, the most relevant legitimacy audience for Operation Sovereign Legitimacy was the Southern African region and the broader community of African states.

The legitimacy judgements of the Congolese public mattered relatively little to Mugabe's government. In part, this was because it assumed that most Congolese welcomed its intervention. Kabila had boosted his domestic popularity by portraying himself as a nationalist defending the DRC against foreign invaders and ethnic Tutsi imperialism.[55] This strategy also improved the legitimacy of Operation Sovereign Legitimacy in the eyes of many Congolese citizens. The remainder, Zimbabwe insisted, were caught up in a foreign-inspired rebellion that was doomed to disappear as soon as Uganda and Rwanda were repulsed. As one senior Zimbabwean diplomat put it, 'Angola, the DRC, Namibia and Zimbabwe view the conflict in the DRC as essentially an invasion of the country by Rwanda and Uganda, with the two countries assisted by a recruited, non-spontaneous and ultimately insignificant rebel element.'[56] Thus Zimbabwe argued that it did not need to be concerned about the legitimacy of Operation Sovereign Legitimacy in the eyes of the Congolese public. It is also worth noting, however, that both Zimbabwe and the DRC were autocracies in which domestic public opinion was routinely disregarded. This also helps explain why Zimbabwe made no direct efforts to persuade Congolese citizens of the legitimacy of its presence in their country.

Zimbabwe's government did not consider its own domestic public a critical legitimacy audience for Operation Sovereign Legitimacy either. The intervention was 'Mugabe's personal decision . . . without prior consultation with parliament, the cabinet, or his party's central committee'.[57] Supporters of the decision argue that the situation left no alternative:

---

[55] International Crisis Group, 'Africa's Seven-Nation War', *ICG Democratic Republic of Congo Report No. 4*, 21 May 1999, p. 14.
[56] Ambassador Gift Punungwe, 'The SADC Organ on Politics, Defence, and Security', in Baregu (ed.), *Crisis in the Democratic Republic of Congo*, p. 139.
[57] Rotberg, 'Africa's Mess, Mugabe's Mayhem', p. 53.

> As regards informing the domestic public, the secretive nature of military operations, and the urgency of the matter at hand, was such that there was no time to waste and the nation could only be informed after the event. Various estimates ... predicting on 17 August that Kinshasa would have fallen within the next 24 hours precluded any dithering ... Parliament was subsequently informed by the Ministry of Defence ... By and large, Parliament upheld the legitimacy and timeliness of Zimbabwe's involvement.[58]

However, Parliament's post hoc approval of Operation Sovereign Legitimacy reflected the fact that Mugabe's tightly controlled Zimbabwe African National Union Patriotic Front held 147 of the 150 parliamentary seats rather than popular support for the intervention. The three opposition MPs condemned Operation Sovereign Legitimacy and a November 1998 Gallup poll in suggested that 70 per cent of Zimbabwe's population opposed the intervention.[59] Risking Zimbabwean lives in the DRC was deeply unpopular, especially because many Zimbabweans saw no reason for the intervention: 'the deployment of troops to the DRC has been ... most odious for citizens, particularly because there was no apparent, "rational" reason for Zimbabwe to become involved.'[60] Zimbabweans also felt that they could not afford a war in the DRC: Zimbabwe's economy was in crisis, with sliding real GDP growth rates, soaring inflation, escalating public debt, and sky-rocketing unemployment.[61] One political commentator summed up the mood: 'the tendency is for an autocratic regime to support an author-itarian regime (but) I would hope that we don't continue pouring money and materiel into that lost cause, let alone offer our men and women to die in that lost battle.'[62]

Zimbabwe's government made virtually no effort to address these concerns. The regime persuaded the country's elites and high military officers to support Operation Sovereign Legitimacy by granting them access to the DRC's mineral wealth.[63] State-owned media praised Operation Sovereign Legitimacy. Beyond this, the government's main

---

[58] Tapfumaneyi, 'Some Reflections on the Current Conflict in the DRC', pp. 114–15.
[59] Economist Intelligence Unit, *Country Report: Zimbabwe*, 1st Quarter (February) 1999, p. 12.
[60] Sandra J. Maclean, 'Mugabe at War: The Political Economy of Conflict in Zimbabwe', *Third World Quarterly*, 23:3 (2002), p. 522.
[61] Rotberg, 'Africa's Mess, Mugabe's Mayhem', pp. 51–3.
[62] 'Mugabe's DRC Move Comes under Fire', *Zimbabwe Independent*, 21 August 1998.
[63] Maclean, 'The Political Economy of Conflict in Zimbabwe', p. 523.

approach was repressive. It refused to reveal the intervention's financial cost to Zimbabwe and suppressed the body count. In June 1999, one Zimbabwean diplomat insisted:

> I don't have figures on how much Zimbabwe is spending on the troops in the DRC. That is a war situation and certain information has to be withheld ... The aggressors in the DRC ... have inundated the international community with fabricated statistics of allied losses, killed or captured. The truth is that while the allies have suffered some losses and have had some troops captured, they have inflicted much heavier damage on the rebels and their supporters than they or their backers have been willing to admit.[64]

The government branded Zimbabwe's independent media as 'unpatriotic' for criticising Operation Sovereign Legitimacy. It also arrested and tortured several journalists who reported a coup attempt by soldiers disgruntled by the DRC adventure.[65] In November 1998, strikes against the regime were banned. There was no major effort to persuade the general Zimbabwean public of the legitimacy of Operation Sovereign Legitimacy, which suggests that it was not considered a crucial legitimacy audience by Mugabe's regime.

Instead, the Zimbabwean government considered other states to be the key legitimacy audience for Operation Sovereign Legitimacy. One of Zimbabwe's explicit foreign policy goals in 1999 was to be 'respected in the comity of Nations'.[66] Although this concern for international renown may seem odd in a regime that disregards domestic public opinion, it can be understood precisely as a consequence of autocracy. Personal rule encourages autocrats to identify their own prestige with that of 'their' state. For Mugabe, Zimbabwe's status was a personal quest, since Zimbabwe was the platform from which he projected his own persona. Moreover, Mugabe, like many autocratic rulers, had placed himself above his fellow citizens. Therefore the international community was the only community of peers he acknowledged and whose rank-ordering remained subject to competition. If Zimbabwe reaffirmed its regional and international leadership credentials through Operation Sovereign Legitimacy, Mugabe's personal prestige as statesman would also increase.

---

[64] Newton Sibanda, 'Zimbabwe/DRCongo: Why We Must Intervene', *Africa News*, 39 (June 1999).
[65] Economist Intelligence Unit, *Country Report: Zimbabwe*, 1st Quarter (February) 1999, p. 6.
[66] Zimbabwean Minister of Foreign Affairs on Zimbabwe's Foreign Policy, 20 January 1999.

Within the 'comity of Nations', however, the ideology of Zimbabwe's regime imposed certain distinctions. One recurrent theme of Mugabe's government was mistrust of the West and willingness to oppose the dominant states in the international system. Mugabe came to power as a Marxist African nationalist who, with the backing of communist China, helped lead Zimbabwe to independence after a brutal war against a British settler regime. The rancour caused by that struggle still persists. In December 2000, one Zimbabwean official declared:

> Because the president . . . tolerates no nonsense about the sovereignty of the state, he is hated and demonised abroad . . . because he is an African leader who speaks for his people. They [the West] want to put puppets in charge of African countries . . . But in Zimbabwe since the early 1950s Mugabe has fought . . . for African rights . . . Where were the advocates of human rights then, where was democracy? Where was transparency when Ian Smith massacred us? . . . This hypocrisy has got to go. We are not equals, some are more equal than others. We are very angry and disappointed.[67]

The US and British policy of 'constructive engagement' with apartheid South Africa in the early 1980s further fuelled Zimbabwe's distrust of the West. Given this mindset, Mugabe's government was relatively unconcerned about the West's opinions on the legitimacy of Operation Sovereign Legitimacy.

By contrast, the Southern African region was a critical legitimacy audience for Zimbabwe. Mugabe announced the intervention in extravagantly pan-regional terms:

> Escalation [of the DRC conflict] will bring a lot of suffering to the people of the Congo as well as to members of this region, member countries of this region . . . The people of the Democratic Republic of Congo are as much our people as those who constitute our individual population as countries. Their welfare is our welfare in the same manner as the welfare of any other state within this region is the welfare of all the other states . . . We shall live up to the expectations of the people in our region . . . May peace and stability reign in the Congo, reign in our region and reign on the whole continent of Africa.[68]

---

[67] Author's interview with Ambassador Munyaradzi S. Kajese, Chief of Protocol, Office of the President and Cabinet of Zimbabwe, Harare, 13 December 2000.
[68] Mugabe, 'Announcement of Zimbabwe's Intervention in the DRC'.

If Southern Africa recognised Operation Sovereign Legitimacy as a genuine regional initiative, leadership of the intervention would dramatically bolster Zimbabwe's regional status. As noted above, some alliances had already been formed in the region: Botswana, Mozambique, and Zambia tended to support South Africa, while Angola and Namibia tended to side with Zimbabwe. Other states remained uncommitted, however. These were the states Zimbabwe most needed to convince. If they recognised Zimbabwe's actions as reflecting the interests of the region, Zimbabwe would gain the critical mass of regional support that it needed to back its claims of regional leadership. With their support, regional and international critics of the intervention could be isolated. Zimbabwe could claim that 'An objective jury drawn from truly patriotic citizens of Southern Africa, and which excludes from its midst some journalists or members of the academia who are playing to the whims of the West, which in turn is seeking to divide and rule Africa, would not only acquit but laud the action taken by the DRC Allies.'[69]

Moreover, winning over the undecided states could have longer-term implications for Zimbabwe's regional leadership status. At best, these states might permanently join Zimbabwe's camp within SADC. At the very least, their support in this particular instance would demonstrate that Zimbabwe continued to lead the region on crucial political issues. South Africa's inaction in the DRC could then be portrayed as a failure of regional leadership, strengthening Zimbabwe's claim that South Africa lacked the will to truly engage the region's problems. As one Zimbabwean military officer argued:

> South Africa is the biggest and strongest country: it should take on that position [of regional lead state] ... For example in the DRC: if the SANDF had joined the operation in the DRC, the crisis would not have lasted, it would not have escalated ... By not coming in, South Africa made a big dent in SADC ... There is still a lot of white control in the structures ... and the armed forces are still predominantly white. Do they accept black regional thinking, are they willing to suffer for those ideals? I'm not sure. I am not sure if I share the same ideals with them as I share with a black man.[70]

Zimbabwe's target legitimacy audience for Operation Sovereign Legitimacy also extended beyond the Southern African region. Zimbabwe's

---

[69] Tapfumaneyi, 'Some Reflections on the Current Conflict in the DRC', p. 123.
[70] Author's interview, remark not for attribution.

external relations have historically centred on the developing world: 'Zimbabwe's foreign policy has been influenced by its revolutionary origins which place emphasis on solidarity with the down-trodden and the dispossessed.'[71] This stance is not purely altruistic. Zimbabwe has chosen to pursue status and influence through prominence in the developing world, rather than through an alliance with the West. Its leadership of the anti-apartheid struggle gave it significant stature in this forum: in addition to chairing the Front Line States from 1991 onward, Zimbabwe was elected to chair the Non-Aligned Movement (NAM) from 1986 to 1989, the Commonwealth in 1991, and the Organisation of African Unity in 1997.

Within the developing world, Zimbabwe's primary foreign policy focus is on Africa. Zimbabwe's position within Africa is a matter of pride to its government. As one diplomat noted with evident satisfaction (and perhaps slight exaggeration): 'No country in Africa commands as much respect as Zimbabwe. Because of our policies, we command respect from Cape Town to Cairo. We walk tall in Africa – anywhere we go we command respect because we are addressing the genuine interests of the people.'[72] More humbly, Zimbabwe's Foreign Minister acknowledged:

> The revolutionary origins of the present Zimbabwean state also lead our country to place at the centre of its foreign policy our relationship to Africa, the continent to which we belong and which expended so much energy and so many resources to assist us to wrest our independence from the enemy, and particularly our relationship with Southern Africa, our sub-region which not only laboured with the rest of Africa for our cause but also endured so much hardship for it.[73]

Showing regional leadership by spearheading a peace enforcement operation in the DRC would further bolster Zimbabwe's continental status. Autonomy and independence from the West remain highly prized within Africa as the continent struggles with the consequences of colonialism. Zimbabwe sought to portray its DRC intervention as a paradigm of constructive and autonomous leadership within Africa. Its Foreign Minister declared: 'Zimbabwe today is ... at the forefront of

---

[71] 'Zimbabwean Minister of Foreign Affairs on Zimbabwe's Foreign Policy', 20 January 1999.
[72] Author's interview with Ambassador Munyaradzi S. Kajese, 13 December 2000.
[73] 'Zimbabwean Minister of Foreign Affairs on Zimbabwe's Foreign Policy', 20 January 1999.

pushing for the fashioning of African means for pursuing African objectives ... Zimbabwe, Angola and Namibia's military involvement in the DRC constitutes implementations of these resolutions.'[74]

As in the Southern African sub-region, however, these claims to continental status based on Zimbabwe's leadership in Operation Sovereign Legitimacy could only be validated if the continent accepted that the operation was in fact conducted to further the interests of the region as a whole. If the intervention was perceived as motivated merely by national interests, Zimbabwe would reap little recognition for its efforts. In other words, for its leadership role to be recognised on the African continent, Zimbabwe had to persuade the continent that its intervention in the DRC was legitimate.

The SADC framework and the legitimacy of Operation Sovereign Legitimacy

To demonstrate that Zimbabwe's decision to launch Operation Sovereign Legitimacy through SADC was motivated by its concerns with the international legitimacy of the intervention, it is not enough to identify and describe these concerns. It must also be established that Zimbabwe expected the SADC framework to help convince its target audiences of the operation's legitimacy. This section makes this case – but it also notes that the actual impact proved less decisive than Zimbabwe had hoped.

Expected effect on regional legitimacy

The potential impact of SADC auspices on Operation Sovereign Legitimacy's regional legitimacy was twofold. First, operating within this framework allowed Zimbabwe to present its actions in the DRC as the fulfilment of a regional obligation. Article 4.b of the SADC Treaty commits members to 'act in accordance with the ... principles ... [of] solidarity, peace and security'. The DRC is a SADC member and thus had a right to expect SADC assistance in a time of crisis. Mugabe stressed, 'we have been appealed to by the ... Head of Government of a country that is a member of our regional organisation and ... with whom we have relations within this organisation that are multilateral ... and therefore we have considered it our duty to respond to the call and

---

[74] Ibid.

appeal, by one of us, for assistance.'[75] Framing the issue in this manner gave Zimbabwe the moral high-ground on the region's own terms. As one commentator put it, Mugabe 'is speaking on the principle that SADC countries have agreed to police their own security ... The principle is that Congo joined SADC and we have to put our money where our mouth is.'[76] Launched within the SADC framework, Zimbabwe's military intervention could be portrayed as a heroic assumption of regional responsibilities. As one Zimbabwean diplomat put it, 'we are sacrificing, but at the end of the day, there will be peace and stability in the region. So we are investing in peace and stability by sacrificing.'[77] Non-participating states were put on the defensive. As a member of Botswana's military noted:

> we did not find intervention in the DRC justifiable ... we thought the conflict was not very directly connected with the affairs of the region. Nevertheless, there is an agreement among [SADC] states to go to the rescue of a colleague against possible coups d'état. So ... we cannot say that we won't go because we don't feel responsibility for the problem in the DRC.[78]

Second, the SADC framework provided a justification for Zimbabwe's leadership of Operation Sovereign Legitimacy as well as a setting that was conducive to generating at least a façade of consensus behind the initiative. The SADC Organ was created to protect the region 'against instability arising from the breakdown of law and order, inter-state conflict and external aggression'.[79] Although it became paralysed in 1997, it was not dissolved and Zimbabwe remained its official Chair. The DRC crisis clearly fell within the Organ's purview, and Zimbabwe used its status as the Organ's Chair to explain its participation in Operation Sovereign Legitimacy. As one official put it, 'as Chair of the SADC Organ on Politics, Defence and Security [Zimbabwe] had to be seen to be leading by example'.[80] According to another observer, 'Zimbabwe, as chair of the Organ on Politics, Defence, and

[75] Mugabe, 'Announcement of Zimbabwe's Intervention in the DRC', 18 August 1998.
[76] 'DRC: Zimbabwe says SADC to back Kabila', *IRIN*, 19 August 1998.
[77] Sibanda, 'Zimbabwe/DRCongo: Why We Must Intervene'.
[78] Author's interview with Lieutenant-Colonel P. S. Manyemba, Staff Officer Air Operations, Botswana Defence Force, Gaborone, Botswana 5 December 2000.
[79] SADC, *Summit Communiqué*, 28 June 1996.
[80] Tapfumaneyi, 'Some Reflections on the Current Conflict in the DRC', p. 122.

Security . . . felt it could not shirk its responsibilities to a neighbor under threat from "imperialism".[81]

Zimbabwe also used its position as Organ Chair to seize the initiative in shaping the regional response to the crisis. It convened the ISDSC meeting of 18 August in Harare on its authority as Organ Chair. The meeting had official SADC status and allowed Zimbabwe to present itself as acting in a multilateral rather than national capacity. From Zimbabwe's point of view, it went very well. One Zimbabwean participant recalled general enthusiasm for the intervention at this meeting: 'I remember when the decision to intervene was taken, everybody was dancing, the chairman was banging his fist on the table, saying let's go now.'[82] Zambia's Defence Minister, who had chaired the meeting, confirmed that 'all SADC countries' had agreed to assist Kabila.[83] At the end of this meeting, still exploiting his role as Organ Chair, Mugabe made himself the mouthpiece of the region and announced a SADC decision to intervene militarily in the DRC.

Given the unequal attendance of the ISDSC meeting as well as the body's lack of formal decision-making powers within SADC, Mugabe must have known that his contention that SADC had unanimously decided to intervene was at best premature. He clearly hoped, however, that SADC members would coalesce behind the position he had outlined. As one observer commented: 'My sense is that . . . [Mugabe] is trying to commit SADC before an agreement is reached.'[84] This was not an unreasonable gamble, because the SADC framework favoured the emergence of official consensus around Mugabe's initiative. The DRC conflict was a genuine regional crisis and a strong appeal to SADC's principle of regional solidarity had been made. The ISDSC had endorsed intervention. The momentum generated by these developments could be expected to bring any recalcitrant SADC members in line behind Zimbabwe's *fait accompli*. Moreover, SADC had no burden-sharing mechanisms for regional peace operations. As Zimbabwean Brigadier Mugoba put it, 'it is enshrined in the SADC principles that while there may be a consensus on intervention, countries decide for themselves whether they will intervene or not . . . Countries are not obliged to

[81] Rupiya, 'A Political and Military Review of Zimbabwe's Involvement in the Second Congo War', p. 96.

[82] Author's interview with Lieutenant-Colonel A. W. Tapfumaneyi, 29 November 2000.

[83] SAPA, 'DR Congo: SADC Defence Ministers Agree to Aid to Kabila against Rebels', BBC, 19 August 1998.

[84] 'DRC: Zimbabwe says SADC to back Kabila', *IRIN*, 19 August 1998.

intervene, there are no binding rules, they decide on their own whether to send troops.'[85] SADC members could therefore accept the creation of a SADC force for the DRC without committing themselves to contributing to it, making acquiescence with Zimbabwe's DRC initiative relatively costless.

In sum, the SADC framework provided a rationale for intervening in the DRC, an institutional reason for Zimbabwe's leadership of the operation, and a forum that favoured the emergence of a regional consensus behind Zimbabwe's leadership. Zimbabwe thus had every reason to expect that operating through SADC would improve Operation Sovereign Legitimacy's legitimacy within Southern Africa.

Expected effect on continental legitimacy

Beyond Southern Africa, SADC's legitimising potential, like that of ECOWAS analysed in the previous chapter, derived from the international trend towards the regionalisation of conflict management efforts that began in the early 1990s. Since Zimbabwe's key extra-regional legitimacy audience for Operation Sovereign Legitimacy was the community of African states, it is particularly relevant that the continental Organisation of African Unity (OAU) was an early proponent of regionalisation. Already in 1991, the Abuja Treaty affirmed that an African Economic Community (AEC) had to be built by strengthening 'regional economic communities'.[86] SADC was recognised as one of the AEC's five regional 'pillars'.[87] When the notion of regionalisation subsequently extended beyond the economic realm, these pillars came to be seen, inter alia, as vehicles for conflict management. The head of the OAU's Conflict Management Centre explained:

> There are lots of complementarities between subregional organisations and our organisation. There are geo-political factors – sometimes proximity helps and sometimes it impedes progress. Generally those closer to a conflict have better information – that is their comparative advantage. They are better placed to understand the conflict and help solve it . . . We

---

[85] Author's interview with Brigadier T. Mugoba, Director-General (Operations and Plans), Zimbabwe Ministry of Defence, Harare, Zimbabwe, 18 December 2000.

[86] *Treaty Establishing the African Economic Community*, 3 June 1991, Abuja, Nigeria.

[87] The four other pillars are the Economic Community of West African States, the Economic Community of Central African States, the Community of Eastern and Southern African States, and the Arab Maghreb Union.

> want to work with them. They are the pillars of regional integration, and our partners in conflict resolution.[88]

Thus by 1998, SADC had been recognised by the OAU as the appropriate structure for dealing with peace and security in Southern Africa. Launching Operation Sovereign Legitimacy within the SADC framework could therefore be expected to improve the intervention's legitimacy in Africa as a whole. As one member of the OAU Crisis Management Centre acknowledged, 'the OAU takes the view that the sub-region is better placed to evaluate the situation and recommend proposals to deal with the security and political crisis. So it makes sense that the organisation should simply endorse the sub-region's proposals.'[89] OAU endorsement of Operation Sovereign Legitimacy would amount to formal continental recognition of the intervention's legitimacy. It would also signal Africa's endorsement of the operation to the rest of the international community, thus facilitating wider international recognition of the intervention's legitimacy. However, while this legitimacy pyramid was crucial for Nigeria's intervention in Liberia (chapter 3) and South Africa's deployment in Lesotho (chapter 5), it was less critical for Operation Sovereign Legitimacy. For Zimbabwe, Africa was a more important legitimacy audience than the wider international community and therefore OAU approval of the operation was primarily an end in itself.

The SADC framework was crucial to obtaining OAU endorsement of Operation Sovereign Legitimacy. The OAU recognised SADC, not individual regional states, as its pillar in Southern Africa. As an anti-colonial organisation strongly committed to the principles of state sovereignty and non-interference, moreover, it was profoundly sceptical of unilateral intervention. SADC's capacity to legitimise Operation Sovereign Legitimacy in Africa thus derived from its multilateral nature as representative of the Southern African region as a whole. To fully exploit this capacity, however, the region had to appear united within SADC. In this context, SADC's internal institutional structures presented a crucial advantage for Zimbabwe.

---

[88] Author's interview with Dr John Tesha, Head of the OAU Conflict Management Centre, Addis Ababa, 20 November 2000.

[89] Interview with Njunga M. Mulikita, UNDP Project for Capacity Building of the OAU Mechanism for Conflict Prevention, Management and Resolution, Addis Ababa, Ethiopia, 31 October 2000.

SADC operates under a consensus rule of decision-making, reflecting a notion of regional solidarity that is fundamental to Southern African politics. This notion has its roots in a shared regional history of anti-colonial struggle: 'SADC has a history of the same revolution. Most countries in the region have gone through colonial war and so the consciousness of countries within SADC is much higher. There is a consciousness among member states – the people who run these states have had similar experiences.'[90] This ideology remained strong through-out the 1990s. As one diplomat warned in 2000: 'It's a very strong solidarity – don't discount it.'[91] However, the consensus rule also reflects the regional sentiment that only a united Southern Africa can emerge from its present marginalisation on the international stage. In 1992, the region's heads of state proclaimed: 'The countries of the region must . . . join together to strengthen themselves economically and poli-tically, if the region is to become a serious player in international relations. No single country of Southern Africa can achieve this status on its own.'[92] SADC's consensus rule is an essential part of this project.

As the lead state in Operation Sovereign Legitimacy, Zimbabwe drew two advantages from this consensus rule. First, SADC could not for-mally condemn the intervention or dispute its appropriation of SADC auspices. As a SADC member, Zimbabwe could veto any such declara-tion. Second, the consensus rule created a pressure cooker atmosphere that favoured Zimbabwe. In consensus decision-making, states face a stark choice between acquiescing to a decision and blocking it, since any voicing of dissent amounts to a veto. The costs of dissent are high: vetoing a collective decision not only alienates the states advocating the decision but also paralyses the organisation and exposes regional divisions. Therefore once Zimbabwe had seized the initiative and built momentum behind an intervention in the DRC, the pressure for acquiescence from other states was considerable. As SADC's Legal Adviser put it, 'if the consensus is against you, what right do you have to resist? The consensus is not absolute, not all have to agree.'[93] Moreover, as noted, SADC's lack of burden-sharing mechanisms made

[90] Author's interview with Colonel (rtd) Tshinga J. Dube, General Manager (Chief Executive), Zimbabwe Defence Industries, Harare, Zimbabwe, 1 December 2000.
[91] Author's interview with Mac Okwechima, Senior Counsellor, Nigeria High Commission, Gaborone, Botswana, 11 December 2000.
[92] 'Towards the Southern African Development Community', pp. 3–4.
[93] Interview with S. Kokerai, SADC Legal Adviser, Gaborone, Botswana, 12 December 2000.

acquiescence with Operation Sovereign Legitimacy relatively inexpensive. The only obligation on acquiescing states was to explain their non-participation without undermining SADC's façade of unity, which could easily be done by invoking financial concerns. Zimbabwe would readily accept this excuse, since its primary concern was being able to claim to be acting in the name of the entire region, and for this it needed SADC approval, not SADC-wide participation. As one member of Zimbabwe's Ministry of Defence put it: 'Where was the resolution taken? That is most important. If it was taken in a SADC forum then it is a SADC operation ... What is important is who resolved to take action, not who participated in that action.'[94]

Thus SADC's consensus rule of decision-making and its lack of burden-sharing mechanisms for peace enforcement operations favoured Zimbabwe's quest to depict itself as operating in the DRC on behalf of the entire Southern African sub-region. This in turn could be expected to increase Operation Sovereign Legitimacy's continental legitimacy, helping to explain why Zimbabwe chose to launch the intervention within the SADC framework.

Expectations and reality

Zimbabwe's decision to launch Operation Sovereign Legitimacy's within the SADC framework can be attributed to SADC's unique capacity to improve the intervention's regional and continental legitimacy. In the event, however, this strategy was only partly successful. As Zimbabwe had hoped, SADC states ultimately coalesced behind the intervention. The SADC Summit in Mauritius on 13–14 September 1998 'commended the Governments of Angola, Namibia and Zimbabwe for ... providing troops to assist the Government and people of the DRC defeat the illegal attempt by rebels and their allies to capture the capital city, Kinshasa, and other strategic areas'.[95] Dissenting states declined to participate in the intervention but publicly justified this decision by pointing to a lack of resources. Botswana, for example, was

> officially unable to participate in the DRC operation because of financial constraints. That is the view of the politicians – we did not send troops to the DRC because we could not afford it ... You may be wondering why

---

[94] Interview with Air Commodore Karakadzai, Deputy Secretary of Policy and Procurement, Zimbabwe Ministry of Defence, Harare, Zimbabwe, 18 December 2000.
[95] SADC, *Summit Communiqué*, Grand Bay, Mauritius, 13–14 September 1998.

I used the word 'officially'. There are certain circles that do not think that
this was the reason. We did not want to go into the DRC, so officially we
said we cannot afford it.[96]

Zimbabwe was thus able to point out: 'Some [SADC countries] felt they
did not have the resources to commit themselves. They were not saying
that it was wrong to assist the Congo, but some realistically felt they did
not have the resources ... nobody came out in the open to condemn the
assistance given to the Congolese.'[97]

At the continental level, the OAU also endorsed Zimbabwe's initiative: OAU Secretary-General Salim Ahmed Salim personally attended
the peace talks Zimbabwe hosted at Victoria Falls on 7–8 September
1998, which represented the first major Zimbabwe-led diplomatic
initiative since the beginning of Operation Sovereign Legitimacy.
Zimbabwe even enjoyed a diplomatic victory at the UN. Security
Council Resolution 1234 of 9 April 1999 confirmed states' 'inherent
right of individual or collective self-defence' and singled out 'uninvited'
forces in the DRC for particular criticism while expressing concern for
the country's national sovereignty and territorial integrity.

However, the legitimising effects of the SADC framework were ultimately less pronounced than Zimbabwe had expected. Despite SADC
institutions, the region did not readily coalesce behind Zimbabwe's
leadership and Operation Sovereign Legitimacy. Instead, as the next
section describes, South Africa openly clashed with Zimbabwe on how
to address the DRC crisis, which prevented SADC's legitimising potential from being used to full effect in the crucial initial phases of the
operation. This came as an unwelcome surprise to the Zimbabwean
leadership – but the risk of encountering such a surprise is an inherent
cost of operating within a multilateral framework.

The costs and benefits of operating through SADC

The best indicator for the value that Zimbabwe placed on the legitimacy
generated by SADC are the costs it incurred by operating in this framework. Chief among these was the political risk Zimbabwe took in submitting the intervention to multinational scrutiny. Claiming a SADC
mandate for Operation Sovereign Legitimacy effectively gave every

---

[96] Author's interview with Lieutenant-Colonel P. S. Manyemba, 5 December 2000.
[97] Author's interview with Colonel (rtd.) Tshinga J. Dube, 1 December 2000.

SADC member a right to comment on or criticise the intervention. Although the organisation was well suited to the task of legitimising Operation Sovereign Legitimacy, it was nonetheless a multilateral forum that by definition escaped the complete control of any one state, including Zimbabwe. In placing Operation Sovereign Legitimacy under SADC auspices, therefore, Zimbabwe assumed the risk that other member states would use the SADC platform to attack the intervention.

This risk was exacerbated by the intense regional rivalry between Zimbabwe and South Africa. As noted, Zimbabwe hoped to use Operation Sovereign Legitimacy to demonstrate its regional leadership and emphasise that it was more responsive to regional needs than South Africa. It therefore consistently sought to sideline South Africa, failing to invite it to the 8 August Victoria Falls summit and ignoring South Africa and Botswana's attempt to undermine the credibility of the 18 August ISDSC meeting in Harare by sending only low-level diplomatic representation. As *coup de grâce*, Mugabe then presented South Africa with a *fait accompli* by announcing a 'SADC' decision to endorse military intervention in the DRC. The very rivalry that made operating through SADC attractive to Zimbabwe also made it dangerous, however, because it gave South Africa an incentive to challenge Zimbabwe. After the Harare meeting, South Africa had two options. It could acquiesce to Zimbabwe's *fait accompli* and thus cede regional leadership to Zimbabwe on this issue. However, it could also use its status as a SADC member to challenge Mugabe's arrogation of SADC auspices for Operation Sovereign Legitimacy. Mugabe had gambled that the traditions of regional solidarity and consensus embodied within SADC would persuade South Africa to opt for acquiescence. Regional rivalry goaded South Africa to break with these conventions.

South Africa countered the Harare overture by attacking the very basis of Zimbabwe's leadership claim. President Nelson Mandela sharply criticised the proposed intervention: 'Our attitude is clear on this problem. It is not to worsen the [DRC's] position by sending a military force.'[98] He added pointedly: 'That is my attitude as chairman of SADC.' Mandela thus both undermined Zimbabwe's claim to be speaking for the entire Southern African region and challenged Mugabe's assertion of SADC leadership. His spokesperson drove the message home: 'Anyone who pretends to be speaking for SADC on this

---

[98] 'Mugabe's Congo adventure must be stopped', *Zimbabwe Independent*, 21 August 1998.

issue is misleading himself and the world.'[99] South Africa's regional allies followed its lead. Botswana's Minister for Foreign Affairs declared that 'it would be unfair to suggest that the [Harare] decision was unanimous'.[100] Its Permanent Secretary for Foreign Affairs added: 'the decision was taken without us ... I would doubt if we would want to be involved ... I am not sure that this is a peacekeeping exercise.'[101] Mozambique's Prime Minister also insisted that the 'individual positions' of certain SADC and OAU members 'cannot be seen as a position of all the countries members of those organisations ... I am sure that the SADC heads of state are in permanent contact, and soon we will know the SADC position, as an organisation, concerning the situation.'[102] He also announced his categorical refusal to allow Mozambican troops 'to take part in offensive operations in the Congo'.[103]

It is worth noting that South Africa and its allies made these critiques as SADC members because Zimbabwe had chosen to place Operation Sovereign Legitimacy under SADC auspices. Had the intervention been presented as an act of collective self-defence, for example, questions of SADC consensus would have been irrelevant and other countries' authority to comment more circumscribed.

Mugabe was furious at this unexpected breaking of SADC ranks and responded sharply and publicly. The newspapers gleefully reported that he told Mandela to 'shut up' – but this summary misses the subtleties of Mugabe's response. His exact phrasing speaks volumes about the norms prevailing in SADC: 'No one is compelled within SADC to go into a campaign of assisting a country beset by conflict. Those who want to keep out ... fine, let them keep out. But let them keep silence about those who want to help.'[104] However, South Africa refused to cede Zimbabwe regional leadership on the DRC issue. Instead, it proposed an alternative SADC approach to the DRC crisis based on diplomatic negotiation. Using its status as SADC Chair, South Africa convened a

---

[99] Fernando Gonçalves, 'The Congo crisis: What is at stake?', *The Zimbabwe Mirror*, 21–27 August 1998.

[100] 'DR Congo: Botswana not bound by Harare move', *Daily News (Botswana)*, 21 August 1998.

[101] Ibid.

[102] 'Mozambique will not send troops to Congo – Mocumbi', *Panafrican News Agency* 22 August 1998.

[103] 'Mocumbi speaks on Congolese conflict', *Pan-African News Agency*, 28 August 1998.

[104] Patrick Laurence, 'Mugabe and Mandela divided by personalities and policies', *The Irish Times*, 21 August 1998.

meeting of the warring parties and an emergency SADC Summit on the DRC in Pretoria on 23 August.

Recognising that this move was calculated to challenge Zimbabwe's regional leadership on the DRC issue, Mugabe declined to attend the Summit. His spokesman declared that 'SADC met and took a decision through its defence ministers last week in Harare and that decision is being implemented so we cannot go back on that decision.'[105] Another Zimbabwean official insisted: 'SADC has already spoken through the ministers of defence and has already taken a position now under implementation. What then is the purpose of this meeting?'[106] Mugabe's allies, DRC President Kabila and Angola's President Dos Santos, also declined to attend the Summit. Nevertheless the Summit proceeded. Its final communiqué called for a ceasefire in the DRC and the initiation of peace talks, and mandated Mandela to cooperate with the Secretary-General of the OAU to create 'the mechanisms for the implementation of this decision'.[107] The Summit thus initiated a regional mediation effort, led by South Africa, that was to persist in parallel with Operation Sovereign Legitimacy for the next several years. South Africa and its allies initially claimed that this, rather than military intervention, was the true SADC initiative on the DRC. Mozambique's Prime Minister, for example, insisted that while SADC countries had responded 'in various ways' to Kabila's request for assistance, 'as an organisation, SADC is in favour of a negotiated settlement'.[108]

Ultimately, this rift within SADC was at least superficially mended. On 3 September, Mandela dropped his public opposition to Operation Sovereign Legitimacy, explaining that he had been misinformed about the nature of the conflict in the DRC but now understood that the intervention had countered a foreign invasion.[109] Zimbabwe and South Africa continued to lead separate initiatives on the DRC: Zimbabwe continued its military presence in the DRC and complemented it by diplomatic negotiations during the Victoria Falls II Summit of 7–8 September, from which South Africa was excluded. South Africa,

---

[105] 'Mugabe snubs Mandela's mediation efforts on Congo', *Xinhua News Agency*, 23 August 1998.

[106] 'Mugabe won't go to Mandela summit', *Deutsche Presse-Agentur*, 22 August 1998.

[107] John Dludlu, 'African leaders seek ceasefire in Congo', *Business Day (South Africa)*, 24 August 1998.

[108] 'Mocumbi speaks on Congolese conflict', *Pan-African News Agency*, 28 August 1998.

[109] Reuters, 'African leaders open door to Congo peace', *The Toronto Star*, 4 September 1998.

meanwhile, continued its quest for a purely diplomatic settlement. However, the two countries no longer publicly criticised each other's initiatives. On 14 September 1998, the SADC Summit affirmed both initiatives: 'The Summit welcomed initiatives by SADC and its Member States intended to assist in the restoration of peace, security and stability in DRC, in particular the Victoria Falls and Pretoria initiatives.'[110]

This sudden compromise had several reasons. South Africa and Zimbabwe recognised that their public row weakened SADC and could cause a permanent rift in the organisation. Both also realised that they were unable to isolate the other enough to credibly claim sole leadership of the regional DRC peace process. In addition, both sides came to recognise that the enormous problems in the DRC were beyond either country's control. Instead of achieving rapid victory, Zimbabwe found its military commitment escalating while South Africa made little progress in promoting the ceasefire called for at the Pretoria Summit. Most importantly, however, as the next chapter will discuss, South Africa was turning its own attention to an escalating crisis in Lesotho, which it hoped to address using SADC auspices. South Africa was willing to allow Zimbabwe to claim SADC auspices for its intervention in the DRC if Zimbabwe agreed not to question South Africa's use of SADC auspices in Lesotho.

Yet despite the comparatively rapid mending of the rift within SADC, South Africa's opposition to Operation Sovereign Legitimacy was costly to Zimbabwe. The West did not accept the intervention as a legitimate regional endeavour: the UN shied away from acknowledging it as a SADC operation and the European Union even threatened sanctions against the intervening states. Yet this outside criticism tended to rally the region around Zimbabwe. Zambia's Permanent Secretary of Foreign Affairs, for example, bristled at the EU threat: 'SADC does not require the approbation of countries from outside the region to intervene in a regional situation.'[111] The greater problem, for Zimbabwe, was that South Africa's objection to Operation Sovereign Legitimacy under-mined the image of regional leadership that Zimbabwe sought to project at the regional and continental level. The public row left no illusions about Zimbabwe's inability to rally the entire Southern African region behind its leadership. Operation Sovereign Legitimacy participants

---

[110] SADC, *Summit Communiqué*, Grand Bay, Mauritius, 13–14 September 1998.
[111] Lazarus Kapambwe, 'The Position of Zambia', in Baregu (ed.), *Crisis in the Democratic Republic of Congo*, p. 110.

continued to refer to their troops as SADC Allied Forces, but Southern Africans tended to treat this appellation with scepticism. A South African journalist called the term 'a fiction that has been difficult to sustain'.[112] A Botswana diplomat noted, 'we have Namibia and Zimbabwe in the DRC operating under the SADC name – but it is not a SADC force, it was never endorsed by SADC. The majority of SADC members wonder why Zimbabwe and Namibia are fighting in the DRC.'[113] A Zambian diplomat was more circumspect. Asked if Operation Sovereign Legitimacy was an SADC operation, he commented only: 'well, three SADC members are there'.[114]

The irony of the situation was that Zimbabwe did not legally need to open itself up to this criticism. From a legal point of view, Operation Sovereign Legitimacy could have been launched without SADC auspices as a collective defence operation. In this case, Zimbabwe would not have had to manoeuvre to seize the initiative within SADC and it would not have been open to charges of usurping SADC auspices. Instead, Zimbabwe chose to operate through SADC. It gambled that SADC's internal institutions would prove strong enough to force the region to coalesce behind its leadership on the DRC issue, but it could not have been oblivious to the risk it incurred. Zimbabwe was defying the sub-region's largest state at a time when its relations with South Africa were already strained. South African President Mandela had enough international and regional stature to publicly challenge Mugabe's bid for regional leadership. There was even a precedent for a dispute between Zimbabwe and South Africa straining SADC's official façade of unity: Mugabe and Mandela's clash over the issue of leadership of the SADC Organ during the 1997 SADC Summit in Blantyre was leaked to the press and only narrowly avoided turning into a public row. Zimbabwe must have realised that seizing leadership of SADC on the DRC issue might provoke South Africa into open dissent despite SADC's code of official unity and regional solidarity.

Nevertheless, Zimbabwe chose to launch Operation Sovereign Legitimacy within the SADC framework. It gained few material advantages from doing so. As argued above, SADC had no military or financial

---

[112] Iden Wetherell, 'Mugabe forms new defence pact', *Mail and Guardian (South Africa)*, 16–22 April 1999.

[113] Author's interview with O. Motswagae, Deputy Director (Multilateral and East Asia) Botswana Ministry of Foreign Affairs, Gaborone, 7 December 2000.

[114] Author's interview, remarks not for attribution.

burden-sharing mechanisms that affected the intervention and did not substantially further Zimbabwe's coalition-building efforts. Angola and Namibia both also preferred to operate under SADC auspices for legitimacy reasons. Angola, however, had a compelling security interest in intervening to prevent UNITA from establishing military bases on the Angolan/Congolese border. Of the three intervening states, it was most likely to intervene in the DRC without the SADC mandate. Namibia had no pressing security or political interests in the DRC and would probably not have participated in an intervention without SADC auspices. The material benefits of Namibia's participation in Operation Sovereign Legitimacy were limited, however. Its initial deployment of 200 troops increased gradually to 2,000 troops by January 1999 but was consistently dwarfed by Zimbabwean and Angolan troop contributions. Namibia's presence arguably increased Operation Sovereign Legitimacy's legitimacy by confirming the regional nature of the operation, but in material terms its contribution was marginal.

Zimbabwe itself would probably not have decided on open military deployment (as opposed to financial or covert military assistance to Kabila) without a SADC mandate, however. Such counterfactuals are notoriously hard to prove, but an unmandated intervention would simply not have served Zimbabwe's regional and continental ambitions. Operating through SADC produced only slight material benefits for Zimbabwe, but only SADC could generate the international legitimacy of Operation Sovereign Legitimacy that would enable Zimbabwe to reaffirm its regional and international leadership credentials. Zimbabwe knew that operating in this framework also made it vulnerable. Attempting to speak for a multilateral organisation is inherently risky, because other member states are not bound to follow the speaker's lead. Zimbabwe had no means of controlling the reactions of its fellow member states to its DRC initiative. In fact, it knew that South Africa might be provoked into open resistance by Zimbabwe's assertion of a regional leadership role with regard to the DRC. Nevertheless, Zimbabwe chose to operate through SADC – it decided that the legitimacy generated by this framework was worth the costs involved by operating through it. Despite the blow that the public dispute with South Africa delivered to Operation Sovereign Legitimacy, moreover, Zimbabwe never questioned the wisdom of this decision. As one Zimbabwean diplomat put it, an ideal regional security mechanism would have differed from the SADC framework only in the strength of regional unity it could muster: 'It would still have intervened, but with less acrimony. We would have intervened as a team, as a regional body, without the squabbles that surfaced afterwards.'[115]

Conclusion

Operation Sovereign Legitimacy provides substantial support for the proposition that states launch peace enforcement operations through international organisations in order to bolster the international legitimacy of their interventions. Zimbabwe's decision to launch the operation within the SADC framework was clearly not motivated by respect for international law. A SADC mandate could not legalise the intervention as a peace enforcement operation without UN Security Council authorisation and was not legally required for a collective self-defence mission. Moreover, Zimbabwe's evident willingness to disregard SADC's internal rules in launching Operation Sovereign Legitimacy does not suggest a deep-seated respect for international law. An explanation based on burden-sharing is equally unconvincing since despite the SADC framework intervening states shouldered the full military and financial costs of their deployments – which Zimbabwe clearly expected, given its efforts to recoup its costs directly from the DRC.

By contrast, Zimbabwe did expect the SADC framework to help address its substantial concerns about Operation Sovereign Legitimacy's regional and continental legitimacy. Zimbabwe hoped to use its leadership of the intervention to support its more general claims to regional and continental leadership. This effect depended entirely on the intervention being accepted as legitimate in Southern Africa and in Africa more widely. SADC was the ideal vehicle for achieving this, since the organisation's internal structures and its status in an international system shaped by regionalisation favoured regional and international coalescing behind Zimbabwe's leadership on the DRC issue. However, launching Operation Sovereign Legitimacy through SADC also presented significant costs, most notably the risk that other member states would reject the intervention allegedly carried out in their name. Zimbabwe took this risk even though it did not have to: if Operation Sovereign Legitimacy had been presented as a collective self-defence mission the SADC framework could legally have been dispensed with. However, Zimbabwe aimed to present the intervention as evidence of its capacity to lead Southern Africa on regional peace and security issues – and only SADC had the capacity to establish the intervention as a legitimate

[115] Author's interview with Lieutenant-Colonel A. W. Tapfumaneyi, 29 November 2000.

regional peace enforcement operation in the eyes of Southern Africa and the continent as a whole.

Thus the fact that Zimbabwe chose to operate in the SADC framework demonstrates the value that it placed on the international legitimacy that SADC auspices could confer on Operation Sovereign Legitimacy. Yet SADC failed to present a united front in the crucial early phases of the operation, which undermined its capacity to legitimise the intervention. For SADC to reach its full potential in generating inter-national legitimacy for regional peace enforcement operations, all of its member states – especially the most influential ones, South Africa and Zimbabwe – had to cooperate. This cooperation was only achieved when South Africa discovered its own need to use SADC to legitimise an intervention. Operation Sovereign Legitimacy represented SADC's troubled infancy as a gatekeeper to international legitimacy for regional peace enforcement operations. South Africa's Operation Boleas in Lesotho, which is examined in the next chapter, marked its coming of age.

5

Peace enforcement through sub-regional organisations: the Southern African Development Community and Operation Boleas in Lesotho

Barely one month after Zimbabwe, Angola, and Namibia claimed SADC auspices for their controversial intervention in the Democratic Republic of Congo, South Africa and Botswana launched a peace enforcement operation into Lesotho. The intervention, codenamed Operation Boleas, was led by South Africa and executed by only two SADC members. However, South Africa and Botswana insisted that they were acting on behalf of SADC. This chapter analyses why South Africa chose to launch Operation Boleas within the SADC framework. It begins by briefly sketching the historical background of the intervention and then argues that neither respect for international law nor a desire for burden-sharing can explain South Africa's choice of the SADC framework. By contrast, the legitimacy-centred theory of the role of international organisations in peace enforcement operations developed in chapter 2 finds considerable support. South Africa had substantial concerns about Operation Boleas's international legitimacy, which operating within the SADC framework helped address. The importance South Africa attached to this legitimacy can be gauged by the considerable costs it incurred to secure the SADC mandate.

Operation Boleas marks SADC's coming of age in the domain of regional peace and security. South Africa and Botswana had hitherto staunchly and publicly sought to deny SADC auspices to the Zimbabwe-led intervention in the DRC. Now, however, they too wished to benefit from the international legitimacy those auspices could bestow on an intervention and recognised that SADC's legitimising potential depended on its presenting a united front to the rest of the international community. This set the stage for a compromise: South Africa stopped its vocal criticism of Operation Sovereign Legitimacy and Zimbabwe did not publicly question South Africa's arrogation of SADC auspices for

Operation Boleas. With SADC's official unity restored, the organisation reached its full potential as a generator of international legitimacy for its members' deployments of military force in the name of regional peace and security.

Operation Boleas: historical background

In stark contrast to the vast DRC, Lesotho is a tiny sovereign mountain kingdom located entirely within the Republic of South Africa. It gained its independence from Great Britain as a constitutional monarchy in 1966 and since then its politics have been marked by intense power struggles involving rival political parties, the king, and the Royal Lesotho Defence Force (RLDF). Lesotho's founding elections were won by the conservative Basotho National Party (BNP), but the populist Basotholand Congress Party (BCP) won the next elections in 1970. BNP Prime Minister Leabua Jonathan promptly annulled the results and established an autocratic regime that was overthrown by a military coup backed by King Moshoeshoe II in 1986. However, the alliance between the monarchy and the military soon foundered on the king's opposition to the new regime's policy of rapprochement with apartheid South Africa. Moshoeshoe was exiled in 1990 and replaced by his son Letsie III, who never forgave his father's dethronement. Lacking royal support, the military regime was overthrown in 1991 and democratic national elections were held in 1993.

The BCP won a landslide victory in these elections, and the first-past-the-post electoral system rewarded it with all sixty-five National Assembly seats. Feeling cheated, the BNP and its military allies urged King Letsie to intervene. In August 1994, offended by the BCP's refusal to reinstate his father, Letsie dismissed Parliament, suspended the constitution, and proclaimed an interim government. However, Presidents Masire of Botswana, Mugabe of Zimbabwe, and Mandela of South Africa intervened and brokered an agreement by which the BCP government was reinstated and Moshoeshoe II resumed his throne. Botswana, Zimbabwe, and South Africa were designated as guarantors of this arrangement.

In 1997, however, the ruling BCP was torn apart by a leadership struggle that resulted in ageing Prime Minister Ntsu Mokhehle and forty of the sixty-five BCP Members of Parliament leaving the party to form the Lesotho Congress for Democracy (LCD). With forty MPs, the LCD became the new ruling party. The twenty-five remaining BCP MPs were left in opposition. By 1998, therefore, both the BNP and the BCP felt that they had been cheated out of power. Both hoped to improve their positions in the 1998 parliamentary elections, and were bitterly disappointed when the LCD gained seventy-nine of the eighty available seats.[1] Adding insult to injury, after this victory Mokhehle retired in favour of his preferred successor, Pakalitha Mosisili.

Both opposition parties contested the results, alleging electoral fraud. When Lesotho's courts rejected their petitions, they organised a series of demonstrations. These rapidly centred around the royal palace, which once again housed King Letsie III, since Moshoeshoe II had died in a car accident in 1996. Mindful of his 1994 experience, Letsie did not accede to the opposition parties' request that he dissolve Parliament, but he also refused to expel the protesters from the palace grounds. With this tacit royal support, demonstrations continued through August and the number of protesters on palace grounds swelled into the hundreds.

Alarmed by these developments, South Africa proposed an international investigation of the election, but the resultant Langa Commission failed to appease tensions. Publication of the Commission's report was repeatedly postponed, leading to suspicions that its findings were being doctored. When the report was finally released on 17 September 1998, its conclusions were disappointing: the Commission declared that due to the disarray in which it found the voting materials, it was 'unable to draw the conclusion ... either that the elections were rigged or that fraud is excluded'.[2] This result pleased nobody. It also came too late to forestall a deterioration in the crisis, because on 11 September a mutiny in the RLDF deprived Mosisili's government of a crucial resource for resisting the continuing protests. RLDF soldiers now refused to intervene against the street demonstrations or to stop armed opposition supporters from enforcing a stay-away by civil servants. The government was paralysed.

On 16 September, Mosisili wrote to the presidents of South Africa, Zimbabwe, Botswana, and Mozambique. Claiming that 'we have a coup on our hands', he submitted 'a formal and urgent request for Your Excellencies, in accordance with SADC agreements, to put together

---

[1] The single opposition seat was won by the BNP. Roger Southall and Roddy Fox, 'Lesotho's General Election of 1998: Rigged or De Rigeur?' *Journal of Modern African Studies*, 37:4 (December 1999), p. 679.

[2] Langa Commission, 'Report of the Commission of Enquiry into the Conduct and Results of the Lesotho General Elections held in May 1998', Article 7.2. Online at www.nul. ls/~mnzmphaka/LangaReport.htm, accessed in January 2002, site no longer accessible.

quickly a strong military intervention to help Lesotho return to normalcy'.[3] He reiterated this plea in a direct letter to South Africa's Acting President Buthelezi on 19 September.[4] Three days later, 600 members of the South African National Defence Force (SANDF) entered Lesotho. They formed the bulk of the Combined Task Force (CTF) for Operation Boleas, a joint military operation by South Africa and Botswana dispatched under SADC auspices 'to prevent any further anarchy and to create a stable environment for the restoration of law and order' in Lesotho.[5]

Operation Boleas was supposed to be a brief intervention with immediate salutary effect. However, the CTF encountered unanticipated resistance by the RLDF and was unable to immediately secure Lesotho's capital, Maseru, where riots sparked by the intervention gave rise to widespread looting and burning. Within 24 hours, the SANDF suffered nine fatalities, fifty-eight RLDF soldiers were killed, there were 'several civilian casualties and hospitals ... [were] treating dozens of people with bullet injuries'.[6] The violence did not subside until early October, when the CTF increased its presence to 3,850 troops and Lesotho's rival political parties grappled towards a peace agreement. CTF forces were significantly reduced by December, and finally withdrew completely on 15 May 1999. What was supposed to be a brief, low-cost intervention had turned into an extended, expensive, and controversial exercise.

---

[3] Letter by Lesotho Prime Minister Pakalitha Mosisili to the presidents of South Africa, Zimbabwe, Botswana, and Mozambique, sent 16 September 1998, read to the South African Parliament by Acting President Mangosuthu Buthelezi on 22 September 1998. South African Hansard, 'Proceedings of the National Assembly, Tuesday 22 September 1998', columns 6763–4.

[4] 'Letter by Lesotho Prime Minister Pakalitha Mosisili to Mangosuthu Buthelezi, Acting President of South Africa, 19 September 1998', read to the South African Parliament by Mangosuthu Buthelezi on 22 September 1998. South African Hansard, 22 September 1998, column 6765.

[5] SANDF, 'Southern African Development Community Combined Task Force Boleas – Operation Boleas and Campaign Charon as presented to the Joint Standing Committee of [the South African] Parliament on Defence and the Portfolio Committee on Foreign Affairs on 2 November 1998', online at www.mil.za/CSANDF/CJOps/Operations/General/Boleas/boleas.htm. Accessed in January 2002, document no longer available.

[6] 'Lesotho fighting intensifies', BBC, 22 September 1998; 'South African Troops Cross Border', *Newsday*, 23 September 1998; Reuters, 'Lawless Lesotho capital "under siege", Mandela praises deputy's decision to send troops to battle "virtual coup" by Maseru mutineers', *The Toronto Star*, 24 September 1998.

Operation Boleas and international law

Why did South Africa decide to launch Operation Boleas under SADC auspices? Since SADC auspices could not remedy doubts about Operation Boleas's legality, respect for international law does not provide a satisfactory explanation for this decision.

The legal basis for Operation Boleas was subject to dispute. The intervention's proponents argued that it did not violate any international laws because it occurred at the express request of Lesotho's legal government. There are two problems with this argument, however. First, although Mosisili was Lesotho's legal head of government, Article 92 of Lesotho's constitution gave King Letsie, as head of state, 'the right to be consulted by the Prime Minister ... on all matters relating to the Government of Lesotho' and to be kept 'fully informed' by the Prime Minister regarding 'the general conduct of the Government of Lesotho'. However, Mosisili believed Letsie to be sympathetic to the opposition parties, and therefore did not consult him before requesting the intervention.[7] This omission arguably made Mosisili's request illegal.

Second, under international law the notion of consent is complicated in situations where a government faces a significant internal threat. As David Wippman points out, 'in cases of civil conflict, questions about the government's authority to speak for the state may arise either because the government is undemocratic and lacks the support of the population as a whole or because the government is only partially representative in character and lacks the support of a significant section of the population'.[8] In such cases, Wippman argues, true consent to an intervention requires the agreement of all the political factions within the state, not merely the accord of the government: 'It appears that states are increasingly coming to accept that, in some internal conflicts, the legal capacity to express the will of the state may again be divided (or shared) between competing subnational communities ... In many such cases, only the collective will of the various warring factions can credibly be treated as the will of the state.'[9] The fact that popular demonstrations had incapacitated Mosisili's government suggests that he could not 'speak for the state' in requesting foreign intervention. Lesotho's

---

[7] SAPA, 'Prime Minister says King Letsie "part of the problem" ', BBC, 24 September 1998.

[8] David Wippman, 'Treaty-Based Intervention: Who Can Say No?' *University of Chicago Law Review*, 62:2 (Spring 1995), p. 624.

[9] Ibid., p. 627.

opposition parties firmly opposed any intervention, insisting that their demonstrations were 'justifiable civil disobedience' in the wake of controversial elections.[10]

Advocates of Operation Boleas countered that the operation sought only to establish the conditions for a negotiated settlement of the crisis, not to impose any particular outcome. Acting South African President Buthelezi insisted: 'Lesotho's problems are the sovereign right of the people of Lesotho to resolve in a manner that they choose ... It is important, however, that ... negotiations take place in an appropriate environment, an environment underpinned by stability ... In the opinion of SADC it was, regrettably, necessary to assist ... in order to create that situation.'[11] According to this argument, Operation Boleas' primary objective was to prevent a military coup that might forestall efforts to negotiate a settlement between Mosisili and the opposition parties.[12] Since this argument did not persuade Lesotho's opposition parties, however, the problem of consent remained. Moreover, there was no threatened coup in Lesotho in September 1998. There was a mutiny, and the mutineers' refusal to enforce order allowed demonstrators to paralyse the government. South African President Mandela called this a 'virtual coup',[13] and Mosisili insisted that 'the happenings in the army and [the protests] at the palace grounds were sides of the same coin, with the same intent of overthrowing the elected government by force'.[14] However, the military did not seize power for itself or for the opposition parties. There was no coup, and no indication that the military was about to move towards a more direct use of force against the government.

Moreover, there is no international law authorising military intervention to prevent coups. Buthelezi insisted that 'SADC has made it clear ... that coups d'état in the region cannot be tolerated by member states.'[15] Indeed, the SADC Organ was charged with protecting the region 'against instability arising from the break-down of law and

---

[10] Wyndham Hartley, 'Incursion Tarnishes SA's Peacemaker Image' *Business Day* (South Africa) 25 September 1998.

[11] South African Hansard, 22 September 1998, columns 6767–8.

[12] Wyndham Hartley, '11 days that led to war', *Sunday Times* (South Africa), 27 September 1998.

[13] Reuters, 'Lawless Lesotho capital "under siege"', *The Toronto Star*, 24 September 1998.

[14] Pakalitha Mosisili, 'Statement by the Right Honourable Prime Minister, Mr Pakalitha Mosisili, to the Nation and the World, 24 September, 1998', online at www.lesotho. gov.ls/speeches/sppm24sep98.htm.

[15] South African Hansard, 22 September 1998, column 6767.

order',[16] and Article 5 of the Draft Protocol on Politics, Defence, and Security sought to commit SADC states 'to defend one another in case of undemocratic attempts at takeover'.[17] However, by 1998 both the draft protocol and the Organ had fallen victim to the dispute over the Organ's leadership described in the previous chapter and were therefore inoperative. Some defenders of Operation Boleas (including Mandela[18]) fell back on the Organisation of African Unity's May 1997 condemnation of unconstitutional changes of government. Although this declaration endorsed military intervention in Sierra Leone, however, it did not formulate a general policy authorising military interventions to reverse coups.[19] In fact, the OAU did not announce a general policy regarding unconstitutional changes of government until July 1999 – and even then it only banned unconstitutional governments from attending OAU summits.[20] In sum, 'no resolution ha[d] been adopted by either the OAU or SADC condemning coups or unconstitutional changes of government in principle. Nor ha[d] any resolution been adopted that authorize[d] member states of the OAU or SADC to intervene if such military coups or unconstitutional changes of government take place, or to prevent them from taking place.'[21] Therefore the focus on preventing a coup did not resolve the doubts about the international legality of Operation Boleas.

Crucially, moreover, SADC auspices could not remedy these doubts. As a response to a legal request for assistance, Operation Boleas would not have required a SADC mandate. As a South African official put it, 'those parts of international law that apply to unsolicited military interventions ... do not apply when a country voluntarily requests military assistance from another.'[22] As a peace enforcement operation,

[16] SADC, *Summit Communiqué*, Gaborone, Botswana, 28 June 1996.
[17] SANDF, 'The SADC Intervention in Lesotho: A Military Perspective', online at www.mil.za/CSANDF/CJOps/Operations/General/Boleas/military_perspective.htm, p. 3. Accessed in January 2002, document no longer available.
[18] SAPA, 'Mandela comments on Lesotho intervention' BBC, 29 September 1998.
[19] OAU Secretary-General, 'Report of the Secretary-General on the Implementation of the Algiers Decisions of the Assembly of [OAU] Heads of State and Government and the Council of Ministers on Unconstitutional Changes of Government', 4–8 July 2000, Article 13.
[20] OAU Assembly of Heads of State and Government, Decisions AHG/Dec.141(XXXV) and AHG/Dec.142(XXXV), Algiers, Algeria, 12–14 July 1999.
[21] Cedric de Coning, 'Conditions for Intervention: DRC & Lesotho', *Conflict Trends*, No.1 (1998).
[22] Willie Hofmeyr, 'Straw men come under fire in Lesotho debate', *Business Day (South Africa)* 14 December 1998.

it was illegal despite SADC auspices, since Article 53 of the UN Charter requires Security Council authorisation for such interventions. In this case, however, the Security Council was not even informed that an intervention was about to take place.

An argument could be made that customary international law was slowly evolving away from the UN Charter insistence on Security Council author-isation for peace enforcement operations. Ruth Wedgwood, for example, notes the precedents set by 1998 in which regional organisations were granted post hoc UN approval for interventions launched without a Security Council mandate.[23] Since Article 5.c of the SADC Treaty estab-lishes the organisation's responsibility to 'promote and defend peace and security' in the region, moreover, it is the most appropriate regional frame-work for conducting peace enforcement operations in Southern Africa. South Africa implicitly affirmed its belief that a SADC mandate did improve the legality of Operation Boleas by insisting: 'The South African Government can . . . at no stage act unilaterally and neither can its military forces do so. All its actions in neighbouring states must have the blessing of the SADC as the legitimate Southern African mandating authority.'[24]

However, South Africa eliminated the possibility of the SADC frame-work improving Operation Boleas's legality by defying internal SADC rules when launching the operation. South Africa launched the inter-vention without official SADC authorisation. The SADC Summit, meet-ing on 13–14 September 1998, welcomed South Africa's mediation efforts and 'expressed concern at the civil disturbances and loss of life following recent elections in Lesotho', but made no mention of a military response.[25] The SADC Organ, meanwhile, was paralysed since 1997 and could not mandate an intervention. To counter this objec-tion defenders of Operation Boleas argued that SADC recognition of the 1994 Memorandum of Understanding that made South Africa, Zimbabwe, and Botswana guarantors of Lesotho's democracy made a separate SADC authorisation for Operation Boleas unnecessary. Yet the SADC Summit never formally endorsed the Memorandum or ratified the extended troika on Lesotho (South Africa, Zimbabwe, Botswana, and Mozambique) as an official SADC institution. Nor was the extended

---

[23] Ruth Wedgwood, 'NATO's Campaign in Yugoslavia' *American Journal of International Law*, 93:4 (October 1999), p. 831.
[24] SANDF, 'The SADC Intervention in Lesotho', Introduction.
[25] SADC, *Summit Communiqué*, Grand Bay, Mauritius, 13–14 September 1998.

troika an appropriate substitute for a Summit meeting since Article 18 of the SADC Treaty sets a quorum of two-thirds of SADC member states for SADC meetings.[26]

Furthermore, even the extended troika was not fully implicated in the decision to launch Operation Boleas. Mozambique and Zimbabwe were not present when Botswana and South Africa agreed to instruct their militaries 'to plan military intervention in Lesotho under the auspices of SADC' on 15 September – just one day after the SADC Summit, whose communiqué had not mentioned intervention.[27] On 16 September, Mosisili's first request for military assistance was sent to all four extended troika members. In response, Acting South African President Buthelezi recalled contacting President Mandela and Vice-President Mbeki, who were both abroad, and consulting with the South African Ministries of Defence and Foreign Affairs.[28] He made no mention of contacting any of his SADC counterparts. Buthelezi then issued presidential Minute 81/172188 authorising an SANDF deployment 'for the purposes of assisting the lawful government of the Kingdom of Lesotho to restore stability to that Kingdom'.[29] By the end of the day, the SANDF was positioned to move into Lesotho.

South Africa postponed its deployment to accommodate an emergency troika meditation effort, but it also proceeded to sign a Status of Forces agreement with Lesotho that identified only South Africa as the 'Sending Party', did not mention SADC, and was not signed by any other SADC member.[30] Mosisili's second request for military assistance on 19 September was addressed to Buthelezi alone.[31] Only then did Buthelezi attempt to consult the other leaders of the extended troika – with only partial success, since he failed to reach the presidents of Zimbabwe and

[26] Jakkie Cilliers, 'Building Security in Southern Africa', *ISS Monograph No.43* (November 1999), section 5.

[27] SANDF, 'SADC Combined Task Force Boleas'.

[28] South African Hansard, 22 September 1998, column 6764.

[29] President's Minute 81/172188 (Z 19E), signed on 16 September 1998 by South Africa's Acting President Mangosuthu Buthelezi and Minister of Defence Joe Modise. Accessed online at www.nul.ls/~mnzmphaka/Invasion.htm in January 2002, site no longer available.

[30] 'Agreement between the Government of the Republic of South Africa and the Kingdom of Lesotho concerning the Status of Armed Forces in the Kingdom of Lesotho Providing Military Assistance', signed by Mangosuthu Buthelezi and Pakalitha Mosisili on 17 September 1998. Accessed online at www.nul.ls/~mnzmphaka/Invasion.htm in January 2002, site no longer available.

[31] 'Letter by Lesotho Prime Minister Pakalitha Mosisili to Mangosuthu Buthelezi', 19 September 1998.

Mozambique.[32] He nevertheless ordered the SANDF to deploy to Lesotho, and Operation Boleas was launched the next morning. The Botswana Defence Force joined the SANDF in Lesotho that evening. Mozambique and Zimbabwe did not participate.

Thus from the beginning of the planning process to the actual deployment of troops, Operation Boleas was a South African enterprise conducted with assistance from Botswana. There was no full consultation with the extended troika, much less with SADC as a whole. Thus SADC's internal rules for launching peace enforcement operations were violated, making it impossible for South Africa and Botswana to claim even the limited legal protection for Operation Boleas that operating within the SADC framework might otherwise have offered. This behaviour does not suggest that respect for international law was a primary concern for either state.

Burden-sharing in Operation Boleas

Burden-sharing considerations also fail to account for South Africa's decision to launch Operation Boleas within the SADC framework. As discussed in the previous chapter, SADC has no mechanisms for promoting financial or military burden-sharing for peace enforcement operations. SADC states launching such interventions must depend on their own resources. Any illusions South Africa might have had about this fact would have been roundly dispelled by the example of Operation Sovereign Legitimacy in the DRC, just weeks prior to the launching of Operation Boleas. Not only were the participants in that operation unable to elicit military or financial aid from their fellow SADC states, but South Africa and other opponents of the operation explicitly argued that their membership in SADC did not bind them to contribute to the intervention.

In the event, there was even less burden-sharing for Operation Boleas than there had been for Operation Sovereign Legitimacy. SADC as an organisation had few resources to contribute: it owned no military assets and in 1998 had no political or military expertise in peace operations. Its average annual budget in the late 1990s was US$16 million, while South

---

[32] South African Hansard, 22 September 1998, column 6765. At a troika delegation meeting on 20 September, Zimbabwe, Botswana, and Mozambique were represented only by their High Commissioners to South Africa and Lesotho (Will Hartley, '11 days that led to war'). The meeting had no authority to approve a military intervention.

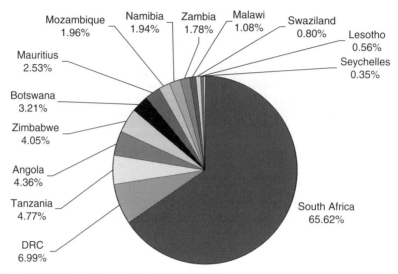

Figure 5.1: National shares of total SADC GDP, 1998

Africa spent over US$4 million in the first ten days of Operation Boleas alone.[33] SADC also failed to attract funding or military assistance for the intervention from outside the Southern African region. As for burden-sharing among SADC members, only two SADC states participated in Operation Boleas. Of course, one of these two states, South Africa, was by far the region's largest military and economic power, and could therefore have been expected to assume the lion's share of any SADC peace operation. Figure 5.1 shows the relative sizes of the region's economies by indicating each country's share of the total GDP generated by all SADC states.[34]

Even taking these wealth differentials into account, however, South Africa assumed a disproportionate share of the financial and military burden for Operation Boleas. South Africa sent, equipped, and paid for an initial 600 troops to launch Operation Boleas, while Botswana pro-vided 200 troops. After the first clashes in Lesotho, both countries sent reinforcements. By October 1998, there were 3,500 SANDF troops and

[33] Theo Neethling, 'Conditions for Successful Entry and Exit: An Assessment of SADC Allied Operations in Lesotho', *ISS Monograph No.44: Boundaries of Peace Support Operations* (February 2000).

[34] Data from SADC, *SADC Statistics: Facts and Figures 1999* (Gaborone: SADC, 1999).

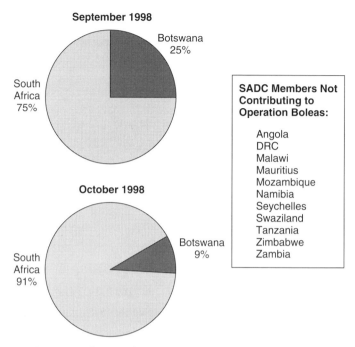

Figure 5.2: Troop contributions for Operation Boleas

350 BDF troops in Lesotho.[35] This distribution of effort within SADC is captured in figure 5.2.

South Africa and Botswana were therefore contributing more to Operation Boleas than would be warranted in a burden-sharing arrangement based on SADC members' relative economic size. The divergences from such a burden-sharing arrangement are captured in figure 5.3. This figure illustrates how much more or less each SADC state contributed to Operation Boleas than its relative economic weight in the region would predict. A score of 0 means that a state shouldered the same proportion of the burden of Operation Boleas as it accounted for in the total GDP of the SADC region in 1998. A negative (positive) score indicates that the country was shouldering a smaller (larger) proportion of the burden than warranted by its economic size.

This figure illustrates a striking disproportion of effort for Operation Boleas in the Southern African region. South Africa and Botswana

---

[35] Neethling, 'Assessment of SADC Allied Operations in Lesotho'.

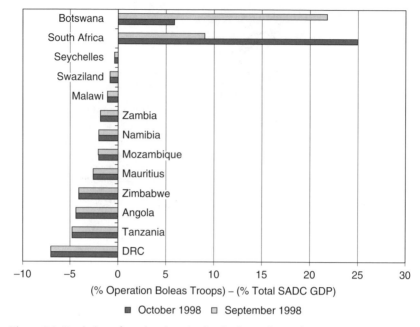

Figure 5.3: Deviations from burden-sharing in Operation Boleas

shouldered a greater share of the personnel burden of intervention than their relative economic size would warrant, while other SADC members failed to contribute troops or resources. Nevertheless, figure 5.3 does not capture the full extent to which the financial and military burden of intervention fell on South Africa. In addition to supplying troops, South Africa provided all of Operation Boleas's air support as well as administrative and logistical support for the intervention. The total cost was considerable: South Africa estimated that it had spent SAR36 million (US$6.5 million) by February 1999, while by March new Defence Minister Patrick Lekota put the costs to the SANDF alone at SAR57 million (US$10.3 million).[36]

South Africa made no serious attempt to spread this cost more evenly among other SADC states. Like Zimbabwe in the DRC, however, it did seek to shift part of the burden to the host state of the intervention,

---

[36] Ibid., p. 5; 'SA to foot the bill for Lesotho intervention', *Mail and Guardian* (South Africa), 12 March 2000.

Lesotho. Articles 13.1 and 13.2 of South Africa's status of forces agreement with Lesotho insist:

> the Receiving Party shall be liable to the Sending Party for all real expenses and costs incurred by the Sending Party, with regard to the provision of military assistance to the Receiving Party . . . The Receiving Party shall be liable to the Sending Party for any losses or damages suffered by the Sending Party, resulting from the provision of the military assistance.

Some US$1.5 million were reportedly transferred from Lesotho to South Africa in December 1999 – much to the fury of Lesotho government critics – but faced with the destruction of its capital and a − 3.5 per cent annual growth rate for 1998, Lesotho was incapable of fully honouring its commitment.[37] By March 2000, South African Defence Minister Lekota abandoned his predecessor's insistence that Lesotho would pay for Operation Boleas, and reverted to the formula of 'each [troop-contributing] country pays its own costs'.[38]

Thus virtually the entire cost of Operation Boleas fell on South Africa and, to a lesser extent, on Botswana. SADC did not prove an effective facilitator of military or financial burden-sharing for Operation Boleas. South Africa must have expected this, given SADC's dearth of burden-sharing mechanisms for peace operations and its inability to generate burden-sharing for Operation Sovereign Legitimacy. South Africa's decision to launch Operation Boleas under SADC auspices thus cannot be attributed to any expectations that the organisation would facilitate burden-sharing for the intervention.

South Africa's legitimacy concerns during Operation Boleas

Chapter 2 suggested that international legitimacy concerns provide a central explanation for states' decisions to launch peace enforcement operations within the framework of an international organisation. This theory finds considerable support in the case of Operation Boleas. This section describes the South African government's legitimacy concerns for the intervention and identifies its primary legitimacy audience.

---

[37] The transfer was reported in Africa News Network, 'Armed Intervention into Lesotho: "Not SADC, But South Africa"', *Africa News Service* 8 January 1999. Lesotho's growth rate from SADC, *SADC Statistics: Facts and Figures 1999*, p. 6.

[38] 'SA to foot the bill for Lesotho intervention', *Mail and Guardian* (South Africa), 12 March 2000.

South Africa's legitimacy concerns

As the lead state in Operation Boleas, South Africa was in a delicate position. Like most states launching peace enforcement operations, it was vulnerable to charges that it was cynically pursuing its national self-interest under the cover of international altruism. Lesotho's mountains house the Lesotho Highlands Water Project, whose primary purpose is to create a reliable water supply for the major South African cities of Johannesburg and Pretoria. South Africa is responsible for 95 per cent of the total project cost, estimated at US$2.3 billion.[39] By September 1998, phase 1A, the construction of the Katse dam, had just been completed at a cost of US$1.4 billion and South Africa had committed itself to generating another US$825 million for phase 1B.[40] South Africa thus had considerable financial interests in Lesotho, which testified to commensurate resource interests. As a Western diplomat put it, 'South Africa could not allow them to cut off the water – Johannesburg would fall apart – and they had put in investments. If Lesotho had resisted, I think they would have had to make it South Africa's tenth province.'[41] Indeed, despite its remoteness from the civil strife unfolding mainly in Lesotho's capital city, the Highlands Water Project was one of the first areas to which the SANDF deployed and saw some of the heaviest fighting of the intervention. For the operation's critics, this confirmed that South Africa was more concerned with its water supply than with Lesotho's democracy.

Just four years after the demise of apartheid, South Africa felt particularly vulnerable to charges of aggression. Apartheid South Africa had launched several hostile military interventions to destabilise anti-apartheid governments in neighbouring states. Its targets included Lesotho, most notoriously in a 1982 raid on ANC safe houses in Maseru during which both South African refugees and dozens of unarmed Lesotho nationals were killed. The new democratic South African government was anxious to distance itself from this past, transcend South Africa's international

---

[39] Figures from the website of TCTA, the construction company working on the project. Online at http://www.metsi.com/projects/lhwp_cos.htm. Accessed 27 October 2003, website now moved to http://www.tcta.co.za/.

[40] TCTA website at http://www.metsi.com/projects/lhwp_cos.htm, accessed 27 October 2003, now moved to www.tcta.co.za; 'World Bank Supports Next Phase of Lesotho Highlands Project With US$45 M Loan', *Water Power and Dam Construction*, 31 July 1998.

[41] Author's interview, remarks not for attribution.

pariah status, and become 'a respected "world citizen"'.[42] Its foreign policy discourse thus stressed peaceful cooperation and equal partnership. President Mandela pledged: 'We have entered this eminent African organisation and rejoined the African community of nations inspired by the desire to join hands with all the countries of our continent as equal partners. It will never again happen that our country should seek to dominate another through force of arms, economic might or subversion.'[43] South Africa especially sought to assuage its immediate neighbours' fears, promising that despite its economic and military power, the 'new' South Africa would not be overbearing, aggressive, or expansionist. Mandela insisted that 'it is [South Africa's] resolve to contribute towards the development of Southern Africa as an equal partner'.[44]

Military intervention in tiny, vulnerable Lesotho stirred up memories of apartheid abuses and imperilled South Africa's efforts to recast itself as a moderate, peaceful team player in regional and international politics. The following reaction from a conference of regional officials and scholars is evidence of the extent of the potential damage:

> The entry of South African forces in Lesotho . . . is a 1986 Apartheid South Africa-style intervention. This reflects the continuing influence of the old guard in the South African military . . . In fundamental terms, South Africa's foreign policy has not changed. South Africa still considers itself inferior to the British but superior to the rest of the region.[45]

The situation was further complicated by the fact that just weeks before Operation Boleas, South Africa had declared that it preferred negotiation to intervention as a response to crises in Southern Africa. As described in the previous chapter, South Africa led the group of SADC states that opposed the Zimbabwe-led military intervention into the DRC. In keeping with the pacific image it wished to project, South

---

[42] South African Department of Foreign Affairs, 'South African Foreign Policy – Discussion Document', South African Government Green Paper, June 1996, Article 3.4. Online at www.polity.org.za/html/govdocs/discuss/foreign.html.

[43] Nelson Mandela, 'Statement of the President of the Republic of South Africa, Nelson Mandela, at the OAU Meeting of Heads of State and Government', Tunis, Tunisia, 13–15 June 1994. Online at www.anc.org.za/ancdocs/history/mandela/1994/sp940613.html.

[44] Nelson Mandela, 'Address at the State Banquet for President Mugabe of Zimbabwe, 16 August 1994'. Online at www.anc.org.za/ancdocs/history/mandela/1994/sp940816.html.

[45] 'Summary of the Discussion on the Regional Response held at the SARIPS Conference on the Crisis in the DRC', Mwesiga Baregu (ed.), *Crisis in the Democratic Republic of Congo* (Harare: SAPES, 1999), pp. 132–3.

Africa had called for peaceful negotiations among the combatants to resolve the crisis and castigated Zimbabwe for excessive militarism in its approach to the DRC. Now the greatest critic of military intervention in the Congo wanted to launch its own intervention into Lesotho.

Despite these challenges, however, Operation Boleas also represented an opportunity. Post-apartheid South Africa felt the need to stake out a positive leadership role for itself in regional and international politics. In part, this reflected an awareness of high international expectations. As (then) Deputy President Thabo Mbeki put it:

> the strength and persistence of the international focus on South Africa puts the South African Government of National Unity under pressure to contribute positively and constructively to the global community. The Southern African region [also] expects a positive contribution from South Africa in terms of their development ... There are also expectations from Africa that South Africa should make a significant contribution towards peace and development on the continent.[46]

South African engagement in peace operations was seen as one way to meet these expectations. In 1996, South Africa pledged that 'as a fully fledged member of the international community, South Africa will fulfil its responsibility to participate in international peace support operations.'[47] In 1998 it reiterated: 'Since the advent of democracy in 1994, domestic and international expectations have grown steadily regarding a new South African role as a responsible and respected member of the international community. These expectations have included a hope that South Africa will play a leading role in international peace missions.'[48] Operation Boleas provided a concrete opportunity to live up to these expectations.

In addition, Operation Boleas allowed South Africa to flex its regional muscles. South Africa sought a role within Southern Africa that was commensurate with its economic, political, and military weight. A 1996 Foreign Affairs discussion document asserted: 'South Africa has a

---

[46] South African Department of Foreign Affairs, 'South African Foreign Policy', section 3.4. The Green Paper also notes that the 'honeymoon' period of international support and admiration for post-apartheid South Africa would not last forever, and that 'many expectations about South Africa's international role have been created'.

[47] Republic of South Africa, *Defence in a Democracy: White Paper on National Defence for the Republic of South Africa*, May 1996, online at www.polity.org.za/html/govdocs/white_papers/defencewp.html, chapter 5, Article 19.

[48] Republic of South Africa, *White Paper on South African Participation in International Peace Missions*, 21 October 1998, online at www.polity.org.za/html/govdocs/white_papers/peacekeeping.html, Executive Summary.

leadership role to play in the SADC'.[49] However, as noted in the previous chapter, South Africa's regional leadership credentials were contested. It was often accused by its neighbours of being both too
aggressive in the region and too disengaged from it – a charge often
summed up in remarks that South Africa remained 'too white'. Angola,
Zimbabwe, and Namibia formed a loose coalition against South Africa
within SADC, which South Africa sought to balance in part by massively
increasing its defence expenditure.[50] Nevertheless, when Angola,
Namibia, and Zimbabwe launched their DRC intervention, projecting
military power and portraying themselves as the only SADC countries
willing to intervene to save a fellow member state, South Africa appeared
once again in danger of being marginalised in regional politics. Lesotho
provided an opportunity for South Africa to demonstrate that it, too,
had the will and the means to respond militarily to a regional security
issue. The leadership struggle in the region thus provided an important
context for Operation Boleas. 'While Zimbabwe's intervention in
Kinshasa was viewed among others as an attempt to challenge
Pretoria's perceived regional hegemony, Lesotho could be South
Africa's response in a regional display of force.'[51]

Thus the challenge for South Africa was to project itself as a force for
regional peace and stability by intervening in Lesotho without stirring
up memories of apartheid aggression and fears of dominance. South
Africa had to be seen as acting forcefully, but legitimately. South Africa
knew that 'the key to the deployment of troops is a legitimate basis ...
[you cannot] move in because you are strongest ... you always need a
legitimate reason, because ... the use of aggressive action today is
prohibited. So it is mandatory that a legitimate basis is established.'[52]

South Africa's legitimacy audiences

The case of Operation Boleas provides an example of the possible
interrelations between the four potential legitimacy audiences identified

---

[49] South African Department of Foreign Affairs, 'South African Foreign Policy',
Article 6.2.
[50] Hein Marais, 'South Africa carries a big stick' *Le Monde Diplomatique*, March 1999.
[51] James Radebe, 'South Africa: Lesotho Intervention Questioned', *Inter Press Service*
7 October 1998.
[52] Author's interview with Colonel Peter Voetmann, Senior Military Advisor, Southern
African Development Community Regional Peacekeeping Training Centre, Harare,
23 November 2000.

in chapter 2. The South African government made some efforts to persuade public opinion in Lesotho of the intervention's legitimacy, but its key concern was with its domestic public opinion, and through this, with the legitimacy judgements of the wider society of states.

As far as Lesotho's population was concerned, South Africa had an obvious interest in seeking to ensure the best possible reception for SANDF troops within Operation Boleas. During the intervention, Boleas troops distributed pamphlets proclaiming 'Attention: People of Lesotho, Your friends in the Southern African Development Community are assisting in resolving the current crisis situation in Lesotho.'[53] South Africa seemed confident that this message would persuade Lesotho's citizens to accept the intervention: SANDF soldiers went into Lesotho under peacekeeping rules of engagement (do not fire unless fired upon) and with blank ammunition in all weapons except soldiers' personal arms.[54]

In fact, however, Lesotho's population was more deeply divided than South Africa anticipated. Reflecting back on the intervention in 2001, 51 per cent of Basotho respondents conceded that it had been necessary, but 21 per cent felt that it had been unnecessary or illegal.[55] Moreover, almost half of the respondents that favoured the intervention in principle (24 per cent of the original sample) also felt that it had been 'badly done'. Indeed, SANDF troops did much to dispel local goodwill upon their arrival. Their unannounced 5 a.m. deployment in Lesotho's capital strongly resembled a surprise attack, after which Boleas troops engaged in a heavy fire fight with Lesotho's defence forces at their Makoanyane barracks, evicted the protesters who had been camping at the royal palace, and hoisted the South African flag on palace premises. Unsurprisingly, many of Lesotho's citizens saw this as an invasion. Popular anger was fanned and channelled by opposition party members, and by 9 a.m. there were riots in the streets. Several buildings associated with South Africa were attacked. As one opposition spokeswoman put it, 'ordinary people came out of their houses to meet the South African invaders. They are burning South African shops. That is our war against

---

[53] Reported in the South African *Mail and Guardian*'s Timeline of the intervention, online at http://www.mg.co.za/news/98sep/23sep-lesotho.html. Accessed January 2002, document no longer available.

[54] SANDF, 'The SADC Intervention in Lesotho', p. 4.

[55] John Gay and Thuso Green, 'Citizen Perceptions of Democracy, Governance, and Political Crisis in Lesotho', *Afrobarometer Paper No.13*, 2001. Online at http://www. afrobarometer.org/abseries.html.

South Africa.'[56] It was a war that South Africa had in large part brought upon itself with its cavalier attitude towards the sensibilities of Lesotho's population. Clearly this was not an audience whose opinion of Operation Boleas's legitimacy the South African government valued very highly.

South Africa's first democratically elected government paid rather more attention to its own domestic public opinion. It had good reason to be anxious about public reactions to the intervention since it had broken South African law in launching Operation Boleas. The 1996 White Paper on Defence had stipulated that:

> South Africa will only become involved in specific peace support operations if the following conditions are met: There should be parliamentary approval and public support for such involvement ... The operation should be authorised by the United Nations Security Council. Operations in Southern Africa should be sanctioned by SADC ... Similarly, operations in Africa should be sanctioned by the Organisation of African Unity.[57]

Operation Boleas had only a questionable SADC mandate and no authorisation from either the UN or the OAU. The South African Parliament was not briefed on the intervention until 2.20 p.m. on 22 September, over nine hours after the first SANDF troops entered Lesotho. Unsurprisingly, opposition MPs had a field day.

Remarkably, however, only one delegate, Freedom Front leader Viljoen, criticised Operation Boleas on grounds of South African law.[58] Virtually all other objecting parties focused on the international status of Operation Boleas. The New National Party registered its 'strongest condemnation' of the intervention, which it charged 'contravenes previous commitments to peaceful solutions for conflict situations on the continent'.[59] It also condemned the hoisting of the South African flag in Maseru, and offered an apology 'to the people of Lesotho for this unnecessary act of aggression'. The PAC chided that 'if we intervene in Lesotho it should be for the sake of defending the people of Lesotho rather than the present government'.[60] The ACDP regretted the shift from South Africa's 'wise and logical' insistence on negotiated

---

[56] *Mail and Guardian*, Timeline.
[57] Republic of South Africa, *Defence in a Democracy*, chapter 5, Article 24.
[58] Viljoen complained that the government had not briefed the political parties before Operation Boleas was launched and questioned the intervention's constitutionality. South African Hansard, 22 September 1998, column 6772.
[59] Ibid., columns 6770–1.   [60] Ibid., column 6775.

settlement in the DRC to aggressive military action in 'tiny' and 'relatively peaceful' Lesotho.[61] It also expressed concern 'that great harm has been done to the potential peacekeeping abilities of South Africa in the region and elsewhere on the continent, as a result of the action of the lone South African contingent operating under cover of the SADC in Lesotho'.

What these opposition MPs realised was that the South African public was primarily concerned about the reactions of a third legitimacy audience for Operation Boleas: the international community. South African newspapers voiced widely held fears that Operation Boleas would tarnish South Africa's international status as a potential force for good in the region. The *Business Day* commented that 'the miracle of the rainbow nation and its negotiated settlement is now gone and the image of [South Africa as] the peacemaker has been considerably tarnished . . . the death of the rainbow nation . . . happened when South Africa invaded Lesotho.'[62] The *Mail and Guardian* opined that 'we have some serious explaining to do' and warned of South Africa looking 'like a thug and an idiot'.[63]

The precise nature of this international legitimacy audience was not always well specified in public discourse. In terms of government policy, the Southern African region seems to have been considered a less crucial audience. South African policy-makers were aware of the fears of South African domination in the region, which were fuelled by both South Africa's aggressive past and its economic, military, and political power. They also knew that their country was seen as excessively aloof and uninterested in Africa: President Mandela himself had been at pains to insist that unlike the apartheid regime, his government saw itself as 'part of the region of Southern Africa and of the continent of Africa'.[64] Some South Africans attempted to portray Operation Boleas as a token of this new commitment. One diplomat argued that the operation 'should crush the argument that South Africa is not concerned in the region . . . we are very much concerned . . . with the stability and social and economic development in the whole sub-region and on the continent'.[65]

[61] Ibid., column 6776. The BDF had not yet joined the SANDF in Lesotho at the time of this debate.

[62] Hartley, 'Incursion Tarnishes SA's Peacemaker Image'.

[63] Howard Barrell, 'Lesotho: we have some serious explaining to do', *Mail and Guardian* (South Africa), 25 September 1998.

[64] Mandela's speech to the UN General Assembly, October 1994, quoted in South African Department of Foreign Affairs, 'South African Foreign Policy', Article 5.3.

[65] Author's interview with Thomas Rambau, First Secretary (Political), South African High Commission, Harare, Zimbabwe, 14 December 2000.

Yet as detailed above, South Africa made very little effort to make Operation Boleas a truly regional military effort. It did not consult fully with its regional neighbours before launching its intervention. It did not seek regional approval for its intervention at the SADC Summit in Mauritius just days prior to the launching of Operation Boleas. And with the exception of Botswana's infantry company, South Africa operated alone in Lesotho.

For the South African government, and perhaps for many South Africans as well, the wider international community was the more important legitimacy audience. South Africa was seeking to establish and affirm its credentials as a good global citizen. It had just emerged from the international pariah status to which its apartheid policies had condemned it. The South African public celebrated their country's 're-entry into the community of nations', including its new or renewed membership in the UN, the Commonwealth, the G77, the OAU, the Non-Aligned Movement (NAM), and SADC. It was a point of national pride to chair SADC and to host the 12th NAM Summit in 1998. South Africa was also thought to be in the running for a UN Security Council seat once the reform of that body began. The South African public did not want to see these developments reversed by international condemnation over Lesotho. And since the South African public cared about the legitimacy of Operation Boleas in the eyes of the international community, the South African government had to do so as well.

The SADC framework and the legitimacy of Operation Boleas

The importance of the SADC framework for Operation Boleas has been succinctly summarised by a Western diplomat: 'it was convenient for both South Africa and Botswana to say it was a SADC operation, not some kind of imperialist venture. Their motivation – it gives legitimacy, it sounds a lot better to be in there as a SADC operation.'[66] As lead nation in Operation Boleas, South Africa sought to use SADC auspices for the intervention to persuade all four of the audiences identified in the previous section. The audience that was most amenable to being convinced by this signal, however, was the international community.

Acting South African President Buthelezi explicitly appealed to Operation Boleas's SADC auspices to legitimise the intervention in the

---

[66] Author's interview with Robert Collingwood, Head of Delegation, European Union Delegation to Botswana. Gaborone, Botswana, 6 December 2000.

eyes of Lesotho's population: 'We would stress, for the benefit of the citizens of Lesotho, that SADC is their organisation and that we are members of one family. This action is not an intervention by an outside power, as it were.'[67] However, this tactic had little success. Not only did South Africa's behaviour in Lesotho undermine its claims of peaceful intent, but Lesotho's opposition parties vehemently disputed South Africa's assumption of the SADC mantle. They insisted that Operation Boleas was a South African invasion rather than a SADC intervention. Vincent Malebo, the Chairman of Lesotho's opposition alliance, asserted: 'it was not SADC which invaded Lesotho but South Africa.'[68] Spokeswoman Mamelo Morrison condemned the new South African government as being 'no better than the apartheid government'.[69] BCP leader Qhubela 'accused Mandela of continuing where former president PW Botha left off with his policy of military destabilisation of Southern African countries' and added: 'This is just big power chauvinism.'[70] In short, Lesotho's opposition leaders deliberately sought to strip Operation Boleas of the legitimacy South Africa had hoped to bestow on it by operating under SADC auspices.

SADC auspices also had only a limited effect on the legitimacy of Operation Boleas in the eyes of the Southern African region. By-passing SADC altogether would certainly have provoked uproar, even among South Africa's closest allies. Botswana would not have been able to join South Africa in its intervention had Operation Boleas not been placed at least nominally under SADC auspices. As one official in Botswana's Foreign Ministry commented: 'because the operation was under SADC, we agreed to participate.'[71] South Africa's more ambitious hope that launching Operation Boleas under SADC auspices would bring it positive recognition for its engagement in the region was not realised, however. South Africa's neighbours were too keenly aware of the extent to which this was a South African rather than a SADC enterprise. It was an open secret that South Africa and Botswana had violated SADC procedures in launching the operation. The region's governments were under no illusion about how little they had been

---

[67] South African Hansard, 22 September 1998, column 6768.
[68] Kekeletso Motopi, 'SANDF are employed in Lesotho not deployed – Malebo', *Mopheme/The Survivor* (Lesotho), 15 December 1998.
[69] *Mail and Guardian*, Timeline.   [70] Ibid.
[71] Author's interview with O. Motswagae, Deputy Director (Multilateral and East Asia) Botswana Ministry of Foreign Affairs. Gaborone, Botswana, 7 December 2000.

consulted prior to the operation. They were simply too intimately aware
of SADC politics for South Africa's arrogation of SADC auspices for
Operation Boleas to substantially bolster the intervention's legitimacy in
their eyes.

With respect to the South African public, the effect of launching
Operation Boleas within the SADC framework was significant but mainly
indirect. Acting President Buthelezi did seek to use the operation's SADC
auspices directly to assuage his domestic critics. He urged Parliament that
Operation Boleas was not 'a matter in which we, as South Africans, should
take political pot shots at one another. This is because we are acting as
members of the SADC family.'[72] As noted above, this did not disarm critics
of the intervention either within Parliament or in the media. However, the
SADC framework did crucially affect the South African public's willingness
to tolerate Operation Boleas. What the South African public feared most
was that the intervention would ruin their country's new international
image – and SADC auspices had a critical positive effect on Operation
Boleas's international legitimacy.

South Africans had reason to fear the international reaction to
Operation Boleas. South Africa's last major incursion into Lesotho –
the raid against anti-apartheid fighters in 1982 – had drawn intense
criticism from the OAU and the UN. Now the newly democratic South
Africa had once again invaded its smaller neighbour virtually unilaterally,
meeting military and popular resistance, causing civilian and military
casualties, and failing to prevent widespread looting and destruction in
Lesotho's capital. Moreover, South Africa and Botswana had acted without
UN authorisation and therefore illegally. One member of the Botswana
Foreign Ministry mused:

> Ordinarily, at the UN we question, for example, when NATO went into
> Kosovo without a Security Council mandate. But even though the opera-
> tion in Lesotho was an enforcement operation, we did not go to the
> Security Council to ask for a mandate ... I don't know [why not].
> When we go to the UN, the developing, non-aligned countries are the
> first to question why big countries tend to intervene without a Security
> Council mandate. But in this case for some reason there was never even
> any discussion about whether it was necessary to raise the issue at the
> Security Council. It was never discussed.[73]

---

[72] South African Hansard, 22 September 1998, column 6769.
[73] Author's interview with O. Motswagae, 7 December 2000.

South Africa had also acted without consulting the OAU, even though it had insisted just weeks earlier that it would 'consider intervening in another country of the region only as part of a joint SADC force acting with the express authority of both the Organisation of African Unity and the United Nations'.[74] Under these circumstances, it was hardly unreasonable to expect international outrage at the intervention.

However, operating within the SADC framework prevented both OAU and UN criticism of Operation Boleas, boosting the intervention's international legitimacy. This framework gave Operation Boleas the status of a regional initiative rather than merely a South African enterprise. As noted in the previous chapter, SADC decisions are made by consensus, reflecting both an ideological solidarity born out of common independence struggles and states' attempt to maximise their international influence by presenting a united regional front. As SADC's Public Relations Officer put it: 'We do not have to wash our dirty linen in public.'[75] The consensus rule of decision-making made SADC disapproval of Operation Boleas impossible, since South Africa would have vetoed such a stance. It also allowed South Africa to put pressure on fellow SADC members hesitant to endorse the operation. Under consensus rules, states could not register dissent without vetoing SADC's imprimatur for Operation Boleas and thus inviting South Africa's wrath. By contrast, assent was cheap since SADC's lack of burden-sharing mechanisms meant that member states incurred no obligation to contribute to Operation Boleas by approving of it. Unsurprisingly, therefore, the 1999 SADC Summit recognised the operation as a 'SADC military intervention in the form of Botswana and South African forces' and 'expressed satisfaction that there is strong determination from the leadership of SADC to bring peace and harmony to the region'.[76] SADC's Secretary-General also praised the operation, arguing that 'recent SADC military and political interventions in Lesotho and the DRC were aimed at preventing the militarization of politics in those countries.'[77]

---

[74] All Africa News Agency, 'South Africa's Move in Lesotho Receives Criticism', *Africa News*, 9 November 1998.
[75] Author's interview with Ester V. Kanaimba, Public Relations Officer, SADC Secretariat, Gaborone, 7 December 2000.
[76] SADC, *Summit Communiqué*, Maputo, Mozambique, 17–18 August 1999.
[77] Government Communications, SADC Information Unit, 'SADC Intervention in Lesotho', 12 October 1998. Online at www.polity.org.za/govdocs/pr/1998/pr1013.html.

Operation Boleas's official status as a regional initiative combined with South African power within Africa to forestall OAU criticism of the intervention. Since, like SADC, the OAU operates by consensus, South Africa could have vetoed any disapproving resolution. Moreover, as one OAU official admitted, the OAU is open to manipulation by strong states: 'Countries tend to use the OAU when it serves them – they intervene first, and then come to the OAU to say that they are maintaining stability, prosperity etc. And not much can be done – South Africa is a military powerhouse, and a huge economic powerhouse.'[78]

However, the SADC framework and the OAU's commitment to regionalisation also prevented criticism of Operation Boleas. The OAU declared its reliance on five regional organisations (including SADC) as essential 'pillars' of African integration and development as early as 1991.[79] As one OAU official explained, a peace enforcement operation under SADC auspices thus had a special status: 'Since SADC is regarded as an integral part of the OAU, it is like a regional outpost of the OAU – all its members are OAU members. They are acting as the OAU – and so since SADC had a presence on the ground, there was not much point in sending OAU observers. Besides, the OAU is perennially short of resources.'[80] Such close dependence does not make for strict supervision and the official acknowledged that in any case the OAU was exceedingly unlikely to criticise a SADC initiative: 'the core principle governing the Member States' meetings [is] consensus – we discuss things in a brotherly way, and avoid arguments. So by and large it is unlikely that an initiative supported by fifteen Member States does not get endorsed at the continental level.'[81]

Thus the OAU accepted being sidelined during Operation Boleas and raised no objections to the intervention. It only re-entered the international scene when a final accord to end the confrontations in Lesotho was signed on 3 December 1999 – and then only by sending OAU Secretary-General Salim Salim to witness (and thus endorse) the accord.

The SADC framework was even more valuable to South Africa at the UN level, where South Africa wields less power than in the OAU and could not have blocked a motion of censure. 'Regionalisation' remained

---

[78] Author's interview. Remark not for attribution.
[79] *Treaty Establishing the African Economic Community*, 3 June 1991, Abuja, Nigeria.
[80] Author's interview with Njunga M. Mulikita, Information Analyst, UNDP Project for Capacity Building of the OAU Mechanism for Conflict Prevention, Management and Resolution, Addis Ababa, 6 November 2000.
[81] Ibid.

a buzzword within the UN in 1998. Just days before Operation Boleas was launched, the UN Security Council reaffirmed 'the need for continued cooperation between the United Nations ... and the OAU and subregional organizations in Africa'.[82] Although formally this did not extend to approval of peace enforcement operations launched without UN authorisation, the slogan of 'African solutions to African problems' was extremely popular, especially after the disastrous UN intervention in Somalia in 1993. SADC's endorsement of Operation Boleas, combined with the OAU's acquiescence to the operation, thus granted the intervention special status within the UN. As one OAU official commented, 'if the OAU accepted it, it was the African position – and that made it hard to criticise from outside.'[83]

Thus the UN refrained from criticising Operation Boleas despite its illegality. Neither the General Assembly nor the Security Council commented on the intervention, while the Secretary-General showed himself sympathetic to it. The day after Operation Boleas was launched, he appealed 'to leaders in Lesotho on all sides to show statesmanship and to work together with the Southern African Development Community for the sake of the people of Lesotho'.[84] Three weeks later, he recognised the negotiations among Lesotho's factions to be held 'under the auspices of the Southern African Development Community'.[85] While not explicitly endorsing the military intervention, he thus validated its SADC auspices and supported its stated goals.

Thanks in large part to its SADC auspices, therefore, Operation Boleas did not provoke the international outrage that many South Africans had feared and that an illegal invasion of a small, sovereign neighbour might be expected to provoke. Indeed, 'there was a marked lack of international condemnation of the incursion.'[86] International reactions fell short of a ringing endorsement but there was no international condemnation of the deployment as illegitimate – a fact the South African government used against its domestic critics. The parliamentary

---

[82] UN Security Council Resolution 1197, 18 September 1998.
[83] Author's interview with Dr Jimmi Adisa, Information Analyst, UNDP Project for Capacity Building of the OAU Mechanism for Conflict Prevention, Management, and Resolution, Addis Ababa, 18 October 2000.
[84] 'Secretary-General Appeals to Leaders in Lesotho to Show Statesmanship and Work Together', UN press release, 23 September 1998.
[85] 'Secretary-General Appeals to All Parties in Lesotho to Reach Agreement on Outstanding Issues', UN press release, 13 October 1998.
[86] Mark Malan, 'Leaner and Meaner? The Future of Peacekeeping in Africa', *African Security Review*, 8:4 (1999).

adviser of then-Vice President Thabo Mbeki, for example, argued that 'in strong contrast to' South African critics, 'the international bodies that have to enforce international law have shown understanding and support for South Africa's position.'[87] He added, somewhat disingenuously, 'this would hardly have been so had we acted in breach of international law.' Lack of international condemnation did not make Boleas legal, however: it just made it legitimate. But then it was international legitimacy, not legality, which most concerned the South African government and the majority of its public.

The costs of operating in the SADC framework

This chapter has argued that South Africa's decision to launch Operation Boleas within the SADC framework was due more to its concerns about the international legitimacy of the operation than to its desire to respect international law or encourage burden-sharing. The significance of this finding, however, depends in part on the costs South Africa incurred in pursuing this strategy. Realists are quick to note that cheap talk and even cheap actions are inadequate indications of states' core motivations. If launching a peace enforcement operation through an international organisation is easy and costless, states need not value legitimacy very highly to do so. South Africa, however, incurred two major costs to secure SADC auspices for Operation Boleas.

The most immediate cost was the additional risk and difficulty associated with multilateral military operations. In order to credibly claim regional auspices, Operation Boleas had to be a multilateral intervention. South Africa thus sought assistance from Botswana, one of its closest allies within SADC. Botswana's officials had no doubts about South Africa's motivation. As the Deputy Director of Botswana's Ministry of Foreign Affairs explained, South Africa 'could not go in alone because ... [it] felt that going in alone would be interpreted in a different way, as interfering with the internal affairs of Lesotho'.[88] Botswana agreed to participate, partly to assist Mosisili and partly to demonstrate its importance in regional politics, but mostly to cement its good relations with its powerful southern neighbour. However, its contribution of a single mechanised infantry company was not only

---

[87] Willie Hofmeyr, 'SA met the letter and spirit of law', *Business Day* (South Africa) 20 November 1998.
[88] Author's interview with O. Motswagae, 7 December 2000.

negligible in purely military terms but also imposed substantial costs on South Africa. Botswana's troops had to be transported through South Africa to Lesotho, and their advance had to be coordinated with that of South Africa's forces. This coordination failed. South African troops entered Lesotho at 5 a.m. on 22 September 1998, but Botswana's soldiers did not deploy until the evening of that day. For the crucial first hours of the intervention, therefore, the so-called Combined Task Force (CTF) for Operation Boleas was purely South African and comprised only 600 rather than the expected 800 troops. South African troops faced the unanticipated resistance by the RLDF and the popular riots in Maseru alone.

Being left with fewer-than-anticipated troops in the face of higher-than-expected resistance is a recipe for military disaster. South Africa assumed this risk even though it was unnecessary from a military point of view. South Africa could easily have deployed an additional 200 soldiers: by October 1998, it had increased its presence in Lesotho from 600 to 3,500 troops. The fact that South Africa nevertheless opted for a joint operation with Botswana demonstrates that it was willing to assume significant costs in its pursuit of international legitimacy through the SADC framework. As one Botswana official put it, South Africa 'felt the need for SADC and approached us as a country'.[89]

The costs to South Africa of operating within the SADC framework were not purely military, however. To claim SADC auspices for Operation Boleas, South Africa also had to make a major foreign policy concession. As noted in the previous chapter, South Africa had vigorously opposed the Zimbabwe-led intervention in the Democratic Republic of Congo when it was launched in August 1998 and resisted Zimbabwean attempts to claim SADC auspices for the operation. South Africa argued that military intervention would aggravate rather than remedy the conflict in the DRC. It also resented Zimbabwe's arrogation of SADC leadership on the issue. However, Operation Boleas's international legitimacy depended on South Africa ending its public dispute with Zimbabwe. If South Africa persisted in opposing Operation Sovereign Legitimacy, Zimbabwe could be expected to retaliate by criticising Operation Boleas and denying the validity of its claimed SADC auspices. Moreover, the public dispute between South Africa and Zimbabwe weakened SADC's international image as the unified voice of Southern Africa. As one observer put it, 'only when SADC

[89] Ibid.

gets its act together and irons out its divergent views will it be able to be effective.'[90]

To maximise Operation Boleas's international legitimacy, therefore, South Africa had to abandon its public opposition to Operation Sovereign Legitimacy. Thus on 3 September President Mandela performed 'an embarrassing *volte face* by endorsing military intervention to prop up Kabila'.[91] Using the public forum provided by the Non-Aligned Movement summit in Durban, Mandela announced that he had been misinformed about the nature of the DRC conflict. He now accepted that it was essentially a foreign invasion, and that it was 'quite reasonable' for a 'legitimate government' to request military assistance from neighbours in such circumstances.[92] He also explained that he 'had dropped his opposition to military intervention when President Sam Nujoma of Namibia explained [that] the initiative was to help Kabila fend off a foreign invasion'.[93] Mandela even went so far as to insist that 'SADC had unanimously supported the military intervention by its member states in the DRC.'[94]

This declaration did not reflect a change of policy preferences within the South African government. South Africa continued to seek a negotiated solution to the DRC conflict and hoped to demonstrate its own leadership capacities in doing so. The inter-Congolese peace agreement signed in Pretoria on 17 December 2002 attests to the persistence of these efforts. In future, however, these negotiations would officially take place in parallel rather than in opposition to the Zimbabwe-led military intervention. This dramatic reversal came just as the situation in Lesotho was deteriorating into a crisis. As one observer delicately put it, 'there may ... have been an expectation of reciprocity should South Africa ever overstep the mark'.[95] The quid pro quo was clear: 'if Zimbabwe, Botswana, and South Africa agree to go into Lesotho, why should South Africa and Botswana condemn the operation into the DRC? And indeed there was a softening of language between Mandela

---

[90] Sanusha Naidu, quoted in Gumisai Mutume, 'Southern Africa: Peace in the Offing for Kabila's DRC', *Inter Press Service*, 3 September 1998.

[91] Marais, 'South Africa carries a big stick'.

[92] Alex Duval Smith, 'Mandela fails in peace initiatives', *The Guardian (London)*, 4 September 1998.

[93] Reuters, 'African leaders open door to Congo peace', *The Toronto Star*, 4 September 1998.

[94] Malan, 'The Future of Peacekeeping in Africa'.

[95] Mark Malan, 'Can They Do That? SADC, the DRC, and Lesotho', *Indicator SA*, 15:4 (Summer 1998), p. 93.

and Mugabe when they met at the NAM summit.'[96] Zimbabwe tacitly accepted the deal. President Mugabe did not make himself available to launch Operation Boleas, but he issued a statement that Zimbabwe supported the 'military intervention by South Africa and Botswana, under the auspices of SADC, [which] was meant to restore law and order to the internal conflict which had threatened peace and security there'.[97]

Thus South Africa had to accept substantial military and foreign policy costs in order to maximise Operation Boleas' international legitimacy through the SADC framework. Neither of these costs procured immediate material benefits. Botswana's small military contribution to Operation Boleas did not compensate for the loss of reliable control that South Africa experienced, particularly during the first days of the intervention. South Africa's reversal of its opposition to the Zimbabwe-led military intervention in the DRC, meanwhile, was quite simply a foreign policy defeat, which South Africa had to humiliatingly concede in a public forum.

Conclusion

This chapter has focused on the second peace enforcement operation launched within the SADC framework, the South African-led military intervention into Lesotho launched in September 1998. Like its immediate antecedent, the Zimbabwe-led intervention into the DRC, this case supports the theory that states' primary motivation for launching peace enforcement operations through international organisations is a desire to bolster the international legitimacy of those interventions. The SADC framework had no significant effect on Operation Boleas' legality, and in any case South Africa displayed little concern with international law in launching the intervention. SADC also failed to promote burden-sharing for the operation. South Africa neither sought nor received widespread military or financial assistance from its fellow SADC members for the intervention. By contrast, South Africa did have significant concerns about the international legitimacy of its intervention, and addressed these successfully by operating through the SADC framework. The fact that South Africa was willing to incur substantial military and

---

[96] Author's interview. Remarks not for attribution.
[97] *Mail and Guardian*, Timeline.

foreign policy costs in order to secure this legitimacy testifies to the value that South Africa attached to it.

While it exhibits similarities with Operation Sovereign Legitimacy, however, Operation Boleas also displays a critical difference: legitimation through SADC was much smoother for this intervention than for its predecessor. When Zimbabwe launched Operation Sovereign Legitimacy, South Africa sought to prevent it from using SADC to legitimise the intervention. The result was an embarrassing public dispute within SADC that not only diminished the international legitimacy of Operation Sovereign Legitimacy but also damaged SADC's credibility as a regional security organisation and thus its ability to act as gatekeeper to international legitimacy for regional military interventions. In this sense, Operation Boleas marked SADC's coming of age. To ensure maximum international legitimacy for this intervention, South Africa dropped its criticism of Operation Sovereign Legitimacy. Zimbabwe, accepting the deal, offered no public resistance to Operation Boleas. It declared that it 'fully supported' the intervention, adding pointedly that 'any military attack to undermine a sovereign government is viewed by all of us in SADC and the OAU . . . [as] a matter of great concern requiring immediate redress wherever it occurs'.[98] South Africa and Zimbabwe had rediscovered their common interest in maximising SADC's capacity to generate international legitimacy for regional military initiatives.

This had institutional consequences, notably for the SADC Organ on Defence, Politics and Security, which had been paralysed since the 1997 SADC Summit in Blantyre. Operation Sovereign Legitimacy and Operation Boleas had been launched without the benefit of a functioning SADC security institution, which created potential legitimacy problems for both operations. As one report noted, 'The lack of formal conflict management procedures in the interventions in Lesotho and the DRC . . . resulted in the perception that they were respectively South African and Zimbabwean rather than SADC operations.'[99] Both South Africa and Zimbabwe now recognised the lack of a functioning security organ within SADC as a liability: the controversies around the 1998

[98] 'Zimbabwe backs SADC intervention in Lesotho', *Xinhua News Agency*, 23 September 1998.
[99] Monde Muyangwa and Margaret A. Vogt, 'An Assessment of the OAU Mechanism for Conflict Prevention, Management and Resolution, 1993–2000', *International Peace Academy report*, online at http://www.ipacademy.org/Publications/Reports/Africa/PublRepoAfriAssessPrint.htm.

interventions 'made it apparent to all parties that a compromise arrangement on the Organ was urgently required'.[100] The process of building the SADC Organ thus resumed.

In August 1999, the SADC Summit mandated the Council of Ministers to 'review the operations of all SADC institutions, including the Organ on Defence, Politics and Security' while agreeing that in the meantime 'the Organ ... should continue to operate and be chaired by President Mugabe.'[101] It was a face-saving compromise. SADC did not have to acknowledge the severity of the Organ dispute, South Africa got a review of the Organ structure as well as a chance of rationalising SADC's economic activities, and Mugabe temporarily remained the Organ Chair. Informally, however, he had to accept consultation by a troika of SADC Chairs (South Africa, Mozambique, and Namibia).[102] Over the next two years, SADC ministers met in a flurry of consultations, and on 31 March 2001 an Extra-Ordinary Summit in Windhoek finalised SADC's new structure. The Organ was integrated into SADC, made accountable to the SADC Summit, and placed under an annually rotating Chair in consultation with his predecessor and successor.[103] Mozambique's Joaquim Cissano became the first Organ Chair under this new dispensation. In 2004, SADC even advanced along the path of creating stand-by arrangements for a regional peacekeeping force, although contrary to burden-sharing imperatives all decisions about the actual deployment of 'ear-marked' troops are likely to remain the prerogative of individual states.

Even more important than this institutional engineering, however, has been a newly strengthened informal commitment to SADC unity. Elements of the rivalry between South Africa and Zimbabwe persist, but their expression has been attenuated. Economic difficulties, initially compounded by the expense of maintaining troops in the DRC but now largely due to a severe domestic political crisis, left Zimbabwe less insistent on regional leadership prerogatives. Moreover, South Africa's current president, Thabo Mbeki, has been conciliatory towards Mugabe, in part because he is less able than Nelson Mandela to command the

---

[100] Cilliers, 'Building Security in Southern Africa'.
[101] SADC, *Summit Communiqué*, Maputo, Mozambique, 17–18 August 1999, Article 46.
[102] Cilliers, 'Building Security in Southern Africa'.
[103] SADC, *Extra-Ordinary Summit Communiqué*, Windhoek, Namibia, 9 March 2001, Article 11. The summit also extended the troika concept to the SADC Summit (Article 10) and changed SADC's approach to economic development, aiming to replace its various sectors with four central economic Directorates by 2003.

regional stature to openly oppose him. Thus the extreme situation of regional rivalry that allowed a brief breach in SADC's façade of regional unity to occur in the immediate aftermath of Zimbabwe's intervention in the DRC no longer obtains. SADC has once again become an organisation whose members speak with a single voice on the international stage. This is not always to the advantage of the people of the region, as SADC's refusal to criticise the forced land reforms and growing authoritarianism of Mugabe's regime in Zimbabwe attests. It does, however, indicate that SADC has now come fully of age as a tool for generating international legitimacy for the policies of its member states.

6

Peace enforcement through a military alliance: the North Atlantic Treaty Organisation and Operation Allied Force in Kosovo

At 8 p.m. local time on 24 March 1999, almost 400 aircraft attacked the Federal Republic of Yugoslavia. Simultaneously, Tomahawk Tactical Land Attack Missiles were launched into Yugoslavia from several warships. Eight member states of the North Atlantic Treaty Organisation (NATO) contributed to this combined, synchronised attack, in which over forty different Yugoslav targets were hit. This was the opening blow in NATO's military campaign over Kosovo, codenamed Operation Allied Force. In the course of the 78-day campaign, thirteen NATO countries deployed over 1,000 aircraft and flew 38,400 sorties, including 10,484 strike sorties that released 26,614 air munitions over the Federal Republic of Yugoslavia (FRY).[1]

This chapter explores why the USA, which led and dominated Operation Allied Force, chose to launch the intervention within a NATO framework. After a brief historical background to the intervention, it demonstrates that neither international law nor burden-sharing concerns explain this decision. By contrast, concerns about the international legitimacy of the intervention played a major role in persuading the USA to accept the considerable costs and inconveniences associated with the NATO framework.

Historical background

Operation Allied Force sought to end government-sponsored repression in Kosovo. The region's predominantly ethnic Albanian population had been increasingly discriminated against since the revocation of its status as an autonomous province of Serbia in July 1990. After initial attempts at non-violent resistance, an armed resistance movement, the Kosovo

---

[1] The Independent Commission on Kosovo, *The Kosovo Report: Conflict, International Response, Lessons Learned* (Oxford: Oxford University Press, 2000), p. 92.

Liberation Army (KLA), emerged in the mid-1990s. Until the late 1990s, however, the international community largely ignored the growing conflict, partly because it was preoccupied with the on-going wars in Croatia and Bosnia-Herzegovina.[2] Only in 1998 did the dramatic escalation of the conflict and the ensuing threat of another ethnic bloodbath in the Balkans galvanise the international community into diplomatic action.

The international community initially operated through a number of international bodies, including the United Nations Security Council, the Organisation for Security and Cooperation in Europe (OSCE), and the Contact Group, an ad hoc body comprising the USA, Russia, the UK, France, Germany and Italy. NATO complemented these efforts, relying on the diplomatic skills of US Ambassador Richard Holbrooke and exerting pressure on the FRY government by moving towards authorising military action in Kosovo from September 1998 onwards. When these efforts did not halt the FRY offensive in Kosovo, the Contact Group invited the FRY government and representatives of the Kosovar Albanians to urgent peace talks in Rambouillet and Paris, France, in February and March 1999. These meetings failed to produce a settlement, and the FRY massed more troops in and around Kosovo. In response, NATO launched Operation Allied Force on 24 March 1999.

The intervention marked several major watersheds in international relations. It was the first major interstate military encounter in Europe since the Second World War. It saw NATO engage in military activity on the very doorstep of its primary Cold War adversary, Russia. It represented the first time a military campaign was waged almost exclusively by air power and with no combat casualties on the part of the attackers. It also witnessed an unprecedented involvement of lawyers in the management of combat operations, especially with regard to target selection for bombing missions.[3] Finally, Operation Allied Force marked the first time that NATO went to war.

NATO was created in 1949 as a Cold War collective self-defence arrangement against the USSR. Its original purpose is stated in Article 5 of the North Atlantic Treaty:

---

[2] The USA first threatened military action against the FRY over Kosovo through President Bush's 'Christmas warning' of December 1992, and the Clinton administration renewed this threat in 1993. However, at the 1995 Dayton peace conference, the Kosovo issue was sidelined to encourage Milosevic's contribution to a settlement.

[3] Richard Betts, 'Command Compromised: Inside NATO's First War', *Foreign Affairs* (July/August 2001), p. 129.

> Parties agree that an armed attack against one or more of them in Europe
> or North America shall be considered an attack against them all and
> consequently they agree that, if such an armed attack occurs, each of
> them ... will assist the Party or Parties so attacked by taking forthwith,
> individually and in concert with the other Parties, such action as it deems
> necessary, including the use of armed forces, to restore and maintain the
> security of the North Atlantic area.

Originally, NATO was no more than a series of forums for ad hoc
meetings among its member states. Even the most important of these,
the North Atlantic Council (NAC), had no regular meeting schedule.
The Alliance had no fixed headquarters, permanent secretariat or independent budget. After the Korean War, however, the NAC was called
into permanent session, a permanent headquarters and secretariat was
created, and an integrated military force was established. This marked
the emergence of NATO as a formal international organisation: 'The
Alliance ... had become NATO, the North Atlantic Treaty Organisation.'[4]
The organisation reinvented itself again after the end of the Cold War,
stressing its contribution to peaceful relations among members and
its importance in confronting the instabilities of the post-Cold War
era. There was also more emphasis on economic collaboration among
Alliance members, based on the long-dormant Article 2 of the North
Atlantic Treaty. NATO membership expanded to comprise nineteen
countries in March 1999 and now stands at twenty-six (Map 6.1).[5] Its
organisational structure also grew: by 2001, NATO's secretariat had
1,300 members and its civil budget exceeded US$130 million.[6]

Ironically, it was this international organisation, rather than the
initial strictly military alliance, that first used force in the international
context. Fortunately, NATO never had to use military force during the
Cold War. In the 1990s, however, increasing emphasis was placed on
possible NATO contributions to international peace support operations.
NATO's very first military operation was enforcing a UN-established

---

[4] *NATO Review*, 50th Anniversary Commemorative Edition (Brussels: NATO, 1999),
p. 11.
[5] NATO's founding members are Belgium, Canada, Denmark, France, Iceland, Italy,
Luxembourg, the Netherlands, Norway, Portugal, the United Kingdom, and the
United States. Subsequent accessions include: Greece and Turkey (1952), the Federal
Republic of Germany (1955), Spain (1982), the Czech Republic, Hungary and Poland
(1999) and Bulgaria, Estonia, Latvia, Lithuania, Romania, Slovakia, Slovenia (2004).
[6] *NATO Handbook* (Brussels: NATO Office of Information and Press, 2001), pp. 219,
204–6.

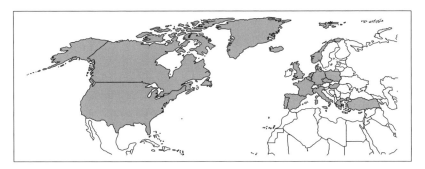

Map 6.1: North Atlantic Treaty Organisation (NATO) in 1999

no-fly zone in Bosnia. Since this occurred in the context of a UN peace-keeping mission, however, it did not constitute an independent NATO campaign. By contrast, Operation Allied Force was launched solely under NATO auspices and explicitly aimed at peace enforcement rather than peacekeeping. Its bombing campaign was intense, and although NATO officials insisted that NATO was not waging war against Yugoslavia, it was hard to avoid that conclusion. Wesley Clark, NATO's Supreme Commander during Operation Allied Force, later conceded: 'We were never allowed to call it a war. But it was, of course. This was modern war, the first war fought in Europe in half a century, and the first ever fought by NATO.'[7]

International law and Operation Allied Force

Why did the USA, the lead state in Operation Allied Force, choose to launch this intervention from within the NATO framework? Despite the extraordinary presence of international lawyers during the campaign,[8] international law does not provide a satisfactory explanation. Like the African sub-regional organisations examined in previous chapters of this book, NATO had no legal authority to launch Operation Allied Force. NATO was created as a defensive alliance, but the intervention did not respond to an armed attack on any NATO member and there-fore was not an act of collective self-defence. According to the UN Charter, all other international uses of military force require a mandate

[7] Wesley Clark, *Waging Modern War: Bosnia, Kosovo, and the Future of Combat* (New York: Public Affairs, 2001), p. xxiii.
[8] Betts, 'Command Compromised', p. 129.

from the UN Security Council. No other organisation can legally authorise peace enforcement operations – and NATO's own Charter recognises 'the primary responsibility of the [UN] Security Council for the maintenance of international peace and security' (Article 7).

From October 1998 onwards, however, Russia and China warned that they would veto a UN Security Council mandate for a NATO campaign in Kosovo. To remain within the bounds of international law under these circumstances, the USA could either refrain from intervening in Kosovo or seek a two-thirds majority vote in the UN General Assembly to override the threatened vetoes through the Uniting for Peace procedure. Instead, Operation Allied Force was simply launched without an explicit UN Security Council mandate.

Nevertheless, efforts to justify Operation Allied Force under international law persisted. Some diplomats argued that the humanitarian situation in Kosovo legally justified the intervention. Thus German Chancellor Gerhard Schroeder declared: 'I consider the legal basis of NATO's action, that is to contain a humanitarian crisis, to be both valid and sufficient.'[9] Stewart Eldon, Britain's representative to the UN, concurred that 'military intervention was justified as an exceptional measure to prevent an overwhelming humanitarian catastrophe.'[10] NATO Secretary-General Javier Solana reinforced this argument by underlining the security implications of a humanitarian catastrophe in Kosovo:

> Our objective is to prevent more human suffering and more repression and violence against the civilian population of Kosovo. We must also act to prevent instability from spreading in the region . . . We must halt the violence and bring an end to the humanitarian catastrophe now unfolding in Kosovo . . . We will do what is necessary to bring stability to the region.[11]

The implication of this argument was that NATO was justified in taking military action precisely because threatened Russian and Chinese vetoes prevented the UN Security Council from responding to the crisis. Thus French Prime Minister Lionel Jospin insisted that because the UN Security Council 'wasn't in a position to [act], because it had become

[9] Heike Krieger (ed.), *The Kosovo Conflict and International Law* (Cambridge: Cambridge University Press, 2001), p. 404.
[10] Hibeaki Shinoda, 'The Politics of Legitimacy in International Relations: A Critical Examination of NATO's Intervention in Kosovo', *Alternatives*, 25:4 (2000), p. 518.
[11] Marc Weller (ed.), *The Crisis in Kosovo 1989–1999: From the Dissolution of Yugoslavia to Rambouillet and the Outbreak of Hostilities* (Cambridge: Documents and Analysis Publishing, 1999), p. 495.

a matter of urgency, it was up to us to shoulder all our responsibilities, particularly in the Atlantic Alliance'.[12]

The second argument in defence of Operation Allied Force's legality was that existing UN Security Council resolutions already provided a legal basis for intervention. In Resolution 1199 of 23 September 1998, the Security Council invoked Chapter VII of the UN Charter and declared itself 'gravely concerned' with 'the excessive and indiscriminate use of force by Serbian security forces and the Yugoslav Army' in Kosovo. NATO issued military activation orders (ACTORDs) under this resolution in October 1998. As the German Minister of Foreign Affairs explained, 'The international community has sharply condemned the behaviour of the government in Belgrade through UN Security Council resolution 1199 . . . Therefore one can state that the threat to use military action aims at the implementation of the unanimously adopted UN Security Council resolution.'[13] The ACTORDs were postponed but not rescinded when the Yugoslav government subsequently bowed to international pressure and partially withdrew its forces from Kosovo. Security Council Resolution 1203 of 24 October 1998 welcomed this development, but remained 'deeply alarmed and concerned at the continuing grave humanitarian situation throughout Kosovo' and reaffirmed that 'the unresolved situation in Kosovo . . . constitutes a continuing threat to peace and security in the region'.

NATO members drew on these two resolutions to justify Operation Allied Force after the failure of the Rambouillet and Paris conferences in March 1999. They insisted that no new UN Security Council resolution was required to authorise NATO intervention. The French Ministry of Foreign Affairs declared, 'NATO's action finds its legitimacy in the authority of the Security Council. The resolutions of the Council concerning the situation in Kosovo (resolution 1199 of 23 September and 1203 of 24 October) have been passed under Chapter VII of the United Nations Charter.'[14] US Secretary of State Madeleine Albright argued that 'Acting under Chapter 7, the Security Council adopted three resolutions – 1160, 119 and 1203 – imposing mandatory obligations on the FRY; and these obligations the FRY has flagrantly ignored. So NATO actions are being taken within this framework.'[15] British Deputy

---

[12] Krieger (ed.), *The Kosovo Conflict and International Law*, p. 394.
[13] Ibid., p. 398.   [14] Ibid., p. 393.
[15] Ibid., p. 419. Security Council Resolution 1160 (31 March 1998) invoked Chapter VII of the UN Charter to impose an arms embargo on the FRY.

Prime Minister John Prescott also insisted that 'Two United Nations Security Council resolutions, 1199 and 1203, underpin our actions',[16] while Belgium claimed that 'the Security Council's resolutions ... provide an unchallengeable basis for the armed intervention'.[17]

Both arguments for Operation Allied Force's legality are flawed. First, there is no clear international law permitting humanitarian intervention in cases short of genocide.[18] As one legal scholar put it, 'No treaty permits humanitarian intervention. Nor is there much, if any, real evidence of a practice followed out of a sense of legal obligation to support a right of humanitarian intervention under customary law.'[19] A British parliamentary committee reached a similar verdict: 'We conclude that, at the very least, the doctrine of humanitarian intervention has a tenuous basis in international customary law, and that this renders NATO action legally questionable.'[20] Although there were substantial human rights abuses in Kosovo and ample reason to fear ethnic cleansing, there was no genocide and therefore no legal basis for military intervention.

Second, although Security Council Resolutions 1199 and 1203 invoke Chapter VII of the UN Charter they do not explicitly authorise the use of force against the FRY. By convention, UN resolutions mandating the international use of force authorise states to use 'all necessary means' to address a particular crisis. The Security Council resolutions on Kosovo did not contain this phrase. They also made no mention of Chapter VIII of the UN Charter, under which a regional organisation might be called upon to engage in enforcement action on behalf of the Security Council. Instead, both resolutions reaffirmed 'the commitment of all Member States to the sovereignty and territorial integrity of the Federal Republic of Yugoslavia'. This undermines attempts to interpret these resolutions as authorising armed intervention.

Thus despite the protestations of NATO members, Operation Allied Force violated international law. The USA appeared relatively untroubled by this fact. Thus when British Foreign Secretary Robin Cook told US Secretary of State Madeleine Albright that his lawyers had warned him that a NATO intervention required a UN mandate, Albright advised

---

[16] Ibid., p. 409.

[17] Mary Ellen O'Connell, 'The UN, NATO, and International Law After Kosovo', *Human Rights Quarterly*, 22:1 (2000), p. 82.

[18] Article 8 of the 1951 International Convention on the Prevention and Punishment of the Crime of Genocide arguably enjoins international military action against genocide.

[19] O'Connell, 'The UN, NATO, and International Law After Kosovo', p. 70.

[20] Krieger (ed.), *The Kosovo Conflict and International Law*, p. 338.

him 'to get himself new lawyers'.[21] In fact, the USA expended very little effort on making a legal case for the intervention, preferring to stress its moral necessity. 'In its explanation of the Kosovo military intervention, the United States ... emphasized the goals of the NATO action, rather than the basis in international law for authorization of the use of force'.[22] President Clinton's first speech announcing the operation made no legal arguments at all. Subsequently, the Clinton administration debated proposing that the operation should be construed as a new precedent in international law establishing NATO's right to act without UN authorisation, but decided not to rely on this argument.[23] The lack of legal justification did not cause the USA to desist either from the intervention itself or from publicly defending it as the appropriate course of action. Equally importantly, NATO's inability to legalise Operation Allied Force did not stop the USA from launching the intervention in this framework. Thus Operation Allied Force yields little support for the claim that lead states launch peace enforcement operations through international organisations out of respect for international law.

Burden-sharing in Operation Allied Force

Burden-sharing provides no more satisfactory explanation for the USA's decision to launch Operation Allied Force through NATO. Despite this framework, the USA had to assume a disproportionate share of the burden of executing and financing the intervention. This could not have surprised the USA, which has criticised the lack of burden-sharing in NATO since the 1950s.

Although it is a military alliance, NATO has no mechanisms to promote military burden-sharing for peace enforcement operations. It does not have a standing army, so any NATO military operation relies on troop contributions from individual member states. Even in cases of collective defence the level of these contributions remains at the discretion of member states: the North Atlantic Treaty only commits a signatory to take 'such action as it deems necessary' to respond to an attack on another NATO member (Article 5). There is no Charter obligation at

---

[21] Madeleine Albright, *Madam Secretary: A Memoir* (New York: Miramax, 2003), p. 384.
[22] Ruth Wedgwood, 'NATO's Campaign in Yugoslavia', *American Journal of International Law*, 93:4 (October 1999), p. 829.
[23] O'Connell, 'The UN, NATO, and International Law After Kosovo'. Thanks to an anonymous reviewer for clarifying this point. For some European reactions, see Krieger (ed.), *The Kosovo Conflict and International Law*, pp. 338, 397.

all for NATO members to contribute to peace enforcement operations and no institutional mechanism for encouraging their participation. The only partial exception is the Allied Command Europe Rapid Reaction Corps (ARRC), which was created in 1991 to undertake a range of military operations including peace support operations. Apart from its permanent headquarters personnel, however, ARRC consists of national units that are earmarked for the Corps but ultimately made available by states only on a case-by-case basis.

NATO's capacity to generate financial burden-sharing for peace enforcement operations is almost equally limited. NATO's three common budgets (military, civil, and security infrastructure) do involve substantial burden-sharing, especially from the point of view of the USA, NATO's largest member. In 1998, the USA accounted for 46.7 per cent of the combined GDP of all NATO countries but was responsible for only 23–28 per cent of these budgets.[24] However, NATO's relatively small budgets are only intended to fund NATO's general operating costs and basic defence infrastructure.[25] They cannot cover the cost of military operations. Thus although NATO can contribute headquarters staff, advance warning aircraft, and elements of military infrastructure, the bulk of troops and equipment in a NATO operation must come from individual NATO members – and each participating state must fund its own contributions.

NATO states' ability to contribute to an operation therefore depends directly on their national military expenditures. Here the USA far outstrips its NATO allies not only in absolute but also in relative terms. In 1999, the USA spent 3 per cent of its GDP on defence, compared to 2.7 per cent, 2.5 per cent, 2 per cent, and 1.5 per cent in France, the UK, Italy, and Germany, respectively. With 47 per cent of NATO's total GDP, the USA was paying for 59 per cent of NATO's total military expenditure. In absolute terms, European NATO members spent only $174 billion on defence, compared to a US expenditure of $283. As a result, their budget for military research and development was just one-quarter of that of the USA, while their joint procurement capacity was only $28 billion, compared to US spending of $47 billion.[26] Consistent

---

[24] Figures calculated on the basis of OECD GDP data, available at www.oecd.org.
[25] In 1998, the civil budget was US$157 million, the military budget US$806.5 million, and the NSIP US$466.4 million. NATO, *NATO Handbook*, chapter 9.
[26] *Strategic Survey 1999/2000* (London: Oxford University Press, 2000), pp. 16–19.

spending constraints of this kind affected European NATO members' capacity to contribute to peace enforcement operations.

From the US point of view, therefore, NATO was not a promising vehicle for military or financial burden-sharing for Operation Allied Force. US policy-makers knew that there were no internal mechanisms in NATO to encourage member states to contribute militarily or financially to a peace enforcement operation. They also knew that even if European NATO allies decided to participate, they would not be able to contribute forces and equipment at the same level of technological sophistication as the USA. The USA has demanded greater military efforts from its European allies for virtually all of NATO's existence, and this debate gained further salience with declining global defence budgets and the question of NATO enlargement after the end of the Cold War. There was no scope for excessive US optimism about NATO's capacity to promote military or financial burden-sharing for Operation Allied Force.

In the event, this burden-sharing was indeed limited. Only fourteen of NATO's nineteen members flew any kind of operational sortie during the Operation Allied Force. Among these fourteen, contributions ranged from substantial to symbolic. Figure 6.1 illustrates the vast differences

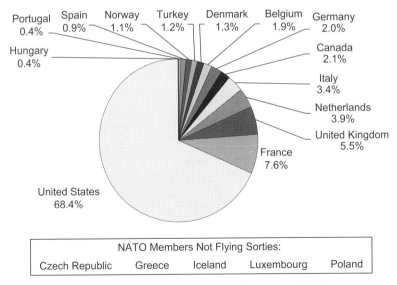

Figure 6.1: National distribution of sorties during Operation Allied Force

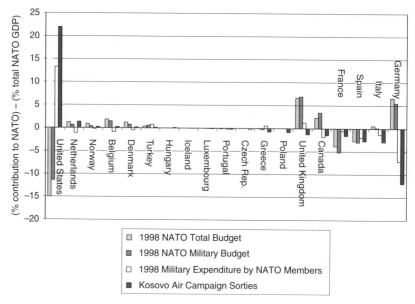

Figure 6.2: National contributions to NATO relative to shares of total NATO GDP

in NATO members' contributions by depicting the national distribution of operational sorties flown during the campaign.[27]

This chart indicates that the USA shouldered by far the largest part of the military burden of intervention, flying over 68 per cent of the sorties in Operation Allied Force. Moreover, the six largest NATO members (USA, France, UK, Italy, Germany, and Canada) accounted for almost 90 per cent of the sorties in the campaign. Thus only five of the USA's eighteen NATO allies made substantial contributions towards sharing the military burden of the Kosovo intervention. The remaining thirteen allies together accounted for only 11 per cent of the campaign's sorties.

This disparity in national contributions to Operation Allied Force is not fully explained by size differences among NATO members. Figure 6.2 takes a country's share of the combined 1998 GDP of all NATO states as a proxy for its relative size within the alliance. It shows the difference between this figure and a country's share of the sorties flown in Operation Allied Force as a measure of how much more or less than its 'fair' share that country contributed to the campaign. For comparison, it also includes

[27] Data from Wesley Clark, Report to NATO Secretary-General Robertson on 'Operation ALLIED FORCE Statistics', 6 January 2000. Unclassified NATO document SHJOC/J3AIR/0500/99.

measures of how much more or less than its expected share the country contributed to NATO's total budget, its military budget, and the total military expenditure by NATO members. This graph makes apparent that, from a US point of view, burden-sharing within NATO works least where it matters most for peace enforcement operations. In 1998, the USA contributed much less to NATO's total budget than its relative economic size would warrant. Other NATO allies, including the UK, Germany, and Canada, paid more than their 'fair' share. The USA came closer to contributing its 'fair' share of NATO's military budget, but again fell significantly short. When it comes to national military expenditure, however, the USA contributed almost 14 per cent more to total NATO expenditure than its relative economic size would seem to warrant. Finally, the USA carried 22 percentage points more than its 'fair' share of the burden created by Kosovo air sorties.

Even this figure does not fully capture the proportion of the burden the USA shouldered during Operation Allied Force, however. The USA flew a disproportionate share of the more dangerous night strikes during the operation as well as 86.7 per cent of the crucial but risky Suppression of Enemy Air Defence missions. US aircraft delivered 80 per cent of the ordinance used during the campaign, in addition to which the USA also had to supply some European aircraft with weapons.[28] The USA launched 90 per cent of the cruise missiles fired during the campaign. In addition, the USA provided the logistic and intelligence backbone of the campaign. It flew 87.45 per cent of the campaign's air-to-air refuelling missions and 70.5 per cent of its reconnaissance flights,[29] as well as providing satellite imagery of the theatre of operations. These contributions were funded exclusively by the USA. Consequently, the USA absorbed 'around 80% of the incremental cost of the Kosovo air campaign and supporting force deployments, with the UK and France contributing most of the balance'.[30]

Thus NATO was spectacularly unsuccessful as a vehicle for interstate burden-sharing during Operation Allied Force. An ad hoc coalition including just the USA, France, the UK, and Italy would have been almost as effective as the nineteen-member NATO framework. Given

[28] *Strategic Survey 1999/2000*, pp. 15–17.

[29] Clark, 'Operation ALLIED FORCE Statistics'.

[30] International Institute for Strategic Studies, *Military Balance 1999–2000* (London: Oxford University Press, 2000), p. 35. The *Military Balance* estimates the total costs of the campaign at US$11 billion.

their long-standing complaints about the lack of burden-sharing within NATO, US policy-makers could not have been surprised by this outcome. This strongly suggests that the USA did not turn NATO in order to promote burden-sharing for Operation Allied Force.

US legitimacy concerns for Operation Allied Force

Given NATO's inability either to legalise Operation Allied Force or to ensure burden-sharing for it, why did the USA choose to launch the operation within this framework? As a senior NATO diplomat put it, it was

> a matter of legitimacy . . . [The NATO framework] gives the operation a wider legitimacy and acceptance. This is important for the operation to succeed. If you have nineteen countries, it is a different thing . . . If there was a unilateral US or British intervention in Serbia, this would lead to serious problems . . . It was a way to deal with the problem more effectively than if it had been only the US and one, two, or three countries together. That would have raised many problems.[31]

This section delineates the USA's legitimacy concerns for Operation Allied Force and identifies its key legitimacy audience.

The nature of US legitimacy concerns

Operation Allied Force generated massive media interest around the world and was highly controversial. The world's strongest alliance had launched a massive military strike against a single, much smaller state because it disapproved of its treatment of an ethnic minority. This prompted accusations of aggression and moral imperialism as well as apprehension among other states that could also be accused of maltreating national minorities. The Yugoslav government protested against the campaign as 'aggression on the Federal Republic of Yugoslavia'[32] and it received important support from other states. India charged 'that the air strikes . . . amount to interfering in the internal affairs of a country'.[33] Russia also declared that 'the NATO military action against sovereign Yugoslavia . . . is nothing other than outright aggression.'[34] To make

---

[31] Author's interview. Remarks not for attribution.
[32] Krieger (ed.), *The Kosovo Conflict and International Law*, p. 304.
[33] Ibid., p. 493 and see pp. 492–7 for other states' reservations.
[34] Philip E. Auerswald and David P. Auerswald (eds.), *The Kosovo Conflict: A Diplomatic History Through Documents* (The Hague: Kluwer Law International, 2000), p. 725.

matters worse, NATO intervened without a UN mandate. China thus called the campaign 'a blatant violation of the UN Charter, as well as the accepted norms of international law', and several other states also officially expressed concern about NATO's recourse to force without a UN mandate.[35]

These protests reflected more than a concern with international law. As chapter 2 argued, sovereignty and non-aggression are basic rules of the international system that can only be overridden in the interest of international peace and security. Thus, Operation Allied Force faced suspicions of illegitimacy as well as accusations of illegality. Non-NATO members worried about militant and unwarranted international activism by an organisation that they could neither influence nor control. As one NATO official recognised, 'if you act ... without a UN Security Council blessing, you need a very strong, convincing case for you to justify what you are doing ... if you go against the grain of the UN system you are obliged to tell your story to the whole world, because the whole world is going to ask.'[36] Inevitably, these accusations reflected on Operation Allied Force's lead state – and while the USA faced allegations of illegality with relative equanimity, it was extremely sensitive about accusations of illegitimate aggression, for two main reasons.

First, the USA had a special stake in the international institutions it had helped to create, because they enshrined the US leadership role in the international community. The Clinton administration was explicit about this:

> After World War II ... America accepted the challenge to lead. We remained engaged overseas and worked with our allies to create international structures – from the Marshall Plan, the United Nations, NATO and other defense arrangements to the International Monetary Fund and the World Bank – that enabled us to strengthen our security and prosperity and win the Cold War ... Without our leadership and engagement, threats would multiply and our opportunities would narrow.[37]

A perceived act of aggression by the USA could undermine these institutions, a possibility India raised when it charged that Operation Allied Force 'seriously undermined the authority of the entire United Nations

---

[35] Ibid., p. 727; Krieger (ed.), *The Kosovo Conflict and International Law*, pp. 492–7.
[36] Author's interview with Michael Rühle, Head of Policy Planning and Speechwriting Section in NATO's Political Affairs Division, Brussels, Belgium, 20 June 2001.
[37] The White House, *A National Security Strategy for a New Century* (National Security Strategy Report to Congress, October 1998), p. 2.

system'.[38] Even if the institutions survived, moreover, the USA's leadership position within them might not. The Clinton administration had already acknowledged the vulnerability of this position in the debate over the USA's failure to fully pay its assessed UN dues in the 1990s: 'If America is to continue to lead the world by its own example ... we must pay our dues to the United Nations.'[39] Accusations of illegitimate aggression could only fuel the longstanding discontent among developing states with the USA's privileged position within the UN and other international institutions. China's official press foreshadowed this line of argument by pointedly noting: 'a self-proclaimed leader of the international community, the United States has shown an increasing disregard for a set of rules of the game in the international arena'.[40]

Second, the USA's unprecedented military and economic power had to be carefully managed to avoid provoking resentment or fear among other states. With the unifying threat of the Cold War over, even the USA's European allies were sensitive to excessive demonstrations of US power.[41] The Clinton administration acknowledged: 'America today is by any measure the world's unchallenged military and economic power ... Indeed, our success is so apparent to others that one of our biggest challenges now is how to avoid the resentment it sometimes generates.'[42] The key to managing this challenge was not to appear to be using US power aggressively. At a minimum, US power had to be seen as non-threatening by other states. At best, placing US power at the service of the international community might strengthen the USA by persuading other states to embrace it more closely as a leader and ally. As Clinton's National Security Adviser put it:

> We should not apologize for being a 'hyperpower'. But to remain strong, we must be a hyperpower that our friends and allies can depend on. We must remember that there is a difference between power and authority. Power is the ability to compel by force or sanctions ... Authority is the ability to lead, and we depend upon it for almost everything we try

---

[38] Ian Black, James Meek, and Ian Traynor, 'War in Europe: Russia and China lead international protests', *The Guardian*, 26 March 1999.

[39] The White House, 'A National Security Strategy for a New Century', p. iv.

[40] Miwa Suzuki, 'Uneasy Asia raises fears over NATO strikes', *Agence France Presse*, 26 March 1999.

[41] William Drozdiak, 'Even Allies resent U.S. dominance', *Washington Post*, 4 November 1997.

[42] Samuel R. Berger, Assistant to President Clinton on National Security Affairs, 'A Foreign Policy for the Global Age', *Foreign Affairs*, 79:6 (2000), p. 23.

to achieve. Our authority is built on qualities very different from our power . . . [including] on the credibility of our commitments and on our willingness to listen to and stand by others. . . . [I]f we use power in a way that antagonizes our friends and dishonors our commitments, we will lose our authority – and our power will mean very little.[43]

Thus the USA had a substantial interest in ensuring that its actions in Kosovo were not widely perceived as aggressive within the international community. To maintain its international leadership position and avoid alienating other states, the USA had to ensure that Operation Allied Force was internationally accepted as a legitimate use of force.

The USA's key legitimacy audience

The Clinton administration showed some sensitivity towards all four potential legitimacy audiences for Operation Allied Force identified in chapter 2. However, it regarded the international community of states as the most critical audience that had to be persuaded of Operation Allied Force's legitimacy.

The USA saw itself as forced to discount Yugoslav public opinion as a legitimacy audience for Operation Allied Force. NATO did stress that its actions were not intended as acts of war against the people of Yugoslavia. Secretary-General Solana emphasised: 'Let me be clear: NATO is not waging war against Yugoslavia. We have no quarrel with the people of Yugoslavia, who for too long have been isolated in Europe because of the policies of their government.'[44] However, Yugoslav public opinion was not seen as an accessible audience. As NATO's spokesman during Operation Allied Force recalled, 'I did not, obviously, expect to get the message across to the Serb people, because I never appeared on Serb TV. When NATO leaders did appear on Serb TV, it was caricatures straight out of Goebbels and the Nazi period.'[45] The only accessible Yugoslav audience, therefore, was seen to be the FRY government, which the USA made no effort to avoid alienating. Secretary of State Albright made it clear that she saw the Milosevic regime as an aggressor that should not be appeased. President Clinton also blamed the regime for making the air campaign necessary: 'if President Milosevic will not make

---

[43] Berger, 'A Foreign Policy for the Global Age', pp. 38–9.
[44] Weller (ed.), *The Crisis in Kosovo*, p. 495.
[45] Author's interview with Dr Jamie Shea, NATO spokesperson during Operation Allied Force, Brussels, Belgium, 28 June 2001.

peace, we will limit his ability to make war'.[46] During the intervention, NATO's major message for Milosevic's government was thus about determination, not legitimacy: 'the idea was to grind them down by showing that NATO was united, that just waiting for NATO to collapse wasn't going to work, that the longer this went on the more determined we would be to prevail.'[47]

The Clinton administration also did not identify US public opinion as a critical legitimacy audience for Operation Allied Force. This reflected an awareness that the US public was not generally sceptical of Operation Allied Force's legitimacy. Unlike other NATO countries like Greece and Italy, in the USA public support for Operation Allied Force consistently ranged above 50 per cent.[48] This support was not particularly robust. It peaked when images of Kosovar refugees flooded TV screens in early April 1999 but declined as NATO bombing errors occurred in April[49] and hopes of a quick victory faltered in May. Debates about target selection and the morality of conducting a war solely from the air also eroded public support for the operation, although most Americans balked at any suggestion of deploying US ground forces in Kosovo.[50] However, most Americans also felt that the USA had no vital interests at stake in Kosovo,[51] and believed that their government was acting for legitimate moral and international reasons: in mid-May 1999, 38 per cent of respondents in a US poll saw humanitarian concerns as the USA's main reason for intervention and an additional 23 per cent cited fears of a larger war.[52] If anything, the US public worried that their government was being too altruistic at the expense of US national interests and resources.

---

[46] Auerswald and Auerswald (eds.), *The Kosovo Conflict*, p. 731.

[47] Author's interview with Dr Jamie Shea, 28 June 2001.

[48] Similar public support existed in France and the UK. Albrecht Schnabel and Ramesh Thakur, *Kosovo and the Challenge of Humanitarian Intervention* (Tokyo: United Nations University, 2000).

[49] NATO erroneously bombed a passenger train in Grdelica Gorge and a civilian convoy in Djakovica on 12 and 14 April, respectively.

[50] Program on International Policy Attitudes, 'Americans on Kosovo: A Study of US Public Attitudes' (27 May 1999), online at www.pipa.org/OnlineReports/Kosovo/kosovo.htm, accessed 19 February 2003, document no longer available at this site.

[51] In March and April 1999, only 35–41 per cent of Americans felt that what happened in Serbia and Kosovo was very important to US interests. American Enterprise Institute Compilation, 'Public Opinion on Kosovo', cached on www.google.com, accessed 19 February 2003.

[52] Program on International Policy Attitudes, 'Americans on Kosovo', p. 12.

From the US point of view, therefore, the most crucial audience that had to be convinced of the legitimacy of Operation Allied Force was the international community of states, within which, as noted above, accusations of aggression were being made. At this level, the USA could distinguish three sets of states. The first were its close allies in Operation Allied Force, including the UK and France, which defended the intervention's legitimacy. The second were the intervention's outspoken critics, headed by Russia and China. The third group comprised states that were alarmed by Operation Allied Force but had not reached a final verdict on the intervention's legitimacy. The importance of this group lay in the fact that it constituted the vast majority of the international community, making its approval a potential substitute for a UN mandate in establishing Operation Allied Force's international legitimacy. After all, as chapter 2 argued, international legitimacy is ultimately a collective value judgement by the international community, and the UN's power to legitimate a peace enforcement operation merely derives from its approximation to that community thanks to its inclusive membership structure. For Operation Allied Force, the USA and its allies circumvented the UN because they feared the Russian and Chinese vetoes in the Security Council. If a critical mass of states could be persuaded that Operation Allied Force reflected the interests and values of the international community, however, the intervention's international legitimacy could be established despite its lack of a UN mandate and the opposition of a few states.

Defenders of Operation Allied Force put forward a complex argument to establish the intervention's legitimacy. They began by distinguishing the operation's legality (which was irreparably damaged by its lack of a UN mandate) from its legitimacy. As a senior NATO official put it, 'I prefer to use the word "legitimate" basis. If you say "legal", you will look at the UN Charter. This was not an article 51 action in self-defence, or an article 107 operation against the defeated powers of World War II. I prefer to go to the notion of legitimate basis.'[53] The next step was to propose a way of measuring the 'legitimate basis' that did not rely on case-by-case UN approval. In this context, the USA and its allies insisted that Operation Allied Force served the interests and values of the international community identified in Chapter One of the UN Charter. These include 'the prevention and removal of threats to the peace' (Article 1.1) and 'respect for human rights and for fundamental freedoms' (Article

[53] Author's interview. Remarks not for attribution.

1.3). Thus President Clinton argued, 'We act to protect thousands of innocent people in Kosovo from a mounting military offensive. We act to prevent a wider war; to diffuse a powder keg in the heart of Europe that has exploded twice before in this century with catastrophic results. And we act to stand united with our allies for peace.'[54] The US delegation to the UN pointedly added: 'The United Nations Charter does not sanction armed assaults on ethnic groups, or imply that the international community should turn a blind eye to a growing humanitarian disaster.'[55]

Advocates for Operation Allied Force contended, moreover, that the UN had already recognised the applicability of these principles. Security Council Resolutions 1199 and 1203 had expressed alarm about the humanitarian situation in Kosovo and pronounced the crisis a threat to international peace and security. NATO was simply more effective at guaranteeing these principles: '[Our] demands were not just NATO demands, but wider demands reflected by UN Security Council resolutions. So we were just trying to use force – that was the difference. We were the ones who were willing to use force to implement the demands.'[56] The fact that the European Union, the OSCE, and the Contact Group had also sought to remedy the crisis further proved that it was a major international concern. NATO firmly situated Operation Allied Force within these wider international efforts. Secretary-General Javier Solana argued:

> We are taking action following the Federal Republic of Yugoslavia Government's refusal of the International Community's demands ... NATO has fully supported all relevant UN Security Council resolutions, the efforts of the OSCE, and those of the Contact Group. We deeply regret that those efforts did not succeed ... This military action is intended to support the political aims of the international community ... We wish thereby to support international efforts to secure Yugoslav agreement to an interim political settlement.[57]

NATO's first press release on Operation Allied Force reiterated: 'NATO's military action ... [is] supporting international efforts to secure FRY agreement to an interim political settlement.'[58] The North Atlantic

[54] Weller (ed.), *The Crisis in Kosovo*, p. 498.
[55] Krieger (ed.), *The Kosovo Conflict and International Law*, p. 434.
[56] Author's interview with Michael Rühle, 20 June 2001.
[57] Weller (ed.), *The Crisis in Kosovo*, p. 495.
[58] Krieger (ed.), *The Kosovo Conflict and International Law*, p. 304.

Council also insisted, 'NATO's military action against the FRY supports the political aims of the international community . . . a peaceful, multi-ethnic and democratic Kosovo in which all its people can live in security and enjoy universal human rights and freedoms on an equal basis.'[59]

Under these circumstances, NATO members argued, the veto threat within the UN was itself illegitimate, because it prevented the UN from reacting to the Kosovo crisis according to the basic interests and values of the international community. For example, the Dutch Permanent Representative to the UN insisted:

> It goes without saying that a country – or an alliance – which is compelled to take up arms to avert such a humanitarian catastrophe would always prefer to be able to base its action on a specific Security Council resolution . . . If, however, due to one or two permanent members' rigid interpretation of the concept of domestic jurisdiction, such a resolution is not attainable, we cannot sit back and simply let the humanitarian catastrophe occur.[60]

Off the record, a NATO official paraphrased the argument as follows: 'Yes, the UN is great, but if these damn Russians decide to allow ethnic cleansing . . . and we, the good guys, can't do anything about it, then to hell with the UN.'[61] The implication was that NATO action in Kosovo was truer to both the UN Charter and the interests and values of the international community than UN Security Council inaction. US President Clinton argued: 'Had we [NATO] chosen to do nothing in the face of this brutality, I do not believe we would have strengthened the UN. We would have risked discrediting the UN. By acting as we did, we helped vindicate the principles and purposes of the UN Charter.'[62]

This argument depended crucially on NATO's interpretation of the international community as a normative community bound by the values of international peace and security and human rights that enjoined intervention in Kosovo. This interpretation was hotly contested, most notably by Russia. Advocates of Operation Allied Force sought to sideline these objectors as unrepresentative of the 'true' international community. They were at pains to point out the 'semi-democratic' or 'authoritarian' nature of their critics. As one NATO official put it, the argument was that 'these damn Russians, who are

---

[59] Ibid., p. 308.   [60] Ibid., p. 427.   [61] Author's interview. Remark not for attribution.
[62] 'Clinton defends NATO military action in Kosovo', *Deutsche Presse-Agentur*, 21 September 1999.

waging war against their own people, want to protect their Slav brother so that he can wage war against his own people'.[63] The implication was that Russia was ill suited to speak for the international community.

Ultimately, however, the success of this argument for Operation Allied Force's legitimacy depended on how widely it was accepted by other states. This is why the large group of states that had not yet decided how to judge Operation Allied Force was a critical legitimacy audience for the USA. If enough states agreed that Operation Allied Force reflected international interests and values, the intervention's international legitimacy would be solidly established and its remaining critics isolated. If most states sided with the critics of the intervention, however, the international community itself would be rejecting the claim that Operation Allied Force was in its interest. In the absence of a UN mandate, the USA and its allies would have nothing else to fall back on to prove their intervention's legitimacy. The stakes for the USA were thus extraordinarily high.

The NATO framework and US legitimacy concerns

The NATO framework played a crucial role in addressing the USA's legitimacy concerns about Operation Allied Force. It made its greatest contribution with regard to the legitimacy audience that most concerned the USA: those members of the international community that initially greeted the intervention with concern but not condemnation.

The NATO framework and Yugoslav and US public opinion

The NATO framework proved least effective with regard to the target state of the intervention. Although NATO insisted that it was fighting against the Milosevic regime rather than the people of Yugoslavia, this distinction was understandably lost on large sections of the Yugoslav public. Many Yugoslavs, including opponents of the Milosevic regime, felt that NATO's attack unacceptably violated their country's sovereignty. 'Many people said they were "opposed to the policy of Milosevic, but NATO strikes against a sovereign country are just going to make him stronger".'[64] On 28 March, four days after the beginning of the air campaign, 10,000 people attended a concert organised by the Belgrade

---

[63] Author's interview. Remark not for attribution.
[64] 'Anti-NATO protests in Europe, US and Australia', *Agence France Presse*, 28 March 1999.

city council to demonstrate against the intervention. Moreover, despite NATO's insistence that it was not at war with the Yugoslav people, its bombing campaign, conducted in all major Yugoslav regions, inevitably affected the country's population. Yugoslav civilians were killed by bombing errors and as the campaign progressed NATO increasingly targeted civilian installations of perceived strategic relevance as well as purely military sites. By mid-April, CNN reported:

> people in Belgrade are getting more and more angry, because they realize, at least in the last few days, that the targets are not military targets, that they are civilian targets ... average people in Belgrade, they think that NATO bombing against Yugoslavia is not a bombing against a regime here, but it's a bombing against average people.[65]

Predictably, the NATO framework failed to convince most Yugoslavs of the intervention's legitimacy. As one man put it, 'They are killing us. They are destroying our cities. They are killing our sons. They are destroying our property. They are bombing our country. And at the same time, they have nothing against us.'[66] Yugoslavs tended to side with their government in condemning the USA's 'aggression on the Federal Republic of Yugoslavia and the use of enormous military and killing potentials'.[67] The multilateral nature of the campaign only led the government to sever diplomatic relations with the UK, France, and Germany as well as with the USA. Among the Yugoslav public, protests extended to the Turkish and Belgian embassies and the German, British, and French cultural centres.[68] The main target of both government and popular resentment, however, remained the USA. As one reporter put it, 'I can tell you that people here [in Belgrade] really hate whatever looks like America.'[69]

As noted above, US public opinion was far less sceptical about the intervention's legitimacy. Even its lack of a UN mandate did not overly concern it: Americans would have preferred a UN mandate for Operation Allied Force but did not think it essential. A US opinion poll in May

[65] Argiris Dinopoulos, 'NATO Bombings Fuel Intense Anti-American Sentiment Among Serbians', CNN, 18 April 1999.
[66] 'Strike Against Yugoslavia: Serbs Remain Defiant', CNN, 28 March 1999.
[67] Auerswald and Auerswald (eds.), *The Kosovo Conflict*, p. 734.
[68] 'Protesters attack US, Turkish, Belgian embassies', BBC, 1 April 1999; 'Anti-NATO protests in Europe, US and Australia', *Agence France Presse*, 28 March 1999.
[69] Dinopoulos, 'NATO Bombings Fuel Intense Anti-American Sentiment Among Serbians', CNN, 18 April 1999.

1999 found that 48 per cent of respondents agreed with the statement 'It concerns me that the UN has not approved NATO military action, but I think NATO's operation should continue'.[70] A further 19 per cent stated, 'It does not concern me that the UN has not approved NATO military action'. Nevertheless, US public opinion was not indifferent to the international setting of Operation Allied Force. There was a strong preference for situating the campaign in a multilateral framework, in part to spread the perceived burden of the intervention, but also because there was unease about the international legitimacy of a unilateral intervention. The US public was willing to dispense with a UN mandate only because it accepted the NATO framework as sufficiently multi-lateral for this purpose. The international status that the formal NATO framework was believed to confer upon Operation Allied Force was important to the US public. Thus one poll found that even among Americans wiling to countenance sending ground troops into Kosovo, only 33 per cent still favoured ground intervention 'if there was no consensus among NATO allies to undertake a ground war, so that the action was not a NATO action and only included the troops of the US and some allies'.[71]

The NATO framework and legitimacy perceptions in the international community

The most important legitimacy effect of the NATO framework occurred at the international level. This effect was not universal since for the USA's Cold War opponents NATO auspices made the intervention seem more rather than less threatening. As one NATO official pointed out, 'Russia and China still consider NATO to be the war machine of the West, and most specifically of the USA.'[72] The Secretary-General of NATO's Parliamentary Assembly confirmed the negative effect of NATO aus-pices on these states: 'our critics, especially the Russians of course, immediately thought it was their nightmares come true: NATO using force – my God! I wonder what they would have done had it been, say for example, the European Union, whether they would have had the

---

[70] Program on International Policy Attitudes, 'Americans on Kosovo', p. 16.   [71] Ibid.
[72] Author's interview with Erik Sandahl, NATO Defence Planning and Operations Division, Crisis Management and Operations Directorate, Crisis Management Section, Brussels, Belgium, 26 June 2001. Author's translation from French.

same reaction. It was the old enemy.'[73] With respect to most other states, however, the NATO framework proved to be a crucial institutional platform for legitimising Operation Allied Force. Its importance has been summarised as follows: 'NATO can claim the legitimacy of a nineteen-nation decision process, and the normative commitments of a democratic Europe . . . NATO's decision deserves more deference than purely unilateral action.'[74]

Many defenders of Operation Allied Force emphasised that NATO regrouped the world's most established democracies. Some argued that this should insulate NATO from suspicions of aggression:

> We are not warmongers. Getting nineteen republics to fight is not an easy thing . . . the governments won't decide unless they can persuade their parliaments. And the Parliaments can't vote for them unless they can convince their electorates that what they are doing is the right thing.[75]

Conversely, the UN was derided as giving excessive power to non-democracies:

> this idea that the UN is by definition right, because it's the big body. [When] you try to set this into real terms, you say wait a minute, then is a semi-democracy like Russia and a . . . dictatorship like China – basically determining whether Europeans can intervene in a European country to stop ethnic cleansing. That doesn't fly. That just doesn't square. That is crazy.[76]

Thus 'NATO created its own legitimacy. It said: we are nineteen democratic nations, if we collectively believe this is the correct thing to do, it's the correct thing to do . . . with NATO, the stress was always on the nineteen democratic nations . . . there is the wider world opinion of other governments, that's why you stress the nineteen democratic nations.'[77] A NATO official emphasised the perceived importance of this argument: 'Multilateralism is one of the elements of legitimation, especially if you're dealing with democratic countries . . . If the countries are democracies, that adds to the legitimacy.'[78]

---

[73] Author's interview with Simon Lunn, Secretary-General of the NATO Parliamentary Assembly. Brussels, Belgium, 27 June 2001.
[74] Wedgwood, 'NATO's Campaign in Yugoslavia', p. 833.
[75] Author's interview with George Katsirdakis, Deputy Director of Defence Partnership and Cooperation Directorate in NATO's Defence Planning and Operations Division, Brussels, Belgium, 20 June 2001.
[76] Author's interview with Michael Rühle, 20 June 2001.
[77] Author's interview with Simon Lunn, 27 June 01.
[78] Author's interview with Erik Sandahl, 26 June 2001. Author's translation from French.

From the point of view of the wider (and in many cases, undemocratic) international community, however, the nature of NATO's members was less important than the multinational nature of the NATO framework itself. By March 1999, NATO had nineteen full members. This had no real significance in strictly legal terms: 'Legally, the Alliance has no greater freedom than its members.'[79] From the point of view of international legitimacy, however, it made a tremendous difference. As noted in chapter 2, in the contemporary international system multilateralism has become accepted as a guarantee that states are acting in the interests of a wider international community. As the world's most inclusive multilateral forum, the UN has primacy in this system, but the auspices of any international organisation help attenuate charges of unilateralism and thus improve the international legitimacy of an intervention. By March 1999, there were several precedents for peace enforcement by international organisations other than the UN, including the ECOWAS intervention in Liberia discussed in chapter 3 of this book. NATO members and officials were keenly aware of this dynamic. One NATO diplomat noted, 'it is important that [intervention] is done by the organisation as a whole rather than by individual nations. If it is done by individual nations, it has a different weight. They look like they are doing it for their own interests. If the organisation gets involved, it's a different activity.'[80] A NATO official concurred:

> vis-à-vis the international community [unilateralism] would send the wrong signal, it could be seen as improper, the intervention might seem biased. Therefore NATO-led operations are composed of 19 Member States . . . The more multilateral an operation is, the more it can offer to the international community a guarantee of objectivity and neutrality.[81]

As with the African sub-regional organisations studied in previous chapters, NATO's capacity to generate international legitimacy for Operation Allied Force was enhanced by its ability to induce its members to unite publicly behind the intervention. Public disputes within the organisation over the intervention would have severely damaged its multilateral credentials. NATO's spokesman during the operation acknowledged the importance of this unity: 'we didn't have a situation

---

[79] Bruno Simma, 'NATO, the UN and the Use of Force: Legal Aspects', *European Journal of International Law*, 1:10 (1999), p. 19.

[80] Author's interview with George Katsirdakis, 20 June 2001.

[81] Author's interview. Remarks not for attribution.

where Italy or Greece or Spain stood up and said "eh, we don't have a legal mandate!", which I think would have made it into a big issue ... But all nineteen agreed, solidly.'[82]

The crucial underpinning of this unity was NATO's consensus rule of decision-making. The decisions of the North Atlantic Council (NAC) must be approved by all member states before they are formally announced in the name of all NATO members. As already noted in previous chapters, in this decision-making system there is no easy way to register dissent from a majority decision. A dissenting state faces a stark choice between vetoing the decision and acquiescing to the majority opinion. The pressure towards acquiescence is considerable, since exercising a veto is costly. The dissenting state faces the wrath of its allies for blocking their decision, which can have material consequences. 'There is a certain pressure being exercised. It is the fate of smaller countries to undergo pressure from bigger countries in a consensus system – political and economic pressures ... It is a game of sticks and carrots.'[83] Casting a veto also invites questions about one's value as an ally. One NATO diplomat explained:

> The process is like a train: you climb up on it, you either get in or get out ... There is an argument about solidarity – we must be all together on this, because later, when our own vital interests are affected, other states will remember this, they will say: in this case you did not follow us or respect what we wanted, why should we help you now? ... We must be part of the whole thing, otherwise we will be left behind. If somebody asks us to do something now, and we say no, then we are in a hard negotiating position next time, when we want something. So it is not easy for a small country ... to block big powers like the US or the UK, unless we are willing to make big sacrifices.[84]

Finally, states realise that public displays of disunity undermine NATO's credibility as an effective alliance, which all NATO members have a stake in:

> The credibility of NATO is an intangible security interest. Maintaining the credibility of NATO is in everybody's interest. And so sometimes just this very goal of being credible, of being seen as a united front, is a value in itself which NATO members will sometimes sacrifice certain interests to.

---

[82] Author's interview with Dr Jamie Shea, 28 June 2001.
[83] Author's interview with Erik Sandahl, 26 June 2001.
[84] Author's interview. Remarks not for attribution.

> Because keeping NATO united is an interest in itself that overrides maybe parochial interests sometimes – if they are not too vital.[85]

In sum, 'It's very hard for one nation to say no if everybody else is willing to say yes . . . It's very hard for one nation – that even includes the US – to say no.'[86]

By contrast, NATO's institutional structures made it very easy for states to acquiesce to Operation Allied Force. Since there is a presumption of consensus as long as no state voices opposition to a proposal, all that was required of dissenting states was to remain silent: 'Consensus is not saying yes, it's just not saying no.'[87] This distinction was salient for states that faced considerable domestic opposition to Operation Allied Force, which they felt unable to openly flout by voting for the air campaign: 'It is easier to sell a decision to one's population if you have simply accepted it without breaking silence . . . This is a clever procedural way for coming to a consensus – if states actually had to vote in favour of a decision, it may be impossible to get a consensus.'[88] Moreover, acquiescing to Operation Allied Force engendered no obligation to participate in it, thanks to NATO's lack of financial and burden-sharing mechanisms for peace enforcement operations. This was crucial for states like Greece, whose publics opposed the campaign, and for impecunious states like Poland, which could not afford the costs of a military operation.

In short, within the NATO framework acquiescence to a decision is cheap and formal opposition expensive. This is crucial for generating a united front among all nineteen NATO members, which many NATO diplomats view as one of their organisation's strongest assets. A British NATO diplomat explained, 'when we do decide to go do something, everybody is actually going to agree, it's not one nation standing up in public and saying no, we do not agree to that. If they're not happy with it, they will stay quiet.'[89] This silence is generally preserved even outside formal NATO structures: 'you can say what you want in the alliance, but not on the free market outside . . . Never accept a NATO operation and

---

85 Author's interview with Michael Rühle, 20 June 2001.
86 Author's interview with Richard Ladd-Jones, UK Permanent Mission to NATO, Brussels, Belgium, 21 June 2001.
87 Author's interview with Simon Lunn, 27 June 2001.
88 Author's interview with Mr Derus, press officer, German Permanent Mission to NATO, Brussels, Belgium, 26 June 2001.
89 Author's interview with Richard Ladd-Jones, 21 June 2001.

then criticise what it is doing.'[90] The USA benefited enormously from this system when it launched Operation Allied Force. The consensus rule helped transform the air campaign from a unilateral US initiative into a multilateral enterprise that bore the collective imprimatur of nineteen states. At the US Permanent Mission to NATO, this unity was identified as the principal benefit of launching Operation Allied Force through the NATO framework: 'it's the solidarity of having nineteen sovereign nations, all saying exactly the same thing. That carries a tremendous amount of strength.'[91] The US Department of Defense stressed that 'Operation Allied Force could not have been conducted without the NATO alliance and without ... most importantly, [the] political and diplomatic support provided by the allies and other members of the coalition.'[92]

NATO also provided an excellent base for lobbying non-NATO members for their endorsement of Operation Allied Force and thus cumulatively reinforcing the intervention's international legitimacy. Most immediately, this included the twenty-four states affiliated with NATO through the Partnership for Peace programme in 1999. NATO had institutionalised avenues for approaching these states through the Euro-Atlantic Partnership Council (EAPC) and Partners' permanent missions to NATO headquarters. The Alliance also provided incentives for Partners to support Operation Allied Force. As one NATO official put it, 'don't forget, of course, there is the tremendous lure of being a NATO member'.[93] Proponents of Operation Allied Force scored a tremendous diplomatic victory when they persuaded virtually all Partner states other than Russia to officially back the Kosovo campaign at the April 1999 EAPC Summit in Washington. Not only was Russia made aware that it was increasingly isolated in its formal opposition to the campaign, but NATO Secretary-General Solana could announce to the world that:

> Our Partners all share our view that the violence resulting from nation-alism and ethnic strife could not be tolerated in the Europe of the 21st

---

[90] Author's interview with Mr Derus, 26 June 2001.
[91] Author's interview with Kenneth Huffman, US Permanent Mission to NATO, Brussels, Belgium 21 June 2001.
[92] US Department of Defence, *Report to Congress: Kosovo/Operation Allied Force After-Action Report*, 31 January 2000, online at www.defenselink.mil/pubs/kaar02072000.pdf, p. 5.
[93] Author's interview. Remarks not for attribution.

century. Our Partners share our resolve and determination to put a stop
to that violent conflict [in Kosovo] and to ensure that justice is upheld . . .
the support of our Partner countries for our political objectives in Kosovo
demonstrates that we share the same values.[94]

NATO could now claim to act in the name of forty-two rather than just
nineteen states, enhancing its ability to present itself as the agent of the
international community as a whole.

NATO's greatest diplomatic victories, however, occurred at the UN.
NATO had two key advantages in this forum: First, NATO had considerable weight within the UN because its members included three
permanent Security Council members and eight of the ten largest financial contributors to the UN. Second, as a multilateral forum NATO
could draw on the precedents the Security Council had set in retroactively legitimising earlier peace enforcement operations by regional
organisations launched without a Security Council mandate by condon-
ing and even supporting these operations. Both factors contributed to
three developments within the UN that enhanced Operation Allied
Force's international legitimacy.

The first was UN Secretary-General Kofi Annan's relatively positive
reaction to Operation Allied Force. As the UN's highest official, Annan
spoke for the international community with more credibility than
any other public figure. His reaction was thus critical for Operation
Allied Force's international legitimacy. Annan publicly disapproved of
NATO's proceeding without a UN mandate. He stressed that 'under the
[UN] Charter the Security Council has primary responsibility for maintaining international peace and security – and this is explicitly acknowledged in the North Atlantic Treaty. Therefore the Council should be
involved in any decision to resort to the use of force.'[95] However, Annan
did not condemn Operation Allied Force and even acknowledged military action to be legitimate: 'It is indeed tragic that diplomacy has failed,
but there are times when the use of force may be legitimate in the pursuit
of peace.'[96] Moreover, on 9 April, Annan echoed NATO's demands on
the FRY government, promising to urge NATO leaders to suspend their
air campaign only 'upon the acceptance by the Yugoslav authorities of

---

[94] Javier Solana, NATO Secretary-General, 'Statement to the Press', 25 April 1999, online
at www.nato.int/docu/speech/1999/s990425a.htm.
[95] Weller (ed.), *The Crisis in Kosovo*, p. 498.   [96] Ibid.

the above conditions'.[97] NATO members were delighted. French authorities immediately declared that Annan's appeal to Belgrade 'meets the expectations expressed by France'.[98] US President Clinton telephoned Annan 'for about 15 minutes to thank him personally for his public statement and to say how grateful . . . the NATO allies were for the show of international support' for the goals of the air campaign.[99]

NATO's second victory within the UN was the resounding defeat on 26 March 1999 of a draft Security Council resolution condemning Operation Allied Force. The draft resolution, sponsored by Belarus, Russia, and India, called NATO's campaign 'a flagrant violation of the UN Charter' and a 'threat to international peace and security', and demanded 'an immediate cessation of the use of force against the Federal Republic of Yugoslavia'.[100] Since France, the UK, and the USA held veto power in the Security Council, this resolution was never likely to pass. However, if these NATO members had had to exercise their veto, Russia would have scored a victory. The Security Council consists of five permanent members (China, France, Russia, the UK, and the USA) and ten non-permanent members elected (subject to regional quotas) by the UN General Assembly to make the Council more representative of the larger international community. In 1999, the Council's non-permanent members were Argentina, Bahrain, Brazil, Canada, Gabon, Gambia, Malaysia, Namibia, the Netherlands, and Slovenia. Draft Security Council resolutions are defeated either if they fail to obtain the required nine-vote majority in the Council or if a permanent

[97] Annan urged the FRY government to end its campaign against Kosovar civilians, withdraw its military forces from Kosovo, accept the return of refugees, and acquiesce to the deployment of an international military force in Kosovo. Krieger (ed.), *The Kosovo Conflict and International Law*, p. 440.

[98] Tani Freedman, 'UN's Annan urges Yugoslavia to stop military action in Kosovo', *Agence France Presse*, 9 April 1999.

[99] Gene Randall, 'Strike Against Yugoslavia: Clinton Thanks Annan for Public Support', CNN, 10 April 1999. After the campaign, Annan argued explicitly that although humanitarian interventions without Security Council mandates were deplorable, they were also understandable if the Security Council failed to take action to halt the gravest crimes against humanity. Kofi Annan, 'Two Concepts of Sovereignty', *The Economist*, 18 September 1999. NATO officials were again delighted: 'That speech by Annan . . . I used it, quoted it all the time in our Kosovo justifications, because here you have the big boss from the UN basically . . . alluding to a failure of the Council. For me this was a revelation, to have the big boss say yes, we messed up here, and so we shouldn't be surprised if others are going ahead.' Author's interview with Michael Rühle, 20 June 2001.

[100] Krieger (ed.), *The Kosovo Conflict and International Law*, p. 432.

member votes against and therefore vetoes them. These two kinds of defeat do not send the same international message: the one signals the international community's rejection of a resolution, the other suggests that a few powerful states have prevailed against the wishes of the international community. If the Council's non-permanent members had supported the draft resolution condemning Operation Allied Force, NATO's isolation in the wider international community would have been painfully obvious. In the event, however, only China and Namibia voted with Russia for the resolution. Canadian representative Fowler stressed: 'There were no vetoes cast this morning. A veto is cast only when it overrides nine positive votes, and that was not the case this morning.'[101]

The resounding defeat of their draft resolution suggested that Russia and China, not NATO, were on the margins of the international community. The British Secretary of State for Defence had predicted this outcome with clear satisfaction:

> NATO's action has received support in the UN Security Council from the United States, France, Argentina, Slovenia, Malaysia, Gambia, Bahrain, the Netherlands and Gabon. Outside of Russia and China, only Namibia disagreed with the military action in the Security Council, and in the wider United Nations, we know only of opposition from India and understandably Belarus and the former Republic of Yugoslavia itself.[102]

With twelve out of fifteen Security Council members voting against the draft resolution, NATO had established its position on Kosovo as the mainstream of the international community. The Dutch permanent representative to the UN put this point succinctly:

> the world has witnessed a gradual shift ... making respect for human rights more mandatory and respect for sovereignty less absolute ... Only if that shift is a reality can we explain how on 26 March the Russian–Chinese draft resolution branding the NATO air strikes as a violation of the Charter could be so decisively rejected by 12 votes to 3.[103]

NATO's final victory in the UN was the passing of Security Council Resolution 1244 on 10 June 1999. On 3 June, the FRY had accepted a peace plan brokered by Finnish President Ahtisaari (for the EU) and Russian special envoy Chernomyrdin. The plan largely reflected NATO's goals in Kosovo, including the withdrawal of FRY troops from Kosovo

[101] Ibid., p. 440. [102] Ibid., p. 410. [103] Ibid., p. 371.

and the deployment of an international civil and military presence in the region. A military-technical agreement for implementing this plan was reached on 9 June. The next day Resolution 1244 established the UN's NATO-led international Kosovo Force (KFOR) and NATO Secretary-General Solana announced an end to NATO air strikes.

Resolution 1244 was a compromise that ultimately greatly benefited NATO members, because through it the international community effectively adopted NATO's campaign and agreed to carry it towards its long-term conclusion. The resolution did pointedly reaffirm the UN as the primary international organisation responsible for peace and security in Kosovo. Russia celebrated this as a defeat for NATO: 'We are pleased that the members of NATO have finally recognised the utter futility of the war they have unleashed and come to understand that there is no alternative to respecting the Charter prerogatives of the Security Council.'[104] However, the resolution, which was co-sponsored by seven major contributors to Operation Allied Force, did not condemn NATO's intervention.[105] It marked the end of direct NATO activity in Kosovo, but neither refuted nor abandoned NATO's goals. As the US representative to the UN pointed out, 'the resolution addresses all our key objectives as set out in the North Atlantic Treaty Organisation.'[106] KFOR's role was to safeguard the achievements of NATO's military campaign as well as of international diplomacy. The UN was essentially providing a follow-on force that allowed NATO to claim victory and escape long-term responsibility for implementing the peace agreement. NATO members maintained a significant presence in Kosovo by contributing to KFOR, but they could shed overall political responsibility for the region's future. Their campaign in Kosovo had become a project of the international community. NATO members thus had good reason to be satisfied with Resolution 1244.

All these diplomatic victories contributed to a single goal: through them, Operation Allied Force was progressively accepted as reflecting the interests and values of the wider international community. NATO members gradually accumulated a critical mass of international support for the operation, which vindicated their original claim that they were

---

[104] Ibid., p. 368.
[105] Resolution 1244 was sponsored by Canada, France, Germany, Italy, the Netherlands, the UK, and the USA, as well as non-NATO members Gabon, Japan, Russia, Slovenia, and Ukraine. Its lack of condemnation of Operation Allied Force caused China to withdraw its support. Ibid., p. 369.
[106] Ibid., p. 371.

acting in the name of the international community. First NATO's Partners for Peace, then the UN Secretary-General, and finally the UN Security Council itself accepted the validity of NATO's aims in Kosovo, if not the way in which the organisation had proceeded. Each successive victory strengthened NATO's claim to be acting for the whole international community and isolated critics like Russia and China. Operation Allied Force's final vindication came in the August 2000 *Kosovo Report* by the Independent International Commission on Kosovo. The report confirmed NATO's core argument:

> The Commission concludes that NATO military intervention was illegal but legitimate. It was illegal because it did not receive prior approval from the United Nations Security Council. However ... the intervention was justified because all diplomatic means had been exhausted and because the intervention had the effect of liberating the majority population of Kosovo from a long period of oppression under Serb rule.[107]

Through these victories, NATO was able to gradually sway a sufficiently large subsection of the international community to lend validity to NATO's overall claim that it was acting in the name of that international community. Thus the NATO framework helped establish Operation Allied Force's international legitimacy, addressing core US concerns about perceptions of the intervention in the international community of states, the USA's key legitimacy audience. As one NATO official observed:

> That is why they went through NATO – they needed the political support and wanted to share the political responsibility for their actions ... vis-à-vis Yugoslavia, Russia, China, and the rest of the world ... the main thing was to show that it was the whole world against one country. The point is political support.[108]

The costs and benefits of the NATO framework

The argument of this chapter so far has been that legitimacy concerns provide a better explanation for the USA's decision to launch Operation Allied Force within the NATO framework than either respect for international law or a desire for burden-sharing. What remains to be established is the significance of this finding. Realists can admit that most

[107] Independent Commission on Kosovo, *Kosovo Report*, Executive Summary.
[108] Author's interview. Remark not for attribution.

states would prefer to act with international legitimacy than without it. Their objection is that this tells us nothing fundamental about states' priorities because international legitimacy is relatively easy and costless to achieve. However, this section demonstrates that the US incurred substantial costs by launching Operation Allied Force within a NATO framework. These most notably included the costs associated with obtaining a NATO mandate and the costs of managing the campaign in a NATO setting.

The costs of obtaining a NATO mandate

Since NATO makes decisions by consensus, NATO auspices could only be obtained for Operation Allied Force if a critical mass of NATO members endorsed the use of force and the remaining minority was persuaded to acquiesce to it. Yet throughout 1998 and into 1999, NATO members differed markedly on how to respond to the growing crisis in Kosovo. It took months of intense diplomatic effort within NATO and the failure of a major international peace initiative to achieve consensus.

Contingency planning for possible NATO military action in Kosovo began as early as May 1998.[109] Until September 1998, however, most European NATO members refused to consider a NATO threat of force without a UN mandate.[110] Encouraged by UN Security Council Resolution 1199 and galvanised by the Gornje Obrinje massacre by Serbian security forces on 28 September, NATO finally united in October 1998 to threaten air strikes against Yugoslavia. This threat was primarily issued to support US Ambassador Holbrooke in his negotiations with President Milosevic, however. NATO states remained divided on the question of the actual use of force, and interest in the military option waned further when Milosevic agreed to comply with Resolution 1199.

For the USA, the 15 January 1999 Racak massacre dramatically reopened the issue of using force against the FRY. The atrocity allowed Secretary of State Madeleine Albright to convince her US colleagues that changing Milosevic's policies in Kosovo required a real commitment to use military force if necessary.[111] US fears of an impending humanitarian

---

[109] John Peters, Stuart Johnson, Nora Bensahel, Timothy Liston, and Traci Williams, *European Contributions to Operation Allied Force: Implications for Transatlantic Cooperation* (Santa Monica: Rand, 2001), pp. 11–12.

[110] Peters et al., *European Contributions to Operation Allied Force*, p. 13.

[111] Ivo Daalder and Michael O'Hanlon, *Winning Ugly: NATO's War to Save Kosovo* (Washington D.C.: Brookings, 2000), pp. 69–72.

disaster escalated when Milosevic sought to expel the head of the OSCE verification mission from Kosovo and denied investigators for the International Criminal Tribunal for the Former Yugoslavia entrance to the region. On 22 January, the USA called on NATO to renew the threat of air strikes unless Milosevic complied fully with the peace deal concluded in October 1998.[112] However, most European NATO members were still not prepared to see NATO use force in Kosovo. They insisted on further diplomatic attempts to resolve the crisis. After simultaneous negotiations within NATO, the Contact Group, and the UN, a compromise was agreed on. On 30 January, the NAC renewed its threat of air strikes against the FRY by delegating authority to launch these strikes to NATO Secretary-General Solana. Before any strikes were launched, however, NATO would allow a last negotiation effort sponsored by the Contact Group to proceed in Rambouillet, France. The USA agreed to pressure both the FRY and the Kosovars to come to an agreement.

The USA doubted that negotiations would resolve the crisis. Secretary of State Albright found it necessary to remind the parties to 'Get serious. Showing up is not going to be good enough.'[113] She also stressed the need to 'maintain a credible threat of force, which has proven again and again to be the only language President Milosevic understands'.[114] When the talks began on 6 February, they seemed to justify US scepticism. The FRY delegation in particular showed little interest in substantive negotiations for a settlement.[115] A Contact Group attempt to break the deadlock through parallel direct negotiations with President Milosevic failed, and alienated the Kosovar delegation. Consequently, neither side was willing to sign an agreement by the appointed end-date of the Rambouillet conference on 20 February. At European and Russian insistence, the USA agreed to a three-day extension of the deadline, but by 23 February, the delegations still refused to sign.[116] Nevertheless, the Contact Group pressed for a follow-on conference in Paris on 15 March,

---

[112] Michael Evans, 'US calls for NATO airstrike threat against Milosevic', *The Times*, 22 January 1999.

[113] Bob Roberts and Gavin Cordon, 'UK urges Kosovo talks as 23 die in raid', *Birmingham Post*, 30 January 1999.

[114] Ian Black, 'Threat of air strikes recedes as Milosevic appears to back down', *The Guardian*, 22 January 1999.

[115] Marc Weller, 'The Rambouillet Conference on Kosovo', *International Affairs*, 75:2 (1999), pp. 227–34.

[116] The Kosovar delegation did indicate its general acceptance of the agreement and an intent to sign after consultations with its constituents.

causing a further delay of NATO military action. The Paris talks ended on 19 March with the Kosovar delegation signing the agreement but the FRY delegation refusing to do so. Only then was the path clear for a NATO intervention. Operation Allied Force began on 24 March.

Thus although the USA was willing to launch NATO air strikes from mid-January onwards, the diplomatic initiatives insisted on by its European allies delayed military action for over two months. During that time, evidence of FRY preparations for a military offensive in Kosovo mounted. By 25 February, US intelligence was reporting thousands of FRY troops and tanks arrayed against Kosovo.[117] By mid-March, according to the US Department of Defense, 'almost one-third of the FRY's total armed forces had massed in and around Kosovo, in preparation for an obvious offensive'.[118] The delay in air strikes allowed the FRY to mass its forces and prepare the offensive campaign the USA was seeking to prevent. It had no benefits for the USA, which was ready to act by mid-January. The delay was, however, necessary for obtaining a NATO mandate for the air strikes. Most European NATO members refused to condone the use of force until all diplomatic means of settling the crisis were exhausted. Rambouillet was the price for bringing them on board:

> [T]he purpose of Rambouillet was not so much to get a deal that few thought attainable. Rather it was to create a consensus in Washington and among the NATO allies that force would have to be used. While the talks failed to get agreement on an interim accord, they did succeed in convincing everybody that diplomacy without the use of force would not succeed in ending the conflict in Kosovo.[119]

As US National Security Adviser Samuel Berger put it, 'we needed to demonstrate real commitment to get a peaceful resolution in order to get the allies to go along with the use of significant force.'[120]

Even after Rambouillet, several obstacles to achieving a NATO mandate remained. Some NATO members continued to have reservations about a military intervention, which the USA sought to accommodate. Hungary, for example, required reassurance that special care would be taken in strikes in Yugoslavia's Vojvodina region, whose inhabitants

[117] Dana Priest, 'US Speaks more softly after failed Kosovo talks', *Washington Post*, 25 February 1999.
[118] US Department of Defense, *Kosovo/Operation Allied Force After-Action Report*, 31 January 2000, p. A7.
[119] Daalder and O'Hanlon, *Winning Ugly*, p. 85.   [120] Ibid.

included ethnic Hungarians. More generally, the fragile consensus for strikes made it impossible to agree on long-term planning for Operation Allied Force. The air campaign plan agreed upon included three phases: attack of Serbian air defence systems, attack of military targets in Kosovo as well as Serbian reinforcements north of Kosovo, and attack of a wide range of military targets throughout Yugoslavia. There was no discussion of what might happen after phase three. In part this reflected optimism that the Milosevic regime would relent within days of the attack. However, it also reflected how contentious any further options were. Several allies, including the USA and Germany, were unwilling publicly to contemplate sending ground troops to Kosovo, and others would not commit to such a step unless the USA did. Therefore, 'NATO deliberately did not prepare contingency plans in case Milosevic remained steadfast in his position and military action beyond the original three-phased plan became necessary. Clinton administration officials and SACEUR Clark worried that if the NAC had to contemplate a more prolonged campaign, it would withdraw its support for *any* air strikes.'[121] From a military point of view, this lack of contingency planning was deplorable. From a political point of view, it was simply part of the cost of obtaining a NATO mandate.

The benefits and costs of operating in the NATO framework

Several of the USA's NATO allies made valuable contributions to Operation Allied Force. The UK, France, and Italy supplied substantial numbers of aircraft, although together they only furnished 19 per cent of NATO's forces, compared with the USA's 65 per cent.[122] European NATO members also provided an indispensable launching pad for the Kosovo campaign. The US Department of Defense has recognised that 'it simply would not have been possible to carry out even the US part of this operation without the NATO members contributing their airspace, their infrastructure, their military bases, and their airfields.'[123]

The most decisive European contribution to Operation Allied Force, however, was British pressure for a NATO ground offensive in Kosovo. Under considerable domestic pressure, US President Clinton had ruled out this option at the beginning of Operation Allied Force, and several

---

[121] Peters et al., *European Contributions to Operation Allied Force*, p. 17.
[122] Clark, 'Operation ALLIED FORCE Statistics' 6 January 2000.
[123] US Department of Defense, *Kosovo/Operation Allied Force After-Action Report*, p. xix.

other members of the campaign, including Italy and Germany, shared his reluctance. This left Allied strategy dangerously open-ended when, contrary to many expectations, the Milosevic regime did not crumble after a few days of bombing. In mid-April, British Prime Minister Tony Blair reopened the issue of a ground initiative in the event that further air strikes proved fruitless.[124] His overture initially alienated the USA and other allies, but as the air campaign wore on Blair's position gained ground. By 19 May, Clinton was publicly edging towards considering a ground campaign: 'we [NATO] intend to see our objectives achieved and . . . we have not and will not take any option off the table.'[125] NATO was slowly shifting towards contemplating a ground offensive. This development was crucial because it persuaded Milosevic that absorbing NATO air strikes was not a long-term option. His decision to negotiate a peace settlement in June 1999 was undoubtedly influenced by this recognition.

However, these contributions to Operation Allied Force cannot explain why the USA chose to operate within the NATO framework. Britain's push for a ground offensive could also have occurred within a coalition of the willing and was in any case not immediately welcomed by the USA. A coalition of the willing could also have effectively united the small handful of NATO allies that carried most of the material burden of Operation Allied Force. These states had trained for joint operations through NATO, but they could have used this training even if the NATO framework had not been used for Operation Allied Force. What the NATO framework added to a potential coalition of the willing alternative was just over a dozen other nations that in military terms contributed little or nothing to the campaign. Worse still, from the US point of view, the NATO framework also generated three major kinds of cost.

First, the NATO framework made it difficult for the USA to issue credible threats and commitments against the Milosevic regime. It took NATO five months of negotiations to make good on its October 1998 threat of air strikes against the FRY and 'the route it travelled to that point was strewn with frequent threats, failed ultimatums, and feeble deadlines that were immediately reset once passed.'[126] Milosevic knew that NATO states were divided on key issues like the need for a UN

---

[124] 'NATO keeps ground troops option open – Blair', *Birmingham Post*, 19 April 1999.
[125] Brian Knowlton, 'Clinton refuses to rule out ground troops in Yugoslavia', *International Herald Tribune*, 19 May 1999.
[126] Daalder and O'Hanlon, *Winning Ugly*, p. 94.

mandate to launch air strikes and the possibility of averting war through a last-minute negotiated settlement. His refusal to bow to NATO's threats was in part a gamble that the Alliance would not be able to unite around an air campaign. Although he was eventually proved mistaken, this was not an unreasonable hope. Thus operating within the NATO framework made it hard for the USA to issue the kind of credible threat that might have eliminated the need to actually resort to military force.

Moreover, the multilateral framework impeded the USA's ability to credibly commit to continuing Operation Allied Force until victory was achieved. Milosevic hoped to outlast NATO. As he commented to Germany's Foreign Minister in March, 'I can stand death – lots of it – but you can't.'[127] Milosevic had reason for optimism: public support for Operation Allied Force fell in nearly all participating countries as air strikes continued and encompassed an ever wider range of targets. Even in the USA, support for air strikes sank to 55 per cent in early May 1999 from a high of 61 per cent in mid-April.[128] Countries where public support for Operation Allied Force was weak to begin with would not be able to sustain this downward pressure indefinitely. While NATO politicians generally kept a united front, popular protests against the air strikes in key NATO countries like Germany and Italy gave Milosevic reason to believe he could outlast NATO's campaign. Thus NATO's spokesman saw a major part of his role as:

> showing that NATO was united, just waiting for NATO to collapse wasn't going to work, that the longer this went on the more determined we would be to prevail, and therefore not to encourage the Yugoslavs who believed that they could win – I mean the Yugoslav government – by allowing them to gain the impression of a fractious, divided alliance with sort of Vietnam-style anti-war protests on the streets of European capitals, giving them the impression, like the Vietnamese had the impression in the 1970s, that ultimately these guys are going to give up and all we have to do is outlast them.[129]

Ultimately, NATO was able to dash Milosevic's hopes, in part by continuing to show a united front at the 23–24 April 1999 Washington Summit of the NAC. Combined with the possibility of a NATO ground offensive and fading Russian support, this convinced Milosevic to agree to a negotiated settlement (on terms favourable to NATO) in June 1999.

---

[127] Ibid. [128] Program on International Policy Attitudes, 'Americans on Kosovo', p. 7.
[129] Author's interview with Dr Jamie Shea, 28 June 2001.

Had the USA and its core allies in Operation Allied Force been able to credibly demonstrate their commitment to stay the course earlier, the campaign might have been over sooner. However, the multilateral NATO framework made such a commitment difficult.

The second set of costs arising from NATO-based multilateralism concerned the day-to-day management of Operation Allied Force. The nature of the campaign itself already made this an extremely complicated issue. This was not a traditional war fought with all available might against a declared enemy but a campaign aimed only at incapacitating the FRY's security forces in Kosovo and ending a humanitarian catastrophe there. Consequently, military operational decisions were politicised to an extraordinary degree. As one NATO official put it:

> In order to do this kind of peace operations there is a tremendous interest and blessing by the political authorities of most of the aspects of an OpPlan [Operational Plan] … What are you authorised to do or not authorised to do? Other than self defence, all the rest needs blessing … This is extremely important, because if you make a mistake there, what kind of message are you sending? So it's politically extremely sensitive.[130]

Wesley Clark, the Commander of Operation Allied Force understood these constraints:

> Operation Allied Force was modern war – limited, carefully constrained in geography, scope, weaponry, and effects. Every measure of escalation was excruciatingly weighed. Diplomatic intercourse with neutral countries, with those opposed to NATO's actions, and even with the actual adversary continued during and around the conflict … The highest possible technology was in use, but only in carefully constrained ways.[131]

Multilateralism made the management of this campaign even more difficult. 'The fact that it's a multinational operation make[s] things even more complicated, because you're not just checking with your government, you're checking with all of them.'[132] This complexity came to the fore during target selection for Operation Allied Force. NATO's political leaders disagreed, at times vehemently, about the appropriate targets for NATO bombers. Some states objected to strikes against facilities with civilian as well as military purposes. Others had geographic concerns: Germany opposed bombing cities for fear of

---

[130] Author's interview. Remarks not for attribution.
[131] Clark, *Waging Modern War*, pp. xxiii–xxiv.
[132] Author's interview. Remarks not for attribution.

civilian casualties, Hungary sought to protect the large ethnic Hungarian population in the Vojvodina region. Some states also emphasised their political importance by insisting on certain targeting priorities. French President Chirac:

> boasted after the conflict that 'there was not one single target that was not agreed upon by France beforehand' ... France intervened within the Alliance to halt attacks on Yugoslav civil installations. It also took credit for steering air raids towards Yugoslav forces deployed in Kosovo itself, for sparing Montenegro as much as possible, and for preventing NATO from proceeding to stage 3 of its operations, which would have entailed intensifying and extending air raids.[133]

Targeting issues also raised legal concerns because the First Additional Protocol to the Geneva Conventions limits legitimate targets in war-time.[134] Many European NATO members had signed the Protocol. The USA had not, but asserted that it would apply the Protocol in Kosovo. The stage was thus set for legal as well as diplomatic wrangling. As Richard Betts notes, 'One of the most striking features of the Kosovo campaign . . . was the remarkably direct role lawyers played in managing combat operations.'[135]

These debates significantly affected the military campaign. With NATO diplomats insisting on specifying the types of targets against which strikes were authorised, the US military, which provided the bulk of Operation Allied Force's firepower, found its doctrine overruled in several ways.[136] It had to escalate air strikes gradually from purely military targets to infrastructure and dual-use targets rather than launch a strategic first attack against all of the opponent's vital interests. The requirement early in the campaign that specific individual targets be approved by NATO's politicians led to a less systematic bombing campaign than US military doctrine called for. Sporadic political approval of

---

[133] Alex Macleod, 'France: Kosovo and the Emergence of a New European Security', in Pierre Martin and Mark K. Brawley (eds.), *Alliance Politics, Kosovo, and NATO's War: Allied Force or Forced Allies?* (New York: Palgrave, 2001), p. 122.

[134] Kathryn Cochran, 'Kosovo Targeting – A Bureaucratic and Legal Nightmare: The Implications for US/Australian Interoperability', Australian Aerospace Centre, June 2001. Online at http://www.defence.gov.au/aerospacecentre/publish/01Paper3.html, accessed 3 December 2002, document no longer available at this site.

[135] Betts, 'Compromised Command', p. 129.

[136] United States General Accounting Office, 'Kosovo Air Operations: Need to Maintain Alliance Cohesion Resulted in Doctrinal Departures', *Report to the US Congress*, July 2001, p. 6.

targets also meant that the military could not concentrate its combat power to the optimal degree. The commander of Operation Allied Force's air forces, US Lieutenant-General Michael Short, protested angrily that 'the operational considerations of NATO's 19 members hampered the conduct of the campaign.'[137] He singled out France as particularly obstreperous, complaining that its vetoing of planned air strike targets impaired NATO's effectiveness and placed US pilots at risk.[138] The US General Accounting Office neatly summarised the trade-off between military effectiveness and effective multilateralism during the Kosovo campaign:

> many US participants in the operation believed that these departures [from US military doctrine] resulted in a longer campaign, more damage to Yugoslavia, and greater risk to alliance forces than likely would have occurred if doctrine had been followed . . . [However] the NATO alliance members remained united throughout the operation, perhaps because of these doctrinal departures.[139]

The final major cost associated with launching Operation Allied Force within the NATO framework was the risk this presented to NATO itself. Part of the problem was public relations. At a time when NATO was contemplating expanding its membership to former Warsaw Pact members, Operation Allied Force damaged public support for the alliance in several Central and Eastern European countries. Among countries waiting to apply for NATO membership, Slovakia showed the largest negative reaction to Operation Allied Force: public support for NATO membership dwindled to 36 per cent, while 50 per cent of respondents did not support Slovakia's entry into NATO.[140] Worse still, Operation Allied Force undermined public support for NATO within several NATO states. In the Czech Republic, support for NATO membership fell from 56 per cent in February 1999 to 49 per cent in March.[141] Some 90 per cent of the Greek public opposed Operation Allied Force, while

---

[137] Andrew Tully, 'Yugoslavia: France Faulted for Limiting Targets During Kosovo Conflict', *Radio Free Europe*, October 1999.

[138] Paul Richter, 'US general says French officials endangers American war pilots', *Los Angeles Times*, 22 October 1999; Tully, 'Yugoslavia: France Faulted for Limiting Targets During Kosovo Conflict', October 1999.

[139] US General Accounting Office, *Kosovo Air Operations*, July 2001, p. 2.

[140] 'Slovak Public Opinion Split on Entry to NATO', *TASS News Agency*, Bratislava, 13 April 1999; 'Half of Slovaks Against Slovakia's Entry to NATO – Poll', *CTK National News Wire*, 13 April 1999.

[141] 'Czechs Show Less Support for NATO than Poles, Hungarians', *CTK National News Wire*, 8 April 1999.

in Italy there was a real chance that Prime Minister D'Alema's coalition government would fall over its support for the campaign. In both cases, populations realised that their countries had other interests that were served through the NATO framework, but nevertheless resented the complicity with Operation Allied Force that NATO membership engendered.

The greatest danger to NATO, however, was the possibility that it might fail in Kosovo. NATO, the world's strongest military alliance, is almost invincible in purely military terms. However, if the alliance had broken apart because of public opposition to the campaign in some of its member states, the results for NATO's credibility would have been disastrous. In choosing to operate within the NATO framework, the USA gambled that the Alliance would remain united and took the risk of severely discrediting NATO. As Paula Dobriansky put it:

> NATO's future is very much linked to what will take place in Kosovo. If there's not a victory in Kosovo, this will have repercussions for NATO's credibility, its operability as well as its effectiveness. This is clearly the most significant challenge confronting NATO in the post-Cold War environment. If NATO fails in Kosovo, this will ... irreparably damage its credibility and its effectiveness.[142]

This was not a prospect that the Clinton administration took lightly. The degree to which it valued NATO's credibility became apparent when it faced the prospect that air strikes alone might not achieve NATO objectives in Kosovo. Rather than admit defeat and damage NATO, the Clinton administration, encouraged by Britain, edged towards a ground offensive in Kosovo.[143] Henry Kissinger, an outspoken critic of the Clinton policy on Kosovo, captured the underlying motivation succinctly:

> NATO cannot survive if it now abandons the campaign without achieving its objective of ending the massacres ... if a ceasefire ... is rejected by Milosevic, there will be no alternative to continuing and intensifying the war, if necessary introducing NATO combat ground forces – a solution which I have heretofore passionately rejected but which will have to be considered to maintain NATO credibility.[144]

---

[142] Jeremy Bransten, 'Crisis in Kosovo to Dominate Historic Summit', *Radio Free Europe*, 21 April 1999.

[143] John F. Harris, 'Clinton says he might send ground troops', *Washington Post*, 19 May 1999.

[144] Henry A. Kissinger, 'Doing Injury to History', 19 April 1999. Online at www.soz.uni-hannover.de/isoz/kosovo/kissin.htm, accessed 9 March 2003, site no longer available.

Thus operating in the NATO framework imposed on-going costs in addition to the delay the US incurred in order to obtain the NATO mandate. This framework made it difficult for the US to issue credible threats, thus precipitating the need for Operation Allied Force and extending its duration. NATO diplomacy about target selection prevented the US military from maximising the effectiveness of its air strikes. The US felt these combined costs keenly: its 2001 decision to intervene unilaterally in Afghanistan despite NATO's declaration that the collective defence provisions of the North Atlantic Treaty had been triggered by the 11 September attacks on the USA in part reflected its experience of the costs of working through NATO in Kosovo.[145] Finally, NATO itself was put at risk, both because its popularity was sapped and because its credibility as a military alliance was at stake in Kosovo. The USA accepted these costs, even though in purely military terms NATO offered virtually no advantage over an ad hoc coalition of the willing. This combination of high costs and low concomitant benefits makes the US decision to launch Operation Allied Force through NATO incomprehensible from a purely military or realist point of view. This decision can only be understood if the fundamental importance of international legitimacy to the USA is fully understood and appreciated.

Conclusion

The evidence from Operation Allied Force fully supports the legitimacy-centred theory of the role of international organisations in peace enforcement operations elaborated in chapter 2. The USA did not demonstrate a strong regard for international law in launching Operation Allied Force and in any case the NATO framework could not guarantee the intervention's legality. NATO also failed to facilitate significant financial or military burden-sharing for Operation Allied Force. Only six of NATO's nineteen member states contributed substantial forces to the intervention, and the USA accounted for around two-thirds of the total military effort. This could not have surprised the USA, whose official complaints about lack of burden-sharing in NATO date back to the 1950s.

By contrast, the NATO framework did bolster Operation Allied Force's international legitimacy. The USA recognised that both its reputation as a relatively benign superpower and its leadership position

---

[145] Thanks to an anonymous reviewer for this point.

in the post-Cold War world would be damaged if it was internationally perceived as engaged in illegitimate aggression. The NATO framework allowed the USA to claim that it was intervening legitimately in the name of the international community. NATO's consensus rule of decision-making encouraged all nineteen NATO members to officially unite behind Operation Allied Force, thereby allaying fears of aggressive uni-lateralism. The organisation also provided a platform from which to convince non-members to endorse the intervention, which ultimately allowed the USA and its allies to sideline the intervention's remaining critics as unrepresentative of the international community.

The USA proved willing to incur substantial costs to secure this international legitimacy for Operation Allied Force. Obtaining the inter-vention's NATO mandate required months of intense negotiations during which the FRY massed its forces for an offensive against Kosovo. Moreover, the NATO framework impaired the USA's ability to make credible threats and commitments and hampered the application of its combat power. Finally, launching Operation Allied Force through NATO also presented a risk to the alliance's credibility and unity. These costs were not offset by any significant military benefits that could not also have been reaped through an ad hoc coalition of the willing. Nevertheless, the USA accepted them – because NATO's core contribu-tion to Operation Allied Force was political rather than military. As one NATO delegate put it, 'You can have a political mandate ... there is a decision, and then only 3–4 countries participate. Others endorse the operation, but they do not participate. If you have a decision, that doesn't matter.'[146] Another delegate concurred:

> The most important thing is to try to build a big coalition. The big powers could have done it [the Kosovo campaign] on their own ... [in fact] the whole thing was done by the big powers. But the political support of a big coalition is important. That way you could present the operation to the world as having NATO and also Partnership for Peace support ... That is why they went through NATO.[147]

In short, the NATO framework provided Operation Allied Force with a degree of international legitimacy that a coalition of the willing could not have matched, and the USA deemed this legitimacy worth the costs of operating through NATO. Thus SACEUR Wesley Clark, while

---

[146] Author's interview. Remarks not for attribution.
[147] Author's interview. Remarks not for attribution.

acknowledging the targeting constraints imposed by the NATO framework, insisted that 'the fundamental lesson of the campaign is that the alliance worked'.[148] The accuracy of this assertion can only be fully appreciated in the context of US concerns about the international legitimacy of Operation Allied Force.

---

[148] Linda Kozaryn, 'Air Chief's Kosovo Lesson: Go for Snake's Head First', *American Forces Press*, October 1999.

7

Peace enforcement through a global organisation: the United Nations and INTERFET in East Timor

On 20 September 1999, 1,500 Australian, British, and New Zealand troops landed at the Komoro airfield in Dili, East Timor. They were the first wave of the International Force East Timor (INTERFET), an Australian-led multinational force under a United Nations mandate to restore, and if necessary enforce, peace and security in East Timor. Over the next five months, INTERFET expanded to include over 14,000 troops from twenty-two countries, and successfully ended the violence that had engulfed East Timor after its population voted overwhelmingly for independence from Indonesia in a UN-administered ballot on 30 August 1999. INTERFET's arrival in East Timor marked several watersheds: It signalled the beginning of the end of Indonesia's twenty-four-year rule over East Timor. It paved the way for East Timor's birth as an independent state on 20 May 2002. It began Australia's largest military operation since the Vietnam War, and the first operation in which Australia was the lead state rather than a junior coalition partner. And it marked the first time that the UN authorised a peace enforcement mission by a coalition of the willing led by a middle power rather than a superpower.

This chapter examines why Australia decided to launch and lead INTERFET within the UN framework. It begins by describing the historical background of the East Timor crisis and Australia's involvement in it. It then argues that neither respect for international law nor burden-sharing considerations satisfactorily account for Australia's decision. By contrast, Australia's significant concerns about INTERFET's international legitimacy can explain why it insisted on a UN mandate for the intervention despite the substantial costs generated by operating within this framework.

Historical background

The 1999 East Timor crisis had roots in the colonial past, when the island of Timor was divided in half, with the Netherlands occupying the western portion and Portugal the eastern one. West Timor gained independence in 1949 as part of Indonesia, but Portugal only recognised East Timor's right to self-determination after its own domestic revolution in 1974. By August 1975, the rivalry between the political parties that emerged in East Timor to exploit this opportunity had escalated into civil war. Portugal was forced to withdraw its government officials to the island of Atauro to the north of Timor. By November, the Timorese Social Democratic Association (ASDT, later the Revolutionary Front for an Independent East Timor – FRETLIN) had gained ascendancy in East Timor and declared the territory independent. In the Cold War context, however, FRETLIN's leftist sympathies caused alarm in Indonesia, Australia, and the USA. On 7 December 1975, with Australian and US complicity, Indonesia invaded and occupied East Timor. Portugal withdrew from its colony under protest. Indonesia's attempt to integrate East Timor as its 27th province encountered persistent local opposition, however, first from FRETLIN guerrillas and then from a growing urban-based popular resistance movement.[1]

International reactions to these developments varied. Portugal opposed the Indonesian occupation of East Timor and lobbied for its condemnation within the United Nations. By contrast, the USA and Australia supported Indonesia. The USA blocked Security Council action against Indonesia in 1975, mostly to protect anti-communist Indonesia as a Cold War ally. Thereafter, the USA extended *de facto* but not *de jure* recognition to Indonesia's rule in East Timor and allowed the issue to fade from its political radar-screen until the Santa Cruz massacre in Dili reignited public sympathy with the East Timorese independence cause in 1991. Australia, by contrast, remained a far more active Indonesian ally. Despite persistent sympathy for the East Timorese among large sections of the Australian public, Australian policy-makers agreed that their country's good relations with Indonesia should not be held hostage to disagreements over East Timor. Australia formally recognised Indonesia's *de facto* sovereignty over the territory in January 1978 and its *de jure* sovereignty in 1979. It sealed its rapprochement with Indonesia in the 1989 Timor Gap Treaty

---

[1] Indonesia gained military ascendancy over FRETLIN by ruthless repression which, combined with famine and dislocation, caused an estimated 200,000 East Timorese deaths. Heike Krieger (ed.), *East Timor and the International Community* (Cambridge: Cambridge University Press, 1997), p. xx.

on joint development of oil resources in the Timor Sea and the 1995 Agreement on Mutual Security.

Over time, most states came to accept Indonesia's *de facto* (if not *de jure*) sovereignty over East Timor. UN resolutions condemning the occupation attracted decreasing interest and were passed by diminishing majorities, until they were replaced in 1982 by a system of consultations between the UN, Portugal, and Indonesia on East Timor. This 'Tripartite Process' became the principal UN forum for dealing with East Timor for the next sixteen years, but made little progress on resolving the issue.

The turning point for East Timor came when the Soharto regime in Indonesia fell victim to internal democratisation pressures and the Asian financial crisis in May 1998. Soharto's Vice President, Dr B. J. Habibie, became interim President and announced his willingness to grant 'special autonomy' to East Timor. This offer reinvigorated the Tripartite Process. Indonesia and Portugal began edging towards an agreement on a medium-term autonomy package for East Timor, having agreed to temporarily set aside their differences on the territory's final status. In August 1998, however, Australia upstaged the Tripartite Process negotiations by emphasising the need for an eventual act of self-determination in East Timor. In doing so, Australia hoped to simultaneously placate domestic critics of its previous East Timor policies, assert itself as the major Western player in the region, and reinforce its alliance with Indonesia.[2] It believed these goals to be compatible because it was convinced that if a sufficiently lengthy transition period was agreed upon the East Timorese could be persuaded to vote for integration in Indonesia, in which case an act of self-determination would promote Indonesia's interests.

Australian Prime Minister Howard was explicit about this prediction in a December 1998 letter to President Habibie reiterating Australia's call for an act of self-determination.[3] Habibie, however, believed that a long transition period would merely allow East Timor to continue absorbing Indonesian resources before gaining independence. Stung by the perceived treachery of his Australian allies, he announced in

---

[2] Richard Leaver, 'Australia, East Timor and Indonesia', *The Pacific Review*, 14:1 (2001), p. 6.

[3] Australian Department of Foreign Affairs and Trade (DFAT), *East Timor in Transition 1998–2000: an Australian Policy Challenge* (Canberra: Brown & Wilton, 2001), Annex 2, pp. 181–2.

January 1999 that East Timor would have to choose immediately between Indonesia's offer of special autonomy and independence.

This proposal voided all previous planning efforts. Despite misgivings about the feasibility or desirability of immediate independence, the UN, Portugal, Australia, and the East Timorese felt unable to turn down the 'window of opportunity' opened by Habibie's offer.[4] Accordingly, the Tripartite Process culminated in the 5 May Agreements, which provided for East Timor's future to be decided in a UN-administered popular consultation offering the East Timorese a choice between autonomy within Indonesia and independence. The UN would provide election officials and civilian police officers, but Indonesia insisted on retaining the responsibility for maintaining peace and security before and during the ballot. Portugal and the UN accepted these terms, despite evidence of Indonesian military (TNI) involvement in on-going violence in East Timor and sponsorship of local pro-integration militias. These security concerns were sacrificed to the overriding aim of seizing the moment to hold the consultation.[5]

Meanwhile in Australia, Defence Department officials feared that the TNI might resort to violence to prevent East Timor's independence and doubted whether Habibie could deliver a peaceful solution on this sensitive issue.[6] They began contingency planning for a possible Australian military role in East Timor in February 1999, with initial plans focusing on an Australian peacekeeping role before or after the ballot and a possible emergency evacuation of UN personnel from East Timor. On 11 March 1999, the Defence Department announced that it was increasing its high readiness forces to two brigades. By contrast, Australia's Department of Foreign Affairs and Trade (DFAT) insisted that Australia's special relationship with Indonesia could be leveraged to ensure a peaceful solution to any crisis. It opposed military contingency planning as being needlessly offensive to Indonesia and militated against 'excessive' international pressure on Indonesia. DFAT thus played down the risks involved in the ballot and maintained that the links between the TNI and East Timorese pro-integration militia involved only 'rogue elements' within the TNI. It insisted on keeping contrary reports from

---

[4] Ian Martin, *Self-Determination in East Timor: The United Nations, the Ballot, and the International Intervention* (Boulder: Lynne Rienner, 2001), p. 25.
[5] Ibid., chapters 3–5.
[6] Desmond Ball, 'Silent Witness: Australian Intelligence and East Timor', *The Pacific Review*, 14:1 (2001), pp. 43–9.

Australia's own intelligence services secret even from its allies. Thus when Mervyn Jenkins, Australia's Defence Attaché in Washington D.C., passed some reports on to colleagues in the CIA, DFAT's reaction was immediate. Jenkins believed that he was acting on Defence Department instructions, but a joint DFAT/Defence Department investigation informed him that he risked imprisonment for espionage. He committed suicide in June 1999.

The ballot was held on 30 August 1999 and on 3 September in New York (4 September in East Timor) UN Secretary-General Kofi Annan announced that 78.5 per cent of registered voters had opted for independence. This announcement unleashed a surge of violence in East Timor by local pro-integration militia supported by the TNI. The UN election-monitoring mission was unable to stem the violence and had to be almost entirely evacuated. Graphic media reports of the carnage aroused public outrage, especially in Australia, whose government announced its willingness to lead an international force to restore peace and security in East Timor. Bowing to international pressure, Indonesia accepted this force on 12 September. On 15 September, UN Security Council Resolution 1264 authorised a multinational force to restore peace and security in East Timor 'by all means necessary'. On 20 September, the first INTERFET troops landed in Dili, East Timor's capital.

INTERFET in international law

Why did Australia, INTERFET's lead state, choose to launch the intervention within the UN framework? Australian policy-makers were keenly aware of the stakes involved in the intervention. A parliamentary briefing report of 21 September 1999 pointed out, 'in many estimates, [INTERFET] will involve almost every element of the Australian Defence Force (ADF) for many months and probably years at an estimated cost of up to $1 billion per year. ADF casualties are to be expected in what has already become the greatest single challenge to Australian foreign and defence policies in a generation.'[7] The report noted that INTERFET troops would be heavily outnumbered by the TNI presence in East Timor. It alluded to the possibility of having to introduce

[7] Adam Cobb, 'East Timor and Australia's Security Role: Issues and Scenarios', *Current Issues Brief No.3 1999–2000*, Information and Research Services, Department of the Parliamentary Library, Australia, p. i.

conscription to sustain even this relatively small ADF deployment, and
raised the spectre of escalation into a full-scale war with Indonesia. All
these possibilities weighed heavily on the minds of Australian policy-
makers – but so did the immense popular demand for action in East
Timor. Not responding to the crisis would have been political suicide for
the government. Thus the Australian government faced an enormous
policy challenge and chose its response strategy – a military intervention
launched under UN auspices – deliberately and with care. International
law did not, however, play the decisive role in these deliberations.

INTERFET is the only peace enforcement operation examined in this
book whose international auspices potentially had major implications
for its legality. By early September 1999, Australian policy-makers knew
that intervening in East Timor would require forceful military action: 'It
is clear that any international presence in East Timor will be *making*
peace.'[8] They were determined to deploy troops that could, if necessary,
not only protect themselves but also impose a settlement to end the
crisis: 'At every step we made absolutely clear that if anybody wanted to
have a fight, they would have a big fight ... What we did is we came
ready to fight. And the result of that was that there was no fight.'[9] Yet
since Australia had not been attacked by Indonesia and the Indonesian
invasion of East Timor predated INTERFET by twenty-four years, this
'ready to fight' deployment could not be defended as an act of individual
or collective self-defence as authorised under Article 51 of the UN
Charter. According to Article 42 of the Charter, therefore, only the UN
Security Council was legally entitled to authorise this kind of enforcement action. INTERFET received this authorisation through Security
Council Resolution 1264 of 15 September 1999. 'Acting under
Chapter VII of the Charter of the United Nations', the resolution
'authorize[d] the establishment of a multinational force' to 'restore
peace and security in East Timor' and permitted 'States participating
in the multinational force to take all necessary measures to fulfil this
mandate'. This provided a legal basis for INTERFET's enforcement
action in East Timor.

It is possible to attack this basis. The UN Charter only empowers the
Security Council to authorise the use of military force when this is
necessary either to counter an act of aggression or to resolve a threat

[8] Ibid.
[9] Author's interview with Professor David Horner, Strategic and Defence Studies Centre,
Australian National University, Canberra, Australia, 5 April 2002.

to international peace (Article 39). East Timor's illegal invasion and occupation by Indonesia in 1975 would legally have warranted such a reaction at the time, but this alone could not justify the timing of the intervention in 1999. Especially from the perspective of Australia, which had recognised Indonesia's legal sovereignty over East Timor, it was hard to argue that a new international act of aggression had taken place. INTERFET thus had to be – and was – defended as a response to a threat to peace and security. Although the renewed violence in East Timor in 1999 clearly undermined *local* peace, security, and human rights, however, it is hard to argue that it threatened *international* peace and security. The tiny half-island of East Timor had been exposed to turmoil and Indonesian repression for twenty-four years without any significant destabilising effect on the region, let alone the world. Indeed, INTERFET threatened international peace and security more than it preserved it. International action to protect East Timor risked encouraging separatist movements in other parts of Indonesia, thus potentially destabilising a major South East Asian power. Even more seriously, INTERFET carried a non-negligible risk of escalating into a direct military confrontation between Australia and Indonesia, which would have had major implications for regional and international peace and security.

Security Council Resolution 1264 acknowledged the absence of a threat to international or regional peace and security. It described the situation in East Timor merely as 'a threat to peace and security', omitting the customary qualifier of 'international' or 'regional'. The fact that a peace enforcement operation was authorised in this context marks a milestone in the on-going evolution towards humanitarian intervention. Since the early 1990s, the Security Council has stretched its prerogative of 'determining the existence' of any threat to international peace to include humanitarian disasters with limited or no real international security implications. In Somalia, for example, the sheer 'magnitude of the human tragedy' was held to constitute a threat to international peace and security, despite the fact that the conflict posed no direct threat to regional peace.[10] However, the standard set by

---

[10] UN Security Council Resolution 794 (1992). This argument about the progression of humanitarian intervention is made in International Institute for Strategic Studies, 'The Shifting Sands of Sovereignty', *Strategic Survey 1999/2000* (London: Oxford University Press, 2000) as well as in Mark Rothert, 'UN Intervention in East Timor', *Columbia Journal of International Law*, 257 (2000–1), p. 276.

the Charter remains relevant to Security Council actions. International Criminal Court President Philippe Kirsch, for example, has criticised UN Security Council Resolution 1422 on the ICC for not responding to a threat to international peace and security.[11] Resolution 1264 represented the first time a peace enforcement operation was authorised under Chapter VII without at least using the language of international peace and security. This precedent may affect the future development of international law, but at the moment it was passed Resolution 1264 represented a departure from international legal practice.

Despite these weaknesses, however, the legal case for INTERFET based on its UN mandate remains strong. The Security Council has the legal ability to authorise peace enforcement operations and there were precedents for the Council adopting a more expansive interpretation of what constitutes a threat to 'international peace and security'. More than any other organisation studied in this book, the UN had the capacity to legalise the enforcement action launched under its auspices, and INTERFET received Security Council authorisation according to the legally specified procedure.

However, Australia's decision to launch INTERFET through the UN was not primarily based on these legal considerations. In fact, Australia declined to exploit the full legal potential of the UN framework. The particularity of an operation mandated under Chapter VII of the UN Charter is that it does not require the consent of the country within which military force is used. From a legal point of view, Indonesian consent was even less necessary in this particular case, since Indonesian legal sovereignty over East Timor had not been accepted within the UN. Nevertheless, the Security Council did not mandate INTERFET until Indonesia had given its assent to the operation, which Resolution 1264 explicitly welcomed. More to the point, Australia itself was as adamant about the need for Indonesian consent as it was about the need for a Chapter VII mandate for the intervention. There were good strategic reasons for this, beginning with the fact that Indonesia had 15,000 troops in East Timor while Australia's entire army only counted around 26,000 troops. From a purely legal point of view, however, a Chapter VII mandate made Indonesian assent redundant – and vice versa. The authorisation to use 'all necessary means' to re-establish peace and

---

[11] Philippe Kirsch, John T. Holmes, and Mora Johnson, 'International Tribunals and Courts', in David Malone (ed.), *The UN Security Council: From the Cold War to the 21st Century* (Boulder: Lynne Rienner, 2004), pp. 289–90.

security was still desirable, because it allowed INTERFET to deal with any militia resistance and ensured that the operation was not hostage to continued Indonesian consent.[12] Legally, however, the Chapter VII mandate was unnecessary, and in fact the passing of Resolution 1264 ultimately proved almost anti-climactic. While that resolution was being debated, Australia and Indonesia were already negotiating about the reception INTERFET troops would receive on their deployment in East Timor.[13] Nevertheless, Australia continued to insist on a Chapter VII UN mandate, which suggests that for Australia the importance of this mandate extended beyond its legal implications.

Burden-sharing during INTERFET

The INTERFET experience also provides little support for the view of international organisations as facilitators of mutually beneficial cooperation among states. Chapter 2 has argued that in the case of peace enforcement operations this cooperation would take the shape of interstate burden-sharing. Theoretically, international organisations could promote burden-sharing either by contributing existing collectively funded internal resources to the intervention or by encouraging their member states to contribute national military or financial resources. However, neither of these avenues generated significant burden-sharing for INTERFET – and Australia did not expect them to.

Internal United Nations resources

With 8,900 employees and a biennial budget of over US$2 billion, the UN has more internal resources to contribute to peace enforcement operations than most other international organisations. Although the UN has no standing army and thus cannot contribute troops to an intervention, it has accumulated considerable experience in launching and administering peace support operations around the world. By 1999, it had launched fifty peacekeeping operations, with an estimated total cost of US$19.2 billion.[14] The repository of this knowledge within the

---

[12] Rothert, 'UN Intervention in East Timor', pp. 273–4.

[13] Author's interview with Major-General Mike Smith, Director-General East Timor in the Australian Defence Headquarters in 1999. Canberra, Australia, 10 April 2002.

[14] United Nations, 'Background Note on United Nations Peacekeeping Operations, 20 March 2000', online at www.un.org/Depts/dpko/dpko/bnote.htm, note is periodically updated, 2000 version no longer available at this site.

UN is the Department of Peacekeeping Operations (DPKO), which in 1999 had some 400 headquarters staff and a biennial programme budget of US$167 million.[15] DPKO also disposes of a Logistics Base in Brindisi, Italy, whose budget for 1999/2000 was US$7.5 million.[16]

However, UN Security Council Resolution 1264 did not create a UN intervention force, but merely 'authorize[d] the establishment of a multinational force' to deploy in East Timor (Article 3). As a multi-national coalition of the willing, INTERFET had no claim on the UN's internal resources. The coalition's lead nation was responsible for planning the operation, negotiating with potential contributors, and harmonising their contributions into a coherent force. Without the benefit of DPKO's expertise and established legal, administrative, and financial procedures, Australia's Department of Defence scrambled to meet these obligations.[17] This was especially clear in Australia's administration of the voluntary Trust Fund established by the UN to help defray developing countries' costs of participation in INTERFET:

> No-one [in Australia] had a clear idea of the prospective cost of the operation, much less how to calculate it . . . this lack of clarity produced confusion and some concern [among potential donors] over Australia's ability to prosecute the mission. The costing mechanism utilised by the UN for its missions . . . was initially overlooked; thus Australian planners and their opposite numbers in other forces were not even speaking the same language. The delay experienced in coming to terms with pre-existing arrangements for multinational operations did not enhance confidence in Australia's ability to manage the coalition.[18]

The Australian Defence Force's supply system was also stretched to its limits, since Australia had to coordinate INTERFET's initial logistics and remained responsible for organising the provision of water, rations,

---

[15] General Assembly Resolution 54/247, 'Programme budget for the biennium 1998–1999', 54th General Assembly Session, Agenda Item 119, 3 February 2000.

[16] General Assembly Resolution 53/236, 'Financing of the United Nations Logistics Base at Brindisi, Italy', 53rd General Assembly Session, Agenda Item 143(a), 6 August 1999.

[17] For example, Australia had to develop and sign bilateral Arrangements of Mutual Logistics Support or Logistics Support as well as subsequent Implementation Agreements with participating countries to codify its logistics supply responsibilities. Author's interview with Wing Commander Peter Wilkinson, SO1 UN Engagement, Strategic Command, Australian Army, Army Headquarters, Canberra, 19 April 2002.

[18] Author's interview with Terry Ilsley, Accounting Policy and Practices Branch, Chief Finance Officer Group, Australian Department of Defence, Canberra, Australia, 15 April 2002.

medical supplies, and petrol to the entire force throughout the operation.[19] None of these burdens was unexpected: Australian policy-makers understood the restrictions of the UN mandate under which they had agreed to launch INTERFET.

UN-based mechanisms for burden-sharing among member states

The UN's internal resources are dwarfed by the resources available to its member states. The second and more substantial way in which it could have generated burden-sharing for INTERFET would thus have been to encourage its member states to participate in the operation. By 1999, the UN had two mechanisms to routinise cooperation for peace operations among its (then) 188 member states. The first was the United Nations Standby Arrangement System (UNSAS), which allows members to earmark military personnel that they would consider making available for peace operations, and which by March 1999 comprised 104,000 personnel from eighty-one member states.[20] These troops were not automatically available for peace operations, but the pledges provided a starting-point for UN-based coalition-building efforts. The second potential burden-sharing mechanism was the UN peacekeeping budget. Through this budget, every UN member state was legally responsible for a predetermined proportion of the costs of any UN peacekeeping operation.[21] Thus a mechanism was in place for the widest possible financial burden-sharing for UN peace operations.

However, Australia did not benefit from these burden-sharing mechanisms during INTERFET. UNSAS is reserved for raising UN forces, not for establishing coalitions of the willing. It was not invoked for INTERFET. More generally, Australia did not use the UN as a primary basis for building the INTERFET coalition. The UN did help focus international attention on East Timor: Security Council and General Assembly debates and a Security Council fact-finding mission dispatched to Indonesia and East Timor in September 1999 raised the

---

[19] Author's interview with Brigadier A. G. Warner, Chief of Staff, Australian Army Land Headquarters, Sydney, Australia, 3 May 2002; author's interview with Terry Ilsley, 15 April 2002.

[20] UN Document S/1999/361, 'Progress Report of the Secretary-General on Standby Arrangements for Peacekeeping', 30 March 1999.

[21] States are assessed for the UN peacekeeping budget in proportion to their per capita GNP. In 1999, the rates of assessment ranged from 30.4 per cent for the USA to 0.001 per cent for the UN's least developed members.

international profile of the crisis. Australia also directed its permanent delegation to the UN to lobby fellow member states for contributions to INTERFET.[22] However, most of the coalition-building for INTERFET was accomplished bilaterally and outside the UN arena. Contrary to expectations raised by Lisa Martin's work on international sanctions,[23] Australia did not make any threats or promises during the UN debates on East Timor to elicit troop contributions. Instead, its coalition-building efforts centred on bilateral negotiations with two groups of states: Australia's traditional Western allies and its regional neighbours.[24]

The first group included the USA, Britain, Canada, and New Zealand, Australia's partners in the ABCA armed forces standardisation agreement. These states had been aware of Australian contingency planning for a possible crisis in East Timor since early 1999. Following Australia's example, both New Zealand and the USA completed speculative planning for a military 'situation' in Timor by July 1999.[25] All four allies responded promptly to Australia's coalition-building efforts in September 1999. Within days of Australia's announcement that it would lead an international force into East Timor, New Zealand, the UK, and Canada had committed infantry troops to INTERFET. The USA lent crucial political support in pressuring Indonesia and the Security Council to accept the deployment of a multinational force, and on 10 September also offered logistical, intelligence, and communications capabilities for the operation. This support was sought and granted in the context of the ABCA alliance system. One senior US official noted: 'In terms of US participation in the INTERFET force ... human rights and regional stability may not have been sufficient factors to prompt US military participation. A critical additional element was the desire on the

---

[22] Penny Wensley, 'East Timor and the United Nations', Speech to the Australian Institute for International Affairs, 23 February 2000, p. 7.

[23] Lisa Martin, *Coercive Cooperation: Explaining Multilateral Economic Sanctions* (Princeton: Princeton University Press, 1992).

[24] Other states were also contacted at the UN, through Australia's diplomatic staff in these countries, and through their missions in Australia. However, while some of these states – notably Jordan, Italy, Fiji, and France – eventually provided significant support for INTERFET, they were given relatively low priority in Australia's initial coalition-building efforts.

[25] John Crawford and Glyn Harper, *Operation East Timor: the New Zealand Defence Force in East Timor 1999–2001* (Reed, Auckland, 2001), chapters 2 and 4. US CinC Pacific, 'US Forces INTERFET (USFI): Operation Stabilise East Timor; Executive Overview', Internal after-action report from the US military, online at www.dod.gov/nii/org/c3is/ccbm/east-timor.pdf, accessed May 2002, document no longer available at this site.

part of US officials to be responsive to a request from Australia – a trusted and valued ally with a highly capable military.'[26] As the ADF recognised, 'the value of Australia's relationships with Canada, New Zealand, the United Kingdom, and the United States was re-confirmed. These ties were a key to the speedy deployment of the INTERFET force.'[27]

The second group of states targeted by coalition-building efforts for INTERFET consisted of Australia's regional neighbours. Since it is not a member of the Association of South East Asian Nations (ASEAN), Australia had no formal alliance with these states, and they had not been informed of Australia's contingency planning. In early September 1999, these states were sceptical of an Australian-led intervention force in East Timor. Some feared the intervention would set a precedent for Western interference in their own internal affairs, and thus stressed the importance of the principle of non-intervention to which they were formally committed as ASEAN members.[28] Others, notably Thailand and the Philippines, were predisposed to support the operation for internal political reasons,[29] but felt that intervening against Indonesia on behalf of the East Timorese was bad *Realpolitik*. 'There was widespread feeling in the region that this was a crisis that didn't need to happen, that it was Australia's responsibility ... [because] the government had been captured by the human rights lobby, subordinating its true strategic interest to the pursuit of human rights and thereby creating problems for everybody.'[30]

Ultimately, several ASEAN states were persuaded to join INTERFET – but this persuasion did not occur in a UN forum. It was the 9–12 September Asia-Pacific Economic Cooperation (APEC) Summit in Auckland that allowed Australian Prime Minister Howard to canvass his regional counterparts for support. Australia's Acting Secretary of Defence during INTERFET recalled the summit's importance:

[26] Eric Schwartz, 'The Intervention in East Timor', Report for the National Intelligence Council, December 2001, p. 4.
[27] Australian Defence Force, 'INTERFET: A Coalition of the Willing. The Australian Defence Experience', Draft report.
[28] Alan Dupont, 'ASEAN's Response to the East Timor Crisis', *Australian Journal of International Affairs*, 54:2 (2000), pp. 164–5.
[29] Filipinos tended to support aiding their fellow Catholics in East Timor, while a confluence of national rivalry with Indonesia and principled support for a more flexible interpretation of non-intervention motivated Thailand's progressive government.
[30] Author's interview with Professor Alan Dupont, Strategic and Defence Studies Centre, Australian National University, Canberra, Australia, 14 April 2002.

> Every so often one feels that . . . the clouds part and there, hovering above
> you in a golden nimbus is a big golden horseshoe. Because, literally, the
> day we wanted to turn around and start building political support,
> complete with real offers of help for a strongly Asia-Pacific oriented
> peacekeeping operation in the Asia Pacific, all of the heads of government
> were assembling in New Zealand.[31]

Australia followed up its APEC overtures by dispatching its Vice Chief of
Defence Force, Air Marshal Douglas Riding, to several of the region's
capitals to seek specific undertakings of troop contributions. He was
disappointed by Malaysia, but subsequent stops in Singapore, Bangkok,
and Manila brought concrete pledges of military support and unexpectedly large troop contributions from the Philippines and Thailand.

These countries were swayed by Indonesia's formal (if reluctant)
acceptance of a UN-mandated force on 12 September, and by effective
bilateral diplomacy. Australia wisely decided to court its neighbours
rather than rely on its political and economic leverage in the region.
Riding reassured his interlocutors that Australia was not seeking confrontation with Indonesia, would shield South East Asian troops from
possible clashes with the Indonesian military, and would help defray
their financial costs of intervention.[32] Australia also enlisted the USA's
political support both to elicit Indonesia's acquiescence to INTERFET
by threatening its access to IMF and World Bank funds and to convince
other South East Asian states to participate in the operation. As one
senior Australian official put it:

> the fact that the Americans were committed to it meant that a whole lot of
> people put in forces who might not otherwise [have done so]. Whenever
> the coalition started to look a bit shaky, somehow somebody talked to
> them and . . . people stopped wavering. I never really asked any questions
> about that, but I don't think it was the brilliance of Australian
> diplomacy.[33]

Combined with the internal predispositions of several ASEAN
nations, these factors ultimately ensured that INTERFET enjoyed a
substantial regional component. Four of the ten ASEAN states participated in INTERFET, and an ASEAN country (Thailand) furnished both

---

[31] Author's interview with Hugh White, Australian Acting Minister of Defence during
INTERFET, Canberra, 15 April 2002.
[32] Author's interview with Air Marshal Douglas Riding, Australian Defence Force,
Canberra, Australia, 1 May 2002.
[33] Author's interview. Remark not for attribution.

the operation's second largest national contingent and its Deputy Force Commander. As with the ABCA countries, however, ASEAN participation was largely negotiated outside the UN framework.

The UN's mechanisms for financial burden-sharing were also ineffective in the INTERFET case. In 1999, Australia was responsible for 1.482 per cent of the UN's peacekeeping budget and could expect the UN's other 187 member states to finance the remaining 98.518 per cent of any UN peace operation. However, INTERFET was not a UN force, and Clause 9 of UN Security Council Resolution 1264 explicitly 'stresse[d] that the expenses of the force will be borne by the participating Member States concerned'. The winners and losers from this dispensation can be seen in the figure 7.1. This graph shows the difference between a country's share of INTERFET troops in October 1999 and its assessment rate for the UN peacekeeping budget. Using the proportion of INTERFET troops furnished by each

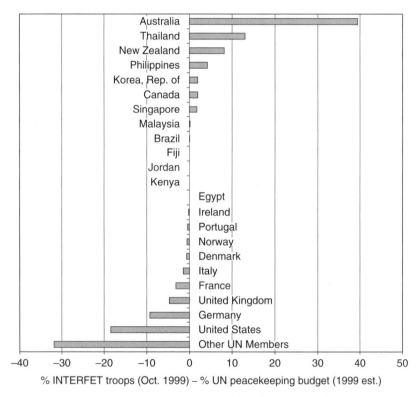

% INTERFET troops (Oct. 1999) – % UN peacekeeping budget (1999 est.)

Figure 7.1: Operating outside the UN assessment system: winners and losers

country as a rough proxy for its share of total INTERFET expenses, each bar represents the financial loss or gain to a particular country of operating as a self-financing member of a coalition of the willing rather than within a UN force paid for out of the peacekeeping budget.

Australia was the biggest loser from this arrangement. It furnished over two-thirds of INTERFET troops in the initial phases of INTERFET, a proportion that declined to 41 per cent by late October. Even assuming that Australian troops cost no more to deploy than Thai or Filipino soldiers, merely funding its own troops put Australia's share of INTERFET's financial burden at almost 28 times the 1.482 per cent of the budget it would have been responsible for had INTERFET been financed out of the UN peace-keeping budget.

Even this graph does not fully capture Australia's full share of INTERFET's financial burden, however, because it does not incorporate expenses countries incurred beyond the deployment and maintenance of their own troops. To reflect these costs, the US bar, for example, would have to be adjusted to the right to reflect the US$50 million in strategic lift that the USA provided for the operation as a whole rather than for its own forces. It is the Australian bar, however, that has to be adjusted most for coalition-related costs. Australia not only shouldered the administrative, logistics, and planning responsibilities for the intervention but also incurred significant costs by subsidising other coalition members. A conservative estimate puts the total Australian Defence Department costs from INTERFET at AU$645 million (US$420 million).[34] Australia's Department of Foreign Affairs and Trade estimated the total cost of INTERFET to Australia at AU$740 million (US$481 million).[35] Given the uneven reporting by other participating governments of their expenses, it is not possible to calculate exactly how large a proportion of the total INTERFET costs this represents. However, the second largest troop contributor, Thailand, estimated its deployment expenses at just under US$21 million.[36] The USA, almost certainly

---

[34] This is the net INTERFET appropriation for the Defence Department, but does not account for existing Defence resources being reallocated to INTERFET. Australian National Audit Office, 'Management of the Australian Defence Force Deployments to East Timor – Department of Defence', *Audit Report No. 38 2001–2002* (Canberra: Commonwealth of Australia, 2002), p. 37.

[35] DFAT, *East Timor in Transition*, p. 144.

[36] Thailand claimed US$20,947,434 from the INTERFET Trust Fund. This would have covered Thailand's costs of deploying and sustaining its troops in East Timor, though not capital investments made for the operation. Thailand also benefited, however, from equipment and strategic lift capabilities provided by the USA and Australia.

INTERFET's second largest financial contributor, spent just under US$57.5 million on the intervention.[37] It thus seems reasonable to estimate that Australia bore some 75 per cent of the total expense of INTERFET.

Australia received no help from other UN member states to lighten this burden. The only UN-based financial burden-sharing mechanism for INTERFET was a Trust Fund created under Article 7 of UN Security Council Resolution 1264, which accumulated US$106 million.[38] Only developing nations were eligible to receive Trust Fund resources, however, and even they could only be reimbursed for force deployment and maintenance costs, not for capital investments such as the purchase of equipment for their contingent. Consequently, only US$38 million were actually disbursed from the Trust Fund – a paltry sum compared to the operation's total cost. The main beneficiaries were developing INTERFET nations, notably Thailand and the Philippines. The benefits to Australia were indirect: it could not seek reimbursement of its own costs, but at least it could shift some of the burden of subsidising other INTERFET states to the Trust Fund donors – a critical issue since both Thailand and the Philippines had made their commitments conditional on international financial support. Even this financial benefit to Australia was offset, however, when Australia volunteered to administer the Trust Fund in exchange for the UN reducing its management fee from 14 per cent to 0.5 per cent. This move saved the Trust Fund money and improved Australia's control over Trust Fund resources, but it produced no financial benefit for Australia while burdening it with the additional administrative costs of managing claims to the fund.[39]

Thus the UN framework did not promote significant financial or military burden-sharing for INTERFET. Australia had to expect this, since the UN's burden-sharing mechanisms are reserved for UN operations rather than UN-mandated coalitions of the willing. In fact, Australia never indicated disappointment with the UN's contribution to INTERFET, which suggests that it did not primarily turn to the organisation to promote burden-sharing.

[37] US Deputy Secretary of Defense Paul Wolfowitz, 'US Participation in and Support of Operation STABILISE', 2 October 2001, report required by Section 127a of Title 10 U.S.C., Article 5.

[38] Australian National Audit Office, 'Management of the Australian Defence Force Deployments to East Timor', Article 2.58, p. 39.

[39] Author's interview with Wing Commander Wilkinson, Canberra, 19 April 2002.

Australia's legitimacy concerns during INTERFET

Chapter 2 argued that states' decisions to launch peace enforcement operations through international organisations owe more to their concerns about their interventions' legitimacy than to respect for international law *per se* or to a desire for burden-sharing. Such concerns were certainly present in Australia's case. They are best understood by examining the legitimacy audiences Australian policy-makers were most anxious to persuade.

Since Australia is a democracy, one might expect that its policy-makers were most preoccupied with their domestic constituents' perceptions of INTERFET's legitimacy. Australia's voters yielded a more direct power over their government than any other potential legitimacy audience. If they decided that INTERFET was illegitimate, the government was unlikely to survive the next election. However, Australian decision-makers had no need to be concerned about the legitimacy perceptions of their domestic audience. Australians favoured intervention even more adamantly than their government. Graphic media coverage of the violence in East Timor and widespread guilt at Australia's historical complicity with Indonesia's occupation of East Timor combined to convince the Australian public that military intervention was not only legitimate but morally necessary. An opinion poll conducted among Australian voters in early October 1999 found 82 per cent of respondents approved of the deployment of Australian soldiers to East Timor.[40] Public support for an intervention was so overwhelming that in an eight-hour-long bipartisan debate in Australia's House of Representatives on 21 September 1999, not a single speaker dared to criticise the government's decision to lead INTERFET.[41] Even when Prime Minister Howard announced a temporary progressive income tax to fund INTERFET in November 1999, he met no significant resistance.[42] Instead of struggling to build support for an intervention, the government found itself seeking to restrain public enthusiasm. Howard

[40] 'Timor stance boosts support for coalition', *Sunday Age*, 3 October 1999.
[41] Hansard of the Parliament of the Commonwealth of Australia, House of Representatives, Votes and Proceedings No. 66, 21 September 1999, online at www.aph.gov.au/hansard/reps/dailys/dr210999.pdf. Partisan criticism was extensive in this debate, but it focused on whether the government had responded early enough to the crisis.
[42] Hansard of the Parliament of the Commonwealth of Australia, House of Representatives, 23 November 1999.

warned that 'the conditions [our forces] encounter could well be violent and disruptive. Any operation of this kind is dangerous. There is a risk of casualties.'[43] Even this did not dampen public support for the intervention.

By contrast, Australian policy-makers were deeply concerned by Indonesia's scepticism of the INTERFET operation. Australia had for decades sought good relations with its populous northern neighbour. Strategically, the threat of a Japanese invasion of Australia during the Second World War imbued Australians with a sense of vulnerability. Friendly relations with Indonesia were long considered essential to guarding the perceived 'sea–air–land gap' to Australia's north. Conversely, conflict with Indonesia was a nightmare scenario for Australian policy-makers, whose 19.5 million constituents were far outnumbered by Indonesia's 210 million inhabitants. Good relations with Indonesia also brought economic benefits, including the joint exploitation of the oil resources in the Timor Sea agreed upon in the 1989 Timor Gap Treaty. And finally, at the political level, Australia recognised that Indonesia's dominant position in ASEAN made it an ideal conduit for Australia's integration in the South East Asian region. Therefore Australian policy-makers 'were very concerned that Indonesia not see what was happening too much as an aggressive Australian move into what had been their territory'.[44]

Most Indonesians resented INTERFET, perceiving Australia's offer to lead the intervention as a betrayal of trust. Many believed that Australia was seeking to humiliate Indonesia, demonstrate its own military prowess, and extend its dominion into the southern Indonesian archipelago. However, Australian policy-makers' concerns over Indonesia's perception of INTERFET were overridden by the Australian public's demand for action in East Timor. Australian public opinion had never been fully comfortable with its government's policy of supporting Indonesia at the expense of East Timor.[45] In September 1999, after hopes of a peaceful transition to independence were disappointed and the media brought tales of carnage in East Timor, the Australian public would not stand for further accommodation of Indonesian sensibilities. Given this domestic imperative, Australian policy-makers were willing

---

[43] Prime Minister John Howard, 'Address to the Nation', televised speech of 19 September 1999, transcript online at http://www.pm.gov.au/news/speeches/1999/address1909.htm.

[44] Author's interview with Hugh White, 15 April 2002.

[45] John Birmingham, 'Appeasing Jakarta – Australia's Complicity in the East Timor Tragedy', *Quarterly Essay*, Issue 2 (Melbourne: Schwartz, 2001).

to discount Indonesia as a legitimacy audience, as long as outright war with Indonesia could be avoided.

From the point of view of the Australian government, the key audience to be persuaded of INTERFET's legitimacy was therefore neither Australian nor Indonesian, but international. More precisely, it was the West, led by the USA, and the South East Asian region. Australian policy-makers have long wrestled with the implications of their country's geography. Australia's dominant European cultural heritage has led to close historical and contemporary alliance ties with the West. However, Australians often suspect that their remote location leads the US superpower to consider them a relatively minor ally. Occasional small slights fuel this suspicion. Just before INTERFET, for example, the July 1999 Australian/US Summit saw Prime Minister Howard fail not only to obtain US trade concessions but also to secure more than 20 minutes of US President Clinton's time. In recent decades, Australia has therefore self-consciously sought to balance its alliance with the USA with greater efforts to reach out to its South East Asian neighbours. The policy of rapprochement with South East Asia was influenced by the end of the Cold War and began under the leadership of Paul Keating (1991–6). Until 1999, its cornerstone was Australia's rapprochement with Indonesia. However, Australia's Western heritage impeded its integration in South East Asia. Australia remained a relative outsider in the region, failing, for example, to join the Association of South East Asian Nations (ASEAN).

Leading INTERFET had the potential of bolstering Australia's position among both its Western allies and its regional neighbours. Leading a successful operation to remedy a regional security problem would help persuade Australia's neighbours of its power and its commitment to regional affairs. Prime Minister Howard sought to encourage this interpretation of INTERFET: 'On East Timor we have shown that we have the capacity under the United Nations to work with our regional partners in putting together a multinational peacekeeping force. It is an example of both our commitment to the region and our capacity to make a constructive and practical contribution to its affairs.'[46] Successful Australian leadership on a South East Asian issue would also demonstrate Australia's value as a regional ally to the USA. It would send two messages: that Australia was capable of addressing regional security

---

[46] Hansard of the Parliament of the Commonwealth of Australia, House of Representatives, 21 September 1999, Article 10030.

issues and that it was able to build and lead regional coalitions of states. If Australia demonstrated a leadership capacity within South East Asia, it would improve not only its regional but also its international stature. Thus INTERFET had to be not only a military success but also an example of effective regional coalition-building.

However, these benefits would only materialise if INTERFET was accepted as legitimate at the regional and international levels. If the South East Asian region did not recognise the intervention as legitimate, Australia's regional isolation would deepen rather than decrease. As the Acting Minister of Defence at the time put it, 'We didn't want to end up looking [like] the Anglo-Saxons charging in, in a way that was out of kilter with regional responses.'[47] Moreover, if states in the region did not view INTERFET as legitimate, they would not join the operation, and Australia would be unable to present itself as a regional leader to the rest of the world. Even a demonstration of regional leadership would be useless, however, if the international community did not accept INTERFET as legitimate. Thus INTERFET's legitimacy was crucial for Australia's status both within the region and in the wider international community.

Achieving legitimacy: the importance of INTERFET's UN mandate

The UN framework allowed Australia to address its core legitimacy concerns for INTERFET. In fact, Australian decision-makers tend to identify the international legitimacy conveyed by INTERFET's UN mandate as the UN's most important contribution to the intervention. As the head of the Australian Defence Department's East Timor Policy Unit in 1999 put it, the UN may have contributed little material or financial support to the operation, but 'what it did give us was some legitimacy for what we did, in an international sense'.[48]

INTERFET's UN mandate did not affect all of Australia's legitimacy audiences equally. It had relatively little impact on Australian domestic public opinion. Australians needed no convincing that, as Prime

---

[47] Author's interview with Hugh White, Canberra, 15 April 2002.

[48] Author's interview with Mike Scrafton, Head Infrastructure, Corporate Services and Infrastructure Group, Australian Department of Defence, Head of East Timor Policy Unit in Australia's Department of Defence during INTERFET, Canberra, Australia, 1 May 2002.

Minister Howard put it, 'our soldiers go to East Timor as part of a great Australian military tradition, which has never sought to impose the will of this country on others, but only to defend what is right.'[49] While they generally welcomed the UN Security Council mandate, it was not necessary to persuade them of INTERFET's legitimacy.

The UN mandate also had only a limited effect on Indonesian perceptions of INTERFET's legitimacy. One senior Australian government official has suggested that concern over Indonesian reactions to INTERFET shaped Australia's determination to operate under a UN mandate: 'we were very keen to do it as an agent of the United Nations . . . We wanted it to be a UN mission . . . we didn't want to be seen as pushing ourselves forward too much. And that related directly to our concerns about the impact of all of this on our long-term bilateral relationship with Indonesia.'[50] However, the degree of legitimacy that a UN mandate could bestow upon INTERFET in Indonesian eyes was strictly limited. Indonesians were keenly aware that Australia was the driving force behind INTERFET, which they viewed as a humiliating assault on Indonesian sovereignty. Indonesian President Abdurrahim Wahid expressed the virulence of Indonesian resentment in January 2000: Australia, he declared, had 'pissed in our face'.[51] Under these circumstances, even a UN Security Council mandate could not fully persuade Indonesia of INTERFET's legitimacy. However, the mandate did help limit the damage INTERFET caused to Australia's relations with Indonesia by providing a face-saving way for Indonesia to accede to the intervention. It was simply 'a lot easier for Indonesia to accept this force if it was UN-mandated rather than if it was not'.[52] As one Australian Defence Department analyst put it: 'without a covering authorisation from the Security Council, the political sense of invasion, of really getting in Jakarta's face in an aggressive and offensive way, would have been hugely amplified.'[53] Australia's Acting Defence Secretary during INTERFET concurred: 'we were right to be worried, but . . . the bad long-term relationship impact without a UN resolution would have been much, much worse.'[54]

---

[49] Howard, 'Address to the Nation'.
[50] Author's interview with Hugh White, Canberra, 15 April 2002.
[51] Peter Hartcher, 'Accent on Positive to Start Again in Indonesia' *Australian Financial Review*, 6 April 2000.
[52] Author's interview with Major-General Mike Smith, 10 April 2002.
[53] Author's interview with Professor Ron Huisken, Australian National University, Canberra, 16 April 2002.
[54] Author's interview with Hugh White, 15 April 2002.

The most important impact of the UN mandate was on international perceptions of INTERFET's legitimacy. As the world's largest and most inclusive interstate organisation, the UN can claim to embody the international community more convincingly than any other body. The UN mandate for INTERFET therefore represented the international community's approval of this operation, making it hard to argue that the intervention reflected only Australia's national priorities. As Brigadier Duncan Lewis, the ADF and INTERFET Spokesman in 1999, noted:

> If you are proximate to the problem in a geographic or emotional sense, you can easily be accused of being partisan, and having an interest – an interest that might not be legitimate. Whereas if you are working under the auspices of the UN, you can't really be accused of that. Because clearly the world community, the wider world community, supports what you are doing.[55]

Australian policy-makers were keenly aware of the UN's legitimising capacity. As one official commented, the UN Security Council mandate conferred upon INTERFET 'the blessing of the international community . . . a Security Council resolution gives you the international cover that can be cited to say that the operation is not an act of war.'[56] This blessing was understood to be crucial for avoiding accusations of aggressive pursuit of narrow national interests. Australia's Acting Secretary of Defence during INTERFET saw this clearly: 'we . . . needed to go in on the basis that the potential risk to us, politically, was managed, and we saw the UN as being essential to that.'[57] Indeed, despite the intense domestic pressure on Australian policy-makers to stop the violence in East Timor, the Australian government insisted that it would not intervene without a Security Council mandate. As one Australian official later put it, going into East Timor without a UN mandate 'would have been a complete policy failure. It wouldn't have occurred.'[58]

In the eyes of the international community, the UN mandate transformed INTERFET from an Australian enterprise to an international

---

[55] Author's interview with Brigadier Duncan Lewis, DSC, CSC, Commander Special Forces, Australian Army, Sydney, Australia, 2 May 2002.
[56] Author's interview, remarks not for attribution.
[57] Author's interview with Hugh White, 15 April 2002.
[58] Author's interview with Stephen Shaw, Project Manager, East Timor, Strategic and International Policy Division, Australian Department of Defence, Canberra, Australia, 19 April 2002.

initiative. It also helped dilute Australia's prominence in INTERFET by allowing Australia to recruit a diverse group of states to join INTERFET. Australian Brigadier Steve Ayling, who coordinated the INTERFFET coalition at the operational level, recalls that in negotiations with prospective participants, 'we had the Security Council resolution on the table – I used to give them a copy of it when they came . . . No one would come without a Security Council resolution . . . I quoted from it all the time.'[59] This international participation reinforced the message sent by the UN mandate that INTERFET was a truly international enterprise. Australia valued this message not only in itself but also because of its effect on Australia's regional neighbours. One senior Defence Department official recalls that:

> The UN Security Council resolution was a nice element, because it gave international legitimacy to the operation. We were . . . concerned because we needed a coalition to downplay the prominence of our involvement, because we wanted the South East Asians to get involved. We didn't want the fact that it was a white Australian intervention force to be the theme of the day. The UN helped us to internationalise that dimension.[60]

Brigadier Ayling concurred:

> we wanted to have a coalition lined up to convince the Indonesians and ASEAN that it wasn't actually Australia doing this. We laboured this point in the briefings: that it's not us, it's all of this – everyone from Norway to Brazil, to Zambia, Mozambique, Egypt. All sorts of countries were interested – the diversity of the coalition was the key to it.[61]

Thus the international legitimacy conveyed by the UN mandate for INTERFET had immediate and concrete repercussions at the regional level. It was indispensable to the process of building a regional coalition of the willing. The dual cover of the international legitimacy generated by the UN mandate and the relatively diverse coalition encouraged by that mandate allowed two of South East Asia's most liberal states to join INTERFET once Indonesia had given its formal assent to the operation. Thailand and the Philippines were the two major South East Asian contributors to INTERFET, and they would not have participated in

---

[59] Author's interview with Brigadier Steve Ayling, Director General INTERFET Branch, Strategic Command, Australian Defence Headquarters during INTERFET, Canberra, Australia, 17 April 2002.
[60] Author's interview. Remarks not for attribution.
[61] Author's interview with Brigadier Steve Ayling, 17 April 2002.

the operation without a UN mandate. A Filipino diplomat noted: 'The UN gave [INTERFET] legitimacy ... The United Nations is the final arbiter, that gave it the mandate to proceed ... we always operate under the aegis of the United Nations.'[62] A Thai diplomat echoed these sentiments, arguing that only a UN mandate offered a 'guarantee that we will do the right thing, and that we will not hurt the other country, that we will not overrule the rights of the people'.[63] Australian Brigadier Ayling was equally clear on the importance of the UN mandate for South East Asian nations: 'Without that international status ... the ASEAN countries wouldn't have come ... It was very important in the marketing of it to say: Look, it's not us. The UN Security Council has recognised that we have to do something to stop women and children being slaughtered ... It was just most important.'[64]

In turn, Thai and Filipino participation gave INTERFET the seal of a regional enterprise and thus further enhanced the operation's legitimacy in the eyes of the international community and particularly among South East Asian nations. Australia had counted on this dynamic:

> It was getting the ASEANs in which really made the difference. So we ended up with Thailand and the Philippines as major contributors ... the reason [that] was important in our eyes was that we felt it would legitimise what we were doing in Asia, and detract from the sense that this action was, if you like, the action of a whole lot of Anglo-Saxons against a whole lot of Asians. We wanted what we were doing to look like a regional enterprise in which we were acting as part of the wider region rather than as an outsider ... at the political level, [Thai and Filipino participation] identified what was happening clearly as a regional rather than an Australian or English action, or European-imposed enterprise.[65]

Thus the UN mandate helped jump-start a virtuous cycle of legitimation for INTERFET: the Security Council mandate provided the initial international legitimacy necessary to begin building a diverse coalition for the intervention, which in turn further enhanced the operation's legitimacy and thus promoted the participation of yet more coalition members.

---

[62] Author's interview with Laureano C. Santiago, Minister and Consul General, Embassy of the Philippines, Canberra, Australia, 10 April 2002.
[63] Author's interview with Captain Kanit Suwannate, Defence Attaché, Royal Thai Embassy, Canberra, Australia, 18 April 2002.
[64] Author's interview with Brigadier Steve Ayling, 17 April 2002.
[65] Author's interview with Hugh White, 15 April 2002.

Through this dynamic, Australia made significant advances towards its strategic objective of enhancing its prestige in the eyes of the USA: 'Australia's standing throughout America was helped by its [perceived] heroic and selfless actions in East Timor. And Australia was on the map in Washington, by making it on CNN, for the first time in many years.'[66] Results were somewhat more mixed with regard to Australia's other objective of improving its regional standing. Australia harmed its own cause by failing to fully incorporate its Asian partners in INTERFET's planning and command structures, and offended them by appearing to entertain the notion of acting as the USA's 'deputy sheriff' in the South East Asian region.[67] Nevertheless, it also proved its capacity and willingness to address regional security issues in conjunction with its neighbours. It also improved its relations with Thailand and the Philippines. Most importantly, however, it avoided being seen as an aggressive Western power expanding into the South East Asian region. Leading INTERFET did not fully integrate Australia into the South East Asian region, but it did not deepen Australia's regional isolation, either. As one senior Australian official recalls, this had been a major Australian concern:

> we didn't want Indonesia particularly to be able to use this to turn the rest of the region against us. As you will have gathered, working well with the region is one of the continual themes of Australian strategic and foreign policy. And so we were very concerned to make sure that this would look like a regional response and not just an Australian response.[68]

Thus the UN framework proved effective in generating legitimacy for INTERFET among the two audiences Australian policy-makers considered most crucial: the West and South East Asian states. As the Vice Chief of Australia's Army noted, this was critical for Australia: the UN 'gave the approval for [INTERFET] to happen, then it subcontracted it to a group coalition to do. [This approval conferred] International legitimacy. There was no way we could have gone there without that.'[69]

---

[66] Bruce C. Wolpe, 'Australia and America: Renewal and Reinvention', *Australian Journal of International Affairs*, 54:1 (2000).

[67] The notion of Australia as a 'deputy sheriff' was first advanced in Fred Brenchley, 'The Howard Defence Doctrine', *The Bulletin*, 28 September 1999, pp. 22–4.

[68] Author's interview with Hugh White, 15 April 2002.

[69] Author's interview with Major General Peter Leahy, Deputy Chief of the Australian Army, Canberra, Australia, 30 April 2002.

The costs and benefits of operating through the United Nations

Does Australia's decision to launch INTERFET within the UN framework attest to the inherent value it placed on international legitimacy? Thus far, this chapter has argued that legitimacy concerns were Australia's primary motivation for operating within this framework. However, if Australia incurred few costs in operating through this framework, or if the costs were balanced by material benefits, this decision tells us little about the inherent value it placed on international legitimacy. To counter this objection, this section demonstrates that Australia accepted substantial costs both to obtain and to operate under UN auspices. Although the legitimacy generated by these auspices helped to build the INTERFET coalition, moreover, the ensuing material benefits to Australia were outweighed by the costs of coalition warfare. In fact, Australia's coalition-building behaviour indicates that it did not simply value legitimacy for instrumental purposes.

The cost of INTERFET's UN mandate

Australia had to overcome three major obstacles to obtain a UN Security Council mandate for INTERFET, and the effort it expended in overcoming them demonstrates the importance it attached to INTERFET's international legitimacy.

First, Australia was an outsider to the UN bodies that addressed East Timor. It was excluded from the Tripartite Process, the official UN forum for discussing East Timor from 1982 to 1999. Consequently, when the possibility of change in East Timor arose in 1998, Australia played a risky positioning game to establish its influence on this issue. It advocated an eventual act of self-determination in East Timor in order to outflank Portugal as an intermediary for the East Timorese. Simultaneously, it sought to maintain close relations with Indonesia by assuring President Habibie that the East Timorese could be persuaded to vote for integration given a sufficiently long transition period. Australia succeeded in raising its negotiating profile, but Habibie, outraged by the perceived treachery of his Australian allies, voided further negotiations by proposing precisely what Australia had hoped to avoid: an early East Timorese vote on independence.

After this set-back, Australia concentrated on mending its relations with Indonesia while also positioning itself within the UN as a key player in possible military operations in East Timor. From April 1999, Australian Brigadier (later Major-General) Mike Smith liaised with the UN about possible Australian contributions to future UN peace operations in East Timor.[70] Later he and Australia's Defence Attaché to the UN provided assistance to the UN in planning the force structure of a possible peacekeeping deployment. This contingency planning ultimately became the basis of INTERFET's force structure planning. Australia also joined the UN monitoring mission for the popular consultation in East Timor, thus positioning itself to participate in the crisis negotiations of September 1999. As Australia's Permanent Representative to the United Nations noted: 'You cannot make "cold calls" in a crisis; you must have invested the effort well beforehand to build up some goodwill and resources on which to draw.'[71]

However, Australia remained an outsider to the UN Security Council, which ultimately gave INTERFET its mandate. It had to rely on the USA and the UK to defend Australia's interests in the Council and to secure a Chapter VII mandate for INTERFET. Australia's Permanent Representative to the UN recalls 'tense moments, which turned into long hours of waiting' as 'we non-members waited like expectant parents outside the delivery room, pouncing on any members who came out of the closed Council for news of what was happening inside.'[72] In short, the UN did not present a hospitable environment for Australian influence on the East Timor issue.

The second obstacle that Australia faced in obtaining INTERFET's mandate was that the Security Council refused to authorise an operation without prior Indonesian assent. As noted above, the Australian government itself was determined to secure this consent before intervening, since it feared open military confrontation with Indonesia. The dynamics of the Security Council reinforced this imperative. China insisted that 'the deployment of any peacekeeping force should be at the request of the Indonesian government', and Russia concurred that 'an international force to East Timor ... will only be possible if ... consent is received from the Indonesian authorities for the acceptance of such a force.'[73] Since both countries hold veto powers over Security

---

[70] Author's interview with Major-General Mike Smith, 10 April 2002.
[71] Wensley, 'East Timor and the United Nations', p. 5.   [72] Ibid.
[73] United Nations Security Council, Record of the 4043rd Meeting, New York, 11 September 1999.

Council decisions, Australia had to gain Indonesian acquiescence before it could obtain a UN mandate for INTERFET. Australian Foreign Minister Downer recognised this emphatically: 'you could say "well, maybe we can get the Security Council to agree without Indonesia", but you wouldn't. You wouldn't. That would not happen. Believe me. That would not happen.'[74]

Indonesia, however, resolutely opposed any intervention. Its eventual grudging acquiescence was obtained only because several factors whittled away at its resolve. One was the international embarrassment that the violence in East Timor caused Indonesia. Under the 5 May Agreements, Indonesia had assumed responsibility for maintaining peace and security in East Timor during the ballot and subsequent transition phase, and it now showed itself either unwilling or unable to do so. A Security Council fact-finding mission and a well-attended open Security Council debate on East Timor on 11 September under-lined the international salience of this failure. Bilateral diplomatic efforts by Indonesia's South and North East Asian neighbors also played a role: Thailand, China, Japan, and South Korea all discretely but emphatically advised Habibie to accept an intervention force.[75] The most crucial factor, however, was US pressure. The Clinton administration underscored its public and private invitations for Indonesia to accept an intervention force with threats of blocking Indonesian access to IMF and World Bank loans should it refuse to do so.[76] This hard-line US position was due in good part to intense Australian lobbying. As one senior US official put it: 'We don't have a dog running in the East Timor race, but we have a very big dog running down there called Australia and we have to support it.'[77]

Ultimately, Indonesia succumbed to these pressures and assented to a multinational intervention force. However, this victory cost Australia intense lobbying efforts and valuable time. Australia agreed to lead an intervention on 6 September, but Indonesia did not acquiesce until 12 September. During this time, East Timor was ransacked and its popula-tion murdered and deported. Yet despite ever-increasing domestic

---

[74] John Moore and Alexander Downer, 'Press Conference', 6 September 1999, online at www.minister.defence.gov.au/1999/mt0699.htm.

[75] Author's interview with Professor Alan Dupont, 13 April 2002.

[76] Nicholas J. Wheeler and Tim Dunne, 'East Timor and the New Humanitarian Interventionism', *International Affairs*, 77:4 (2001), p. 819.

[77] Anonymous, quoted in Peter Hartcher, 'The ABC of Winning US Support', *Australian Financial Review*, 13 September 1999.

pressure to act, the Australian government waited for Indonesian assent not only to limit the chance of military confrontation between Australia and Indonesia but also to unblock the Security Council mandating process. Once Indonesia did acquiesce, the Security Council mandate was obtained on 15 September, and troops began arriving in Dili on the 20th. Waiting for Indonesian assent thus caused the single longest delay in the launching of INTERFET.

The final obstacle Australia faced in obtaining a Security Council mandate for INTERFET was that Council members did not want to have to pay for the operation. Under the 1999 dispensation, the five Permanent Members of the Security Council were required to fund almost half the UN peacekeeping budget and could therefore expect any UN peace enforcement operation they authorised to cost them hundreds of millions of dollars. Consequently, the UN burden-sharing arrangements for peacekeeping operations became a liability for Australia. It overcame this problem by agreeing to lead a coalition of the willing rather than a UN force, thereby waiving all burden-sharing claims on Security Council members. Australia was involved in the drafting negotiations for clause 9 of Security Council Resolution 1264, which stressed 'that the expenses of the force will be borne by the participating Member States concerned'. It knew that this clause would dramatically increase the financial burden it would have to shoulder – but it also realised that this would be the price of obtaining a Security Council mandate and the international legitimacy this entailed. By accepting to pay that price, Australia demonstrated that it regarded the international legitimacy generated by the Security Council mandate as more important than any burden-sharing mechanism the UN had to offer.

Legitimacy, coalition-building, and the cost of coalition

Even the fact that obtaining a UN mandate for INTERFET was costly does not conclusively demonstrate that Australia valued the legitimacy that this mandate generated as an end in itself. Realist sceptics might argue that the material benefits of operating within the UN framework outweighed its costs. As argued above, the legitimacy conveyed by the UN mandate allowed Australia to recruit contributors to INTERFET. Some of these contributors provided crucial resources for INTERFET. The USA supplied critical capabilities in strategic lift, communications, and intelligence.[78] Thailand, the Republic of Korea, and the Philippines contributed badly needed infantry forces, easing Australian worries about the operation's sustainability given the ADF's limited troop numbers. Nevertheless, the argument that Australia's motivation for operating within the UN framework was not legitimacy itself but effective coalition-building fails on both theoretical and empirical grounds.

At the theoretical level, realism provides no adequate explanation for why legitimacy should help coalition-building. If states are essentially power or security maximisers and international organisations exert no independent influence on international politics, why would a UN mandate entice a state that would not otherwise contribute to a peace enforcement operation to do so? By contrast, constructivism, as noted in chapter 2, does highlight the possibility that international rules can not only constrain but also enable state action by allowing governments to mobilise otherwise unavailable resources.[79]

Chapter 2 also argued, however, that states do not in fact value international legitimacy only for the resources it helps to mobilise, and this is borne out in the INTERFET case. Although INTERFET's legitimacy paved the way for burden-sharing through coalition-building, Australia's coalition-building strategy cannot be fully explained with reference to burden-sharing. In fact, three factors suggest that rather than pursuing legitimacy purely in order to build a coalition, Australia built its coalition in large part in order to enhance its intervention's legitimacy.

First, Australia assiduously courted and praised all INTERFET contributors, regardless of the size and timing of their contributions. Although INTERFET eventually included twenty-two states, Australia bore the brunt of the burden during its most dangerous early phases. Australia provided most of INTERFET's initial deployment force, joined only by the UK and New Zealand. Ten days later, when INTERFET began expanding beyond Dili, Australia accounted for over two-thirds of INTERFET' troops, and was joined by only seven INTERFET partners. Australia's share of INTERFET troops only began to decline when INTERFET's most dangerous moments were over. Figure 7.2 shows the troop distribution in INTERFET on 29 October.

---

[78] INTERFET Force Commander Peter Cosgrove also used the 31st Military Expeditionary Unit aboard the USS Belleau Woods (which arrived in Dili harbour on 5 October) as a strategic reserve, even though these troops were not formally committed as ground forces.

[79] Thanks to an anonymous reviewer for stressing this point.

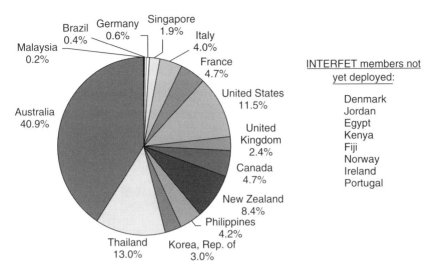

Figure 7.2: INTERFET troop contributions, 29 October 1999

This chart shows not only that Australia was still providing 41 per cent of INTERFET's troops on 29 October 1999, but also that more than a month into the operation, ten of INTERFET's eventual twenty-two members had not yet deployed any troops to East Timor. The last TNI soldier left East Timor three days later, on 1 November. Thus just under half of INTERFET's members arrived in the theatre of operations well after the chance that they would have to make any significant military contribution to the peace enforcement mission had passed. Nevertheless, Australia praised these countries' contributions unreservedly, and regardless of the size of the contributions they eventually made. Brigadier Ayling recalled his strategy as follows:

> we took the view that . . . large or small didn't matter. If they wanted to send one person, we gave them the same Rolls Royce treatment, if they wanted to send a hundred people, if they wanted to send 1001 people . . . And you do everything that you can as a coalition leader to bolster each and every one's support. We used to say: By golly, we're glad the Norwegians have sent two officers, because without them we'd have this deficiency, and they're doing a terrific job, etc. – so that everyone gets the kudos out of it.[80]

This behaviour would have made no sense if Australia's main objective in coalition-building had been to ease its own burden in launching

---

[80] Author's interview with Brigadier Steve Ayling, 17 April 2002.

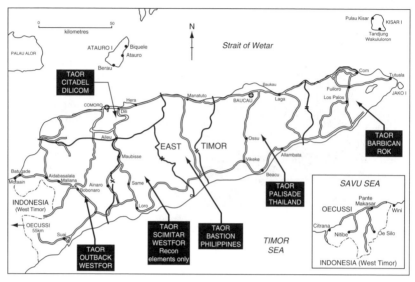

Map 7.1: Geographical distribution of INTERFET forces
Source: Cartographic Services, Research School of Pacific and Asian Studies, The Australian National University © Cartography, The Australian National University

INTERFET. However, Australia was not building the coalition solely to elicit military support but also to further the virtuous cycle of legitimation described in the previous section. Brigadier Ayling was clear on this: 'we gave them [all] the Rolls Royce treatment because at the strategic level it was the number of countries within the coalition – that was the strength: the diversity of the coalition.'[81]

The second indication that Australia's coalition-building strategy did not primarily aim at burden-sharing is the geographical distribution of INTERFET troops. Many INTERFET members – notably its major Asian contributors – were extremely wary of offending Indonesia. They therefore stressed the humanitarian nature of their deployment and sought to avoid using their troops in a combat capacity. Their greatest fear was becoming involved in a direct military confrontation with Indonesian troops. Consequently, they made their participation conditional on being assigned a geographical sector of East Timor where the risk of military confrontation was low and the scope for humanitarian action abundant. Australia acquiesced. Map 7.1 provides a map

---

[81] Ibid.

of the resultant distribution of areas of INTERFET members' areas of operation.

South Korea, Thailand, and the Philippines were all assigned sectors in the east of East Timor. Meanwhile, Dili Command (DILICOM) and West Force (WESTFOR) were composed of troops from Australia and New Zealand. These forces assumed responsibility for the 'hot zone' of the border between East Timor and Indonesia, where militia activity was intense and there was a high risk of clashes with the Indonesian military. This geographical distribution of troops ensured that Australia shouldered a disproportionate share of INTERFET's military risks. Yet Australia was no less concerned about its future relations with Indonesia than its Asian neighbours, and Australian military planners had warned that any confrontation with the TNI risked escalating into a full-scale war. Why, then, did Australia agree to this division of labour? Again, the answer revolves around the legitimacy effects of having these countries' flags and troops on the ground with INTERFET. Brigadier Ayling saw this clearly:

> The purist would say: oh, they can get stuffed, they will go where we want them to go. I say: well hang on a minute: if you say that they are going to be sent to the western end of the island, then politically, they won't come. Or they'll come light. Or they'll send money. Or they'll send toys. But if you want an infantry battalion, on part of the island, you accommodate them.[82]

The third indication of Australia's key motivation in building the INTERFET coalition was that despite the limited military contributions provided by most INTERFET members, Australia accepted considerable costs associated with coalition-building. Some of these costs reflected general issues in coalition warfare. In any coalition, members need to understand the force's command structure, objectives, division of labour, and rules of engagement. To facilitate this understanding, Australia spent US$1.5 million on flying planning teams from potential troop contributors to Australia and East Timor for an elaborate five-stage briefing process.[83] It also insisted that all INTERFET troops spend one to two weeks at its training facilities at Townsville, where they were accommodated and offered a range of training modules, again at

---

[82] Ibid.   [83] Author's interview with Michael Scrafton, 1 May 2002.

Australian expense.[84] Coalition warfare also imposes political costs, notably the impossibility of maintaining a united front for the operation because of interstate rivalries within the coalition. Thus the commander of the British contingent publicly accused Australia of excess caution in deploying beyond Dili, while the Malaysian contingent vociferously complained that Australia was being too aggressive. Coming from an ASEAN INTERFET member, this latter claim was particularly problematic for Australia, but it was hardly unexpected, given Malaysia's often vocal hostility to Australia. Nevertheless, Australia accepted Malaysia's participation in INTERFET – not because the twenty-seven interpreters Malaysia eventually sent had any particular military significance but because even a token Malaysian contribution had implications for INTERFET's international legitimacy.

Australia also faced coalition-building costs arising specifically from its desire to include a strong non-Western and regional component in INTERFET. Most of INTERFET's non-Western participants were developing nations whose defence forces disposed of only limited financial resources and equipment stocks. While these countries were eligible for funding from the UN Trust Fund for INTERFET described above, two problems arose. First, since the Trust Fund only issued reimbursements at the end of the operation, several countries faced cash flow problems. Australia addressed these by providing financial loans to two countries (Fiji and the Philippines) and promising similar support to Thailand if this became necessary. It also made what amounted to in-kind loans to developing INTERFET members by supplying their troops with goods and services for which it later sought reimbursement from the Trust Fund in their name. The most striking case of this kind of assistance was to the Philippines, which reclaimed just under US$2 million from the Fund while Australia reclaimed over US$3 million in support costs. Australia had advanced more money for the Filipino deployment than the Philippines themselves. In total, Australia eventually reclaimed over US$9 million from the Trust Fund, which amounted to over one-third of the total Trust Fund resources disbursed, implying that Australia advanced over one-third of the deployment costs of developing INTERFET members.

The second problem with the UN Trust Fund was that it did not cover capital investments such as the purchase of equipment. Australia stepped into the gap to provide the necessary equipment, ranging from socks and

---

[84] Author's interview with Wing Commander Peter Wilkinson, 19 April 2002.

uniforms to engineering equipment. The full cost of this effort has not yet been documented. The ADF has acknowledged directly gifting AU$3.5 million (US$2.3 million) in equipment to developing INTERFET members,[85] but this is only the tip of the iceberg. The hidden costs of unofficial or informal equipment use or lending were much higher, and still remain unclear, though one senior Defence Department official has placed them at several hundred million Australian dollars. Australia's first priority was to gain and maintain international momentum behind INTERFET, and it was willing to shoulder the costs of doing so. As the head of the Defence Department's East Timor Policy Unit put it, 'It was conceived to be in our interest, strongly in our strategic interest, that this didn't fail. And we, I think, funded a range of things that we were never confident that we were going to get reimbursed even partially for from the UN.'[86]

The resources Australia provided to developing INTERFET members could have been spent directly on the Australian INTERFET effort. This would have been a more efficient distribution of resources from Australia's point of view, both because Australia had more control over its own troops than over those of other coalition members and because it was the Australian and New Zealand troops that manned East Timor's 'hot zones'. The fact that Australia nevertheless chose to divert these resources to other INTERFET members shows that far from seeking to spread the burden of intervention to its partners, Australia was willing to shoulder extra costs just to have these partners in East Timor. This willingness can only be understood in the context of Australian concerns about INTERFET's international legitimacy.

Thus the realist challenge to a legitimacy-based theory of the role of international organisations in peace enforcement operations is not supported by empirical evidence in the INTERFET case. Both obtaining the UN Security Council mandate and operating within the UN framework generated costs for Australia. Although the legitimacy generated by this framework did help INTERFET coalition-building, moreover, this was not Australia's primary reason for valuing this legitimacy. While some coalition members made substantial military contributions to INTERFET, most did not. Australia nevertheless accommodated these states' deployment preferences and subsidised its developing INTERFET

---

[85] Australian National Audit Office, 'Management of the Australian Defence Force Deployments to East Timor', Article 2.62, p. 40.
[86] Author's interview with Mike Scrafton, 1 May 2002.

partners. It thus sought to ease the burdens of deployment on other INTERFET members rather than to exploit their cooperation in military or financial terms. Simultaneously, Australia shouldered the costs of coalition warfare, including not only coordination problems but also internal criticism of INTERFET strategy. This strongly suggests that Australia valued the legitimacy effects of states' participation in the INTERFET coalition above their specific military or financial contribution to the force. In short, it saw coalition-building as a means to enhancing INTERFET's legitimacy rather than the other way around.

Conclusion

The evidence of the INTERFET case overwhelmingly supports the legitimacy-centred theory of the role of international organisations in peace enforcement operations formulated in chapter 2. Neither international law nor burden-sharing considerations can explain Australia's decision to launch INTERFET within the UN framework. The UN is the only international organisation that has the legal ability to authorise peace enforcement operations, but this was not Australia's primary motivation for seeking a UN mandate for INTERFET. In fact, Australia chose not to rely on the Security Council's legal ability to authorise military intervention without the consent of the host state. Australia also agreed to launch and lead INTERFET as a coalition of the willing, forgoing both the UN's internal resources and its mechanisms for eliciting financial or troops contributions from UN member states. Nevertheless, Australian policy-makers insist that INTERFET could only have been launched through the UN.

The UN mandate was crucial because Australia had significant legitimacy concerns for INTERFET, which grew out of Australia's historical background and geographical location and reflected its quest for increased regional and international status. Australian policy-makers hoped to use INTERFET to demonstrate Australia's importance as a net contributor to regional peace and security. This could only be achieved if the intervention was accepted as legitimate both within South East Asia and in the wider international community. The UN mandate bestowed the international legitimacy necessary for Australia to launch the operation and for other states to participate in it, which in turn further increased the intervention's international legitimacy, beginning a virtuous cycle of legitimation. Australian policy-makers consistently acknowledge that the international legitimacy generated by INTERFET's UN mandate was crucial to the intervention's success.

Obtaining this legitimacy was neither costless nor easy for Australia. To secure the Security Council mandate, Australia had to manoeuvre carefully within the UN, coax Indonesian acquiescence to an intervention, and sacrifice any claims on UN burden-sharing mechanisms. Once issued, the mandate was vital to persuading other members of the international community, and in particular Australia's South East Asian neighbours, to participate in INTERFET. However, Australia did not seek the legitimacy of a UN mandate because of its burden-sharing implications. From Australia's point of view, the INTERFET coalition was vital because it further confirmed the intervention's international legitimacy, not because of the military contributions of its coalition partners. For this legitimacy, Australia was willing to shoulder the considerable costs of coalition-building and coalition warfare.

8

Conclusion

This book has argued that in the contemporary international system states launch peace enforcement operations within the framework of international organisations primarily because they wish to ensure the international legitimacy of these operations. This concluding chapter summarises and juxtaposes the findings of the five case studies in this project, noting differences but above all stressing the remarkable similarities among them. Overall, the empirical findings in this book support the legitimacy-centred theory of the role of international organisations against its main alternatives. This chapter then takes a step back from the focus on peace enforcement operations that has pervaded this project to situate these findings in the broader universe of international military activity. It also considers the one conspicuous exception to the trend studied here: the 2003 US-led invasion of Iraq, which portrayed itself as akin to a peace enforcement mission but did not occur under the auspices of an international organisation. It argues that this case illustrates not only the limits but also the strength of a legitimacy-based conception of the role of international organisations. Finally, the chapter reflects on the theoretical and practical implications of recognising international organisations as gatekeepers to legitimacy in the contemporary international system.

Summary of empirical evidence

This book has analysed five peace enforcement operations launched on three continents: Europe (Kosovo), Asia (East Timor), and Africa (Liberia, Democratic Republic of Congo, and Lesotho). These operations were launched in three types of institutional setting: the global United Nations, the NATO military alliance, and two African sub-regional organisations, the Economic Community of West African States (ECOWAS) and the Southern African Development Community (SADC). The lead states in these operations varied in both their international stature and the nature of their regimes, ranging from the US superpower to relatively small powers like Zimbabwe, and from established democracies (Australia, USA) to a dictatorship (Nigeria). Despite this diversity, several common trends emerged, all of which support the proposition that in the contemporary international system states launching peace enforcement operations turn to international organisations primarily to ensure the international legitimacy of their interventions. Table 8.1 summarises the key findings of the five case studies.

The first thing to note about this table is the consistency with which two main rival explanations of the role of international organisations in peace enforcement operations are rejected. In four of the five case studies, respect for international law was clearly an inadequate explanation for the intervening states' decisions to launch their peace enforcement operations through international organisations. The interventions in Liberia, Lesotho, and Kosovo occurred without a UN Security Council mandate and therefore violated international law despite their international auspices. The Zimbabwe-led intervention in the Democratic Republic of Congo, which also occurred without a UN mandate, can be partially defended as an act of collective self-defence in the face of international aggression. In that case, however, its SADC auspices were superfluous, since international law does not require collective security operations to be approved by any international organisation. The only case in which the mandating international organisation could arguably have guaranteed the legality of the peace enforcement operation launched under its auspices was the Australian-led intervention in East Timor. However, Australia's simultaneous insistence on obtaining Indonesian consent for the intervention made the UN mandate redundant in terms of international law and suggests that compliance with international law was not Australia's primary reason for operating within the UN framework.

The evidence of the five case studies is even more emphatically at odds with the neo-liberal institutionalist view of international organisations as facilitators of interstate cooperation and burden-sharing. No significant burden-sharing took place in any of the five peace enforcement operations studied. The lead states consistently furnished the vast majority of the troops and equipment deployed. Where reasonable cost estimates can be made, it is clear that lead states assumed at least three-quarters of the total cost of the operations. The remaining burden was never evenly spread among the other members of the mandating organisations. In each operation except NATO's Kosovo campaign, only

Table 8.1: *Summary of case studies*

Target state (date)	Liberia (1990–1997)	D. R. Congo (1998–2002)	Lesotho (1998–1999)	Kosovo (1999)	East Timor (1999–2000)
International organisation	ECOWAS	SADC	SADC	NATO	UN
Lead state (regime type)	Nigeria (dictatorship)	Zimbabwe (autocracy)	South Africa (democracy)	USA (democracy)	Australia (democracy)
International legal status	No UNSC mandate	No UNSC mandate, but collective security	No UNSC mandate	No UNSC mandate	UNSC mandate
Burden-sharing	5 of 15 members join Nigeria: 62–86% troops, 90% cost	3 of 13 members join Zimbabwe: 50–83% troops	2 of 13 members join South Africa: 75–91% troops	14 of 19 members join USA: 68% sorties 80% cost	22 of 188 members join Australia: 41–66% troops, 75% cost
Legitimacy concerns? (Audience)	Yes (International Community)	Yes (Southern Africa, Africa)	Yes (Domestic, International Community)	Yes (International Community)	Yes (South East Asia, International Community)
Effect of international framework	Substantial	Africa: substantial International: modest	Domestic: modest International: high	Substantial	High
Cost of mandate	• Risk to ECOWAS • Buy acquiescence • No burden-sharing • Finance coalition • Coalition warfare	• Defy South Africa • Deadlock SADC • No burden-sharing	• Accept Zimbabwe DRC operation • Coalition warfare • No burden-sharing	• Coalition warfare • No burden-sharing • Finance coalition	• Delay • No burden-sharing • Finance coalition • Coalition warfare

a tiny minority of the mandating organisation's members participated in the intervention. Even in the NATO case, only five of the USA's eighteen allies made substantial military or financial contributions. The remaining NATO members made only token efforts, collectively accounting for only 11 per cent of the campaign's aircraft and sorties.

Moreover, none of the lead states expected better burden-sharing performances from their organisations. Neither SADC nor ECOWAS had formal military burden-sharing mechanisms when the interventions into Liberia, the DRC, and Lesotho were launched. NATO's 55-year history is marked with persistent but generally ineffectual US complaints that its allies are not shouldering enough of the common defence burden. The UN has formal burden-sharing mechanisms, but in the East Timor case Australia was explicitly given a mandate to lead a multinational rather than a UN force – the key distinction being that multinational forces are not funded by the UN. Thus none of the lead states examined here expected or obtained the kind of burden-sharing that neo-liberal institutionalism predicts from international organisations.

By contrast, table 8.1 shows that all five case studies supported the theory that states turn to international organisations because of the international legitimacy these organisations can bestow on peace enforcement operations. All five lead states had substantial concerns about the international legitimacy of their interventions. In two instances, the perceived audience for these legitimacy concerns had a regional dimension. Because of its foreign policy posture as champion of the developing world and Africa in particular, Zimbabwe was most concerned with Southern and continental African perceptions of the legitimacy of its DRC intervention. Australia, meanwhile, feared a strong South East Asian backlash if its East Timor intervention was not perceived as legitimate. In all but the Zimbabwean case, however, there was also a concern for the legitimacy of the peace enforcement operations in the eyes of the wider international community. This international community was not always well defined. In the Australian and South African cases, it most notably included the West, but also extended to the more general audience of the world's states. For the USA, the international community was defined partly in terms of its Western allies but mostly as a more amorphous world opinion that might affect states' perceptions of the benevolence of the US superpower.

Interestingly, domestic legitimacy audiences mattered much less than international ones in the case studies analysed here – at least as far as states' decisions to seek international auspices for their peace enforcement operations were concerned. Autocracies like Nigeria and Zimbabwe largely ignored domestic cynicism about their motives and dissatisfaction with their decision to allocate scarce resources to peace enforcement. Established democracies like the USA and Australia benefited from their citizens' confidence in their own countries' fundamentally good intentions. Australians overwhelmingly supported the East Timor intervention and had little doubt that it was fully justified. US citizens were less enthusiastic about NATO's air campaign in Kosovo, but media images of fleeing Kosovar refugees combined with widespread confidence in the essential altruism of the US government's actions to eliminate most public doubts about the legitimacy of the intervention. Only in newly democratic South Africa, where citizens remembered past abuses, mistrusted their government's intentions, and feared renewed international disapprobation, did domestic legitimacy present the government with a challenge it could not ignore. Even in South Africa, however, domestic legitimacy concerns did not overshadow international ones. Instead, they underscored the need for the South African government to secure international legitimacy for its intervention in order to counter domestic criticism. Thus all five lead states were intensely concerned with their operation's legitimacy in the eyes of a key international audience.

Moreover, in all five cases the fact that the peace enforcement operation was launched under the auspices of an international organisation improved its legitimacy in the eyes of the key audience. This effect was most pronounced in the case of the Australian-led UN intervention in East Timor, whose Security Council mandate swayed not only the broad international community but also key South East Asian countries like Thailand and the Philippines to view the intervention as legitimate. This is consistent with the prediction made in chapter 2 that the more an international organisation's membership approaches universality, the greater the legitimising effect of its mandate will be. A UN mandate does not matter only or even mostly because of the organisation's unique status in international law. As a global international organisation, the UN is better placed than any other international body to signal the world's endorsement of an intervention and thus establish it as a collective operation for the common good rather than a unilateral initiative for national ends. Given the rules governing the international use of force in the contemporary international system, this amounts to certifying the international legitimacy of an intervention.

As a result of the global trend towards endorsing the regionalisation of conflict management, however, international organisations that do not aspire to universal membership can also affect the international legitimacy of peace enforcement operations. Despite the fact that they violated international law, none of the interventions in Liberia, Lesotho, and Kosovo faced official condemnation in any international body. UN follow-up missions in Liberia and Kosovo amounted to post hoc approval of the interventions. Only in the case of the DRC, which ironically was in better compliance with international law than any of the other regional enforcement operations, did the legitimising effect of an international organisation's auspices falter a little on the world stage. This anomaly was caused by South Africa's initial condemnation of the operation, which temporarily raised doubts about the validity of the operation's SADC auspices. Given early post-apartheid South Africa's position as a relative outsider in sub-Saharan Africa, however, its criticism had relatively little effect on African perceptions of the intervention's legitimacy. Moreover, once South Africa dropped its objections in exchange for Zimbabwe's approval of SADC auspices for South Africa's intervention in Lesotho, the legitimising effect of operating within the SADC framework was restored. This benefited not only Zimbabwe but also South Africa, which faced no international criticism of its Lesotho operation despite Basotho protests and domestic opposition to the intervention.

Finally, as the last row of table 8.1 indicates, the realist challenge to a legitimacy-based theory of the role of international organisations in modern peace enforcement operations failed. Although mandating organisations are subject to political pressures and manipulations, they are not simply cheap figleaves for powerful states. In all five cases studied in this book, intervening states incurred substantial costs in their pursuit of the legitimacy generated by an international organisation's mandate. Some of these costs were material. In all five cases, lead states declared themselves willing to bear the brunt of the military and financial burden of operations as long as their fellow member states acceded to their use of the international organisation's auspices. In direct opposition to neo-liberal institutionalism, they explicitly waived any burden-sharing requirements that might otherwise have arisen from the international organisation's mandate. Moreover, in at least three of the five cases (Liberia, Kosovo, and East Timor), the lead state effectively subsidised other participants in their interventions. In the Liberian case, Nigeria also disbursed funds to persuade fellow ECOWAS members to acquiesce to the operation's ECOWAS auspices.

Another common cost of operating within the framework of an international organisation was the complexity and loss of control associated with coalition warfare. In the Lesotho case, South African troops were left exposed because inadequate coordination with their Botswana allies resulted in lower-than-expected troop strengths on the first day of the deployment. In East Timor, Australia expended much energy on constructing a coalition and meeting its allies' geographical deployment preferences. Other costs were more idiosyncratic to individual cases. For Australia, a major cost of operating through the UN system was the delay it caused to the deployment, which cost East Timorese lives and infuriated the Australian public. For Zimbabwe, invoking SADC auspices opened its intervention in the DRC up for criticism by its regional rival and fellow SADC member, South Africa. South Africa, in turn, had to make the major foreign policy compromise of reversing its opposition to the DRC intervention in order to secure SADC auspices for its own peace enforcement operation in Lesotho.

Thus there is remarkable consistency in the evidence generated by this book's five case studies despite the variety of lead states and international organisations examined. Neither strict compliance with international law nor burden-sharing adequately explained any lead state's decision to launch its peace enforcement operation through an international organisation. By contrast, all lead states had strong concerns about their peace enforcement operation's international legitimacy, and found international organisations a suitable framework for addressing this challenge. To obtain the auspices of these international organisations, all five lead states incurred substantial costs, indicating that their concern for international legitimacy was neither frivolous nor superficial. Thus this study suggests that regardless of their regime type and international status, states in the contemporary system recognise the need to ensure that the peace enforcement operations they launch appear legitimate to the international community. It also indicates that international organisations play a major role in peace enforcement operations because they are the gatekeepers of international legitimacy.

Generalising beyond peace enforcement operations

How much can we learn about the nature of politics in the contemporary international system by examining peace enforcement operations? Is it possible to derive general claims about the importance of international legitimacy and the role of international organisations in military affairs from the case studies examined here? This book cannot claim to have proven the centrality of legitimacy concerns to all arenas of international politics, and it does not seek to imply that international organisations are important only as gatekeepers to this legitimacy. Nevertheless, it does suggest that legitimacy is a central concern of states when they engage in international activity – even and especially in that most controversial of activities, the use of military force abroad. It has also argued that the role of international organisations in this respect has been undeservedly neglected by international relations theory. If states care about legitimacy when they launch peace enforcement operations, it seems reasonable to suppose that they will also care about legitimacy in at least some other circumstances. If international organisations are gatekeepers to international legitimacy during peace enforcement operations, they may serve a similar function in other endeavours. Yet critics may object that peace enforcement operations are in important ways *sui generis* and therefore do not provide a good window on other areas of international politics. This case for peace enforcement 'exceptionalism' can be made from two directions.

Exceptionally controversial?

One challenge contends that peace enforcement operations are exceptional because they are by their very nature more controversial than most other international activities. While states are correctly concerned with legitimacy when they engage in such spectacular and often illegal activities, this concern need not carry over into other, more mundane spheres of international politics. This objection is only partially valid. Chapter 2 of this book has conceded that legitimacy and legality often overlap. An international activity that is in full accordance with international law is unlikely to be viewed as illegitimate. In general, therefore, a state that is acting legally need not be as concerned about international legitimacy as one that is acting illegally. Peace enforcement operations raise the problem of legitimacy acutely at least in part because their legality is often in question. Nevertheless, three considerations attenuate the extent to which this makes peace enforcement operations exceptional in world politics.

First, even if it were the case that legitimacy concerns are particularly acute for peace enforcement operations *only* because they stretch the bounds of international law, this would not put these operations in a class of their own. Many states engage in illegal activities from time to time: they refuse to allow refugees to apply for asylum, fail to stop genocide, maintain barriers to free trade, or continue environmentally damaging production techniques despite treaty obligations to the contrary. States engaged in these activities have as much incentive as those launching peace enforcement operations to ensure that their actions are not perceived as illegitimate. Their strategies may differ, however, since in cases that do not involve the use of military force international organisations may not be the primary gatekeepers of legitimacy. In such cases, other means of establishing the international legitimacy of one's actions are likely to exist – one avenue of future research would be to explore how states learn what measures are necessary to ensure the international legitimacy of technically illegal activities. Empirically, they frequently seem to succeed in their quest for legitimacy. Illegal activities seldom produce an international outcry and formal condemnation by fellow states is rare.

Second, as chapter 2 argued, peace enforcement operations are not controversial only because they violate international law, but also and more importantly because they involve the use of military force abroad. They thus impinge on such fundamental rules of the contemporary international system as the respect of state sovereignty and the prohibition of aggression. If this gives states launching peace enforcement operations particular reason to be concerned about international legitimacy, the same logic should hold for states engaged in other kinds of international military activity. If international organisations act as gatekeepers of international legitimacy for peace enforcement operations, they should fulfil similar roles for these other military activities. A wide spectrum of international military activities seems to bear this out. Contemporary peacekeeping and peace-building operations almost universally take place within the framework of international organisations, even though legal concerns weigh much less heavily in these consent-based operations than in peace enforcement operations.[1] Moreover, as chapter 1 noted, the two major campaigns against international aggression since World War Two, the Korean War (1950–53), and the Gulf War (1991), were both fought under United Nations mandates. Chapter 1 also noted that Cold War interventions in Czechoslovakia

---

[1] Peacekeeping has long been the province of the United Nations, but other international organisations are also entering this field, as NATO's first out-of-area mission in Afghanistan attests.

and Grenada took place under the auspices of international organisations, while more recent interventions in Moldova, Somalia, and Sierra Leone were also associated with international organisations. Thus peace enforcement operations are not isolated controversial phenomena. They seem to be part of a continuum of international military activities that give rise to concerns about international legitimacy and therefore take place within international organisations.

Finally, although the controversial nature and disputed legal status of peace enforcement operations may bring states' legitimacy concerns into particular relief, it does not follow that legitimacy is of no importance to states engaged in less spectacular activities. Diplomats in the modern age are keenly aware that every foreign policy move has an immediate international audience. States routinely monitor each other's behaviour and evaluate it against commonly accepted standards of behaviour that may or may not be codified in international law. Not only, as just mentioned, is there substantial international tolerance for certain impingements of international law but, as chapter 2 noted, some legal international actions are condemned as illegitimate. Both North Korea's withdrawal from the Nuclear Non-Proliferation Treaty and the USA's 'renegotiation' of the Anti-Ballistic Missile Treaty, while perfectly legal, were widely perceived as illegitimate. This suggests that states routinely judge each other's actions according to standards that can differ from international law – in other words, they judge the legitimacy rather than the legality of each other's policies. Thus even routine, mundane, and legal activities are subject to legitimacy judgements – and states must keep the requirements of legitimacy in mind when engaging in all such activities.

Exceptionally low stakes?

The charge of peace enforcement exceptionalism can also be made from the opposite direction. Peace enforcement operations are at least ostensibly altruistic operations. Their justification is the collective good of international peace and security. These interventions are not formally intended for the individual benefit of the intervening state, which may not occupy the target country or appropriate its resources. States might not launch peace enforcement operations for entirely altruistic reasons, but they are nonetheless rarely motivated by such essential concerns as state security or national survival. Thus sceptics contend that although legitimacy may play a role in these non-essential operations, when the real fundamentals of state politics are affected, such niceties fall by the wayside. The key flaw in this objection is that it mistakes the ordinary and the exceptional.

It is clear that there are limits to the constraint that legitimacy concerns pose to state policies. Occasionally, states seek to evade this constraint by pursuing national interests secretly. Between 1984 and 1986, for example, the USA secretly sold arms to Iran and diverted the proceeds to support a rebel movement in Nicaragua. Legitimacy concerns did not prevent this activity because the USA believed it would be able to hide it from public view. However, this use of subterfuge and secrecy affirms the importance of legitimacy in international politics at the same time as it seeks to circumvent its constraints: by attempting to evade censure through dissimulation, states demonstrate their fear of international condemnation. More important from the theoretical point of view are cases in which states deliberately and openly defy international rules and thus invite charges of illegitimacy. Concern about international legitimacy will not deter states from actions that they believe to be essential to the preservation of core national interests. In 1981, for example, Israel braved international condemnation to bomb the Osirak nuclear reactor in Iraq because it believed the facility constituted 'a mortal danger to the people of Israel'.[2] Legitimacy concerns can also fail to prevent states from seizing opportunities for national aggrandisement. Thus Iraq was willing to draw international condemnation for its occupation of Kuwait in 1991 – wrongly believing that such condemnation would not be accompanied by military action.[3]

Critics who dispute the centrality of legitimacy concerns in contemporary international politics portray these cases as the essence of international politics. They conceive the core of international activity to be the pursuit of national interests regardless of any rules or norms in the international community. For them, peace enforcement operations are optional and anomalous enterprises that occur on the fringes of the world stage and reveal little about the real nature of world politics. However, deliberate disregard for international legitimacy is the exception in world politics, not the norm. Because the right to self-defence is a fundamental feature of the contemporary international system, there are

[2] BBC, '7 June 1981: Israel bombs Baghdad nuclear reactor' online at http://news.bbc.co.uk/onthisday/hi/dates/stories/june/7/newsid_3014000/3014623.stm.
[3] Saddam Hussein allegedly concluded after meeting with April Glaspie, the US Ambassador to Iraq, that the USA would not intervene to counter an invasion of Kuwait.

relatively few occasions on which states feel pushed to the extreme of having to act despite the anticipated condemnation of their fellow states. States reacting to attacks can and do invoke the principle of self-defence to secure international approval for their actions. This includes reactions to invasions and less direct responses to attack: the US invasion of Afghanistan in 2002, for example, was widely accepted as an act of self-defence following the terrorist attacks of 11 September 2001. In a few cases, however, the applicability of the right to self-defence is in dispute. The Osirak bombing was a pre-emptive strike rather than a reaction to an attack, and thus invited international condemnation despite Israel's claim to be acting in self-defence. The 2003 US invasion of Iraq, examined in more detail later in this chapter, followed the same pattern. Such cases are relatively rare, however, since the exigencies of national survival are normally clearly discernible. Thus the favourite scenario of many critics in which a state disregards the constraints of international legitimacy in order to save itself, is in fact exceedingly rare: it applies only in cases where the international community is not convinced that an act of self-defence is necessary.

The other scenario advanced by those sceptical of the importance of legitimacy in international relations is the self-interested invasion. If states believe their national interests will be greatly furthered by an invasion, they will not let legitimacy concerns deter them. Examples of such behaviour are more frequent than cases of disputed self-defence. They include Iraq's 1991 invasion of Kuwait, the USSR's occupation of Hungary in 1956, Vietnam's 1978 intervention in Cambodia, and Yugoslavia's attacks on Slovenia, Croatia, and Bosnia in the 1990s. However, as Mark Zacher has documented, support for the norm of territorial integrity has greatly increased since World War Two, the incidence of territorial wars has been relatively low, and there has been a marked decline in successful wars of aggrandisement.[4] Zacher correctly acknowledges that this trend is due to instrumental as well as ideational reasons. The power of the norm of territorial integrity is bolstered by the declining economic and strategic benefits of territorial occupation, as well as by Western states' commitment to oppose territorial aggression in the developing world. The crucial consideration here is simply that the most common type of self-interested invasion, war for territorial aggrandisement, is on the decline as an international

---

[4] Mark W. Zacher, 'The Territorial Integrity Norm: International Boundaries and the Use of Force', *International Organization*, 55:2 (Spring 2001).

phenomenon. Rather than being the essence of international politics, it is an exception.

Thus while there are limits to the constraints that legitimacy concerns impose on international politics, these limits are not so narrow as to relegate this book into irrelevance. Peace enforcement operations are not exceptional instances where stakes are so low that states can afford to take legitimacy considerations into account. The opposite is true: instances where states choose to brave international condemnation in pursuit of perceived national interests are the real exceptions in contemporary world politics.

In short, charges of peace enforcement exceptionalism are easily exaggerated. Peace enforcement operations are extraordinary international phenomena, since they involve the use of military force for ostensibly altruistic ends. However, they are not so exceptional as to make their study irrelevant for general international relations theory. The legitimacy concerns that accompany peace enforcement operations are not unique to these operations, though their controversial nature puts these concerns in relief. Moreover, peace enforcement operations are not unique in the degree to which states allow themselves to be constrained by legitimacy concerns. States brave international condemnation when they perceive their survival to be threatened or envisage great national benefits. In such exceptional circumstances, pre-emptive strikes and territorial aggression occur. In all other instances of international military activity, however, from peacekeeping to wars against aggression, concerns about international legitimacy arise that are similar to those that preoccupy states launching peace enforcement operations. Thus while international legitimacy may not be states' overriding concern in all their international activities, it is sufficiently important in enough spheres of world politics to warrant recognition in contemporary international relations theory.

The 2003 US invasion of Iraq

The 2003 US invasion of Iraq vividly demonstrated both the limits and the importance of international legitimacy concerns in contemporary international politics. On 1 June 2002, in the shadow of the terrorist attacks of 11 September 2001 and with the Taliban regime already overthrown in Afghanistan, US President George W. Bush outlined a new military strategy for the USA: 'the war on terror will not be won on the defensive. We must take the battle to the enemy, disrupt his plans, and confront the worst threats before they emerge ... our security will require all Americans to be forward-looking and resolute, and be ready for preemptive action when necessary.'[5] Iraq was the first target of this doctrine of pre-emption. In September 2002, Bush presented the United Nations with a challenge: 'Iraq has answered a decade of UN demands with a decade of defiance. All the world now faces a test, and the United Nations a difficult and defining moment ... Will the United Nations serve the purpose of its founding, or will it be irrelevant?'[6] He also threatened unilateral action if the UN failed to act: 'We will work with the UN Security Council for the necessary resolutions. But the purposes of the United States should not be doubted. The Security Council resolutions will be enforced ... or action will be unavoidable. And a regime that has lost its legitimacy will also lose its power.' On 20 March 2003, the Bush administration fulfilled its threat, launching an invasion of Iraq with the help of its British and Australian allies, but without the mandate of the UN or of any other international organisation.

This intervention, codenamed Operation Iraqi Freedom by the USA (and Operation Telic and Operation Falconer by the UK and Australia, respectively) seems to provide a dramatic counter-example to the central claims of this book. I have argued that states care about international legitimacy, that they launch peace enforcement operations through international organisations to achieve that legitimacy, and that their concerns about legitimacy significantly shape their international behaviour. Operation Iraqi Freedom was not a peace enforcement operation, since it did not respond to an on-going civil war in Iraq. However, it did claim to be serving international peace and security by pre-emptively combating terrorism and the USA could be expected to seek the mandate of an international organisation to certify (and thus legitimise) the intervention as a genuinely international endeavour. Yet in launching Operation Iraqi Freedom the USA showed considerable disregard for both international legitimacy and the United Nations, the international organisation most capable of bestowing legitimacy on the intervention. When it became clear that the UN would not issue an enforcement mandate, the Bush administration decided to defy world opinion and intervene without a UN mandate. Nevertheless, Operation Iraqi Freedom

---

[5] George W. Bush, 'President Bush Delivers Graduation Speech at West Point', 1 June 2002, online at www.whitehouse.gov/news/releases/2002/06/20020601-3.html.
[6] George W. Bush, 'President's remarks at the United Nations General Assembly', 12 September 2002, online at www.whitehouse.gov/news/releases/2002/09/20020912-1.html.

underlined the importance as well as the limitations of legitimacy concerns in contemporary international politics.

It should be noted that an extraordinary confluence of factors made the USA perhaps singularly impervious to international legitimacy concerns. The governing Bush administration was remarkably wary of multilateralism and tended to assert the USA's special status as the world's sole superpower, in contrast to previous administrations' concern with projecting the USA as a benign world leader anxious to work in partnership with other states. Moreover, the 11 September 2001 terrorist attacks had sparked enormous anger, fear, and (at times militant) patriotism among the US public, which was channelled against Iraq by government claims that Saddam Hussein had connections to the terrorist network of Al Qaeda. Thus conditions within the USA greatly favoured unilateralism: the world's sole superpower, acting under a sense of threat and led by a hawkish regime with low regard for multilateralism, might be expected to ignore international legitimacy concerns more readily than virtually all other states. This, then, was an exceptionally hard case for the theory that legitimacy matters in international politics. In fact, however, even under these conditions the USA did not simply abandon concerns for the international legitimacy of its actions.

The US case for the international legitimacy of Operation Iraqi Freedom

First, the USA acknowledged the importance of its international audience and demonstrated the value it placed on international legitimacy by seeking to justify its intervention according to the rules that currently prevail in the international system. It invoked two core international principles to establish the international legitimacy of Operation Iraqi Freedom. The first was the right to self-defence. The Bush administration repeatedly sought to link Saddam Hussein's regime to Al Qaeda and thereby to the 11 September terrorist attacks on the USA. While this tactic resonated with the domestic US public, however, it gained little credence internationally.

Therefore the key argument with which the USA sought to persuade its international audience centred on the threat that Iraq's failure to disarm posed to international peace and security. Bush consistently sought to locate US action in Iraq in this framework. In June 2002, he stressed that the doctrine of pre-emption served the whole world: 'we will not leave the safety of America and the peace of the planet at the mercy of a few mad terrorists and tyrants. We will lift this dark threat from our country and from the world.'[7] His September 2002 speech to the UN depicted the USA as defending 'the just demands of peace and security' and 'the permanent rights and hopes of mankind'.[8] Announcing the beginning of Operation Iraqi Freedom, Bush again described the aim of the intervention in global terms: 'to disarm Iraq, to free its people and to defend the world from grave danger'.[9] After major combat had officially ended, he still insisted that the US-led 'coalition of nations acted to defend the peace, and the credibility of the United Nations'.[10] This theme has been consistently upheld since the intervention. In his September 2004 address to the United Nations General Assembly President Bush argued that in Iraq 'a coalition of nations enforced the just demands of the world'.[11] During the October 2004 US presidential debates, he reiterated: 'Saddam Hussein now sits in a prison cell. America and the world are safer for it.'[12] Commemorating the second anniversary of the intervention on 19 March 2005, Bush recalled: 'On this day two years ago, we launched Operation Iraqi Freedom to disarm a brutal regime, free its people, and defend the world from a grave danger.'[13] Thus Bush consistently emphasised that the intervention increased international security, which would bring it into accordance with the international rule allowing the use of force to preserve international peace and security and thus 'qualify' it for international legitimacy.

In addition, the Bush administration respected the international convention that intervention should be multilateral to limit the scope for aggression in the pursuit of purely national interests. Coalitions of the willing are less able to convey unbiased multilateralism than international organisations because they are created on an ad hoc basis for a

[7] Bush, 'President Bush Delivers Graduation Speech at West Point', 1 June 2002.
[8] Bush, 'President's Remarks at the United Nations General Assembly', 12 September 2002.
[9] George W. Bush, 'President Bush Addresses the Nation', 19 March 2003 (N.B. 20 March in Iraq), online at www.whitehouse.gov/news/releases/2003/03/iraq/20030319-17.html, accessed 29 September 2003, document no longer available at this site.
[10] George W. Bush, 'President Bush Addresses United Nations General Assembly', 23 September 2003, online at www.whitehouse.gov/news/releases/2003/09/iraq/20030923-4.html, accessed 29 September 2003, document no longer available at this site.
[11] George W. Bush, 'President Speaks to the United Nations General Assembly', 21 September 2004, online at www.whitehouse.gov/news/releases/2004/09/print/20040921-3.html.
[12] 'Transcript of First Bush-Kerry Presidential Debate, September 30, 2004', Commission on Presidential Debates website at www.debates.org/pages/trans2004a.html.
[13] George W. Bush, 'President's Radio address', 19 March 2005, online at www.whitehouse.gov/news/releases/2005/03/20050319.html.

particular intervention. Thus in contrast to existing international organisations whose memberships are more likely to reflect a full spectrum of reactions to a proposed intervention, a coalition of the willing by definition unites only states that support the intervention, while critical states are excluded. Nevertheless coalitions do certify that the intervention is endorsed by more than one state and thus suggest that international as well as particularistic interests are being served. The size of the coalition thus matters crucially for its capacity to improve the legitimacy of an intervention: the more states participate, the harder it is to present the intervention as serving the particularistic interests of a single state.

The Bush administration acknowledged and responded to this reality. Even though it bore the overwhelming majority of the costs and burdens of the operation, the USA insisted that it was merely the leader of an international coalition. Announcing Operation Iraqi Freedom, Bush stressed: 'In this war, our coalition is broad, more than 40 countries from across the globe.'[14] This insistence that the intervention was a coalition effort has continued throughout the USA's deployment in Iraq and became an important issue in the 2004 US presidential election. During the first presidential debate, for example, presidential hopeful John Kerry criticised George Bush's coalition building: 'when we went in, there were three countries: Great Britain, Australia and the United States. That's not a grand coalition. We can do better.'[15] Bush's reply acknowledged the importance of this attack: 'Well, actually, he forgot Poland. And now there's 30 nations involved, standing side by side with our American troops . . . Our coalition is strong. It will remain strong, so long as I'm the president.' To those concerned only about burden-sharing, this response was risible, and pundits were quick to point out the very limited military contributions of these allies. In terms of legitimacy, however, this was a critical debate. Once it became apparent that the invasion of Iraq would probably proceed without a UN mandate, the multilateralism of the coalition became the central characteristic to which the USA appealed to make the case for the intervention's legitimacy. The intended message was clearly articulated by White House spokesman Ari Fleisher even before the invasion began: 'There will be another international organization that will be the coalition of

---

[14] George W. Bush, 'President Discusses Beginning of Operation Iraqi Freedom', 22 March 2003, online at www.whitehouse.gov/news/releases/2003/03/iraq/2030322.html, accessed 26 September 2003, document no longer available at this site.
[15] 'Transcript of First Bush-Kerry Presidential Debate'.

the willing that will be made up of numerous nations that will disarm Saddam Hussein. It'll be multilateral. It will be international. It just won't be the United Nations.'[16]

US attempts to situate Operation Iraqi Freedom in the UN framework

The second consideration that limits the extent to which Operation Iraqi Freedom undermines a legitimacy-centred theory of international relations is that the USA did implicitly recognise the pre-eminent role of international organisations as gatekeepers to international legitimacy. At the urging of both moderates in the administration such as Colin Powell and key outsiders like the UK's Tony Blair, the Bush administration took considerable pains to claim a UN mandate.

The administration engaged in protracted if ultimately unsuccessful attempts to secure explicit UN authorisation for its intervention. In September 2002, Bush asked the UN to enforce its own resolutions against Iraq and indicated the USA's preference for working within the UN framework: 'My nation will work with the UN Security Council to meet our common challenge ... We will work with the UN Security Council for the necessary resolutions.'[17] Although the US Congress gave President Bush the right to go to war against Iraq on 11 October 2002, the administration did not immediately launch a unilateral intervention. Instead, it began intense negotiations for a UN mandate. These ultimately yielded Security Council Resolution 1441 of 8 November 2002, which declared Iraq's 'material breach' of previous Council resolutions a threat to international peace and security and called for the immediate return of UN weapons inspectors to Iraq, but did not explicitly authorise the use of force. The USA further suspended its threat of intervention pending the report of chief UN weapons inspector Hans Blix. In March 2003, when the long-awaited report noted problems with Iraq's compliance but also identified a 'substantial measure of disarmament', the USA agreed to a further British initiative to secure an explicit Security Council mandate for military action. Although France and Russia were likely to veto such a resolution, the USA persisted, persuaded

---

[16] 'White House: Blix report shows Iraq not disarming', *Deutsche Presse-Agentur*, 7 March 2003.
[17] George W. Bush, 'President's Remarks at the United Nations General Assembly', 12 September 2002.

by the UK that even a vetoed resolution would enhance an intervention's international legitimacy, provided it had the support of a majority in the Security Council. Only when it became apparent that this Security Council majority could not be obtained did the USA abandon UN-based diplomacy and launch the invasion of Iraq without an explicit international mandate.

Even then, however, the USA insisted that it was in fact acting on a UN mandate. Speaking at the UN in September 2002, Bush had framed the proposed Iraq intervention by appealing to Security Council Resolutions 686, 687, and 688 of 1991. He insisted that US action to end Iraqi defiance of these resolutions would uphold the UN: 'We want the United Nations to be effective, and respectful [sic], and successful. We want the resolutions of the world's most important multilateral body to be enforced.'[18] When Security Council Resolution 1441 was passed, the Bush administration insisted that it already authorised military action if Iraq was found to be in continued 'material breach' of its obligations to disarm. Both the USA and the UK argued that the March 2003 Blix report confirmed this breach. This formed the basis of the US justification for intervening in Iraq. Just days before the intervention, Bush made this very clear:

> The United Nations Security Council, in Resolution 1441, has declared Iraq in material breach of its longstanding obligations, demanding once again Iraq's full and immediate disarmament, and promised serious consequences if the regime refused to comply. That resolution was passed unanimously and its logic is inescapable: the Iraqi regime will disarm itself, or the Iraqi regime will be disarmed by force. And the regime has not disarmed itself.[19]

Bush brushed away the objection that the majority in the Security Council would not support another resolution authorising the use of force:

> Resolution 1441, which was unanimously approved, said that Saddam Hussein would unconditionally disarm, and if he didn't, there would be serious consequences. The United Nations Security Council looked at

---

[18] Ibid.
[19] George W. Bush, 'President Bush: Monday "Moment of Truth" for World on Iraq', press conference in the Azores, Portugal, 16 March 2003. Online at www.whitehouse. gov/news/releases/2003/03/iraq/20030316-3. html, accessed 26 September 2003, document no longer available at this site.

this issue four and a half months ago and voted unanimously to say: Disarm immediately and unconditionally, and if you don't, there are going to be serious consequences. The world has spoken. And it did in a unified voice. Sorry.

Thus even when it could not secure an explicit mandate for Operation Iraqi Freedom, the USA insisted on locating the intervention within the UN framework. It even suggested, echoing an argument made about the Kosovo campaign, that action in Iraq in fact supported the UN more than inaction.[20] President Bush reiterated this theme in his September 2004 address to the UN General Assembly: 'the Security Council promised serious consequences for [Saddam Hussein's] defiance [of Security Council resolutions]. And the commitments we make must have meaning. When we say "serious consequences," for the sake of peace, there must be serious consequences.'[21] This emphasis on linking the intervention to the UN is a tribute to the strength of the Bush administration's conviction that legitimate international military action required the approval of that international organisation. As one observer noted, 'what is most important here is that contending sides continue to regard United Nations approval as a necessary component of the use of force ... consider [the contrast to] what much of the world expected to happen back in August [2002]: that the United States would lead an invasion of Iraq without any reference to the United Nations at all.'[22]

The aftermath of intervention

US attempts to establish the international legitimacy of Operation Iraqi Freedom by claiming to act for international peace and security and seeking to situate the intervention within the UN framework were countered by key Security Council members. France and Russia insisted that Resolution 1441 did not automatically authorise the use of force even if Iraq was found to be in breach of its international obligations to disarm. France, Russia, and Germany opposed the US and British

[20] Unlike in the Kosovo case, French and German opposition to the Operation Iraqi Freedom meant that the USA did not have the option of sidestepping the UN by launching the intervention through NATO.
[21] Bush, 'President Speaks to the United Nations General Assembly', 21 September 2004. For similar arguments about Kosovo, see chapter 6 of this book.
[22] Anne-Marie Slaughter, 'Good reasons for going around the UN', *New York Times*, 18 March 2003.

interpretation of the Blix report, arguing that rather than demonstrating the need to use force, the report reaffirmed the possibility of peaceful disarmament. The public and humiliating failure of the USA and the UK to assemble majority support for a resolution authorising the use of force in Iraq in the Security Council in March 2003 was in large part due to their anti-war diplomacy. Finally, France, Germany, and Russia publicly condemned Operation Iraqi Freedom once it was launched. Together, these three countries undermined the USA's claim that Operation Iraqi Freedom was taking place in a UN framework and thus with a global mandate. The ensuing damage to the Operation Iraqi Freedom's international legitimacy did not deter the USA from launching the intervention. However, both the USA's strategy for responding to this damage in the aftermath of the intervention and its limited success in doing so reaffirm the importance of international organisations as gatekeepers to international legitimacy.

The Bush administration's strategy for remedying Operation Iraqi Freedom's lack of international legitimacy was to renew its efforts to locate the campaign within a UN framework once the occupation was established. On 23 September 2003, President Bush reiterated before the UN General Assembly that Operation Iraqi Freedom had taken place within the UN framework. Alluding to Resolution 1441, he declared: 'The Security Council was right to be alarmed. The Security Council was right to demand that Iraq destroy its illegal weapons ... The Security Council was right to vow serious consequences if Iraq refused to comply. And because there were consequences, because a coalition of nations acted to defend the peace, and the credibility of the United Nations, Iraq is free.'[23] He also announced that 'the United Nations can contribute greatly to the cause of Iraqi self-government. America is working with friends and allies on a new Security Council resolution, which will expand the UN's role in Iraq. As in the aftermath of other conflicts, the United Nations should assist in developing a constitution, in training civil servants, and conducting free and fair elections.' While the USA continued to insist that coalition forces should retain authority within Iraq until a new Iraqi government was installed, it had come to accept the need for a UN presence in post-war Iraq.

This vision faced significant obstacles. Many UN members opposed the proposition that the UN should play an auxiliary role in Iraq, hoping

---

[23] Bush, 'President Bush Addresses United Nations General Assembly', 23 September 2003.

instead to see the UN assume interim authority and set limits to the sweeping powers of the US-dominated occupation forces (the Coalition Provisional Authority). Some UN diplomats believed that the notion of the UN serving an occupation force whose deployment it refused to authorise was in itself preposterous. As one UN diplomat commented about the Bush speech: 'He said he wanted the United Nations to assist. But assist what? Assist who? The Coalition Provisional Authority? Please.'[24] Another key obstacle, however, was that a UN deployment in Iraq would confer at least a modicum of post hoc international legitimacy on the intervention. Both France and Russia had predicted as early as 22 March 2003 that the USA would eventually turn back to the UN for the legitimacy the organisation could provide. They had vowed to use their veto in the Security Council to fight any such initiative. Russian Foreign Minister Igor Ivanov stated: 'Without a doubt, there will be attempts to confer legitimacy on military operations or post-war reorganization in Iraq through the UN Security Council. We, of course, will not give this military action legitimacy through possible Security Council resolutions.'[25] France's President Chirac declared, 'France will not accept a resolution that would legitimise military intervention and give the US and British the powers of administration in Iraq.'[26]

In the event, the diplomatic deadlock over the intervention did shift with the unanimous passing of Security Council Resolution 1511 on 16 October 2003. Sponsored by the USA and supported by the UK and Spain, this resolution offered critics of Operation Iraqi Freedom a trade-off. It reaffirmed Iraq's sovereignty and territorial integrity, emphasised the 'temporary nature' of the US-led Coalition Provisional Authority in Iraq and placed it (albeit loosely) under Security Council supervision by requesting it 'to report to the Council on the progress being made' (§6). Coupled with a call for a stronger UN role in Iraq, the resolution offered opponents the promise of a speedy US cession of power in Iraq. In return, the USA and its allies obtained a mandate for their forces in Iraq: citing Chapter VII of the UN Charter, Resolution 1511 'authorizes a multinational force under unified command to take all

---

[24] Steven R. Weisman, 'Audience unmoved during Bush's address at the UN', *The New York Times*, 24 September 2003.

[25] 'Russia says it will block US bids to seek retroactive UN approval for war', *Agence France Presse*, 22 March 2003.

[26] Judy Dempsey, Krishna Guha, and George Parke, 'Chirac plans to resist the control of post-war Iraq by US allies; French condemn "illegal" war', *Financial Times*, 22 March 2003.

measures necessary to contribute to the maintenance of security and stability in Iraq' (§13).

This development echoed the case studies in this book in several important ways. Resolution 1511 provided legal cover for future US-led deployments in Iraq but it did not endorse the earlier US-led deployment and could not legalise it. As in the case studies, therefore, respect for international law was no adequate explanation for the USA's renewed attempt to garner UN auspices for its intervention. Second, again mirroring this book's case studies, Resolution 1511 did not promote burden-sharing, despite a clause urging UN member states to contribute to the newly authorised multinational force. The force was explicitly not a UN force and thus had no claim on funding through the UN peacekeeping budget. Germany, France, Russia, and Pakistan announced immediately after the vote that they had no intention of contributing to the force financially or militarily, and India and Kenya followed suit a few days later, scuttling any US hopes of the UN mandate generating significant burden-sharing benefits. Such hopes would anyway have been extremely limited among knowledgeable observers of international organisations' record in launching peace enforcement operations. Indeed, US Secretary of State Colin Powell affirmed that he was not expecting any 'major contributions' to the USA's Iraq efforts.[27]

The USA's primary motivation for seeking Resolution 1511 mirrored those of the lead states in this book's case studies. Even the US superpower eventually had to recognise the importance of international legitimacy. British Foreign Secretary Jack Straw candidly remarked about the proposed Resolution 1511: 'The main purpose of the resolution is much more what I would describe as psychological-political rather than providing an extra thousand troops here or thousand troops there.'[28] The USA stood isolated on the Iraq issue, having squandered the international goodwill and sympathy that flowed towards the USA after the terrorist attacks of 11 September 2001. To end this isolation and regain at least an element of international legitimacy for its activity in Iraq, the USA needed a UN mandate. This was why the Bush administration reluctantly returned to the United Nations. 'In the end, some of Mr. Bush's advisers say, what is needed from the United Nations is

---

[27] Bryan Bender and Joe Lauria, 'Rebuilding Iraq: Triumph, Setback for Bush on Iraq', *Boston Globe*, 17 October 2003.
[28] Brian Knowlton, 'US and Germany look to move past discord over Iraq', *International Herald Tribune*, 25 September 2003.

legitimacy – for a new government in Iraq, for the American occupation and any new countries that choose to send troops.'[29]

The dynamics of the Security Council decision also deserve notice. Unlike other institutions examined in this book, the Council does not take decisions by consensus. However, the Iraq crisis had taken its toll on the Council's international credibility, creating incentives towards unanimity since continued paralysis might condemn the body to increasing irrelevance. In six weeks of intensive lobbying led by Colin Powell, the defining moment came when the USA persuaded first China and then Russia to support the resolution. Russia helped persuade its anti-war allies France and Germany to follow suit. Germany explicitly cited the (political, if not procedural) need for Council unanimity in justifying its vote: 'This can only succeed when the Security Council appears as unified as possible. We therefore did not want to stand in the way of unity of the Council.'[30] The pressure towards consensus was even stronger on Syria, the last hold-out against the resolution, whose ambassador to the UN called his US counterpart at 1.30 a.m. on the night before the vote to announce that his government, too, would back the plan.[31] As in the cases studied in previous chapters, moreover, acquiescence was eased by the lack of burden-sharing obligations. As one diplomat put it, Security Council members 'could have it both ways: Give the US a symbolic victory and do what they [the member states] want.'[32]

Finally, echoing lead states in other chapters of this book, the USA was willing to incur costs for this symbolism: it accepted an increased political role for the UN in Iraq's reconstruction, agreed to report its activities to the Security Council and to have the Council review the multinational force's mandate within twelve months, and committed itself 'to return governing responsibilities and authorities to the people of Iraq as soon as possible'.[33] It also implicitly recognised the Security Council's right to supervise, monitor, and mandate any multinational deployment in Iraq, although this has not subsequently occurred to any meaningful extent.

[29] David Sanger, 'Bush's day at the UN: it's chilly, still, there', *New York Times*, 24 September 2003.
[30] Felicity Barringer, 'UN hands US symbolic victory on Iraq', *New York Times*, 20 October 2003.
[31] Bender and Lauria, 'Rebuilding Iraq'.   [32] Ibid.
[33] United Nations Security Council Resolution 1511, 16 October 2003, Article 6.

Resolution 1511 signalled the end of the USA's diplomatic isolation on Iraq, but in the wake of months of bitter controversy, this could only be a first step towards remedying the international illegitimacy of the deployment. The next big step was Security Council Resolution 1546, adopted unanimously on 8 June 2004 in anticipation of the assumption of authority by Iraq's interim government at the end of the month. Citing Chapter VII of the UN Charter, the resolution welcomes this step in the transition towards an elected Iraqi government, cedes the UN 'a leading role' in the further political process in Iraq, and recognises the continued importance of the multinational force in maintaining peace and stability in Iraq. The force's legitimacy is affirmed in two respects. First, it is accepted that the UN presence in Iraq will need to rely on the force for its own security, suggesting that the force fulfils a vital function in the reconstruction effort. Second, and even more importantly, Resolution 1546 notes that the force is deployed at the request of Iraq's incoming Interim Government and appends Iraq's letter to that effect. The deployment is thus presented as invited and peaceful rather than imposed and aggressive. UN Secretary-General Kofi Annan furthered the resolution's legitimising effect by emphasising that it was 'a genuine expression of the will of the international community'.[34] Again, the USA incurred costs to obtain this legitimacy. The Iraqi government was not given a veto over coalition movements in Iraq but it did, against US wishes, retain the right not to participate in these deployments and therefore the ability to signal its approval or disapproval of them. More generally, the USA traded off control over Iraq for international legitimacy. The interim government was chosen by UN envoy Lakhdar Brahimi, albeit in consultation with the USA. The presence of US troops now had to be justified by invitation from the host government. And on 28 June 2004, the USA formally handed governing authority in Iraq over to an Iraqi government.

In the aftermath of its invasion, therefore, the USA displayed a renewed interest in international legitimacy. Its decision to turn to the UN to remedy Operation Iraqi Freedom's lack of international legitimacy implicitly acknowledged the organisation's gatekeeper role in this respect. The USA supplemented these efforts by asking NATO to take up a larger role in Iraq's multinational force, perhaps hoping to benefit from the kind of legitimacy pyramid described in earlier chapters. Due

[34] 'Annan pledges UN will play its role in Iraq's next phase', *UN News Service*, 25 June 2004.

to the reticence of European NATO members, however, the Istanbul Summit of 29 June 2004 yielded only a decision to offer assistance in training Iraq's security forces. US diplomats seized the opportunity to insist that the twenty-six NATO allies had endorsed 'a collective NATO mission inside Iraq'[35] although in fact no formal NATO force had been created.[36] Bridling at the US announcement, French President Chirac declared himself 'firmly opposed to seeing the alliance's flag fly in Iraq'.[37] This argument was motivated by both sides' awareness of the importance of symbols, and in particular of the international legitimacy that a NATO framework could generate for the US policy in Iraq. The struggle over this legitimising capacity remained unresolved during the Istanbul Summit and was apparent in the final statement's carefully worded acknowledgement of 'the efforts of nations, including many NATO Allies, in the Multinational Force for Iraq, which is present in Iraq at the request of the Iraqi government and in accordance with UNSCR 1546'.[38] The text endorses and thus helps promote the legitimacy of the UN-authorised force, but shies away from doing the same for Operation Iraqi Freedom.

Yet US strategy in the aftermath of its invasion is not the only evidence that the Iraq case yields for the role of international organisations as gatekeepers to international legitimacy. The consequences of the USA's decision to intervene without an international mandate are just as significant. As this study predicts, Operation Iraqi Freedom was widely viewed as illegitimate. Days before the intervention, the UN Secretary-General Kofi Annan warned: 'If the action is to take place without the support of the [Security] council, its legitimacy will be questioned and the support for it will be diminished.'[39] On the day Operation Iraqi Freedom was launched, he remarked pointedly:

> Perhaps if we had persevered a little longer, Iraq could yet have been disarmed peacefully or – if not – the world could have taken action to solve this problem in a collective decision, endowing it with greater legitimacy, and therefore commanding wider support, than is now the

---

[35] Reuters, 'Uneasy peace as Chirac needles US at NATO', *New York Times*, 29 June 2004.

[36] 'Statement on Iraq' issued by NATO Heads of State and Government participating in the meeting of the North Atlantic Council in Istanbul on 28 June 2004, online at www.nato.int/docu/pr/2004/p04-098e.htm.

[37] Reuters, 'Uneasy peace as Chirac needles US at NATO'.

[38] NATO Heads of State and Government, 'Statement on Iraq'.

[39] 'Failed efforts to gain UN Security Council resolution to deal with disarmament of Iraq', *All Things Considered – (USA) National Public Radio*, 17 March 2003.

case . . . Over the past weeks, the peoples of the world have shown what great importance they attach to the legitimacy conveyed by the authority of the United Nations. They have made clear that, in confronting uncertainty and danger, they want to see power harnessed to legitimacy. They want their leaders to come together, in the United Nations, to resolve the problems shared by all humanity.[40]

The USA faced both short- and longer-term consequences from ignoring these warnings. The immediate effects of Operation Iraqi Freedom's international illegitimacy were evident as the USA struggled to recruit members for its coalition of the willing in Iraq. Traditional US allies both in Europe and in the Arab world refused to participate in the operation, in marked contrast to their positions during the 1991 UN-authorised campaign against Iraq's occupation of Kuwait. Even some of the states that did respond to US pressure to join the coalition initially asked not to be identified for fear of the repercussions of being associated with an illegitimate operation.[41] US hopes of sharing the costs of peacekeeping and peace-building in the aftermath of the intervention also failed to materialise. In the summer of 2003, Turkey, India, Pakistan, Bangladesh, and South Korea were approached by the USA for troop contributions to the stabilisation effort in Iraq but hesitated to associate themselves with the intervention. As noted above, even the USA's return to the UN in September 2003 could only partially remedy international reticence to contribute troops. Bush administration officials also had to abandon hopes announced in August 2003 that a meeting of donor nations in Madrid in October would generate 'billions of dollars . . . for Iraq'.[42] Democratic presidential hopeful Howard Dean summed up the USA's dilemma succinctly: Bush 'really poisoned the well with the allies on the way into Iraq and now, of course, he's going to have a hard time getting any help from them to get out'.[43]

The consequences of illegitimacy also went beyond these material factors, however. The USA's international standing plummeted as a result of the intervention. Widely seen as an essentially benign (if not always benevolent) superpower in the 1990s, the USA is now perceived

[40] Kofi Annan, 'Statement of the UN Secretary-General on Iraq', 20 March 2003, online at www.un.org/apps/sg/printsgstates.asp?nid=292, accessed 20 March 2003, document no longer available at this site.
[41] Steve Schifferes, 'US says "coalition of willing" grows', BBC, 21 March 2003.
[42] Weisman, 'Audience unmoved during Bush's address at the UN'.
[43] Associated Press, 'Schroeder and Bush agree past differences on Iraq are behind them', *New York Times*, 24 September 2003.

as undermining global security. UN Secretary-General Kofi Annan has argued that the US doctrine of pre-emption threatens world peace:

> until now it has been understood that when States go beyond [self-defence] and decide to use force to deal with broader threats to international peace and security, they need the unique legitimacy provided by the United Nations. Now, some say this understanding is no longer tenable, since an 'armed attack' with weapons of mass destruction could be launched at any time, without warning, or by a clandestine group. Rather than wait for that to happen, they argue, States have the right and obligation to use force pre-emptively . . . According to this argument, States are not obliged to wait until there is agreement in the Security Council. Instead, they reserve the right to act unilaterally, or in ad hoc coalitions. This logic represents a fundamental challenge to the principles on which, however imperfectly, world peace and stability have rested for the last 58 years. My concern is that, if it were to be adopted, it could set precedents that resulted in a proliferation of the unilateral and lawless use of force, with or without justification.[44]

World public opinion went further. In January 2003 US moves towards intervening in Iraq led 83.3 per cent of respondents to a poll by *Time* magazine's European edition to identify the USA as the greatest threat to world peace.[45] In 2005, a BBC poll found that George Bush's re-election as US president was seen as negative for world peace and security by a majority of respondents in sixteen of the twenty-one countries polled, a plurality in two further countries, and by 58 per cent of all respondents.[46] A plurality of 47 per cent of all respondents viewed US influence in the world as 'mostly negative'.[47] Seventy per cent of respondents opposed their country's contributing troops in Iraq.

The results for overall perceptions of the US have been dramatic. Pew Center surveys found that from 1999 to 2004, favourable perceptions of the USA had decreased from 83 per cent to 40 per cent in the UK, from 78 per cent to 38 per cent in Germany, from 62 per cent to 37 per cent in

---

[44] 'Adoption of Policy of Pre-Emption Could Result in Proliferation of Unilateral, Lawless Use of Force, Secretary-General Tells General Assembly', *UN Press Release*, 23 September 2003.

[45] Eric Margolis, 'Europe urges restraint, but Bush knows best', *Toronto Sun*, 26 January 2003. Only 8.9 per cent of readers named Iraq as the greatest threat.

[46] Steven Kull and Doug Miller, 'In 18 of 21 Countries Polled, Most See Bush's Reelection as Negative for World Security', joint report by Program on International Policy Attitudes and GlobeScan, 19 January 2005, online at www.pipa.org/archives/global_opinion.php, p. 1.

[47] Ibid., p. 2.

France, and from 77 per cent to 27 per cent in Morocco.[48] This sea-change in attitudes towards the US will complicate almost every aspect of US foreign policy for years if not decades to come. As Democratic presidential nominee John Kerry put it in the 2004 presidential debates, even former US allies no longer assume that US international policies are benign and legitimate: 'You have to earn that respect. And I think we have a lot of earning back to do.'[49]

It is significant that even the world's undisputed superpower could not avoid these consequences of launching a military intervention without the mandate of an international organisation. Chapter 2 argued that while powerful states may be able to break international rules with a degree of impunity, they can neither change these rules at will nor freely manipulate the international organisations that serve as their guardians. Operation Iraqi Freedom confirmed that international rules can be broken, although it also showed that even the world's most powerful country, led by hawkish politicians and with a population that believed itself to be under attack, hesitated to openly violate these rules. Instead, the USA tried to establish Operation Iraqi Freedom's legitimacy by defending the intervention as necessary for international peace and security, seeking a UN mandate for it, linking it to previous Security Council resolutions, and returning to the UN after the invasion to seek international endorsement of its stabilisation and reconstruction efforts. Operation Iraqi Freedom also showed what the USA could not do. It could not alter the international rules governing the use of force to render pre-emptive action without an international mandate legitimate. It could not force the UN to issue a mandate for the operation. And it could not escape the material and foreign policy consequences of launching an illegitimate military intervention. Thus Operation Iraqi Freedom demonstrated the relative resilience of international rules and the inability of even powerful states to control international organisations. In short, it confirmed that the constraint of international legitimacy cannot be eliminated by an exercise of power.

---

[48] Steven Kull and Doug Miller, 'Global Public Opinion on the US Presidential Election and US Foreign Policy', joint report by Program on International Policy Attitudes and GlobeScan, 8 September 2004, online at www.pipa.org/archives/global_opinion.php, p. 4.
[49] 'Transcript of First Bush-Kerry Presidential Debate'.

Practical and theoretical implications

In 1935, French Foreign Minister Pierre Laval advised Josef Stalin to institute greater religious tolerance in the Soviet Union in order to win favour with the Pope. Stalin famously replied: 'The Pope? How many divisions has he got?'[50] The same kind of logic has tended to cloud perceptions of the importance of international organisations in the contemporary international system. International organisations are no match for states in terms of either military power or the capacity for independent agency on the world stage. They can neither exist nor take sustained action without their member states' support. This fundamental fact has led both politicians and academics to dismiss international organisations as epiphenomenal to world politics, especially where the crucial issue of the use of military force is concerned. Yet as Inis Claude noted with respect to the UN as early as 1966, scepticism about the role of international organisations in international politics often derives from an excessively narrow understanding of what constitutes relevance on the international stage: 'Our action-oriented generation has concentrated on the question of what the United Nations can and cannot *do* . . . rather than on its verbal performance.'[51] Like the Pope, international organisations have no standing armies. They cannot launch peace enforcement operations on their own. They cannot even guarantee substantial burden-sharing for these operations among their members. They can, however, endow an intervention with international legitimacy by granting it an international mandate – and this makes them critical actors in modern peace enforcement.

This central insight has both practical and theoretical ramifications. The most obvious policy implication concerns states launching peace enforcement operations. The temptation to proceed without the mandate of an international organisation can be considerable. The ponderous process of securing an international mandate is often at odds with the urgency of the situation the lead state wishes to address. International organisations' capacity to promote burden-sharing for peace enforcement operations is limited and in any event multilateral warfare is frustrating and inefficient. States that have the material capacity to launch peace

---

[50] *The Columbia World of Quotations* (New York: Columbia University Press, 1996), number 55130. Online at www.bartleby.com/66/30/55130.html.

[51] Inis L. Claude, 'Collective Legitimization as a Political Function of the United Nations', *International Organization*, 20:2 (1966), p. 372.

enforcement operations alone or with a small group of close allies may wonder why they should bother operating in the framework of a formal international organisation. International law is unlikely to be a decisive constraint: it provides no reason for operating through any organisation other than the UN and in any case this book has shown that states rarely feel bound to strictly follow international law in launching peace enforcement operations. Throughout the 1990s, states nevertheless consistently sought to place their interventions under the mandate of an international organisation. However, as UN Secretary-General Kofi Annan noted, there is a danger that the USA's Operation Iraqi Freedom in 2003 might be seen as setting a precedent for a less constraining way of launching enforcement operations.[52]

Recognising that international organisations are gatekeepers to international legitimacy for peace enforcement operations counteracts the temptation to launch such an operation without an international mandate. It reveals that lead states in previous peace enforcement operations were not blindly following social conventions or making unnecessary sacrifices to obtain an empty symbol. Instead, these states recognised that international rules are critical parts of the international society of states to which they inextricably belonged. They also knew that an international organisation's mandate translated into an international legitimacy that not only facilitated coalition-building for their interventions but also helped safeguard or even bolster their own international status. They calculated that this legitimacy more than compensated for the disadvantages of operating through an international organisation. By contrast, the Bush administration underestimated the importance of international organisations as gatekeepers to international legitimacy. It believed that it could justify Operation Iraqi Freedom without an explicit international mandate by affirming that it served international peace and security, appealing to previous UN Security Council resolutions, and returning to the UN in the aftermath of the invasion. This strategy failed, and the USA's international status has deteriorated as a result. Future lead states will do well to avoid this mistake.

This book also yields policy recommendations for those who wish to safeguard and strengthen international organisations' role in contemporary peace enforcement. There have been many reform efforts in this respect, but most focus on an organisation's material capacities, such as

---

[52] 'Adoption of Policy of Pre-Emption Could Result in Proliferation of Unilateral, Lawless Use of Force, Secretary-General Tells General Assembly', *UN Press Release*, 23 September 2003.

improved stand-by force arrangements, rapidly deployable headquarters, units and equipment, or surge capacity among staff specialists in peace operations. These are important initiatives, but they cannot alter the fact that unless international organisations gain substantial military capacities of their own they will remain marginal to the operational aspects of peace enforcement operations. Recognising that the primary reason for international organisations' importance in peace enforcement lies in their legitimising capacity implies that reformers should focus more on protecting and enhancing that fragile capacity.

As chapter 2 argued, contemporary international organisations owe their ability to endow an intervention with legitimacy to their status as interpreters of prevailing international rules and mouthpieces of the international community. Their capacity to legitimise peace enforcement operations thus ultimately depends on their own legitimacy as truly international bodies. This legitimacy can be damaged in a number of ways. An international organisation that appears to be controlled by a single state loses its special claim to speaking for a community of states and thus transcending the particularistic interests of individual members. Several of the organisations in this book are vulnerable to such perceptions, and their member states and bureaucrats must be especially careful to avoid appearing to rubber stamp large states' initiatives. This problem is aggravated if an organisation's decision-making institutions are seen as insufficiently representative of its membership. Thus the debate about restructuring the UN Security Council should not be thought of only in terms of efficiency and whether individual states deserve to be included in the Council. Another critical consideration is what kind of representation will permit the Council to improve its claim to speak for the whole UN membership and thus its ability to ensure the international legitimacy of interventions launched under its mandate. Finally, inaction can also be detrimental to an international organisation's legitimacy. During the Kosovo campaign, the USA argued that Russian and Chinese veto threats were preventing the Security Council from enacting the will of the international community. It was the obstruction of the Security Council that permitted the USA to present NATO as a more credible agent of the international community on this occasion. Similarly, African sub-regional international organisations derived much of their capacity to legitimise regional peace enforcement operations from the perception that the Security Council is unwilling to serve the international community by assuming its responsibility to protect international peace and security in Africa.

To maximise their organisations' influence in peace enforcement, therefore, reformers should focus on ensuring that they are relatively independent of major member states, consistently committed to the peace and security in their sphere of influence, and that their decision-making bodies are recognised as broadly representative of their members. The balance between these factors is delicate and difficult to maintain. Without it, however, international organisations will gradually lose their capacity to generate legitimacy for peace enforcement operations and with it much of their relevance to these interventions.

At the theoretical level, this book has sought to contribute to the on-going scholarly debate about the role of international organisations in world affairs and focus attention on the politics of international legitimacy. Most basically, it has shown that at least in peace enforcement operations, international organisations matter. Chapter 1 noted that these organisations are virtually ubiquitous in contemporary peace enforcement and the subsequent chapters established that, contrary to realist expectations, they are not mere figleaves for power politics. Chapter 2 advanced the theoretical argument that international organisations cannot legitimise peace enforcement operations at the sole behest of powerful states. They are constrained by both their multilateral membership and the limited flexibility of the rules that govern which types of behaviour can be considered legitimate in the contemporary international system. The empirical chapters confirmed that lead states incurred significant costs in order to obtain and operate under the auspices of an international organisation. Power politics and/or outright manipulation played a role in each of the case studies, but lead states still found themselves having to adjust the composition and tactics of their intervention forces and shouldering the military and financial costs of multilateral warfare. These were inherent costs of operating within the framework of an international organisation that lead states expected and chose to assume.

This study also demonstrated that, contrary to neo-liberal institutionalist expectations, in peace enforcement operations international organisations do not matter primarily as facilitators of mutually beneficial interstate cooperation. None of the case studies found evidence that international organisations were effective at facilitating burden-sharing for peace enforcement operations. Lead states found themselves shouldering a disproportionate share of the costs of their interventions while other member states contributed little or nothing to the operation. They did receive substantial support from some fellow member states, but two points are worth noting about this support. First, in all cases an ad hoc coalition of the willing would have achieved the same degree of burden-sharing without the costs and constraints associated with operating through a formal international organisation. Second, international organisations did not contribute to coalition-building in the ways a neo-liberal institutionalist would predict. Institutionalised burden-sharing mechanisms were either non-existent or explicitly deactivated for the peace enforcement operations studied, monitoring of defection was unnecessary, and lead states did not use international organisations as platforms for credible commitments in order to recruit partners for their interventions.

What international organisations did contribute to coalition-building was the legitimacy generated by their mandate, which enabled some states to join the intervention. However, this observation sits more easily with constructivism's suggestion that norms empower as well as constrain states than with neo-liberal institutionalism's emphasis on states as rational utility-maximisers. Moreover, it does not fully capture why lead states in peace enforcement operations turn to international organisations. Chapter 2 argued that states are consciously social actors that recognise themselves as members of an international society of states and value their standing within that society. Since the legitimacy of their peace enforcement operations can affect this standing, states value this legitimacy in itself as well as for instrumental coalition-building purposes. Indeed, the case studies in this book confirm empirically that lead states' legitimacy concerns extended far beyond the desire to build a functional coalition for their intervention. These states invariably had significant concerns about their standing in either the international community as a whole or a particular sub-section of it, and they recognised that this standing would be significantly affected by the perceived legitimacy or illegitimacy of their interventions. All five case studies show this to be the primary motivation of lead states for launching their peace enforcement operations within the framework of an international organisation.

This book thus presents an essentially constructivist argument. As chapter 2 noted, legitimacy is a public status judged according to the prevailing rules of a particular society. Contemporary international organisations are uniquely well positioned to speak for the society of states, identify its prevailing rules, and apply them to a particular case. This gives extraordinary weight to their mandates as indicators of the international legitimacy of a military intervention. In addition to advancing a constructivist argument for the role of international organisations in world politics, however, this book has also sought to advance the study of legitimacy more specifically. It makes three main contributions. The first is to focus attention on the international legitimacy of actions as well as of actors or institutions. There is a significant body of thought on what constitutes a legitimate actor on the international scene, but there has been much less consideration of how actions come to be perceived as either legitimate or illegitimate. The second contribution is to highlight the importance of thinking about legitimacy in terms of legitimacy audiences. Legitimacy is a social judgement according to social rules and it is therefore critical to consider *which* society is making the judgement. The case studies in this book consistently found that lead states' legitimacy concerns could only be fully understood when their key legitimacy audience was identified.

Finally, this book contributes to the study of international legitimacy by exploring the nature of the rules that underlie international judgements. Chapter 2 argued that these rules need not reflect substantive normative agreement among states, which makes it possible to speak of international legitimacy judgements despite the profound divisions that separate states in the contemporary international system. States can and do differ in their assessment of the moral worth of the content of international rules. This does not rob these rules of their significance as long as states continue to value the international society that recognises them as sovereign entities and recognise prevailing international rules as an integral part of this society. Indeed, the case studies in this volume yield relatively little evidence of states seeking to comply with international rules because they value their content. Instead, the overwhelming dynamic is that of states wanting to maintain or improve their standing in the 'club' by being seen *by other members* to obey its rules.

Even more importantly, this study distinguished the rules that underlie international legitimacy judgements from international laws. Legality and legitimacy often overlap in the international system because law generally reflects the rules that also provide standards for international legitimacy judgements. As chapter 2 argued, however, the evolution of customary international law in particular cannot be explained unless legitimacy is distinguished from legality. It is international *legitimacy* judgements that determine whether an action that violates current customary law simply remains an illegal act or becomes a precedent shaping the future development of international law. The case studies of this book show that states care deeply about this distinction. Lead states are willing to act illegally. Four of the five peace enforcement operations studied were arguably illegal. States are much less willing to be perceived as acting illegitimately, however, which is ultimately why they turn to international organisations to launch their interventions. Thus the well-known finding of the Independent International Commission on Kosovo that NATO's Kosovo campaign was 'illegal but legitimate'[53] did not merely draw a semantic distinction. It captured an essential but hitherto insufficiently studied dimension of legitimacy in the contemporary international system.

---

[53] The Independent International Commission on Kosovo, *The Kosovo Report: Conflict, International Response, Lessons Learned* (Oxford: Oxford University Press, 2000).

Epilogue: UN intervention in Lebanon

As this book goes into press, the United Nations Interim Force in Lebanon (UNIFIL) is being dramatically expanded to help address the conflict between Israel and Hizbollah that has devastated Lebanon. The manner in which this crisis was addressed should dispel any remaining doubts about the political relevance of the United Nations raised by the US intervention in Iraq. It also reaffirms the central proposition of this book, which is that the key contribution of international organisations to contemporary peace enforcement operations lies in the international legitimacy provided by their mandate.

The violence that flared in Lebanon and Israel in July and August 2006 has roots in the longstanding Arab–Israeli conflict, but its immediate trigger was the abduction of two Israeli soldiers by Hizbollah on 12 July 2006. Hizbollah, the 'Party of God', was founded following Israel's occupation of southern Lebanon in 1982 and, with Iran's help, developed into an important political and military player in Lebanon. It poses a persistent threat to Israel despite the call for the disarmament of all militias in the Taif Accords, which ended Lebanon's civil war in 1989. Hizbollah maintained its commitment to the struggle against Israel despite the latter's withdrawal from southern Lebanon in 2000 and declared 2006 'the year of retrieving the prisoners' held by Israel.[1] It hoped to use the two captured Israeli soldiers in a prisoner exchange with Israel. Instead, Israel launched an economic blockade and intensive air strikes against Beirut and southern Lebanon. Hizbollah retaliated with missile attacks against Israeli cities, and the violence rapidly escalated. By 7 August 2006, Lebanon had suffered over 1,000 civilian

---

[1] International Crisis Group, 'Israel/Palestine/Lebanon: Climbing Out Of The Abyss' *Middle East Report* No. 57, 25 July 2006, online at http://www.crisisgroup.org/home/index.cfm?id=4282&l=1

fatalities and Israel around 100,[2] while over 500,000 Lebanese had been displaced from their homes.

Discussions about a possible international intervention began within days of the first air strikes and were further fuelled when Israel announced that it would support the deployment of a 'serious' intervention force.[3] One early US proposal allegedly called for a force that would eventually deploy throughout Lebanon to disarm Hizbollah,[4] while a subsequent plan envisioned up to 30,000 NATO and UN troops being deployed only in a buffer zone of southern Lebanon.[5] On 27 July 2006, a major summit meeting in Rome specified that any intervention force should have a UN mandate, but failed to endorse any particular deployment option or to produce promises of troop contributions.[6] The summit ended in acrimony because the USA and the UK insisted on the need to find an enduring solution rather than call for an immediate ceasefire, a position other participants rejected as giving Israel time to achieve its military aims in Lebanon.[7] Thereafter, negotiations shifted into the UN framework. After meeting with US President Bush on 28 July, British Prime Minister Blair announced that the UN Security Council would meet on 31 July to discuss a resolution authorising a stabilisation force.[8] On 29 July, Bush specified that the US would be seeking a Chapter VII enforcement mandate for the intervention.[9] France, however, introduced its own draft Security Council resolution on 30 July. Over the next week, France and the USA merged their proposals and submitted a joint draft resolution to the Council after confirming Israel's support for it.

However, Lebanon had presented its own seven-point peace plan at the Rome summit. This proposal called for the Lebanese government

---

[2] Salim Yassine, 'Lebanese PM wins full Arab backing for truce plan', *Agence France Presse*, 7 August 2006.

[3] Patrick Bishop, 'Britain and US step up campaign for Lebanon peace force', *The Daily Telegraph*, 25 July 2006.

[4] Sandro Contenta, 'US wants peacekeepers: Bold proposal sees international force deployed across breadth of Lebanon' *Toronto Star*, 25 July 2006.

[5] 'Rice proposes international force for southern Lebanon', *Deutsche Presse-Agentur*, 25 July 2006.

[6] John Hooper, Ewen MacAskill and Jonathan Steele, 'Middle East crisis', *The Guardian*, 27 July 2006.

[7] Ibid.

[8] George Jones and Alec Russell, 'Blair and Bush launch peace plan', *The Daily Telegraph*, 29 July 2006.

[9] 'Bush renews calls for multinational force for Lebanon', *Agence France Presse*, 29 July 2006.

to extend its authority throughout its territory 'through its own legitimate armed forces' and thus advocated simply expanding the existing UN peacekeeping force in southern Lebanon, UNIFIL, rather than creating a new intervention force.[10] Thus on 6 August, Lebanon publicly rejected the Franco-American draft resolution, objecting both to its failure to call for an immediate ceasefire and to the suggestion of a new intervention force that was not under direct UN command.[11] Lebanon sought and received formal support from the Arab League and the Organisation of the Islamic Conference, and thus launched a new round of negotiations. Ultimately, France and the USA altered their draft resolution to acknowledge Lebanon's seven-point plan, emphasise the need to end violence as well as address its root causes, call for a Lebanese deployment into southern Lebanon and a parallel Israeli withdrawal from the area, and expand UNIFIL to facilitate this process. On 11 August 2006 the Security Council unanimously endorsed this text, which thus became Council Resolution 1701.

Unlike in the other case studies in this book, however, there was some uncertainty about which state would lead the expanded UNIFIL force. France was identified as a possible lead state for a multinational intervention as early as 25 July 2006.[12] Unlike the USA, it is perceived as relatively neutral in the Middle East. Moreover, France has strong historical ties to Lebanon, it was already providing UNIFIL's Force Commander (as well as 200 of the force's troops), and it had placed itself at the forefront of diplomatic efforts to address the crisis. UN officials thus openly hoped that France would provide the military 'backbone' of the expanded UNIFIL.[13] However, France initially offered only 200 new troops for the operation, and it was not until 24 August that it increased its offer and thus put itself in a position to act as UNIFIL's lead state. On 25 August UN Secretary-General Kofi Annan officially requested France to take this responsibility for the first six months of the new mission.

As the remainder of this epilogue will show, France's prevarications underline the central message of this book. France's primary – and indeed only – incentive for working within the UN framework was the legitimacy

---

[10] 'Full text: Lebanon's seven-point proposal', *BBC News*, online at http://news.bbc.ca.uk/go/pr/fr/-/1/hi/world/middle_east/5256936.stm

[11] 'Lebanon's speaker rejects US-French draft resolution', *BBC Monitoring*, 6 August 2006.

[12] Bishop, 'Britain and US step up campaign for Lebanon peace force'.

[13] Steven Erlanger, 'As Israel begins to pull troops out, Lebanon and the UN prepare to replace them', *New York Times*, 16 August 2006.

provided by the organisation's mandate. The problem, from France's point of view, was that this legitimacy came at an almost prohibitive price.

International law

As in the INTERFET case, the UN Security Council mandate made an expanded and more robust UNIFIL legal. However, multiple rounds of negotiation made resolution 1701 deliberately vague about the nature of the mission. Both France and the USA initially envisioned a multinational force mandated (in a separate Security Council resolution) under Chapter VII of the UN Charter and thus authorised to take enforcement action.[14] By contrast, Lebanon insisted on the immediate deployment of a force under direct UN command and with a Chapter VI peacekeeping mandate. By 11 August, France and the US had agreed to the UN force, but were still negotiating for a Chapter VII mandate.[15] The final compromise was not to mention any chapter at all in Resolution 1701. The text identifies the crisis as a threat to peace and security and authorises UNIFIL 'to take all necessary action ... to ensure that its area of operations is not utilized for hostile activities of any kind' as well as to protect itself and threatened civilians. However, the references to Chapter VII and 'all necessary means' that are customary in UN enforcement mandates are missing. Thus, as one US official put it, the text 'walks like, talks like and acts like a Chapter VII resolution'[16] – but it is not quite one.

France attributed its reluctance to lead the expanded UNIFIL to this ambiguity, but the solution it eventually acquiesced to suggests that its concern was more pragmatic than legal. Faced with French reticence, the USA proposed considering a new Security Council resolution clarifying the mission's enforcement mandate.[17] If approved, such a resolution would have eliminated all legal doubts about an enforcement mission. However, France explained its position by referring not to international law but to its experiences as part of the UN forces in Bosnia. What it sought was not a new Security Council resolution but assurances from

[14] 'The draft UN resolution', *The Guardian Unlimited*, 6 August 2006, online at http://observer.guardian.co.uk/world/story/0,,1838369,00.html

[15] 'French-US draft ready for UN Security Council', *Deutsche Presse-Agentur*, 11 August 2006.

[16] Warren Hoge and Steven Erlanger, 'UN Council backs measures to halt war in Lebanon', *New York Times*, 12 August 2006.

[17] 'UN has received no new troop offers from Lebanon force', *Deutsche Presse-Agentur*, 21 August 2006.

the UN secretariat about the mission's chain of command and rules of engagement (ROEs). Once it obtained assurances that the force would report to military rather than civilian officials at UN headquarters and that its ROEs would permit the use of deadly force in implementing its mandate, France increased its troop contributions.[18] This suggests that France had other priorities in helping to launch UNIFIL in the UN framework than strict compliance with international law.

Burden-sharing

As in the other cases reviewed in this book, UNIFIL's mandating international organisation contributed little to coalition-building for the force. Five days after Resolution 1701 was passed, the UN had no firm troop commitments for the force.[19] By 18 August, Indonesia, Malaysia, Bangladesh and Nepal had offered troops[20] but there were no concrete pledges from the European countries that UN officials had envisioned as providing the core of the expanded UNIFIL. Several of these states shared France's concerns about the mission's chain of command and ROEs, and French reticence to spearhead the force further diminished their enthusiasm for the mission. Only Italy indicated its willingness to provide a substantial number of troops: its offer of 2,000–3,000 troops established it as a potential alternative lead state for the mission, and indeed on 20 August Israeli Prime Minister Ehud Olmert invited Italy to assume this role.[21]

It was only after France had obtained the guarantees it sought from the UN and agreed to significantly support and lead UNIFIL that European troop contributions began to increase. In addition to France, Italy, and Spain, which had already offered troops, Finland, Portugal, Poland and Belgium pledged ground troops for the mission, allowing Annan to announce that 'We can now put together a credible force'.[22] Significantly, these troop commitments were negotiated at an

---

[18] Craig S. Smith, 'France offers many more troops for Lebanon', *New York Times*, 25 August 2006.

[19] Erlanger, 'As Israel begins to pull troops out, Lebanon and the UN prepare to replace them'.

[20] 'UN makes urgent appeal to Europe for Lebanon peacekeepers', *Agence France Presse*, 18 August 2006.

[21] 'UN has received no new troop offers from Lebanon force', *Deutsche Presse-Agentur*, 21 August 2006.

[22] Shada Islam, 'EU to send up to 6,900 troops as part of Lebanon force', *Deutsche Presse-Agentur*, 25 August 2006.

EU rather than a UN summit and were prompted more by French and US than UN lobbying. Thus the UN's contribution to building the coalition for UNIFIL's vanguard force was limited.

Legitimacy

France's reluctance to lead the UNIFIL mission described in Resolution 1701 should not obscure the value it placed on a UN mandate for an intervention force. In fact, the draft resolution France introduced to the Security Council on 30 July suggests that the *only* thing it sought from the UN was its mandate. In the text, the Council 'expresses its intention . . . to authorize under Chapter VII of the Charter the deployment of an international force' to southern Lebanon.[23] As in the INTERFET case examined earlier in this book, this would have meant minimal UN involvement in forming, financing, and commanding the intervention force. The UN Security Council mandate was nevertheless indispensable for a French deployment because only this mandate could establish the deployment's local and international legitimacy.

Like all lead states in peace enforcement operations, France faced several legitimacy audiences. What is unique in this case, however, is the prominence of legitimacy audiences in the host region. In part, this prominence derived from Lebanon's *de jure* sovereignty over the deployment area and Israel and Hizbollah's military capacities: if any side rejected the intervention as illegitimate, UNIFIL would quickly find itself under attack. In addition, however, local legitimacy audiences mattered because of their extraordinarily close ties to global and domestic legitimacy audiences. The cleavages of the Arab–Israeli conflict are widely reproduced both at the international level and within states. Domestically, Jewish groups tend to favour Israel while Arab and Muslim communities tend to be sympathetic to Palestinian and Arab causes. Globally, the USA staunchly supports Israel but Arab and developing states tend to align themselves with its regional opponents. Crucially, these domestic and global actors are highly responsive to emotional appeals from the regional protagonists that they support. Consequently, UNIFIL is unique among the case studies in this book in the extent to which international and domestic legitimacy audiences take their cues from audiences in the host region.

---

[23] 'Text of draft UN resolution on Lebanon', *Agence France Presse*, 30 July 2006.

France is keenly aware of the globally polarising nature of the Arab–Israeli conflict. Like many European states, it has historically hesitated to criticise Israel, in part because of domestic Jewish lobbies but especially because of its experience of and complicity in the Holocaust. However, it has increasingly sought to play a mediating role in the conflict, a policy that reflects not only France's ambition to extend its influence in the Middle East but also the influence of the growing French Arab and Muslim communities. This relative neutrality combined with France's considerable military capacity make it a prime candidate to lead the expanded UNIFIL. For France this meant an opportunity to simultaneously bolster its profile in the Middle East, satisfy domestic constituents, and reaffirm its status in the international system. The prestige associated with leading such a mission was evident when Italy catapulted to international prominence by offering to provide UNIFIL with the troops and leadership France seemed unwilling to provide in the days after Resolution 1701 was passed. Italian Prime Minister Romano Prodi celebrated this offer as heralding 'a new phase in Italian foreign policy', and it was probably no coincidence that France reopened the issue of a larger French contribution to UNIFIL just two days later.[24] However, France could only benefit from leading the expanded UNIFIL if the deployment was seen as legitimate both internationally and within France itself. As in other cases reviewed in this book, a UN mandate was essential to establishing this legitimacy. Given the unique alignment of domestic, regional, and global legitimacy audiences in the Middle East conflict, however, in this case it was also crucially important that all the parties on the ground should accept the intervention as legitimate.

This prominence of local legitimacy audiences generated a unique dynamic because, as the previous case studies already suggested, local audiences are more concerned with the practical impact of an intervention than their international or lead state counterparts. Perceived impartiality in the pursuit of international peace and security remains crucial: although some actors would prefer an intervention that is biased in their favour, perceived impartiality is the minimum condition for persuading local audiences of a deployment's legitimacy. What distinguishes local audiences is that they rely less on the intervention's mandate to assess its impartiality because, unlike their international counterparts, they have both intimate knowledge of and a direct stake

---

[24] 'Italy approves participation in United Nations forces in Lebanon', *Deutsche Presse-Agentur*, 18 August 2006. Helene Cooper, 'Bush calls need for robust Lebanon force "urgent" ', *New York Times*, 22 August 2006.

in the deployment's impact on the ground. Thus while in the other deployments in this book international legitimacy was established primarily through the mandate of an international organisation and then reinforced by a diverse multinational force composition, in the UNIFIL case force composition gained greater immediate prominence.

Thus Lebanon made it clear that it required not only a UN mandate but also UN command to accept an intervention force. It believed that only the global UN could launch a force that would genuinely serve regional peace and security rather than the particularistic aims of Israel and its Western allies. However, it did not believe that a UN mandate alone could guarantee this impartiality and therefore insisted that the deployment should also be placed under UN command. This would not only increase the UN's control over the force but also encourage the participation of developing nations that might not be invited to join a multinational force – and these troops would help guarantee the force's neutrality on the ground. Interestingly, US Secretary of State Condoleezza Rice initially sought to dismiss Lebanon's reservations: 'I think we . . . have to vote the resolution, and then I think you will see parties recognise that they have an obligation to respond to UN Security Council resolutions.'[25] Had she been successful, the intervention would have resembled the other case studies in this book in being mandated but not controlled by an international organisation. The fact that Resolution 1701 ultimately incorporated Lebanon's demands suggests that other countries (including France) had a less cavalier attitude towards local legitimacy, in part for security reasons and in part because they appreciated the unique alignment of their domestic, host, and global legitimacy audiences.

Force composition was equally important to Israel, though its substantive preferences differed markedly from Lebanon's. Israel indicated early in the crisis that it favoured a NATO mission,[26] a preference that sprang from the perception that such a deployment would be both more robust and more sympathetic towards Israel than a UN force. It was also willing to accept the Franco-American proposal of an eventual UN mandated multinational force, in part because this force was to be deployed under Chapter VII and led by Europeans. In addition, the draft resolution that would have created the force favoured Israel by insisting that Hizbollah immediately cease 'all attacks' while Israel only

---

[25] William Wallis, 'Arabs unite with Beirut against UN resolution', *Financial Times*, 7 August 2006.
[26] Bishop, 'Britain and US step up campaign for Lebanon peace force'.

had to cease 'all offensive military operations' and by stressing that an intervention force would only be created (by a second Council resolution) once both Israel and Lebanon agreed to a set of principles for a long-term settlement, which would give Israel a chance to consolidate its gains in southern Lebanon.[27] Because Lebanon rejected this draft resolution, however, Resolution 1701 was ultimately less favourable to Israel, notably in authorising the immediate expansion of UNIFIL under UN command but with ambiguous enforcement powers.

Israel could not summarily reject this plan as illegitimate because it corresponded perfectly to prevailing international rules about the use of military force: it expanded a mission that existed since 1978 with the explicit consent of the host state (Lebanon), and it was endorsed by the UN Security Council. However, Israel did not share the perceptions of impartiality upon which the UN's role as gatekeeper to international legitimacy is based. In Israel's view the UN's universal membership has led to bias, with the steadily growing majority of developing state members passing a barrage of General Assembly resolutions condemning Israel. Any indication that the expanded UNIFIL reflected this bias would give Israel not just an incentive but also an internationally defensible reason to reject the force. The problem was particularly acute because several of the first states to volunteer troops for the force (including Malaysia and Indonesia) had not officially recognised Israel as a state. The UN's desperation to convince European states to join UNIFIL thus reflected not only a need for troop contributions but even more importantly the need to create a force that would be considered legitimate by all local stakeholders. As UN Deputy Secretary-General Mark Malloch Brown put it, 'It's very important that Europe now steps forward ... We said before that a European-Muslim force (would be preferable) because of both groups' interest in this situation ... They bring when you combine them a legitimacy that satisfies both sides to this conflict.'[28]

Thus in part because of the unique global influence of local legitimacy audiences in this case, negotiations on force composition rapidly took centre stage in the struggle over UNIFIL's international legitimacy. This should not, however, obscure the importance of the UN mandate, which was an essential condition for Lebanon to accept the deployment and for developing and European states to contribute to the force. Moreover,

---

[27] 'The draft UN resolution', *Guardian Unlimited*, 6 August 2006.
[28] 'UN makes urgent appeal to Europe for Lebanon peacekeepers', *Agence France Presse*, 18 August 2006.

the insistence on balanced force contributions complemented rather than replaced the insistence on a UN mandate: for both Lebanon and Israel, it was a means of ensuring that the impartiality promised by the mandate would in fact be attained on the ground.

Costs

Like the lead states in the other interventions studied in this book, France incurred significant costs in obtaining the mandate of an international organisation for its deployment. As in the INTERFET case in East Timor, one cost was time: because of the complexity of the international negotiations that eventually resulted in Resolution 1701, the UN mandate for intervention came almost exactly one month after the violence in Lebanon erupted. Some 700–1,000 Lebanese citizens and 124 Israelis died from the fighting in these 30 days and UN Secretary-General Kofi Annan publicly deplored the delay, adding that he was 'convinced that my frustration and disappointment are shared by hundreds of millions of people around the world'.[29] Unlike Australia in the East Timor case, however, France faced no overwhelming domestic pressure to act immediately and did not appear to place a high value on an immediate response. It contributed to the lengthy process of determining how the international community would respond to the Lebanon crisis and although it took the lead in introducing the first draft UN Security Council resolution on the issue it did not do so until 30 July, eighteen days after the crisis began. Even more tellingly, France did not immediately launch a major deployment effort once Resolution 1701 was passed. Instead, it took six days to offer only 200 additional troops to UNIFIL and then began lengthy negotiations with the UN Secretariat regarding the force's command structure and ROEs. This suggests that France did not regard time as a major cost in obtaining a UN mandate for its deployment.

The main cost in France's eyes was that, on Lebanon's insistence, the UN mandate was tied to the deployment of a UN force. France made no secret of the fact that it would have preferred to lead a UN-mandated multilateral force. It clearly doubted the UN's capacity to undertake robust military deployments and cited its experiences in Bosnia to justify insisting on a military command unit in UN headquarters and explicit

---

[29] J. T. Nguyen, 'Security Council unanimously adopts Lebanon resolution', *Deutsche Presse-Agentur*, 12 August 2006.

clarification of the mission's ROEs. France will also have less control over a UN force than over a multilateral one: whereas INTERFET's Australian commander reported to his own government, the French UNIFIL commander must report to the UN and faces a higher level of UN supervision. Moreover, a UN force implies greater UN Secretariat involvement in designing the intervention, and a fully diverse UN force raises greater diplomatic, logistical, and military challenges than a multinational force composed of carefully selected allies. These costs caused France to reassess its desire to lead the intervention, and since Italy offered to fill the vacuum, reasserting French leadership came at the additional price of agreeing to a limited six-months' command span and Italian leadership of UNIFIL's military command unit in New York. For the purposes of this book, however, the key insight is that France assessed the costs of obtaining a UN mandate so highly that it almost backed away from leading the deployment altogether. Nevertheless it persisted in its efforts to obtain a mandate even after it became clear that Lebanon would insist on a UN force and ultimately not only voted for but co-sponsored UN Security Council Resolution 1701 as the only means of launching a legitimate intervention in Lebanon.

Conclusion

In the wake of the USA's 2003 intervention in Iraq, pundits were willing to dismiss the UN as irrelevant to world politics, at least as far as international security and the Middle East are concerned. The intervention also threatened to cast doubt on the core assertion in this book that international organisations play a central role as gatekeepers to international legitimacy for modern peace enforcement operations, although I have already argued that careful assessment of the case does not warrant this conclusion. The Lebanon crisis, while fuelling further debates about the Security Council's responsiveness to international security threats, reaffirmed the UN's centrality to the politics of international legitimacy in the contemporary international system. Italy's Foreign Minister Massimo d'Alema declared that Italy was 'contributing to the start of a new phase in the world, characterised by the end of the unilateral approach triggered on September 11th 2001, and a return to the multilateral approach [with] the UN back in the lead'.[30] French foreign

---

[30] Gianni Riotta, 'D'Alema: the end of unilateralism, UN back in the lead', *Corriere della Sera*, 29 August 2006, online at www.esteri.it/eng/0_1_01.asp?id=1633

minister Philippe Douste-Blazy also identified renewed multilateralism as one of the lessons of the crisis: 'Collective action and cohesion in the international community must prevail. No state can meet the challenge of international security alone. No unilateral approach can hope to have sufficient legitimacy. Effectiveness and legitimacy must not be at odds, quite the contrary. This is the reason Security Council action must be central in dealing with crises.'[31] As this book has shown, these are not new insights. The Lebanon crisis has, however, served to reaffirm this position in the wake of the challenge posed to it by US actions in Iraq.

[31] Embassy of France in the United States, 'Daily Press Briefing', 30 August 2006, online at www.ambafrance-us.org/news/briefing/us300806.asp

APPENDIX: SUMMARY OF INTERVIEWS CONDUCTED

Country	Research date	Location reason	Interviews	Interviewees
Australia	April–May 2002	Lead state INTERFET	30	30
Belgium	June 2001	NATO Headquarters	15	15
Botswana	December 2000	SADC Headquarters	9	9
Ethiopia	October–November 2000	OAU (now AU) Headquarters	41	34
Nigeria	September–October 2000	ECOWAS Headquarters; Lead state Operation Liberty	31	25
USA	2000–2003	UN Headquarters; Lead state Operation Allied Force	7	7
Zimbabwe	November–December 2000	SADC Organ Headquarters; Lead state Operation Sovereign Legitimacy	16	16

BIBLIOGRAPHY

Primary documents and news reports

Abel, David, 'N.E. kin grieve for 2 killed in Iraq' *Boston Globe*, 3 September 2003

Africa News Service, 'Armed intervention into Lesotho: "not SADC, but South Africa" ', 8 January 1999

Agence France Presse, 'Bush renews calls for multinational force for Lebanon', 29 July 2006

   'ECOWAS to sanction defaulting member sates', 18 June 1991

   'Anti-NATO protests in Europe, US and Australia', 28 March 1999

   'Russia says it will block US bids to seek retroactive UN approval for war', 22 March 2003

   'Text of draft UN resolution on Lebanon', 30 July 2006

   'UN makes urgent appeal to Europe for Lebanon peacekeepers', 18 August 2006

All Africa News Agency, 'South Africa's move in Lesotho receives criticism', *Africa News*, 9 November 1998

American Enterprise Institute Compilation, 'Public opinion on Kosovo' cached on www.google.com, accessed 19 February 2003, no longer available at this site

Annan, Kofi, 'Two Concepts of Sovereignty', *The Economist*, 18 September 1999

'Annan pledges UN will play its role in Iraq's next phase' *UN News Service*, 25 June 2004

Associated Press, 'Schroeder and Bush agree past differences on Iraq are behind them', *New York Times*, 24 September 2003

Australian Defence Force, Draft report: 'INTERFET: a coalition of the willing. The Australian Defence Experience'

Australian Department of Foreign Affairs and Trade, *Australia and the Indonesian Incorporation of Portuguese Timor, 1974–76* (Carlton: Melbourne University Press, 2000)

   East Timor in Transition 1998–2000: an Australian Policy Challenge (Canberra: Brown & Wilton, 2001)

Australian National Audit Office, 'Management of the Australian Defence Force Deployments to East Timor – Department of Defence', *Audit Report No. 38 2001–2002* (Canberra: Commonwealth of Australia, 2002)

Barrell, Howard, 'Lesotho: we have some serious explaining to do', *Mail and Guardian* (South Africa), 25 September 1998

Barringer, Felicity, 'UN hands US symbolic victory on Iraq', *New York Times*, 20 October 2003

Bartlett, Lawrence, 'War and riches inspire new African economic deal making', *Agence France Presse*, 30 September 1999

Bauer, Dominik, 'Ein Illegaler Krieg', *Spiegel*, 20 March 2003

BBC, 'Full text: Lebanon's seven-point proposal', online at http://news.bbc.ca.uk/ go/pr/fr/-/1/hi/world/middle_east/5256936.stm

'Lebanon's speaker rejects US-French draft resolution', 6 August 2006

'Lesotho fighting intensifies', 22 September 1998

'Protesters attack US, Turkish, Belgian embassies', 1 April 1999

'7 June 1981: Israel bombs Baghdad nuclear reactor', online at http://news.bbc. co.uk/onthisday/hi/dates/stories/june/7/newsid_3014000/3014623.stm

'US ambassador responds to Putin address on Iraq action', 20 March 2003

Bender, Bryan and Joe Lauria, 'Rebuilding Iraq: triumph, setback for Bush on Iraq', *Boston Globe*, 17 October 2003

Benin, Republic of, 'Draft Proposal Establishing a Mechanism for Peace-Keeping, Security and Stability in West Africa', presented by the delegation for the Republic of Benin to the ECOWAS Ministerial Meeting on the Establishment of a Mechanism for Peace-Keeping, Security and Stability in West Africa at Yamoussoukro, 9–12 March 1998

Bishop, Patrick, 'Britain and US step up campaign for Lebanon peace force', *The Daily Telegraph*, 25 July 2006

Black, Ian, 'Threat of air strikes recedes as Milosevic appears to back down', *The Guardian*, 22 January 1999

Black, Ian, James Meek, and Ian Traynor, 'War in Europe: Russia and China lead international protests', *The Guardian*, 26 March 1999

Bone, James, 'UN rejects call for a peacekeeping force in Timor', *The Times*, 2 September 1999

Boot, William, 'The two versions of the Langa Report', *Weekly Mail and Guardian*, 25 September 1998

Boutros-Ghali, Boutros, *An Agenda for Peace* (New York: UN, 1992)

Supplement to An Agenda for Peace (New York: UN, 1995)

Bransten, Jeremy, 'NATO: crisis in Kosovo to dominate historic summit', *Radio Free Europe*, 21 April 1999

Bush, George W., 'Graduation Speech at West Point', 1 June 2002, online at www.whitehouse.gov/news/releases/2002/06/20020601-3.html

'Remarks at the United Nations General Assembly', 12 September 2002, online at www.whitehouse.gov/news/releases/2002/09/20020912-1.html

'Monday "Moment of Truth" for World on Iraq', press conference in the Azores, Portugal, 16 March 2003, online at www.whitehouse.gov/news/

releases/2003/03/iraq/20030316-3.html. Accessed 26 September 2003, document no longer available at this site

'President Discusses Beginning of Operation Iraqi Freedom', 22 March 2003. Online at www.whitehouse.gov/news/releases/2003/03/iraq/2030322.html. Accessed 26 September 2003, document no longer available at this site

'President Speaks to the United Nations General Assembly', 21 September 2004, online at www.whitehouse.gov/news/releases/2004/09/print/20040921-3.html

'President's Radio address', 19 March 2005, online at www.whitehouse.gov/news/releases/2005/03/20050319.html

Buthelezi, Mangosuthu, President's Minute 81/172188 (Z 19E), signed on 16 September 1998 by South Africa's Acting President Mangosuthu Buthelezi and Minister of Defence Joe Modise. Online at www.nul.ls/~mnzmphaka/Invasion.htm, accessed in January 2002, site no longer available

Buthelezi, Mangosuthu and Pakalitha Mosisili, 'Agreement between the Government of the Republic of South Africa and the Kingdom of Lesotho concerning the Status of Armed Forces in the Kingdom of Lesotho Providing Military Assistance', 17 September 1998. Online at http://www.nul.ls/~mnzmphaka/Invasion.htm, accessed in January 2002, site no longer available

Clark, General Wesley, 'Press Conference at NATO Headquarters', Brussels, Belgium, 25 March 1999, online at http://www.nato.int/kosovo/press/p990325a.htm

Report to NATO Secretary-General Robertson on 'Operation ALLIED FORCE Statistics', 6 January 2000. Unclassified NATO document SHJOC/J3AIR/0500/99. Courtesy of the NATO Secretariat

Contenta, Sandro, 'US wants peacekeepers: bold proposal sees international force deployed across breadth of Lebanon', *Toronto Star*, 25 July 2006

Cooper, Helene, 'Bush calls need for robust Lebanon force "urgent"', *New York Times*, 22 August 2006

'Czechs show less support for NATO than Poles, Hungarians', *CTK National News Wire*, 8 April 1999

Dempsey, Judy Krishna Guha and George Parke, 'Chirac plans to resist the control of post-war Iraq by US allies; French condemn "illegal" war', *Financial Times*, 22 March 2003

Deutsche Presse-Agentur, 'Amid protests, Schroeder dismisses doubts over NATO strikes', 10 April 1999

'Clinton defends NATO military action in Kosovo', 21 September 1999

'Fischer: Blix report shows "peaceful disarmament is possible"', 7 March 2003

'French–US draft ready for UN Security Council', 11 August 2006

'Italy approves participation in United Nations forces in Lebanon', 18 August 2006

'Mugabe says Southern African states will back Kabila', 18 August 1998
'Mugabe won't go to Mandela summit', 22 August 1998
'Rebels close on Kinshasa, give Kabila a week to quit', 18 August 1998
'Rice proposes international force for southern Lebanon', 25 July 2006
'UN has received no new troop offers from Lebanon force', 21 August 2006
'White House: Blix report shows Iraq not disarming', 7 March 2003
'Zimbabwe defence minister says SADC to send men, arms to DRC', 19 August
    1998
Dinmore, Guy and Mark Turner, 'Complex Blix report gives hope to both sides in
    UN', *Financial Times*, 8 March 2003
Dludlu, John, 'African leaders seek ceasefire in Congo', *Business Day (South
    Africa)*, 24 August 1998
'DR Congo: Botswana not bound by Harare move', *Daily News (Botswana)*,
    21 August 1998
Drozdiak, William, 'Even allies resent US Dominance', *Washington Post*,
    4 November 1997
Duval Smith, Alex, 'Mandela fails in peace initiatives', *The Guardian (London)*,
    4 September 1998
ECOWAS Administration and Finance Commission, 'ECOWAS Budget 2000',
    prepared by the Executive Secretariat in Abuja and approved by the 24th
    Session of the ECOWAS Administration and Finance Commission,
    26 November–2 December 1999. Courtesy of ECOWAS Secretariat
ECOWAS Council of Ministers, Final Report, 47th Session of the ECOWAS
    Council of Ministers, Bamako, Mali, 9–12 December 2000
ECOWAS Defence, Interior, and Security Ministers, Projet de Mécanisme de
    Prévention, de Gestion, de Maintien de la Paix et de la Sécurité, signed at
    Banjul, Gambia, 24 July 1998. Online at www.cedeao.org/sitecedeao/francais/
    peace-3.htm, accessed summer 2000, document no longer available at
    this site
ECOWAS Heads of State and Government, 'Protocol on Non-Aggression', signed
    in Lagos, Nigeria, on 22 April 1978, *The West African Bulletin*, No. 3, June
    1996
    'Protocol Relating to Mutual Assistance on Defence', signed in Freetown,
        Sierra Leone, on 29 May 1981, *The West African Bulletin*, No. 3, June 1996
    'Final Communiqué of the First Extra-Ordinary Session of the Authority of
        Heads of State and Government held in Bamako, Mali, 27–28/Nov/1990',
        Official Journal of the Economic Community of West African States, Vol. 21
        (1992)
    Declaration A/DCL.1/7/91 of Political Principles of the Economic Community
        of West African States, signed at the Fourteenth Session of the Authority of
        Heads of State and Government in Abuja, 4–6 July 1991. Courtesy of
        ECOWAS Secretariat

'Treaty of the Economic Community of West African States', signed 24 July 1993 in Cotonou, Benin. Online at www.ecowas.int/sitecedeao/english/stat-1.htm, accessed summer 2000, document no longer available at this site

'Final Communiqué of the Fourth Extraordinary Session of the Authority of Heads of State and Government of the Economic Community of West African States', issued from Lomé, Togo, 17 December 1997. Courtesy of ECOWAS Secretariat

'Decision A/Dec.11/10/98 Relating to the ECOWAS Mechanism for Conflict Prevention, Management, Resolution, Peacekeeping and Security', signed in Abuja, Nigeria, 31 October 1998. *Official Journal of the Economic Community of West African States*, Vol. 35, October 1998

'Decision A/DEC.12/10/98 Creating the Post of Deputy Executive Secretary for Political Affairs, Defence and Security in the Executive Secretariat', *Official Journal of the Economic Community of West African States*, Vol. 35, October 1998, pp. 27–8

'Protocol Relating to the Mechanism for Conflict Prevention, Management, Resolution, Peacekeeping and Security', signed on 10 December 1999 in Lomé, Togo. Courtesy of the ECOWAS Secretariat

'Rules of Procedure of the Mediation and Security Council', approved in Abuja, Nigeria, 27 May 2000. Courtesy of the ECOWAS Secretariat

Ellis, S., 'Profiteering from war', *Weekly Mail and Guardian* (South Africa), 25 July 1997

Embassy of France in the United States, 'Daily Press Briefing' 30 August 2006, online at www.ambafrance-us.org/news/briefing/us300806.asp

Evans, Michael, 'US calls for NATO airstrike threat against Milosevic', *The Times*, 22 January 1999

'Failed efforts to gain UN Security Council resolution to deal with disarmament of Iraq', *All Things Considered – (USA) National Public Radio*, 17 March 2003

'Final report of the Panel of Experts on the Illegal Exploitation of Natural Resources and Other Forms of Wealth of the Democratic Republic of the Congo, 8 October 2002', online at www.un.org/Docs/journal/asp/ws.asp?m=S/2002/1146

Freedman, Tani, 'UN's Annan urges Yugoslavia to stop military action in Kosovo', *Agence France Presse*, 9 April 1999

Gonçalves, Fernando, 'The Congo crisis: what is at stake?' *The Zimbabwe Mirror*, 21–27 August 1998

'Half of Slovaks against Slovakia's entry to NATO – Poll', *CTK National News Wire*, 13 April 1999

Hansard of the Parliament of the Commonwealth of Australia, House of Representatives. Votes and Proceedings No. 66, 21 September 1999. Online at www.aph.gov.au/hansard/reps/dailys/dr210999.pdf

Harris, John F., 'Clinton says he might send ground troops', *Washington Post*, 19 May 1999

Hartcher, Peter, 'The ABC of winning US support', *Australian Financial Review*, 13 September 1999

  'Accent on positive to start again in Indonesia', *Australian Financial Review*, 6 April 2000

Hartley, Wyndham, 'Incursion tarnishes SA's peacemaker image', *Business Day (South Africa)*, 25 September 1998

  '11 days that led to war', *Sunday Times (South Africa)*, 27 September 1998

Hofmeyr, Willie, 'Straw men come under fire in Lesotho debate', *Business Day (South Africa)*, 14 December 1998

  'SA met the letter and spirit of law', *Business Day (South Africa)*, 20 November 1998

Hoge, Warren and Steven Erlanger, 'UN Council backs measures to halt war in Lebanon', *New York Times*, 12 August 2006

Hooper, John, Ewen MacAskill and Jonathan Steele, 'Middle East crisis', *The Guardian*, 27 July 2006

Howard, John, 'Address to the Nation', televised speech of 19 September 1999, transcript online at http://www.pm.gov.au/news/speeches/1999/address1909.htm

IRIN (UN Integrated Regional Information Networks), 'DRC: Zimbabwe says SADC to back Kabila', 19 August 1998

  'Kinshasa bids farewell to allied forces', 30 October 2002

  'Secretary-General appeals to leaders in Lesotho to show statesmanship and work together', 23 September 1998

  'Secretary-General appeals to all parties in Lesotho to reach agreement on outstanding issues', 13 October 1998

  'DRC: Zimbabwe says SADC to back Kabila', 19 August 1998

  'Adoption of policy of pre-emption could result in proliferation of unilateral, lawless use of force, Secretary-General tells General Assembly', 23 September 2003

Islam, Shada, 'EU to send up to 6,900 troops as part of Lebanon force', *Deutsche Presse-Agentur*, 25 August 2006

Jones, George and Alec Russell, 'Blair and Bush launch peace plan', *The Daily Telegraph*, 29 July 2006

Knowlton, Brian, 'Clinton refuses to rule out ground troops in Yugoslavia', *International Herald Tribune*, 19 May 1999

  'US and Germany look to move past discord over Iraq', *International Herald Tribune*, 25 September 2003

Kouyate, Lansana, *2000 Interim Report of the Executive Secretary*. ECOWAS publication courtesy of the ECOWAS Secretariat

Kozaryn, Linda, 'Air chief's Kosovo lesson: go for snake's head first', *American Forces Press*, October 1999

Kull, Steven and Doug Miller, 'Global Public Opinion on the US Presidential Election and US Foreign Policy', joint report by Program on International Policy Attitudes and GlobeScan, 8 September 2004, online at www.pipa. org/archives/global_opinion.php

'In 18 of 21 Countries Polled, Most See Bush's Reelection as Negative for World Security', joint report by Program on International Policy Attitudes and GlobeScan, 19 January 2005, online at www.pipa.org/archives/ global_opinion.php

Langa Commission, 'Report of the Commission of Enquiry into the Conduct and results of the Lesotho General Elections held in May 1998', online at www.nul.ls/~mnzmphaka/LangaReport.htm. Accessed in January 2002, site no longer accessible

Laurence, Patrick, 'Mugabe and Mandela divided by personalities and policies', *The Irish Times*, 21 August 1998

Lekic, Slobodan, 'Anti-NATO protests continue in Europe', *Associated Press*, 27 March 1999

Lesotho Constitution, online at www.lesotho.gov.ls/constitute/gconstitute.htm

Machipisa, Lewis, 'D. R. Congo: Southern African could send troops to crush rebellion', *Inter Press Service*, 12 August 1998

Maletsky, Christof, 'Regional defence organ wrested from Mugabe', *The Namibian*, 12 March 2001

Mandela, Nelson, President of the Republic of South Africa, 'Statement at the OAU Meeting of Heads of State and Government, Tunis, Tunisia, 13–15 June 1994'. Online at www.anc.org.za/ancdocs/history/mandela/1994/ sp940613.html

'Address at the State Banquet for President Mugabe of Zimbabwe, 16 August 1994'. Online at www.anc. org.za/ancdocs/history/mandela/1994/sp940816.html

Marais, Hein, 'South Africa carries a big stick', *Le Monde Diplomatique*, March 1999

Marshall, Andrew, 'Clinton rebuked Blair for "warmonger talk"', *The Independent*, 21 May 1999

Masamvo, Sydney, 'Government owed $100 billion', *Financial Gazette (Harare)*, 12 September 2002

Mills, Greg, 'Is the Lesotho foray a lesson learned?', *Business Day (South Africa)*, 28 October 1998

Moore, John and Alexander Downer, 'Press Conference', 6 September 1999, online at www.minister.defence.gov.au/1999/mt0699.htm

Mosisili, Pakalitha, 'Letter to the presidents of South Africa, Zimbabwe, Botswana, and Mozambique', sent 16 September 1998, read to the South African Parliament by Acting President Mangosuthu Buthelezi 22 September 1998. South African Hansard, 'Proceedings of the National Assembly, Tuesday 22 September 1998', columns 6763–4

'Letter to Mangosuthu Buthelezi, acting president of South Africa, 19 September 1998', read to the South African Parliament by Mangosuthu Buthelezi, 22 September 1998. South African Hansard, 22 September 1998, column 6765

'Statement by the Right Honourable Prime Minister, Mr Pakalitha Mosisili, to the Nation and the World, 24 September 1998', online at www.lesotho. gov.ls/speeches/sppm24sep98.htm

Motopi, Kekeletso, 'SANDF are employed in Lesotho not deployed – Malebo', *Mopheme/The Survivor (Lesotho)*, 15 December 1998

Mugabe, Robert, 'Announcement of Zimbabwe's intervention in the DRC', Harare, 18 August 1998, accessed online through the Zimbabwe government's website at www.gta.gov.zw on 16 April 2003, site not currently accessible

'Mugabe's Congo adventure must be stopped', *Zimbabwe Independent*, 21 August 1998

'Mugabe's DRC move comes under fire', *Zimbabwe Independent*, 21 August 1998

Mutume, Gumisai, 'Southern Africa: peace in the offing for Kabila's DRC', *Inter Press Service*, 3 September 1998

NATO Heads of State and Government, 'Statement on Iraq', issued by NATO Heads of State and Government at the meeting of the North Atlantic Council in Istanbul on 28 June 2004, online at www.nato.int/docu/pr/ 2004/p04-098e.htm

'NATO bombings fuel intense anti-American sentiment among Serbians', CNN, 18 April 1999

'NATO keeps ground troops option open – Blair', *Birmingham Post*, 19 April 1999

Nguyen, J. T., 'Security Council unanimously adopts Lebanon resolution', *Deutsche Presse-Agentur*, 12 August 2006

North Atlantic Council, Decision Council D-1/1, First Session of the North Atlantic Council, Washington DC, 17 September 1949. Courtesy of NATO Archives

'Statement on Kosovo', 23 April 1999. Online at www.nato.int/docu/pr/1999/ p99-062e.htm

OAU, 'Report of the Secretary-General on the Implementation of the Algiers Decisions of the Assembly of [OAU] Heads of State and Government and the Council of Ministers on Unconstitutional Changes of Government', delivered to the 7th Ordinary Session of the Council of Ministers in Lomé, Togo, 4–8 July 2000. Courtesy of the OAU Secretariat

OAU Assembly of Heads of State and Government, Decisions AHG/Dec.141(XXXV) and AHG/Dec.142(XXXV), made at the 35th Ordinary Session of the OAU, held in Algiers, Algeria, 12–14 July 1999. Courtesy of OAU Secretariat

Official Journal of the Economic Community of West African States, Vol. 21, Special Supplement on 'ECOWAS Decisions on the Liberian Crisis'. Courtesy of the ECOWAS library

Pan-African News Agency, 'Mozambique will not send troops to Congo – Mocumbi', 22 August 1998

'Mocumbi speaks on Congolese conflict', 28 August 1998

'Peace, they say, but the killing goes on', *The Economist*, 27 March 2003

Pearce, Justin, 'Mugabe's costly Congo venture', *BBC News Online*, 25 July 2000

Priest, Dana, 'US speaks more softly after failed Kosovo talks', *Washington Post*, 25 February 1999

Program on International Policy Attitudes, 'Americans on Kosovo: A Study of US Public Attitudes' (27 May 1999), online at www.pipa.org/OnlineReports/Kosovo/kosovo.htm, accessed 19 February 2003, document no longer available at this site

Radebe, James, 'South Africa: Lesotho intervention questioned', *Inter Press Service*, 7 October 1998

Randall, Gene, 'Strike against Yugoslavia: Clinton thanks Annan for public support', CNN, 10 April 1999

'Reaction to S. African operation in Lesotho' *BBC Summary of World Broadcasts*, 11 December 1982

Reuters, 'African leaders open door to Congo peace', *The Toronto Star*, 4 September 1998

   'Lawless Lesotho capital "under siege", Mandela praises deputy's decision to send troops to battle "virtual coup" by Maseru mutineers', *The Toronto Star*, 24 September 1998

   'Uneasy peace as Chirac needles US at NATO', *New York Times*, 29 June 2004

   'Zimbabwe, Congo set up joint ventures to fund war', *GO Network News*, 23 September 1999

Richter, Paul, 'US general says French officials endangers american war pilots', *Los Angeles Times*, 22 October 1999

Riotta, Gianni, 'D'Alema: the end of unilateralism, UN back in the lead', *Corriere della Sera*, 29 August 2006, online at www.esteri.it/eng/0_1_01.asp?id=1633

Roberts, Bob and Gavin Cordon, 'UK urges Kosovo talks as 23 die in raid', *Birmingham Post*, 30 January 1999

'Russia digs in against NATO Strikes', *The Guardian* (London), 7 October 1998

SADC, *SADC Statistics: Facts and Figures 1999* (Gaborone: SADC, 1999)

SADC Heads of State and Government, *Summit Communiqué*, Gaborone, Botswana, 28 June 1996. Courtesy of SADC Secretariat

   Summit Communiqué, Grand Bay, Mauritius, 13–14 September 1998. Courtesy of the SADC Secretariat

   Summit Communiqué, Maputo, Mozambique, 17–18 August 1999. Courtesy of the SADC Secretariat

   Extra-Ordinary Summit Communiqué, Windhoek, Namibia, 9 March 2001

SANDF, 'Southern African Development Community Combined Task Force Boleas – Operation Boleas and Campaign Charon as presented to the Joint Standing Committee of [the South African] Parliament on Defence and the Portfolio

Committee on Foreign Affairs on 2 November 1998', online at www.mil.za/ CSANDF/CJOps/Operations/General/Boleas/boleas.htm. Accessed in January 2002, document no longer available

'The SADC Intervention in Lesotho: A Military Perspective', undated report, online at www.mil.za/CSANDF/CJOps/Operations/General/Boleas/military_ perspective.htm. Accessed in January 2002, document no longer available

Sanger, David, 'Bush's day at the UN: it's chilly, still, there', *New York Times*, 24 September 2003

SAPA (South African News Agency), 'Prime Minister says King Letsie "part of the problem" ', BBC World, 24 September 1998

'Mandela comments on Lesotho intervention', BBC, 29 September 1998

'DR Congo: SADC defence ministers agree to aid to Kabila against rebels', BBC, 19 August 1998

'Mandela rules out sending military assistance to DR Congo's Kabila', BBC, 20 August 1998

'S. Africa gives up Lesotho mediation', BBC World, 21 September 1998

'SA to foot the bill for Lesotho intervention', *Mail and Guardian*, 12 March 2000

Sawyer, Dr Amos, 'Liberian interim president address to the nation on the outcome of the Lome cease-fire talks', Radio ELBC, Monrovia, 19 February 1991, transcribed by BBC Summary of World Broadcasts, 22 February 1991

Schifferes, Steve, 'US says "coalition of willing" grows', BBC News Online, 21 March 2003, online at http://news.bbc.co.uk/2/hi/americas/2870487.stm

Seelye, Katherine, 'Clinton resists renewed calls for ground troops in Kosovo', *New York Times*, 19 May 1999

Sibanda, Newton, 'Zimbabwe/DR Congo: why we must intervene' *AfricaNews*, Issue 39 (June 1999)

Slaughter, Anne-Marie, 'Good reasons for going around the UN', *New York Times*, 18 March 2003

Smith, Craig S., 'France offers many more troops for Lebanon', *New York Times*, 25 August 2006

Solana, Dr Javier, NATO Secretary-General, 'Statement to the Press', 25 April 1999, online at www.nato.int/docu/speech/1999/s990425a.htm

South Africa, Republic of, *Defence in a Democracy: White Paper on National Defence for the Republic of South Africa*, May 1996, online at http://www. polity.org.za/govdocs/white_papers/defencewp.html

White Paper on South African Participation in International Peace Missions, Approved by Cabinet 21 October 1998, online at http://www.polity.org.za/ govdocs/white_papers/peacekeeping.html

South African Department of Foreign Affairs, 'South African Foreign Policy – Discussion Document', South African Government Green Paper, June 1996, online at www.polity.org.za/html/govdocs/discuss/foreign.html

'South African troops cross border', *Newsday*, 23 September 1998

'Strike against Yugoslavia: Serbs remain defiant', CNN, 28 March 1999

Suzuki, Miwa, 'Uneasy Asia raises fears over NATO strikes', *Agence France Presse*, 26 March 1999

TASS, 'Slovak public opinion split on entry to NATO', 13 April 1999

'The draft UN resolution', *The Guardian Unlimited*, 6 August 2006, online at http://observer.guardian.co.uk/world/story/0,,1838369,00.html

Thoenes, Sander, 'UN in urgent talks over E Timor fears', *Financial Times*, 2 September 1999

'Time to stop the "patriotic" warmongers', *Zimbabwe Independent*, 5 March 1999

'Towards the Southern African Development Community', Declaration by the Heads of State or Government of Southern African States, 17 August 1992 (Gaborone, Botswana: Associated Printers, 1998)

Treaty Establishing the African Economic Community, 3 June 1991, Abuja, Nigeria. Courtesy of the OAU Secretariat

Tully, Andrew, 'Yugoslavia: France faulted for limiting targets during Kosovo conflict', *Radio Free Europe*, October 1999

United Nations, *Charter of the United Nations* (New York: United Nations Department of Public Information, 1993)

United Nations General Assembly, Resolution 53/236 'Financing of the United Nations Logistics Base at Brindisi, Italy', 53rd General Assembly Session, 6 August 1999

Resolution 54/247 'Programme budget for the biennium 1998–1999', 54th General Assembly Session, 3 February 2000

United Nations Secretary-General, 'Progress Report of the Secretary-General on Standby Arrangements for Peacekeeping', 30 March 1999

Statement of the Secretary-General on Iraq, 20 March 2003, online at www.un.org/apps/sg/printsgstates.asp?nid=292, accessed 20 March 2003, document no longer available at this site

United Nations Security Council, Record of the 4043rd Meeting, New York, 11 September 1999, online at www.un.org/peace/etimor/docs.9985750E.htm, accessed 27 February 2002, document no longer available at this site

Resolution 1264 (1999), 15 September 1999

United States CinC Pacific, 'US Forces INTERFET (USFI), 'Operation Stabilise East Timor; Executive Overview', internal after-action report from the US military, online at www.dod.gov/nii/org/c3is/ccbm/east-timor.pdf, accessed May 2002, document no longer available at this site

United States Congressional Budget Office, 'NATO Burdensharing after Enlargement', Report to Congress, August 2001

United States Department of Defence, *Report to Congress: Kosovo/Operation Allied Force After-Action Report*, 31 January 2000, online at www.defenselink.mil/pubs/kaar02072000.pdf

United States General Accounting Office, *Kosovo Air Operations: Need to Maintain Alliance Cohesion Resulted in Doctrinal Departures*, Report to the US Congress, July 2001

United States White House, 'A National Security Strategy for a New Century', October 1998, online at http://www.globalsecurity.org/mlitary/library/policy/national/nss-9810.htm, accessed 20 February 2003, document no longer available at this site

Wallis, William, 'Arabs unite with Beirut against UN resolution', *Financial Times*, 7 August 2006

Weisman, Steven R., 'Audience unmoved during Bush's address at the UN', *The New York Times*, 24 September 2003

Wensley, Penny, Ambassador and Permanent Representative of Australia to the United Nations. 'East Timor and the United Nations', speech to the Australian Institute for International Affairs, 23 February 2000

West African Heads of State and Government, *Treaty of the Economic Community of West African States*, signed 25 May 1975 in Lagos, Nigeria. Courtesy of the ECOWAS Secretariat

Wetherell, Iden, 'Mugabe forms new defence pact', *Mail and Guardian (South Africa)*, 16–22 April 1999

'Why we went to war', *The Namibian*, 14 September 1998

Wolfowitz, Paul, 'US Participation in and Support of Operation STABILISE', report to Congress, required by Section 127a of Title 10 U.S.C.

Xinhua News Agency, 'Most Zimbabweans support intervention in Congo: paper', 23 August 1998

'Mugabe snubs Mandela's mediation efforts on Congo', 23 August 1998

'Zimbabwe backs SADC intervention in Lesotho', 23 September 1998

Yassine, Salim, 'Lebanese PM wins full Arab backing for truce plan', *Agence France Presse*, 7 August 2006

'Zimbabwe to send troops to Congo', CNN, 19 August 1998

'Zimbabwean Minister of Foreign Affairs on Zimbabwe's Foreign Policy', 20 January 1999, online through the Zimbabwe government's website at http://www.gta.gov.zw. Accessed on 16 April 2003, site not currently accessible

Secondary literature

Abbott, Kenneth, Robert O. Keohane, Andrew Moravcsik, Anne-Marie Slaughter, and Duncan Snidal, 'The Concept of Legalization', *International Organization*, 54:3 (2000)

Abbott, Kenneth W. and Duncan Snidal, 'Why States Act through Formal International Organizations', *Journal of Conflict Resolution*, 42:1 (February 1998)

Aboagye, Lt. Col. Festus B., *ECOMOG: A Sub-Regional Experience in Conflict Resolution, Management and Peacekeeping in Liberia* (Accra: Sedco Publishing, 1999)

Adebajo, Adekeye, *Liberia's Civil War: Nigeria, ECOMOG, and Regional Security in West Africa* (Boulder: Lynne Rienner, 2002)

Adibe, Clement, 'The Liberian Conflict and the ECOWAS-UN Partnership', *Third World Quarterly*, 18:3 (1997)

Auerswald, Philip E. and David P. Auerswald (eds.), *The Kosovo Conflict: A Diplomatic History Through Documents* (The Hague: Kluwer Law International, 2000)

Axelrod, Robert M., *The Evolution of Cooperation* (New York: Basic Books, 1984)

Babangida, Ibrahim, 'The Imperative Features of Nigerian Foreign Policy', *Contact*, 2:3 (Nov. 1990) (Publication of the Economic Community of West African States)

Ball, Desmond, 'Silent Witness: Australian intelligence and East Timor' *The Pacific Review*, 14:1 (2001)

Baregu, Mwesiga (ed.), *Crisis in the Democratic Republic of Congo* (Harare: SAPES Books, 1999)

Barnett, M. N. and M. Finnemore, 'The Politics, Power, and Pathologies of International Organizations', *International Organization*, 53:4 (Fall 1999)

Bennis, Phyllis, *Calling the Shots: How Washington Dominates Today's UN* (New York: Olive Branch Press, 2000)

Berger, Samuel R., 'A Foreign Policy for the Global Age', *Foreign Affairs*, 79:6 (2000)

Berman, Eric, 'The Security Council's Increasing Reliance on Burden-Sharing: Collaboration or Abrogation?', *International Peacekeeping*, 4:1 (Spring 1998)

' "Successful" Elections in Liberia: Hold the Applause', *UN Watch*, online at http://unwatch.org/pas/97/pas008.htm, document no longer available at this site

Berman, Eric G. and Katie E. Sams, *Peacekeeping in Africa: Capabilities and Culpabilities* (Geneva: United Nations, 2000)

Betts, Richard, 'Command Compromised: Inside NATO's First War', *Foreign Affairs* (July/August 2001)

Birmingham, John, 'Appeasing Jakarta – Australia's Complicity in the East Timor Tragedy', *Quarterly Essay*, Issue 2 (Melbourne: Schwartz, 2001)

Boulden, Jane, *Peace Enforcement: the United Nations Experience in Congo, Somalia, and Bosnia* (Westport: Praeger, 2001)

Braeckman, Colette, *L'Enjeu Congolais: L'Afrique Centrale Après Mobutu* (Paris: Fayard, 1999)

Brenchley, Fred, 'The Howard Defence Doctrine', *The Bulletin* 28 September 1999

Buchanan, Allen, 'From Nuremberg to Kosovo: The Morality of Illegal International Legal Reform', paper presented at the Princeton University Law and Public Affairs Seminar, Princeton, 6 February 2001
  'Recognitional Legitimacy and the State System', *Philosophy and Public Affairs*, 28:1 (1999)
Bukovansky, Mlada, *Legitimacy and Power Politics: The American and French Revolutions in International Political Culture* (Princeton: Princeton University Press, 2002)
Bull, Hedley, *The Anarchical Society: A Study of Order in World Politics* (New York: Columbia University Press, 1995)
Burley, A. M. and W. Mattli, 'Europe Before the Court: A Political Theory of Legal Integration', *International Organization*, 47:1 (Winter 1993)
Buzan, Barry, 'From International System to International Society: Structural Realism and Regime Theory Meet the English School', *International Organization*, 47:3 (Summer 1993)
Byers, Michael, *Custom, Power and the Power of Rules: International Relations and Customary International Law* (Cambridge: Cambridge University Press, 1999)
  'Not Yet Havoc: Geopolitical Change and the International Rules on Military Force', forthcoming
Caron, David D., 'The Legitimacy of the Collective Authority of the Security Council', *American Journal of International Law*, 87:4 (October 1993)
Chayes, Abram, and Antonia Chayes, 'On Compliance', *International Organization*, 47:2 (1993)
Chesterman, Simon, 'Legality Versus Legitimacy: Humanitarian Intervention, the Security Council, and the Rule of Law', *Security Dialogue*, 33:3 (2002)
Cilliers, Jakkie, 'Building Security in Southern Africa', *ISS Monograph No. 43* (November 1999)
Clark, General Wesley, *Waging Modern War: Bosnia, Kosovo, and the Future of Combat* (New York: Public Affairs, 2001)
Clarke, Walter and Jeffrey Herbst (eds.), *Learning from Somalia: the Lessons of Armed Humanitarian Intervention* (Boulder: Westview Press, 1997)
Claude, Inis L., 'Collective Legitimization as a Political Function of the United Nations', *International Organization*, 20:3 (1966)
Cobb, Adam, 'East Timor and Australia's Security Role: Issues and Scenarios' *Current Issues Brief No. 3 1999–2000*, Information and Research Services, Department of the Parliamentary Library, Australia
Cochran, Kathryn, 'Kosovo Targeting – A Bureaucratic and Legal Nightmare: The Implications for US/Australian Interoperability', Australian Aerospace Centre, June 2001, http://www.defence.gov.au/aerospacecentre/publish/01Paper3.html, accessed 3 December 2002, document no longer available at this site

Cohen, Herman, Assistant Secretary of State for African Affairs, 'Statement to Subcommittee on African Affairs of the US Senate Foreign Relations Committee' 27 November 1990

Coicaud, Jean-Marc and Veijo Heiskanen, *The Legitimacy of International Organizations* (Tokyo: United National University Press, 2001)

Coicaud, Jean-Marc, *Legitimacy and Politics: A Contribution to the Study of Political Right and Political Responsibility* (Cambridge: Cambridge University Press, 2002)

Coning, Cedric de, 'Conditions for Intervention: DRC & Lesotho', *Conflict Trends*, No. 1 (1998)

Conteh-Morgan, Earl, 'Ecowas: Peace-making or Meddling in Liberia?', *Africa Insight*, 23:1 (1993)

Contact Magazine, Vol. 2, No. 3, 'Sixteen States, One Destiny' (Lagos: ECOWAS, November 1990)

Crawford, John and Glyn Harper, *Operation East Timor: the New Zealand Defence Force in East Timor 1999–2001* (Auckland: Reed, 2001)

Daalder, Ivo and Michael O'Hanlon, *Winning Ugly: NATO's War to Save Kosovo* (Washington, D.C.: Brookings, 2000)

Downs George W., David M. Rocke and Peter N. Barsoon, 'Is Good News about Compliance Good News about Cooperation?', *International Organization*, 50:3 (Summer 1996)

Dowty, A. and G. Loescher, 'Refugee Flows as Grounds for International Action', *International Security*, 21:1 (Summer 1996)

Doyle, Michael W., *Ways of War and Peace: Realism, Liberalism, and Socialism* (New York: W.W. Norton & Company, 1997)

Doyle, Michael W. and Nicholas Sambanis, 'International Peacebuilding: A Theoretical and Quantitative Analysis', paper prepared for delivery at the 2000 Annual Meeting of the American Political Science Association, Washington, D.C., 31 August–3 September 2000

Doyle, Michael W., Ian Johnstone, and Robert C. Orr (eds.), *Keeping the Peace: Lessons from Multidimensional UN Operations in Cambodia and El Salvador* (New York: Cambridge University Press, 1997)

Dupont, Alan, 'ASEAN's Response to the East Timor Crisis', *Australian Journal of International Affairs*, 54:2 (2000)

Economist Intelligence Unit, *Country Report: Zimbabwe*, 1st Quarter (February) 1999

Farer, Tom, 'A Paradigm of Legitimate Intervention', in Lori F. Damrosch (ed.), *Enforcing Restraint: Collective Intervention in Internal Conflicts* (New York: Council on Foreign Relations Press, 1993)

Finnemore, Martha, 'Military Intervention and the Organization of International Politics', in Joseph Lepgold and Thomas G. Weiss (eds.), *Collective Conflict Management and Changing World Politics* (Albany: State University of New York Press, 1998)

National Interests in International Society (Ithaca: Cornell University Press, 1996)

The Purpose of Intervention: Changing Beliefs About the Use of Force (Ithaca: Cornell University Press, 2003)

Finnemore, Martha and K. Sikkink, 'International Norm Dynamics and Political Change', *International Organization*, 52:4 (Fall 1998)

Franck, Thomas M., 'Interpretation and Change in the Law of Humanitarian Intervention', in J.L. Holzgrefe and Robert O. Keohane (eds.) *Humanitarian Intervention: Ethical, Legal, and Political Dilemmas* (Cambridge: Cambridge University Press, 2003)

The Power of Legitimacy among Nations (New York: Oxford University Press, 1990)

Gilpin, Robert, *War and Change in World Politics* (New York: Cambridge University Press, 1981)

Goldstein, Judith and Robert Keohane (eds.), *Ideas and Foreign Policy: Beliefs, Institutions, and Political Change* (Ithaca: Cornell University Press, 1993)

Gonzales-Pelaez, Ana and Barry Buzan, 'A Viable Project of Solidarism? The Neglected Contributions of John Vincent's Basic Rights Initiative', *International Relations*, 17:3 (2003)

Gordon, Chris, 'Africa's Wars All Becoming One', *Jane's Intelligence Review*, 5:10 (October 1998)

Hartigan, Kevin, 'Matching Humanitarian Norms with Cold, Hard Interests: The Making of Refugee Policies in Mexico and Honduras, 1980–89', *International Organization*, 46:3 (Summer 1992)

Henkin, Louis, 'Kosovo and the Law of "Humanitarian Intervention"', *American Journal of International Law*, 93:4 (1999)

Hirsch, John L. and Robert B. Oakley, *Somalia and Operation Restore Hope: Reflections on Peacemaking and Peacekeeping* (Washington, D.C.: United States Institute of Peace Press, 1995)

Howe, Herbert, 'Lessons from Liberia', *International Security*, 21:3 (Winter 1996/97)

Hurd, Ian, 'Legitimacy and Authority in International Politics', *International Organization*, 53:2 (Spring 1999)

'Legitimacy, Power, and the Symbolic Life of the UN Security Council', *Global Governance*, 8 (2002)

Hurrell, Andrew, 'International Society and the Study of Regimes: A Reflective Approach', in Volker Rittberger (ed.), *Regime Theory and International Relations* (Oxford: Oxford University Press, 1997)

Hutchful, Eboe, 'The ECOMOG Experience with Peacekeeping in West Africa', in Marc Malan (ed.), *Whither Peacekeeping in Africa?* Institute for Security Studies Monograph No. 36 (ISS, Pretoria, South Africa, April 1999)

Independent Commission on Kosovo, *The Kosovo Report: Conflict, International Response, Lessons Learned* (Oxford: Oxford University Press, 2000)

Inegbedion, John, 'ECOMOG in Comparative Perspective', in E. Keller and D. Rothchild (eds.), *Africa in the New International Order* (Boulder: Lynne Rienner, 1996)

International Commission on Intervention and State Sovereignty, *The Responsibility to Protect* (Ottawa: International Development Research Centre, 2001)

International Crisis Group, 'Africa's Seven-Nation War', *ICG Democratic Republic of Congo Report No. 4*, 21 May 1999

  'How Kabila Lost His Way: The Performance of Laurent Désiré Kabila's Government', *Republic of Congo Report No. 3*, 21 May 1999

  'Scramble for the Congo: Anatomy of an Ugly War', *ICG Africa Report No. 26*, 20 December 2000

International Institute for Strategic Studies, 'Congo: Less Fighting, but No Peace', *Strategic Survey 2000/2001* (London: Oxford University Press, 2001)

  Military Balance (London: Oxford University Press), annual reports 1990–2000

  Strategic Survey 1998/99 (London: Oxford University Press, 1999)

  Strategic Survey 1999/2000 (London: Oxford University Press, 2000)

Iweriebor, Ehiedu E. and Martin I. Uhomoibhi, *UN Security Council: A Case for Nigeria's Membership* (Lagos: Times Books Ltd., 1999)

Jackson, Robert H., *Quasi-States: Sovereignty, International Relations, and the Third World* (Cambridge: Cambridge University Press, 1990)

Jardine, Matthew, 'East Timor, the United Nations, and the International Community: Force Feeding Human Rights into the Institutionalised Jaws of Failure', *Pacifica Review*, 12:1 (February 2000)

Keck, Margaret E. and Kathryn Sikkink, *Activists Beyond Borders: Advocacy Networks in International Politics* (Ithaca: Cornell University Press, 1998)

Keohane, Robert, *After Hegemony: Cooperation and Discord in the World Political Economy* (Princeton: Princeton University Press, 1984)

  'The Contingent Legitimacy of UN-Based Multilateralism', paper presented at a conference on 'Legitimacy and Power in the Post-9/11 World', University of Southern California, 27 April 2005

Keohane, Robert and Joseph S. Nye, 'The Club Model of Multilateral Cooperation and Problems of Democratic Legitimacy', paper presented at the American Political Science Convention, Washington, D.C., 31 August–3 September 2000

Khobe, Mitikishe Maxwell, 'The Evolution and Conduct of ECOMOG Operations in West Africa', in Mark Malan (ed.), *Boundaries of Peace Operations: The African Dimension*, Institute for Security Studies Monograph No. 44, February 2000

Kirsch, Philippe, John T. Holmes, and Mora Johnson, 'International Tribunals and Courts', in David Malone (ed.), *The UN Security Council: From the Cold War to the 21st Century* (Boulder: Lynne Rienner, 2004)

Kissinger, Henry A., 'Doing Injury to History', 19 April, 1999, online at www.soz. uni-hannover.de/isoz/kosovo/kissin.htm, accessed 9 March 2003, site no longer available

Koh, Harold Hongju, 'Why do Nations Obey International Law?' *The Yale Law Journal*, 106:2599 (1997)

Krasner, Stephen D., 'Global Communications and National Power: Life on the Pareto Frontier', *World Politics*, 43:3 (April 1991)

'State Power and the Structure of International Trade', *World Politics*, 28:3 (1976)

Sovereignty: Organized Hypocrisy (Princeton: Princeton University Press, 1999)

'Structural Causes and Regime Consequences: Regimes as Intervening Variables', in S. Krasner, *International Regimes* (Ithaca: Cornell University Press, 1983)

Krieger, Heike (ed.), *East Timor and the International Community: Basic Documents*, Vol. 10, Cambridge International Documents Series (Cambridge: Cambridge University Press, 1997)

The Kosovo Conflict and International Law (Cambridge: Cambridge University Press, 2001)

Lamb, Guy, 'The Realities of Regional Security in Southern Africa', paper presented at the Globe Southern Africa Conference on 'Partnership for Sustainability II', Environmental Security in Southern Africa, at the Parliament of South Africa, Cape Town, 21–22 September 2000

Laoye, Col. Larinde, 'Logistics Support in ECOMOG Operations', *Defence Studies*, Special Issue on ECOMOG (1996)

Leaver, Richard, 'Australia, East Timor and Indonesia', *The Pacific Review*, 14:1 (2001)

Luck, Edward C. and Michael W. Doyle (eds.), *International Law and Organization: Closing the Compliance Gap* (Lanham: Rowman and Littlefield, 2004)

Maclean, Sandra J., 'Mugabe at War: the Political Economy of Conflict in Zimbabwe', *Third World Quarterly*, 23:3 (2002)

Malan, Mark, 'Can They Do That? SADC, the DRC, and Lesotho', *Indicator SA*, 15:4 (Summer 1998)

'Leaner and Meaner? The Future of Peacekeeping in Africa', *African Security Review*, 8:4 (1999)

Malan, Mark and Jakkie Cilliers, 'SADC Organ on Politics, Defence and Security: Future Development', *ISS Occasional Paper*, No. 19 (March 1997)

Mandaza, Ibbo (ed.), *Reflections on the Crisis in the Democratic Republic of Congo* (Harare: Sapes Books, 1999)

March, James G. and Johan P. Olsen, 'The Institutional Dynamics of International Political Orders', *International Organization*, 52:4 (Autumn 1998)

Martin, Ian, *Self-Determination in East Timor: The United Nations, the Ballot, and the International Intervention* (Boulder: Lynne Rienner, 2001)

Martin, Lisa L., 'Interests, Power, and Multilateralism', *International Organization*, 46:4 (Autumn 1992)

   Coercive Cooperation: Explaining Multilateral Economic Sanctions (Princeton: Princeton University Press, 1992)

Martin, Pierre and Mark K. Brawley (eds.), *Alliance Politics, Kosovo, and NATO's War: Allied Force or Forced Allies?* (New York: Palgrave, 2001)

Milgrom, P., D. North, and B. Weingast, 'The Role of Institutions in the Revival of Trade', *Economics and Politics*, 2 (1990)

Mill, John S., 'A Few Words on Non-intervention', in J. S. Mill, *Essays on Politics and Culture*, Gertrude Himmelfarb (ed.), (Garden City: Doubleday, 1963)

Mingst, Karen, 'International Organization', *Encyclopædia Britannica*, online at www.search.eb.com/eb/article?eu=43555

Morgenthau, Hans Joachim, *Politics Among Nations; The Struggle for Power and Peace* (New York: Knopf, 1960)

Mortimer, Robert, 'ECOMOG, Liberia, and Regional Security in West Africa', in E. Keller and D. Rothchild (eds.), *Africa in the New International Order* (Boulder: Lynne Rienner, 1996)

Muyangwa, Monde and Margaret A. Vogt, 'An Assessment of the OAU Mechanism for Conflict Prevention, Management and Resolution, 1993–2000', *International Peace Academy Report*, online at www.ipacademy. org/Publications/Reports/Africa/PublRepoAfriAssessPrint.htm

Nardin, Terry, *Law, Morality, and the Relations of States* (Princeton: Princeton University Press, 1983)

NATO, *NATO Handbook* (Brussels: NATO Office of Information and Press, 2001)

   NATO Review, 50th Anniversary Commemorative Edition (Brussels: NATO, 1999)

Neethling, Theo, 'Conditions for Successful Entry and Exit: An Assessment of SADC Allied Operations in Lesotho', *ISS Monograph No. 44: Boundaries of Peace Support Operations* (February 2000)

Nest, Michael, 'Ambitions, Profits and Loss: Zimbabwean Economic Involvement in the Democratic Republic of Congo', *African Affairs*, 100 (2001)

O'Connell, Mary Ellen, 'The UN, NATO, and International Law After Kosovo', *Human Rights Quarterly*, 22:1 (2000)

Omitoogun, Wuyi, 'Military Expenditure in Africa', *SIPRI Yearbook 2000* (Oxford University Press, Oxford, 2000)

Pedlow, Gregory W., *NATO Strategy Documents 1949–1969* (Brussels: NATO, 1997)

Peters, John, Stuart Johnson, Nora Bensahel, Timothy Liston, and Traci Williams, *European Contributions to Operation Allied Force: Implications for Transatlantic Cooperation* (Santa Monica: Rand, 2001)

Price, Richard, *The Chemical Weapons Taboo* (Ithaca: Cornell University Press, 1997)

Regan, Patrick M., *Civil Wars and Foreign Powers – Outside Intervention in Intrastate Conflict* (Ann Arbor: University of Michigan Press, 2000)

Reno, William, *Warlord Politics and African States* (Boulder: Lynne Rienner, 1998)

Reus-Smit, Christian, *The Moral Purpose of the State* (Princeton: Princeton University Press, 1999)

(ed.), *The Politics of International Law* (Cambridge: Cambridge University Press, 2004)

Reyntjens, Filip, 'Briefing: the Democratic Republic of Congo, from Kabila to Kabila', *African Affairs*, 100:399 (2001)

Richardson, Louise, 'The Concert of Europe and Security Management in the Nineteenth Century', in Helga Haftendorn, Robert O. Keohane, and Celeste A. Wallander (eds), *Imperfect Unions: Security Institutions over Time and Space* (London: Oxford University Press, 1999)

Rotberg, Robert I., 'Africa's Mess, Mugabe's Mayhem', *Foreign Affairs*, 79:5 (September/October 2000)

Rothert, Mark, 'UN Intervention in East Timor', *Columbia Journal of International Law*, 257 (2000–2001)

Rupiya, Martin R., 'A Political and Military Review of Zimbabwe's Involvement in the Second Congo War', in John F. Clark (ed.), *African Stakes of the Congo War* (New York: Palgrave Macmillan, 2002)

Sandholtz, Wayne, 'Dynamics of International Norm Change: the Case of Wartime Art Plunder', forthcoming

Schnabel, Albrecht and Ramesh Thakur, *Kosovo and the Challenge of Humanitarian Intervention* (Tokyo: United Nations University, 2000)

Schwartz, Eric, 'The Intervention in East Timor', Report for the National Intelligence Council, December 2001, online at www.puaf.umd.edu/ CISSM/Projects/NIC/Schwartz.htm, accessed May 2002, document no longer available at this site

Sesay, Max, 'Civil War and Collective Intervention in Liberia' *Review of African Political Economy*, 67 (1996)

Seybolt, Taylor, 'The War in the Democratic Republic of Congo', *SIPRI Yearbook 2000* (Oxford University Press, Oxford, 2000)

Shinoda, Hibeaki, 'The Politics of Legitimacy in International Relations: A Critical Examination of NATO's Intervention in Kosovo', *Alternatives*, 25:4 (2000)

Simma, Bruno, 'NATO, the UN and the Use of Force: Legal Aspects', *European Journal of International Law*, 1:10 (1999)

Southall, Roger and Roddy Fox, 'Lesotho's General Election of 1998: Rigged or De Rigeur?', *Journal Of Modern African Studies*, 37:4 (December 1999)

Stedman, S. J., 'Spoiler Problems in Peace Processes', *International Security*, 22:2 (Fall 1997)

Steffek, Jens, 'The Legitimation of International Governance: A Discourse Approach', *European Journal of International Relations*, 9:2 (2003)

Stone Sweet, Alec, 'Judicialization and the Construction of Governance', *Comparative Political Studies*, 32:2 (April 1999)

Thucydides, *History of the Peloponnesian War*, translated by Rex Warner (London: Penguin Classics, 1972)

Trachtenberg, Marc, 'Intervention in Historical Perspective', in Laura W. Reed and Carl Kayson (eds.), *Emerging Norms of Justified Intervention* (Cambridge, Mass.: American Academy of Arts and Sciences, 1993)

United Nations, *The Blue Helmets: A Review of United Nations Peace-keeping* (New York: UN Department of Public Information, 1996)

Vincent, R. John, *Human Rights and International Relations* (Cambridge: Cambridge University Press, 1986)

Voeten, Eric, 'The Political Origins of the UN Security Council's Ability to Legitimize the Use of Force', *International Organization*, 59:3 (2005)

Vogt, Margaret A. (ed.), *The Liberian Crisis and ECOMOG: A Bold Attempt at Regional Peace Keeping* (Lagos: Gabumo Publishers, 1992)

Waltz, Kenneth N., *Theory of International Politics* (Reading: Addison-Wesley, 1979)

Walzer, Michael, *Just and Unjust Wars: A Moral Argument with Historical Illustrations* (New York: Basic Books, 1992)

'The Politics of Rescue', *Dissent*, Winter 1995

Wedgwood, Ruth, 'NATO's Campaign in Yugoslavia', *American Journal of International Law*, 93:4 (October 1999)

Weller, Marc (ed.), *The Crisis in Kosovo 1989–1999: From the Dissolution of Yugoslavia to Rambouillet and the Outbreak of Hostilities* (Cambridge: Documents and Analysis Publishing Ltd., 1999)

'The Rambouillet Conference on Kosovo', *International Affairs*, 75:2 (1999)

(ed.), *Regional Peace-keeping and International Enforcement: The Liberian Crisis* (Cambridge: Grotius Publications, Cambridge University Press, 1994)

Wendt, Alexander, 'Anarchy Is What States Make of It', *International Organization*, 46:2 (Spring 1992)

'The Agent-Structure Problem in International Relations Theory', *International Organization*, 41:3 (1987)

Wheeler, Nicholas J., *Saving Strangers: Humanitarian Intervention in International Society* (Oxford: Oxford University Press, 2002)

Wheeler, Nicholas J. and Tim Dunne, 'East Timor and the New Humanitarian Interventionism', *International Affairs*, 77:4 (2001)

Wight, Martin, 'International Legitimacy', in Hedley Bull (ed.), *Systems of States: Martin Wight* (Leicester: Leicester University Press, 1977)

Wippman, David, 'Treaty-Based Intervention: Who Can Say No?', *University of Chicago Law Review*, 62:2 (Spring 1995)

Wolpe, Bruce C., 'Australia and America: Renewal and Reinvention', *Australian Journal of International Affairs*, 54:1 (2000)

Zacher, Mark W., 'The Territorial Integrity Norm: International Boundaries and the Use of Force', *International Organization*, 55:2 (Spring 2001)

INDEX